HERETICAL THOUGHT

Series editor: Ruth O'Brien,
The Graduate Center,
City University of New York

ASSEMBLY

MICHAEL HARDT
AND
ANTONIO NEGRI

OXFORD
UNIVERSITY PRESS

Oxford University Press is a department of the University of Oxford.
It furthers the University's objective of excellence in research, scholarship,
and education by publishing worldwide. Oxford is a registered trade mark of
Oxford University Press in the UK and certain other countries.

Published in the United States of America by Oxford University Press
198 Madison Avenue, New York, NY 10016, United States of America.

Library of Congress Cataloging-in-Publication Data

Names: Hardt, Michael, 1960– author. | Negri, Antonio, 1933– author.
Title: Assembly / Michael Hardt & Antonio Negri.
Description: New York : Oxford University Press, 2017. |
Includes bibliographical references and index.
Identifiers: LCCN 2016052875 | ISBN 9780190677961 (hardback : alk. paper) |
ISBN 9780190677985 (epub)
Subjects: LCSH: Representative government and representation. | Democracy. |
Social movements—Political aspects. | Power (Social sciences)
Classification: LCC JF1051 .H37 2017 | DDC 321.8—dc23 LC record available at
https://lccn.loc.gov/2016052875

1 3 5 7 9 8 6 4 2
Printed by Sheridan Books, Inc., United States of America

Keeping faith with people who, in the teeth of relentless oppression, spontaneously resist, is all right on the night. But it is not enough when the next day dawns, since all it means is that, sooner or later, the frontline troops, with their superior weapons and sophisticated responses, will corner some of our young people on a dark night along one of these walkways and take their revenge.

—STUART HALL, "Cold Comfort Farm"

To know the allure of the commons is to know that one is not simply commencing something but instead fortunate enough to be participating in something vaster, partial, incomplete, and ever expanding.

—JOSÉ MUÑOZ, "The Brown Commons"

Contents

To your most excellent Majesty

In olden times authors were proud of the privilege to dedicate their works to Majesty—a noble custom, which we should revive. For whether we recognize it or not, Magnificence is all around us. We do not mean the remnants of the royal lines that grow more ridiculous by the day, and certainly not the pompous politicians and captains of finance, most of whom should be brought up on criminal charges. We are more sympathetic to the tradition of Thoreau, Emerson, and Whitman, who revere the glory of the mountains and mystery of the forests—but that is not what we mean either. We dedicate this book instead to those who, against all odds, continue to fight for freedom, those who suffer defeat only to stand up again, indefatigable, to combat the forces of domination. Yours is true Majesty.

—following Melville, following Machiavelli

Preface

Here poetry equals insurrection.

—Aimé Césaire

The script is by now familiar: inspiring social movements rise up against injustice and domination, briefly grab global headlines, and then fade from view. Even when they topple individual authoritarian leaders they have been unable thus far to create new, durable alternatives. Save few exceptions, these movements either have abandoned their radical aspirations and become players in the existing systems or have been defeated by ferocious repression. Why have the movements, which address the needs and desires of so many, not been able to achieve lasting change and create a new, more democratic and just society?

This question becomes all the more urgent as right-wing political forces rise and take power in countries throughout the world, suspending normal legal procedures in order to attack political opponents, undermining the independence of the judiciary and the press, operating extensive surveillance operations, creating an atmosphere of fear among various subordinated populations, posing notions of racial or religious purity as conditions for social belonging, threatening migrants with mass expulsion, and much more. People will protest the actions of these governments, and they are right to do so. But protest is not enough. Social movements also have to enact a lasting social transformation.

Today we are living in a phase of transition, which requires questioning some of our basic political assumptions. Rather than asking only how to take power we must also ask what kind of power we want and, perhaps more important, who we want to become. "Everything turns," as Hegel says, "on grasping and expressing the True not only as Substance, but equally as Subject."[1] We must train our eyes to recognize how the movements have the potential to redefine fundamental social relations so that they strive not to take power as it is but to take power differently, to achieve a fundamentally new, democratic society and, crucially, to produce new subjectivities.

The most powerful social movements today treat leadership as a dirty word—and for many good reasons. For more than a half century activists have rightly criticized how centralized, vertical forms of organization, including charismatic figures, leadership councils, party structures, and bureaucratic institutions, become fetters to the development of democracy and the full participation of all in political life. Gone are the days, on the one hand, when a political vanguard could successfully take power in the name of the masses; the claims of political realism and the presumed effectiveness of such centralized leadership have proved completely illusory. And yet, on the other, it is a terrible mistake to translate valid critiques of leadership into a refusal of sustained political organization and institution, to banish verticality only to make a fetish of horizontality and ignore the need for durable social structures. "Leaderless" movements must organize the production of subjectivity necessary to create lasting social relations.

Instead of dismissing leadership completely we should start by individuating its core political functions and then invent new mechanisms and practices for fulfilling them. (Whether this still is called "leadership" matters little.) Two key leadership functions are decision-making and assembly. To guard against the cacophony of individual voices and the paralysis of the political process, the thinking goes, leaders must be able to bring people together in a coherent whole and make the difficult choices necessary to sustain the movement and ultimately to transform society. The fact that leadership is defined by a decision-making capacity presents a paradox for modern conceptions of democracy: leaders make decisions at a distance, in relative solitude, but those decisions must in some sense be connected to the multitude and represent its will and desires. This tension or contradiction gives rise to a series of anomalies of modern democratic thought. The ability of leaders to assemble the multitude demonstrates this same tension. They must be political entrepreneurs who gather people, create new social combinations, and discipline them to cooperate with one another. Those who assemble people in this way, however, stand apart from the assembly itself, inevitably creating a dynamic between leaders and followers, rulers and ruled. Democratic leadership ultimately appears as an oxymoron.

Our hypothesis is that decision-making and assembly do not require centralized rule but instead can be accomplished together by the multitude, democratically. There are, of course, and will continue to be, issues that because of their urgency or technical nature require centralized decision-making of various sorts, but such "leadership" must be constantly subordinated to the multitude, deployed and dismissed as occasion dictates. If leaders are still necessary and possible in this context, it is only because they serve the productive multitude. This is not an elimination of leadership, then, but an inversion of the political relationship that constitutes it, a reversal of the polarity that links horizontal movements and vertical leadership.

So what do today's movements of the multitude want? They certainly demand equality, freedom, and democracy, but they also want well-being and wealth—not to possess more but instead to create sustainable relations of access and use for all. Long ago these demands were conceived together in terms of happiness. Today political, social happiness is not an unrealistic dream, but instead is embedded in the reality of social production, the result of together producing society, producing social relations in conditions of freedom and equality. That is the only path to a really democratic society.

If we treat the potential effectiveness of democratic organizing to transform the world only in political terms, however, if we treat the political as an autonomous realm detached from social needs and social production, then we will constantly and inevitably find ourselves spinning in circles or running into dead ends. In effect, we need to leave the noisy sphere of politics, where everything takes place on the surface, and descend into the hidden abode of social production and reproduction. We need to root the questions of organization and effectiveness, assembly and decision-making in the social terrain because only there will we find lasting solutions. That is the task of the central chapters of our book. We can verify the potential of the multitude to organize itself, to set the terms for how we cooperate, and to make decisions together only by investigating what people are already doing, what are their talents and capacities, in the field of social production.

Today production is increasingly social in a double sense: on one hand, people produce ever more socially, in networks of cooperation and interaction; and, on the other, the result of production is not just commodities but social relations and ultimately society itself. This double terrain of social production is where the talents and capacities of people to organize and rule themselves are nurtured and revealed, but it is also where the most important challenges and the most severe forms of domination facing the multitude are in play, including the ruling mechanisms of finance, money, and neoliberal administration.

One key struggle on the terrain of social production plays out over the uses, management, and appropriation of the common, that is, the wealth of the earth and the social wealth that we share and whose use we manage together. The common is increasingly today both the foundation and primary result of social production. We rely, in other words, on shared knowledges, languages, relationships, and circuits of cooperation along with shared access to resources in order to produce, and what we produce tends (at least potentially) to be common, that is, shared and managed socially.

There are primarily two approaches to the common today, which point in divergent directions. One affirms the right to appropriate the common as private property, which has been a principle of capitalist ideology from the outset. Capitalist accumulation today functions increasingly through the extraction of the common, through enormous oil and gas operations, huge mining enterprises, and monocultural agriculture but also by extracting the value produced in social forms of the common, such as the generation of knowledges, social cooperation, cultural products, and the like. Finance stands at the head of these processes of extraction, which are equally destructive of the earth and the social ecosystems that they capture.

The other approach seeks to keep access to the common open and to manage our wealth democratically, demonstrating the ways that the multitude already is relatively autonomous and has the potential to be more so. People together are ever more able to determine how they will cooperate with each other socially, how they will manage their relations to each other and their world, and how they will generate new combinations of human and nonhuman forces, social and digital machines, material and immaterial elements. From this standpoint we can see, in fact, that transforming the common into private property, closing access and imposing a monopoly of decision-making over its use and development, becomes a fetter to future productivity. We are all more productive the more we have access to knowledges, the more we are able to cooperate and communicate with each other, the more we share resources and wealth. The management of and care for the common is the responsibility of the multitude, and this social capacity has immediate political implications for self-governance, freedom, and democracy.

And yet—whispers some evil genius in our ears—the conditions in the world today are not propitious. Neoliberalism seems to have absorbed the common and society itself under its dominion, posing money as the exclusive measure of not only economic value but also our relations to each other and our world. Finance rules over almost all productive relations, which it has thrust into the icy waters of the global market. Maybe, the evil genius continues, your inversion of political roles could have made some sense if entrepreneurs were like what capitalists boasted about in the old days, that is, figures who promoted the virtues of innovation. But those entrepreneurs are fewer and fewer. The venture capitalist, the financier, and the fund manager are the ones who now command—or more accurately, money commands and those are merely its vassals and administrators. Today's capitalist entrepreneur is no Ahab leading his ship in uncharted seas but a sedentary priest officiating over an unending orgy of financial accumulation.

Moreover, neoliberalism not only has imposed a reorganization of production for the accumulation of wealth and the extraction of the common toward private ends but also has reorganized the political powers of the ruling classes. An extraordinary violence that compounds and exacerbates poverty has been structured into the exercise of power. Police forces have become kinds of militias that hunt the poor, people of color, the miserable, and the exploited; and, correspondingly, wars have become exercises of global police, with little concern for national sovereignty or international law. From the politics of exception have been stripped every varnish of charisma, if there really ever was any, and the state of exception has become the normal state of power. "Poor little deluded ones," concludes our evil genius, with all the arrogance, condescension, and disdain of the powerful for the rebels' naiveté.

And yet there is much more at play. Fortunately, there are myriad forms of daily resistance and the episodic but repeated revolt of potent social movements. One has to wonder if the contempt with which the powerful hold the travails of rebels and protesters (and the insinuation that they will never succeed in organizing if not subordinated to traditional leadership) does not mask their dread that the movements will proceed from resistance to insurrection—and thus their fear of losing control. They know (or suspect) that power is never as secure and self-sufficient as it pretends to be. The image of an omnipotent Leviathan is just a fable that serves to terrify the poor and the subordinated into submission. Power is always a relationship of force or, better, of many forces: "subordination cannot be understood," Ranajit Guha explains, "except as one of the constitutive terms in a binary relationship of which the other is dominance."[2] Maintaining social order requires constantly engaging and negotiating this relationship.

This conflict is today part of our social being. It is, in this sense, an ontological fact. The world as it is—this is how we understand ontology—is characterized by social struggles, the resistances and revolts of the subordinated,
and the striving for freedom and equality. But it is dominated by an extreme
minority that rules over the lives of the many and extorts the social value created by those who produce and reproduce society. In other words, it is a
world constructed in social cooperation but divided by the domination of the
ruling classes, by their blind passion for appropriation and their insatiable
thirst for hoarding wealth.

Social being thus appears as either a totalitarian figure of command or a
force of resistance and liberation. The One of power divides into Two, and
ontology is split into different standpoints, each of which is dynamic and
constructive. And from this separation also follows an epistemological divide:
on one side is an abstract affirmation of truth that, however it is constructed,
must be considered a fixed order, permanent and organic, dictated by nature;
on the other is a search for truth from below that is constructed in practice.
The one appears as the capacity of subjugation and the other as subjectification, that is, the autonomous production of subjectivity. That production of
subjectivity is made possible by the fact that truth is not given but constructed, not substance but subject. The power to make and to construct is
here an index of truth. In the processes of subjectivation that are developed
and enacted in practice, a truth and an ethics thus arise from below.

Leadership, then, if it is still to have a role, must exercise an entrepreneurial
function, not dictating to others or acting in their name or even claiming to
represent them but as a simple operator of assembly within a multitude that
is self-organized and cooperates in freedom and equality to produce wealth.
Entrepreneurship in this sense must be an agent of happiness. In the course of
this book, then, in addition to investigating and affirming the resistances and
uprisings of the multitude in recent decades, we will also propose the hypothesis of a democratic entrepreneurship of the multitude. Only by assuming
society as it is and as it is becoming, that is, as circuits of cooperation among
widely heterogeneous subjectivities that produce and use the common in its
various forms, can we establish a project of liberation, constructing a strong
figure of political entrepreneurship in line with the production of the
common.

It may well seem incongruous for us to celebrate entrepreneurship when
neoliberal ideologues prattle on ceaselessly about its virtues, advocating the

creation of an entrepreneurial society, bowing down in awe to the brave capitalist risk takers, and exhorting us all, from kindergarten to retirement, to become entrepreneurs of our own lives. We know such heroic tales of capitalist entrepreneurship are just empty talk, but if you look elsewhere you will see that there is plenty of entrepreneurial activity around today—organizing new social combinations, inventing new forms of social cooperation, generating democratic mechanisms for our access to, use of, and participation in decision-making about the common. It is important to claim the concept of entrepreneurship for our own. Indeed one of the central tasks of political thought is to struggle over concepts, to clarify or transform their meaning. Entrepreneurship serves as the hinge between the forms of the multitude's cooperation in social production and its assembly in political terms.

We have already developed in our other work some of the economic claims that are necessary for this project and we will continue to develop them in this book. Here is a partial list in schematic form. (1) The common—that is, the various forms of social and natural wealth that we share, have access to, and manage together—is ever more central to the capitalist mode of production. (2) In step with the common's growing economic relevance, labor is being transformed. How people produce value both at work and in society is increasingly based on cooperation, social and scientific knowledges, care, and the creation of social relationships. The social subjectivities that animate cooperative relationships, furthermore, tend to be endowed with a certain autonomy with respect to capitalist command. (3) Labor is being changed also by new intensive relationships and various kinds of material and immaterial machines that are essential for production, such as digital algorithms and "general intellect," including extensive banks of social and scientific knowledges. One task we will propose is that the multitude reappropriate and make its own such forms of fixed capital that are essential means of social production. (4) The center of gravity of capitalist production is shifting from the exploitation of labor in large-scale industry toward the capitalist extraction of value (often through financial instruments) from the common, that is, from the earth and from cooperative social labor. This is not primarily a quantitative shift and indeed, considered globally, there may be no reduction of the numbers of workers in factories. More important is the qualitative significance of the extraction of the common in various forms from the earth (such as oil, mining, and monocultural agriculture) and from social production (including education, health, cultural production, routine and creative cognitive work, and care work), which tends to reorganize and recompose the global capitalist economy as a whole. A new phase in capitalist development is emerging after manufacture and large-scale industry, a phase characterized by social production, which requires high levels of autonomy, cooperation, and "commoning" of living labor. (5) These transformations of capitalist production and the labor-power at its heart change the terms of how resistance can be organized against exploitation and the extraction of value. They make it possible for the situation to be inverted such that the multitude now reappropriates the common from capital and constructs a real democracy. The problem of organization (and the verticalization of the horizontal movements) resides here with the problem of the "constitutionalization" of the common—as objectives of social and workers' struggles, certainly, but also as the institutionalization of free and democratic forms of life.

These are some of the arguments that lead us to believe it is possible and desirable for the multitude to tip the relations of power in its favor and, ultimately, to take power—but, crucially, to take power differently. If the movements are becoming capable of formulating the strategy necessary to transform society, then they will also be able to take hold of the common, and thus to reconfigure freedom, equality, democracy, and wealth. The "differently," in other words, means not repeating the hypocrisies that pose freedom (without equality) as a concept of the Right and equality (without freedom) a proposition of the Left, and it means refusing to separate the common and happiness. By taking power, the movements need to affirm their most incisive differences and most extensive pluralities, that is, as a multitude. But that is not enough. This "differently" also means that by taking power the multitude must produce independent institutions that demystify identities and the centrality of power—unmasking state power and constructing nonsovereign institutions. Producing subversive struggles against power to vanquish sovereignty: this is an essential component of that "differently." But even that is not enough. All this must be constructed materially. And that opens a path to be traveled, one that leads the multitude to reappropriate wealth, incorporating fixed capital in its schemes of productive social cooperation, a path that roots power in the common.

A new Prince is emerging on the horizon, a Prince born of the passions of the multitude. Indignation at the corrupt policies that continually fill the feeding troughs of bankers, financiers, bureaucrats, and the wealthy; outrage at the frightening levels of social inequality and poverty; anger and fear at the destruction of the earth and its ecosystems; and denunciation of the seemingly unstoppable systems of violence and war—most people recognize all this but feel powerless to make any change. Indignation and anger, when they fester and drag on without outcome, risk collapsing into either desperation or resignation. On this terrain, a new Prince indicates a path of freedom and equality, a path that poses the task of putting the common in the hands of all, managed democratically by all. By Prince, of course, we do not mean an individual or even a party or leadership council, but rather the political articulation that weaves together the different forms of resistance and struggles for liberation in society today. This Prince thus appears as a swarm, a multitude moving in coherent formation and carrying, implicitly, a threat.

The title of this book, *Assembly*, is meant to grasp the power of coming together and acting politically in concert. But we do not offer a theory of assembly or a detailed analysis of any specific practice of assembly. Instead we approach the concept transversally and show how it resonates with a broad web of political principles and practices—from the general assemblies instituted by contemporary social movements to the legislative assemblies of modern politics, from the right to assemble asserted in legal traditions to the freedom of association central to labor organizing, and from the various forms of congregation in religious communities to the philosophical notion of machinic assemblage that constitutes new subjectivities. Assembly is a lens through which to recognize new democratic political possibilities.[3]

At various points, punctuating the rhythm of the book, we propose calls and responses. These are not questions and answers, as if the responses could put the calls to rest. Calls and responses should speak back and forth in an open dialogue. Classic African American styles of preaching are something like what we have in mind because they require the participation of the entire congregation. But that reference is not really right. In preacherly mode, the roles of those who call and those who respond are strictly divided: the preacher makes a statement and the congregation affirms it, "amen to that," urging the preacher on. We are interested in fuller forms of participation in which the roles are equal, interchangeable. A better fit is call-and-response work songs, such as the sea shanties that were common on nineteenth-century merchant sailing vessels. Songs serve to pass the time and synchronize labor. But really, with such industrious obedience, work songs are not the right reference either. A clearer inspiration for us, to return to the history of African American culture, is the call and response songs sung by slaves in the plantation

PART I

THE LEADERSHIP PROBLEM

No good comes from having many leaders.
Let there be one in charge, one ruler,
who gets from crooked-minded Cronos' son
sceptre and laws, so he may rule his people.

—HOMER, *The Iliad*

I have no fear that the result of our experiment will be that
men may be trusted to govern themselves without a master.

—THOMAS JEFFERSON TO DAVID HARTLEY, 1787

CHAPTER 1

WHERE HAVE ALL THE LEADERS GONE?

We continue to witness each year the eruption of "leaderless" social movements. From North Africa and the Middle East to Europe, the Americas, and East Asia, movements have left journalists, political analysts, police forces, and governments disoriented and perplexed. Activists too have struggled to understand and evaluate the power and effectiveness of horizontal movements. The movements have proven able to pose democratic ideals, sometimes to force reforms, and to pressure and even overthrow regimes—and, indeed, widespread social processes have been set in motion in coordination with or as a consequence of them—but the movements tend to be short-lived and seem unable to bring about lasting social transformation. They don't grow the roots and branches, as Machiavelli says, to be able to survive adverse weather.[1] Many assume that if only social movements could find new leaders they would return to their earlier glory and be able to sustain and achieve projects of social transformation and liberation. Where, they ask, are the new Martin Luther King Jr.'s, Rudi Dutschkes, Patrice Lumumbas, and Stephen Bikos? Where have all the leaders gone?

Leadership has become a conundrum that today's movements seem unable to solve, but the leadership problem in revolutionary and progressive movements is not entirely new. To leap over the contemporary impasse let's take a few steps back and get a running start.

"Errors" of the Communards

In March 1871, while the bourgeois government and its army retreats to Versailles, the Communards take control of Paris and quickly set about inventing institutional structures for a radically new kind of democracy, a government of the people, by the people: universal suffrage and free education are established, standing armies are abolished, representatives are paid workingmen's wages, and, perhaps most important, the mandates of all politicians are revocable at any time. The Communards seek to create the means for everyone to participate actively in all political decision-making and to represent themselves.

Karl Marx, writing from London, admires the audacity of the Communards and celebrates their powers of institutional innovation, their capacity to reinvent democracy. But he also claims that, from too good intentions, the Communards commit two crucial errors. First, by too quickly dissolving the central committee of the Commune and putting decision-making immediately in the hands of the people, the Communards are overly dogmatic in their attachment to democracy. Second, by not pursuing the retreating troops of the Third Republic to Versailles while they have the military advantage in March, the Communards are led astray by their devotion to nonviolence and peace. The Communards are too angelic in Marx's view, and their lack of leadership contributes to their defeat in May, just two months after their historic victory. The Commune is destroyed and by the thousands Communards are executed or exiled by a victorious bourgeoisie untroubled by any angelic inhibitions. But if the Communards had not committed these "errors," wouldn't they have—even if they had survived—negated the inspiring democratic core of their project? For many that is the Gordian knot.[2]

Now almost a century and a half has passed since the victory and defeat of the Paris Commune, and still, when discussing the dilemmas of progressive and revolutionary political organization, we hear repeated denunciations of both those who naively refuse leadership and, on the contrary, those who fall back into centralized, hierarchical structures. But the idea that these are our only options has lasted much too long.

Attempts to get beyond this impasse are blocked, in large part, by the strategic ambiguity or, rather, an excess of "tactical realism" on the part of our predecessors, that is, those who politically and theoretically guided revolutions after the Commune throughout the world—communists of the First, Second, and Third Internationals, guerrilla leaders in the mountains of Latin America and Southeast Asia, Maoists in China and West Bengal, black nationalists in the United States, and many others. The tradition maintains, with many variations, a double position: the strategic goal of revolution is to create a society in which together we can rule ourselves without masters or central committees, but from the realist point of view we must recognize that the time is not right. Modern liberation movements are devoted to democracy as the future goal but not under present conditions. Neither the external nor the internal conditions, the thinking goes, yet exist for a real democracy. The continuing power of the bourgeoisie and the Prussians at the gates of Paris (or, later, the white armies from Siberia to Poland or, later still, the counter-revolutionary forces led by the CIA, COINTELPRO, death squads, and innumerable others) will destroy any democratic experiment. Moreover, and this is the greater obstacle, the people are not yet ready to rule themselves. The revolution needs time.

This double position has characterized a widely shared conviction, but it is interesting nonetheless to note that already 150 years ago it made many communists uneasy. They shared the utopian desire for a real democracy but feared that the delay would extend indefinitely, that if we expect a mystical event eventually to realize our dreams we will wait in vain. We are not that interested in the ideological critiques directed at Marx and the leaders of the International by Pierre-Joseph Proudhon, Giuseppe Mazzini, or Mikhail Bakunin but rather those brought by the mutualists and anarcho-communists from Holland, Switzerland, Spain, and Italy to contest the organizational centralism of the International and its organizational methods as a repetition of the modern conception of power and the political.[3] These revolutionaries foresaw that a Thomas Hobbes lurks even within their own revolutionary organizations, that the assumptions of sovereign authority infect their political imaginations.

The relationship between leadership and democracy, which is a political dilemma that has plagued liberals as much as socialists and revolutionaries throughout modernity, is expressed clearly in the theory and practice of representation, which can serve as an introduction to our problematic. Every legitimate power, the theory goes, must be representative and thus have a solid foundation in the popular will. But beyond such virtuous-sounding declarations, what is the relationship between the action of representatives and will of the represented? In very general terms, the two primary responses to this question point in opposite directions: one affirms that power can and must be grounded solidly in its popular constituents, that, through representation, the people's will is expressed in power; and the other claims that sovereign authority, even popular sovereignty, must through the mechanisms of representation be separated and shielded from the will of the constituents. The trick is that all forms of modern representation combine, in different measures, these two seemingly contradictory mandates. Representation connects and cuts.

"'Representative democracy' might appear today as a pleonasm," writes Jacques Rancière. "But it was initially an oxymoron."[4] In modern history and the history of capitalist societies, the possibility of putting together power and consent, centrality and autonomy, has been revealed as an illusion. Modernity has left us the legacy, both in its socialist and liberal figures, of at once the necessity of the sovereign unity of power and the fiction of its being a relation between two parties.

The Communards clearly recognized—and this was no error—the falsity of the claims of modern representation. They were not satisfied to choose every four or six years some member of the ruling class who pledges to represent them and act in their interests. It took many years for others to catch up with the Communards and see through the falsity of modern representation—and if you want one particularly tragic episode in this monstrous history, ask someone who lived through the passage from the "dictatorship of the proletariat" to the "all people's state" in the era of Khrushchev and Brezhnev—but now this perception is becoming generalized. Unfortunately, though, the recognition that leaders don't really represent our desires is most often met with resignation. It's better than authoritarian rule, after all. In effect, the modern paradigm of representation is coming to an end without there yet taking shape a real democratic alternative.

False assumption: Critique of leadership = refusal of organization and institution

Today's social movements consistently and decisively reject traditional, centralized forms of political organization. Charismatic or bureaucratic leaders, hierarchical party structures, vanguard organizations, and even electoral and representative structures are constantly criticized and undermined. The immune systems of the movements have become so developed that every emergence of the leadership virus is immediately attacked by antibodies. It is crucial, however, that the opposition to centralized authority not be equated with the rejection of all organizational and institutional forms. Too often today the healthy immune response turns into an autoimmune disorder. In order to avoid traditional leadership, in fact, social movements must devote more not less attention and energy to the invention and establishment of such forms. We will return below to investigate the nature of some of these new forms and the existing social forces that can nourish them.

The path to realize these alternatives, however, is at times circuitous, with numerous pitfalls. Many of today's most intelligent political theorists, often ones with rich activist experiences, regard the problematic of organization as a festering wound that remains from past defeats. They agree in general and in theory that organization is necessary, but seem to have a visceral reaction to any actual political organization. You can taste in their writing a hint of bitterness from dashed hopes—from inspiring liberation movements that were thwarted by superior forces, revolutionary projects that came to naught, and promising organizations that went bad and fell apart internally. We understand this reaction and we lived together with them through many of these defeats. But one has to recognize defeat without being defeated. Pull out the thorn and let the wound heal. Like the "unarmed prophets" whom Machiavelli ridiculed, social movements that refuse organization are not only useless but also dangerous to themselves and others.

Indeed many important theoretical developments of recent decades, including ones we have promoted, have been cited to support a generalized refusal of organization. Theoretical investigations, for instance, of the increasingly general intellectual, affective, and communicative capacities of the labor force, sometimes coupled with arguments about the potentials of new media technologies, have been used to bolster the assumption that activists can organize spontaneously and have no need for institutions of any sort. The philosophical and political affirmation of immanence, in such cases, is mistakenly translated into a refusal of all norms and organizational structures—often combined with the assumption of radical individualism. On the contrary, the affirmation of immanence and the recognition of new generalized social capacities are compatible with and indeed require organization and institution of a new type, a type that deploys structures of leadership, albeit in new form.

In short, we endorse in general the critiques of authority and demands for democracy and equality in social movements. And yet we are not among those who claim that today's horizontal movements in themselves are sufficient, that there is no problem, and that the issue of leadership has been superseded. Behind the critique of leadership often hides a position we do not endorse that resists all attempts to create organizational and institutional forms in the movements that can guarantee their continuity and effectiveness. When this happens the critiques of authority and leadership really do become liabilities for the movements.

We do not subscribe either, at the opposite extreme, to the view that the existing horizontal movements need to dedicate their efforts to resuscitating either a progressive electoral party or a vanguardist revolutionary party. First of all, the potential of electoral parties is highly constrained, particularly as the state is ever more occupied (or sometimes actually colonized) by capitalist power and thus less open to the influence of parties. Second, and perhaps more important, the party in its various forms is unable to make good on its claims to be representative (and we will return to the question of representation in more detail). Progressive electoral parties, in the opposition and in power, can tactically have positive effects, but as a complement to not a substitute for the movements. We have no sympathy with those who claim that, because of the weakness of the movements and the illusions of reform through electoral means, we need to resuscitate the corpse of the modern vanguard party and the charismatic figures of liberation movements past, propping up their rotting leadership structures. We too recognize ourselves as part of the modern revolutionary and liberation traditions that gave birth to so many parties, but no act of necromancy will breathe life into the vanguard party form today—nor do we think it desirable even if it were possible. Let the dead bury the dead.

Leaderless movements as symptoms of a historical shift

To confront the leadership problem we need to recognize, first, that the lack of leaders in the movements today is neither accidental nor isolated: hierarchical structures have been overturned and dismantled within the movements as a function of both the crisis of representation and a deep aspiration to democracy. Today's leadership problem is really a symptom of a profound historical transformation, one that is currently in midstream—modern organizational forms have been destroyed and adequate replacements have not yet been invented. We need to see this process to its completion, but to do so we will eventually have to extend our analysis well beyond the terrain of politics to investigate the social and economic shifts at play. For now, though, let us focus on the political terrain and the challenges of political organization.[5]

One simple answer to the question—Where have all the leaders gone?—is that they are behind bars or buried underground. The ruling powers and the forces of reaction (often in collaboration with the institutional parties of the Left) have systematically imprisoned and assassinated revolutionary leaders. Each country has its own pantheon of fallen heroes and martyrs: Rosa Luxemburg,

Antonio Gramsci, Che Guevara, Nelson Mandela, Fred Hampton, Ibrahim Kaypakkaya—you can make your own list. Although targeted killing and political imprisonment are the most spectacular, a host of other weapons of repression are continually employed that, although less visible, are often more effective: specialized legal persecution, from measures that criminalize protest up to extraordinary rendition and Guantanamo-style imprisonment; covert operations, including counterinformation programs, provocations by undercover law agents, and entrapment by goading potential activists into illegal acts; censorship, or using dominant media outlets to spread false information, create ideological confusion, or simply distort events by translating social and political questions into matters of style, fashion, or custom; the making of leaders into celebrities in order to co-opt them; and many, many more.[6] And don't forget the collateral damage of each of these methods of repression, not only those bombed or imprisoned "in error" but also the children of the imprisoned, the communities disrupted, and the generalized atmosphere of fear. The ruling powers deem such damage as acceptable costs of achieving the objective. Every counterinsurgency manual preaches the importance, by one means or another, of removing revolutionary leaders: cut off the head and the body will die.

No one should underestimate the effects and damages of such forms of repression, but on their own they reveal little about the decline of leadership in social movements. The repression and targeting of revolutionary and liberation leaders, after all, are not new and, in fact, focusing on such external causes gives us a poor understanding of the movements' evolution, in which the real motor of change is internal. The more profound answer to the question—Where have all the leaders gone?—is that leaders have constantly been critiqued and torn down from within the movements, which have made antiauthoritarianism and democracy their central foundations. The goal is to raise the consciousness and capacities of everyone so that all can speak equally and participate in political decisions. And such efforts are often accompanied by undermining all who claim to be leaders.

One powerful moment in this genealogy—one that still resonates with activists throughout the world—is constituted by the efforts of many feminist organizations in the late 1960s and early 1970s to develop tools to promote democracy within the movement. The practice of consciousness-raising, for instance, and making sure that everyone speaks at meetings, serves as a means to foster the participation of all in the political process and to make it possible for decisions to be made by everyone involved. Feminist organizations also developed rules to prevent members from taking the position of representative or leader, dictating, for example, that no one should speak to the media without the group's permission. An individual being designated as leader or representative of the group would undermine the hard-won accomplishments of democracy, equality, and empowerment within the organization. When someone did present herself or accepted being designated as a leader or spokesperson, she was subject to "trashing," a sometimes brutal process of criticism and isolation. Behind such practices, however, was an antiauthoritarian spirit and, more important, the desire to create democracy. The feminist movements of the 1960s and '70s were an extraordinary incubator for generating and developing the democratic practices that have come to be generalized in contemporary social movements.[7]

Such democratic practices and critiques of representation also proliferated in other social movements of the 1960s and '70s. These movements rejected not only the way male legislators claimed to represent the interests of women and the way the white power structure claimed to represent black people but also the way movement leaders claimed to represent their own organizations. In many segments of the movements, participation was promoted as the antidote to representation, and participatory democracy as the alternative to centralized leadership.[8]

Those who lament the decline of leadership structures today often point, especially in the US context, to the history of black politics as counterexample. The successes of the civil rights movement of the 1950s and '60s are credited to the wisdom and effectiveness of its leaders: most often a group of black, male preachers with the Southern Christian Leadership Conference and with Martin Luther King Jr. at the head of the list. The same is true for the Black Power movement, with references to Malcolm X, Huey Newton, Stokely Carmichael (Kwame Ture), and others. But there is also a minor line in African American politics, most clearly developed in black feminist discourses, that runs counter to the traditional glorification of leaders. The "default deployment of charismatic leadership," Erica Edwards writes, "as a political wish (that is, the lament that 'we have no leaders') and as narrative-explanatory mechanism (that is, the telling of the story of black politics as the story of black leadership) is as politically dangerous... as it is historically inaccurate." She analyzes three primary modes of "violence of charismatic leadership": its falsification of the past (silencing or eclipsing the effectiveness of other historical actors); its distortion of the movements themselves (creating authority structures that make democracy impossible); and its heteronormative masculinity, that is, the regulative ideal of gender and sexuality implicit in charismatic leadership.[9] "The most damaging impact of the sanitized and oversimplified version of the civil rights story," argues Marcia Chatelain, "is that it has convinced many people that single, charismatic male leaders are a prerequisite for social movements. This is simply untrue."[10] Once we look beyond the dominant histories we can see that forms of democratic participation have been proposed and tested throughout the modern movements of liberation, including in black America, and have today become the norm.

Black Lives Matter (BLM), the coalition of powerful protest movements that has exploded across the United States since 2014 in response to repeated police violence, is a clear manifestation of how developed the immune system of the movements against leadership has become. BLM is often criticized for its failure to emulate the leadership structures and discipline of traditional black political institutions, but, as Frederick C. Harris explains, activists have made a conscious and cogent decision: "They are rejecting the charismatic leadership model that has dominated black politics for the past half century, and for good reason."[11] The centralized leadership preached by previous generations, they believe, is not only undemocratic but also ineffective. There are thus no charismatic leaders of BLM protests and no one who speaks for the movement. Instead a wide network of relatively anonymous facilitators, like DeRay Mckesson and Patrisse Cullors, make connections in the streets and on social media, and sometimes "choreograph" (to use Paolo Gerbaudo's term) collective action.[12] There are, of course, differences within the network. Some activists reject not only orderly centralized leadership but also explicit policy goals and the practices of "black respectability," as Juliet Hooker says, opting instead for expressions of defiance and outrage.[13] Others strive to combine horizontal organizational structures with policy demands, illustrated, for example, by the 2016 platform of the Movement for Black Lives.[14] Activists in and around BLM, in other words, are testing new ways to combine democratic organization with political effectiveness.

The critique of traditional leadership structures among BLM activists overlaps strongly with their rejection of gender and sexuality hierarchies. The dominant organizational models of the past, Alicia Garza claims, keep "straight [cisgender] Black men in the front of the movement while our sisters, queer and trans, and disabled folk take up roles in the background or not at all."[15] In BLM, in contrast, women are recognized, especially by activists, to play central organizational roles. (The creation of the hashtag #BlackLivesMatter by three women—Garza, Cullors, and Opal Tometi—is often cited as indicative.) The traditional assumptions regarding gender and sexuality qualifications for leadership, then, tend to obscure the forms of organization developed in the movement. "It isn't a coincidence," Marcia Chatelain maintains, "that a movement that brings together the talents of black women—many of them queer—for the purpose of liberation is considered leaderless, since black women have so often been rendered invisible."[16] The BLM movement is a field of experimentation of new organizational forms that gathers together (sometimes subterranean) democratic tendencies from the past. And like many contemporary movements it presents not so much a new organizational model as a symptom of a historical shift.

The same people who lament the lack of leaders in the movements today bemoan too the dearth of "public intellectuals." We shouldn't forget that sometimes the refusal of leadership in political organizations corresponds to a plea to academics or intellectuals to represent the movement. This issue was powerfully present in the revolts of 1968, when new social subjects "took the floor" and spoke out. Michel de Certeau, a great moralist and attentive historian of that period, rightly emphasized that this prise de parole (literally: "taking the word") itself constituted a revolution, which is certainly true.[17] But the act of speaking out alone does not resolve the question of what to say. Hence the plea, often tacit but constant, to recognized intellectuals to become public, political intellectuals, that is, to indicate the political line. In France and elsewhere Jean-Paul Sartre functioned as a primary model. But in the late 1960s, as some students asked professors to represent the movements, they recognized the potential danger that such representatives would drown out the voices of others. Take, for example, the case of Jürgen Habermas in Frankfurt. He supported the movements and combatted Theodor Adorno's unfounded critiques of them, but he also undermined the movements by trying to rein them in to an ethics of individualism and the respect for formal democracy.[18] The activists themselves, however, tried to express (against individualism) their collective project and (against the merely formal democracy of the dominant parties and the state bureaucracy) the truth of the exploited and the necessity of revolution.

The most intelligent intellectuals have taken this lesson to heart. When they support movements rather than presenting themselves as spokespeople they seek to learn from the movements or even to play a role functional to them. Gilles Deleuze and Michel Foucault are good examples of this, as are

Edward Said and Gayatri Spivak, Judith Butler and Stuart Hall. Intellectuals, at least the best of them, have learned a fundamental lesson: never speak in the name of others. The movements instead must serve as guide, marking the political direction for intellectuals. Already in the early 1960s Mario Tronti understood well that the role of the "party intellectual" is over since all theoretical knowledge tends to be embedded in practical activity. So, let's be done with public intellectuals! That is not to say, of course, that academics should stay closed in their ivory towers or write in incomprehensible jargon, but that those with the talent and inclination should engage cooperatively in processes of co-research, valorizing and contributing to the theoretical knowledges and political decision-making that emerge from the movements.[19]

The first step, then, to understanding today's "leadership problem" is to reconstruct its political genealogies. As we said, leaders have been attacked by state and right-wing forces with a wide range of legal and extralegal tactics, but, more important, they have been prevented from emerging within the movements themselves. The critique of authority and verticality within the movements has become so generalized that leadership is viewed as contrary to the movements' goals. Liberation movements can no longer produce leaders—or, better, leadership is incompatible with the movements due to their challenges to authority, undemocratic structures, and centralized decision-making along with the critiques of representation and the practice of speaking for others. The movements have cut off their own head, so to speak, operating under the assumption that their acephalous body can organize itself and act autonomously. The internal critique of leadership thus leads us directly to the problematic of organization.

One exception that proves the rule: when leaders of liberation movements appear today they must be masked.[20] The masked subcomandante Marcos, until recently the primary voice of the Zapatistas, is emblematic. His mask served not only to prevent recognition by the Mexican police and the army but also to maintain an ambiguous relation with the democracy of the Zapatista communities. The mask marked his status as a *sub*comandante (undercutting the traditional military title) and allowed him to insist that "Marcos" is not an individual but a placeholder for all the subordinated: "Marcos is a gay person in San Francisco," he asserted, "a black person in South Africa, an Asian person in Europe, a Chicano in San Isidro, an anarchist in Spain, a Palestinian in Israel, an indigenous person in the streets of San Cristobal."[21] Beatriz (Paul) Preciado recognizes in Marcos's mask an act of disidentification in line with the most radical queer and transgender practices: "Zapatista, queer, and trans experiences invite us to de-privatize the face and the name so as to transform the body of the multitude into a collective agent of revolution."[22] But even the mask is not enough. On May 25, 2014, Marcos announced that his figure had always been merely a hologram for the movement and would cease to exist.[23] Even the mask of the leader must fade away.

The problem today. We need to take up the problem of leadership under current conditions and investigate two primary tasks: how to construct organization without hierarchy; and how to create institutions without centralization. Both of these projects contain the materialist intuition that constructing a lasting political framework does not need a transcendent power standing above or behind social life, that is, that political organization and political institutions do not require sovereignty.

This marks a profound break from the political logics of modernity. And it should be no surprise that the clear light that allows us to recognize these truths today, at the twilight of modernity, resembles the illumination of modernity's dawn. In the sixteenth and seventeenth centuries, for example, several authors in central Europe, including Johannes Althusius and Baruch Spinoza, fought against the theorists of sovereignty and the absolutist state in England and France, such as Thomas Hobbes and Jean Bodin, to pose alternative political visions. For centuries, princes and the social classes they ruled, the governors and the governed, clashed in assemblies in tests of their respective power. The first charters and constitutional documents, Sandro Chignola explains, were granted as recognition of the power of the ruled. The rulers and ruled, he says, formed the geometrical figure not of a circle (with a single center) but an ellipse (around two central points): "Historically, the governed social classes are the ones that provoked the princes and constrained them to draft statutes and documents that recognized libertates and immunity. And, vice versa, the incitement that the princes exercised on those social classes, trying to manage their challenges and to govern their otherwise irreducible resistance, is what helps to trace the outline of the ellipse."[24] We have no desire, of course, to return to the political arrangements of premodern Europe, but some of the truths of those struggles can still serve us today. Yes, we need to resist every form of leadership that repeats modern sovereignty, but we also need to rediscover what many knew long ago: sovereignty does not define the entire field of politics, and nonsovereign forms of organization and institution can be powerful and lasting.

CHAPTER 2

STRATEGY AND TACTICS OF THE CENTAUR

A commonplace of modern politics—from revolutionary organizations to bureaucratic structures, from electoral political parties to civic organizations—is not only that some must lead and others follow but also that the responsibilities for strategy and tactics are divided between these two. Leaders are responsible for strategy. As its Greek etymology tells us, strategy indicates the command of a general, a *strategus*, and the analogy between politics and warfare in this conception is not coincidental. The primary requirement of the strategist is to *see far*, across the entire social field. From the hilltop, leaders must have the power to analyze the strengths and weaknesses of the forces we are up against. The strategist must also adopt the standpoint of the general interest, setting aside or balancing partial interests and factions. Finally, the strategic role of leadership requires seeing far in the temporal sense, prudence, planning for the long term and creating a continuous arc of activity.

Tactics, which involves the arrangement of forces, is the domain of followers, who are limited because they act on the interests of a specific group and their concerns are short-term. Their operations require knowing the immediate surroundings in space and time. Only when aligned with the strategic vision can tactical work contribute to the general efforts over the long term.

The centaur, half human and half beast, is emblematic of the union of the leaders and the led. The upper, human half designates the strategic capacities and thus intelligence, knowledge of the social whole, understanding of the general interest, and ability to articulate comprehensive long-term plans. The lower half instead needs only knowledge of its immediate surroundings to accomplish its tactical efforts. Partial, tactical struggles express our visceral revulsion toward the forms of domination we face and our passion for freedom.

Museum of revolutions past

Modern revolutionary theorists continuously grappled with the problem of leadership, of strategy and tactics. Their solutions generally fall into two groups, both of which pose a dialectic between spontaneity and authority. The first group focuses on quantities: spontaneity and authority need to be combined in just measure so that the force of the people will be both expressed and contained in structures of representation. Popular struggles and worker revolts are the dynamo that drives the political process but the will of the people alone, according to this view, lacks constancy, wisdom, expertise, and knowledge. Leaders must represent the people but with safeguards to stop the expression of the popular will when necessary. A balance is thus required between secrecy and transparency, the clandestine and the public. The centaur is again the imagined beast of this balance. Its human half, functioning through reason and law, seeks the people's consent and solicits popular action, whereas the animal half applies the force of authority and coerces when necessary. The one without the other, as Machiavelli would say, is not lasting, but they must be balanced. Too much authority for the leaders or too much power to the people, too much coercion or too much reliance on consent, too much secrecy or too much transparency will prove disastrous. The key is the correct balance, just measure.[1]

Leon Trotsky articulates what few modern theorists of politics are able or willing to express in such explicit terms: "In order to conquer the power, the proletariat needs more than a spontaneous insurrection. It needs a suitable organization; it needs a plan; it needs a conspiracy."[2] In effect, the modern problem of revolutionary organization can be expressed in the general formula: revolution = spontaneity + conspiracy. The primary line of debate, in Trotsky's view, is about proportions: he criticizes Louis Auguste Blanqui for too much conspiracy while condemning Bakunin for too much spontaneity. The science of politics appears in the form of a recipe book providing the cook with the proper quantities.

A second group of modern solutions to the organization problem emphasizes temporal sequence. The spontaneity and the will of the people come first, and thus the people have priority over the authority of the leaders. Rosa Luxemburg, for example, rightly mocks "the lovers of 'orderly and well-disciplined' struggles," who think that political actions should be initiated from above and "carried out by the decision of the highest committees."[3]

Leaders, she argues, must appreciate the power and learn from the intelligence of popular revolts and workers' struggles. Mass action is educational and recruits more to the struggle. And yet even Luxemburg, who is chastised by Georg Lukács for overestimating "the spontaneous, elemental forces of the Revolution," insists that such spontaneous action must at the proper moment be brought into a dialectic with authority.[4] Although the role of the party is not to initiate political action, she argues, once the struggle has fully emerged, the party must "assume political leadership in the midst of the revolutionary period" and take responsibility for "the *political leadership* of the whole movement."[5] Whereas the revolt and even insurrection of the masses are given the initial role, their actions must then be unified in the form of a constituent power: the strategic direction of leadership or the party "completes" the movements and dictates the general interest. Popular action may come first, but the authority of leadership prevails in the end. The temporal sequence of this second group of solutions thus repeats the substance of the dialectic between spontaneity and authority expressed in the first group.

Even modern revolutionary projects that have attempted to put workers at the center have often fallen back into the same framework of leadership. Consider, for example, the notion that the "technical composition" of the proletariat should guide the "political composition" of revolutionary organization. "Technical composition" here refers to the organization and socialization of labor-power in economic production, and recognizing the present technical composition requires a thorough investigation of what people do at work, how they produce and cooperate productively. The idea that the technical composition should guide the political composition undermines notions that workers can't represent themselves: the same capacities for cooperation and organization that workers develop in production can be deployed in politics too. Such efforts, however, although born of healthy instincts, have sometimes had perverse effects in the context of modern workers' struggles, leading back to the same dynamic between leaders and followers, reformulating schemas of hierarchy and representation. For a long period the urban, white, male factory worker, recognized as being at the pinnacle of capitalist production, was thought to be able to represent all those engaged in other forms of labor, waged and unwaged—a formulation that peasants, feminists, people of color, indigenous activists, and others have rightly refused. The hierarchies of capitalist production are effectively transferred onto revolutionary organization.[6]

The various modern revolutionary and progressive conceptions of the relationship between leadership and the people, between authority and democracy, can be summed up with the paradoxical expression "democratic centralism." The tension between the two terms serves both to recognize the separation and to indicate their possible or progressive synthesis. Antonio Gramsci imagines this dual relation—division and synthesis—in dynamic topological terms. Democratic centralism, he explains, "is a centralism in movement, so to speak, that is, a continuous adequation of the organization to the real movement, a bringing together in sync [*un contemperare*] of the thrusts from below with the command from above, a continuous insertion of the elements that bloom [*sbocciano*] from the depths of the masses in the solid frame of the apparatus of direction that assures the continuity and regular accumulation of experiences."[7] Democratic centralism thus appears as a unity of opposites, the result of a properly dialectical process. The two halves, however, democratic initiative and central leadership, are not really opposites but instead have different capacities and fulfill different roles—tactics and strategy, spontaneity and political planning—which is why they fit together in Gramsci's imagination like gears that line up and mesh.

First call: Strategy to the movements

The political division of labor within revolutionary and liberation movements between leaders and followers, strategy and tactics, rests on an appraisal of the capacities of the different actors. Only the few, the thinking goes, have the intelligence, knowledge, and vision needed for strategic planning and therefore vertical, centralized decision-making structures are required. What if we were able to verify, instead, that capacities for strategy today are becoming generalized? What if democratic, horizontal social movements were developing the ability to grasp the entire social field and craft lasting political projects? This would not mean that centralized decision-making structures can be abolished, that a pure horizontality would be sufficient. In our view, in fact, under present conditions, a dynamic between verticality and horizontality, between centralized and democratic decision-making structures, is still necessary. But recognizing today's changing social capacities allows us to reverse the polarity of the dynamic, and that shift could have extraordinary effects. Our first call is thus to invert the roles: *strategy to the movements and tactics to leadership.*[8]

Throughout modernity, of course, movements continually arose that refused leadership. After 1807, for example, after the king of Prussia's armed forces had failed, organized Prussian and Austrian peasants (Carl von Clausewitz called them a powerful torch) fought back Napoleon's army. The result, however, was the establishment of a universal draft by the Prussian monarchy, subjecting the guerrilla forces to national ideology.[9] The experience of popular revolts in Spain from 1808 to 1813 had similar characteristics.[10] More relevant for us are the various phases of Vietnamese popular war against France and the United States, which had characteristics similar to many other antiimperialist struggles of the twentieth century. Popular rebellions were the foundation of the anticolonial struggle, but they were eventually absorbed under the direction of the party and the military organization. Today it is both possible and desirable that the movements develop autonomous and lasting political strategic capacities.

Tactical leadership

Whereas social movements and structures of democratic decision-making should chart the long-term course, leadership should be limited to short-term action and tied to specific occasions. Saying that leadership is tactical, and thus occasional, partial, and variable, then, does not mean that organization is not necessary. To the contrary, organizational issues require more attention but a new type of organization is necessary, one subordinated to and in service of the movements.

We will return later to analyze more fully the conception of tactical leadership, but for now we can simply indicate in general terms situations that require swift response, the most obvious of which involve threats of violence. Although many recent social movements have experimented with participatory decision-making on a large scale, we do not (yet) have adequate means to confront immediate problems in a democratic way. One type of threat that needs a tactical leadership can be grouped under the theme of counterpower: confronting the existing power structures, especially regarding questions of force and under the threat of violence, often requires prompt decision-making. It is irresponsible for even the most democratic street protest not to have a security team to protect activists against violence—to change the route, for example, when the police or thugs attack. The same need applies at a larger

scale when progressive or revolutionary movements are threatened by the violence of oligarchies, death squads, media attacks, militias, right-wing reaction, and the like.

The issue becomes much more complex when we confront the traditional
assumption that leadership is required for effective political organization and
in order to sustain and guide institutions. As we said earlier, we view the needs
for political organization and institutionalization to be not only still necessary
but even greater than before. We will need to approach this from both sides.
On the one hand, we will investigate how the multitude has become and can
become capable of organizing politically and also of sustaining and innovating
institutions; the multitude is achieving, for instance, an entrepreneurial role in
society and politics (as well as in economic relations). On the other hand,
when leadership structures are necessary within organizations and institutions
their functioning must be limited to tactical judgments regarding how to
apply the general social strategy in changing circumstances, and leadership
must be completely subordinated to and submerged in the multitude.

You're playing with fire, many of our friends will say—or simply deluding
yourselves! You'll never limit the power of leaders, even the honest ones.
Once you give them a little, they will take more and more. How many times
have you heard autocratic politicians claim they are merely servants of the
people? How many times have you seen a political activist lifted up into a
position of power by social movements only then arrogantly to rule over
them? These friends are right that no legal safeguards or formal structures or
divisions of power will effectively guard against the usurpation of power. This
is ultimately a relation of force, even among allies. The only sure means to
constrain leadership to a merely tactical role is for the multitude to occupy
completely and firmly the strategic position and defend it at all costs. We
should focus on developing the strategic capacities of the multitude, in other
words, and limiting leadership to tactics will follow.

Strategic movements

To equate movements with strategy means that the movements already have
(or can develop) adequate knowledge of the social reality and can plot their
own long-term political direction. We must recognize, on the one hand, the
knowledges and organizational capacities that people already possess and, on

the other, what is necessary for the entire multitude to participate actively in the construction and implementation of lasting political projects. People do not need to be given the party line to inform and guide their practice. They have the potential to recognize their oppression and know what they want.

The capacities for strategy that are already widespread in social movements are often not immediately evident. A good first step toward unearthing them is to demystify the concept of "spontaneity." Distrust anyone who calls a social movement or a revolt spontaneous. Belief in spontaneity, in politics as in physics, is based simply on an ignorance of causes—and, for our purposes, ignorance of the existing social organization from which it emerges. When in February 1960, for instance, four young black men sat at the whites-only lunch counter of a Woolworth's in Greensboro, North Carolina, and refused to leave, journalists and many academics described it as a spontaneous protest—and from the outside it certainly appeared to come from nowhere. But when you look within the movement, as Aldon Morris argues, you can see the rich organizational structures from which it emerged, including student associations, church and community groups, and sections of the NAACP, as well as the cycle of sit-in protests that spread throughout the US South in the 1950s. The Greensboro sit-in was not spontaneous but an expression of a broad network of ongoing organizational activity.[11] The same is true of many workers' struggles throughout Europe in the 1960s and '70s, which the dominant trade unions and party leaders called "spontaneous" in order to discredit them. They too, however, were the fruit of continuous, tireless agitation inside and outside the factories.[12] Belief in spontaneity is an ideological position— ignorance is never really innocent—that serves (consciously or not) to eclipse and discredit the work, knowledge, and organizational structures that stand behind events of protest and revolt. We need to investigate the structures and experiences from which "spontaneity" arises and reveal what those social bodies can do.[13]

To discover how widespread capacities for strategy are, however, we have to look beyond activist organizations and beyond the realm of politics; we need to delve into the social terrain. For this reason, in parts II and III we will descend from the realm of politics to investigate the social and economic relationships of cooperation that constitute contemporary society. Only in this way will we be able to gauge accurately people's current capacities, to recognize the existing wealth but also the deficiencies, and thus to plot what must be done.

Toward a new problem The inversion of strategy and tactics promises (or alludes to) a substantially new problem. Rather than posing the proper relationship between the masses and leadership, spontaneity and centralism, democracy and authority, as do the theories of the modern revolutionary, progressive, and liberal traditions, this inversion fundamentally alters the meaning of the two poles and thus transforms the entire political paradigm. Action of the multitude is (or must be) no longer tactical, short-sighted, and blind to the general social interest. The calling (*Beruf*) of the multitude is strategic. And, correspondingly, leadership must become something fundamentally different: a weapon to wield and dispose of as the occasion dictates.

A party of movements?

Progressive political parties in Latin America and southern Europe, which emerged from powerful social movements, have seemed at certain moments and in certain respects already to respond to our call to invert the roles of strategy and tactics. In Latin America from the 1990s to the first decade of this century a series of progressive parties were carried to power on the backs of social movements. The Brazilian Workers' Party, first elected to power in 2002, emerged from the opposition to the military dictatorship and a long history of trade union organizing. The Bolivian Movement for Socialism, first elected to power in 2005, emerged directly from the massive antineoliberal and indigenous struggles of the early years of the decade. In different respects, for certain periods, and with various limitations, progressive parties elected in Ecuador, Venezuela, Argentina, and Uruguay have shared connections to the power of social movements. Syriza in Greece and, even more clearly, the Podemos Party founded in Spain in 2014 follow on the Latin American experiences. Podemos was born from the wave of social struggles including the "15M movement" of encampments in major cities in the summer of 2011 that expressed indignation at austerity policies and social inequality; the "mareas" protesting cuts in healthcare, education, and other sectors; the antieviction "Platform of those affected by mortgages"; and various other metropolitan and grassroots initiatives. These parties experiment with new relationships between horizontal and vertical elements, but do they actually constitute a

new organizational form—a party of movements—in which strategy and tactics have been inverted?

We are not in the position yet to evaluate in detail any of these specific
experiences and the fates of several of them are still open. Based on our analysis so far, though, we can offer a few criteria for evaluating these experiments
and some warnings regarding the pitfalls they face. One danger facing these
projects can be expressed in terms of populism, when populism is understood
as the operation of a hegemonic power that constructs "the people" as a unified figure, which it claims to represent.[14] Populist political formations may
recognize their source in the movements that brought them to power, but
they always end up separating themselves from that source and affirming that
political power is a domain autonomous from the social, claiming that they
can discern and represent the general will of the people. Populists overesti-
mate the importance of state power and underestimate the political expressions of social movements for not only their own legitimacy but also the
effectiveness of the project. Populism is thus characterized by a central paradox: constant lip service to the power of the people but ultimate control and
decision-making by a small clique of politicians. In this respect left populism
and right populism are too often uncomfortably close. And don't trust politicians, even ones who have emerged from the movements, who tell you that
they first need to achieve state control and then they will restore the power
to the movements. Populism, in this framework, retains strategy in the hands
of leadership and limits the movements to tactical actions.

In all the recent political experiences in Latin America and the Mediterranean, however, the relationship between leadership and movements is one
of constant internal struggle that often coincides with important synergies.
The wager of many Spanish activists who were deeply engaged in the 15M
movement and who decided to support Podemos, for example, is that the
strength of the movements can overcome any tendency on the part of leaders to assert the "autonomy of the political" and, indeed, the autonomy of
leadership's own strategic, decision-making powers. Even more significant
may be the interplay of national organizations and successful municipal initiatives, such as Ahora Madrid, Barcelona en comú, and Coalició compromís
in Valencia. Certainly, the outcome will be decided by a relation of force.
Activists in each of the other experiences have made similar wagers and few,
if any, can be said to have been completely successful. But a wager lost is not
always a bad bet.

Let's end with an historical example—an improper one as are all such historical references, and yet one that has some truth in it. The revolutionary period of 1848 in Europe has strong resonances with the season of rebellions that followed the economic crises of 2007–2008 and that broke out into the open in 2011, especially in the Mediterranean and extending into the Middle East. And very similar are their fates. In 1848 the democratic uprisings in Europe could not transform themselves into revolutionary movements. They developed as social powers, demanding rights and wealth, but quickly they were either brutally defeated by the ruling powers or stripped of their subversive roots and co-opted in national and nationalist ideologies aimed at constructing modern nation-states. Today, many uprisings and protest movements are subjected to similar forms of repression and even more dangerous forms of blackmail. In some instances, for instance, those who fought for freedom and democracy against the illiberal, military, and dictatorial regimes that had been grafted together with projects of capitalist development find themselves confronted on the other side by forces of religious mystification, fanaticism, and ferocious priestly creeds. Fighting against the one seems to throw you, willingly or not, into the arms of the other. The multitudes are certainly right to rebel, but it is no surprise that many have shipwrecked trying to navigate through such brutal hazards. Marx noted that the proletariat first appeared as an organized political force in June 1848 on the Paris barricades and the fact that it was quickly crushed did not dull the historical significance of its combat. Don't underestimate today the lasting power of those who fight and are defeated.

CHAPTER 3

CONTRA ROUSSEAU; OR, POUR EN FINIR AVEC LA SOUVERAINETÉ

The reduction of leadership to a tactical role and the elevation of the multitude to the level of strategy undermine the position of sovereignty in modern politics. If sovereign is the one who decides, as Carl Schmitt famously writes, then sovereignty cannot survive this inversion, at least not in recognizable form.[1] Leaders can still decide over tactical matters tied to specific occasions in short-term mandates, but such decisions are firmly subordinated to the dictates of the multitude. Regarding core, strategic political decisions, "the one" should never decide. The many must make decisions.

Do not mourn the loss of sovereignty—on the contrary! Sovereignty is too often confused with independence and self-determination, but in contrast to those concepts sovereignty always marks a relationship of power and domination: sovereignty is the exclusive right to exercise political authority. The sovereign always stands in relation to subjects, above them, with the ultimate power to make political decisions. The autonomy of sovereign authority was born in Europe when, in the transfer of imperial power from Rome to Constantinople, the Roman concept of *imperium* was transformed by Christian theology. From that moment on, sovereign power took on absolutist characteristics—and later, with the territorial dissolution of the empire and, eventually, with the birth of nation-states, this was reinterpreted as the basis of the modern state, becoming the motor of a continuous concentration of power. This notion of sovereignty was instrumental to the formation of Westphalian international law, an order built of national sovereignties.[2]

Keep in mind that the concept of sovereignty that functioned in early modern Europe was also a pillar of the ideological justification of conquest and colonization. As Alvaro Reyes and Mara Kaufman argue convincingly, for European political thinkers from Juan Gines de Sepulveda to Thomas Hobbes and John Locke, the concept of sovereignty emerges from the colonial mentality and is conceived explicitly in relation to the natives of "America," who are considered populations that remain in the state of nature. The sovereign must rule over those who cannot rule themselves. Sovereignty, however, is not limited to the colonies. Reyes and Kaufman note that, whereas many political models and institutions are transported from Europe to the colonies as part of the conquistador's armory and the colonial administrator's operations manual, some also flow back and are established at the center of European structures of rule. Although born as part of the ideological framework justifying the conquest and colonization of the Americas, colonial sovereignty migrates to Europe and sustains there a kind of internal colonialism, a lasting structure of political domination that divides rulers from ruled and centralizes political decision-making.[3]

One modern strategy to contain the powers of sovereignty has been to subordinate it to the rule of law, that is, to limit the decision-making powers of the sovereign within the established system of norms. This indeed has been an effective defensive maneuver, but it really displaces rather than resolves the problem. No notion of custom or tradition or natural right can negate the need for political decision-making, and the rule of law does not provide an alternative decision-making power. Another modern strategy has been to appropriate sovereignty from rulers, reverse positions within the structure, and establish a new sovereign power: the third estate will be sovereign, the nation will be sovereign, even the people will be sovereign. The dictatorship of the proletariat—a concept invented to counter the existing dictatorship of the bourgeoisie—stands in a long line of modern attempts to reverse positions within the relationships defined by sovereignty. Not only are the structures of domination preserved by such alternative conceptions of sovereignty, but they also require, as we said earlier, the unity and homogeneity of the sovereign, decision-making subject. The people or the nation or the proletariat can be sovereign only when it speaks with one voice. In contrast, a multitude, since it is not one but many, can never be sovereign.

The sovereign decision is always in some sense the judgment of god, a god on earth, whether the monarch, the party, or the people. Let's finally be done, as Antonin Artaud proclaims in a radio transmission by that title, with the judgment of god. To be done with sovereignty more not less attention on political decision-making is required. We must focus more intensely on the processes and structures that can support collective decisions. Opposing sovereignty in this way poses a central task for our analysis: to discover how the many can decide—and rule themselves together without masters.

Critique of representation

Our call—"strategy to the movements, tactics to leadership"—rests on the assumption that social movements and political institutions can be interwoven, nourishing and advancing one another so that people do not need representatives to make political decisions for them, that people, in effect, can represent themselves. "To represent oneself" is an intriguing limit concept, but really it is an oxymoron. Representation, like sovereignty, is necessarily founded on a relationship of unequal power of political decision-making. People claiming their own decision-making powers undermines both sovereignty and representation.

Rousseau is well known for pronouncing the impossibility of political representation. The will, he explains, cannot be represented: either it is yours or it isn't; there is no middle ground.[4] One might take his rejection of representation and delegation as an affirmation of participation and direct democracy. But really when he celebrates the "general will" in contrast to the "will of all," Rousseau theorizes a form of representation that underwrites sovereign power. The general will constructs a representative public, not as a forum of plural voices but a unified, unanimous political subject that mystifies and stands in for all. How could you differ with or oppose the general will? After all, Rousseau tells us, it's *your* will and expresses *your* interest. Whereas the will of all, because of its plurality, is inimical to sovereignty, the general will, unified and indivisible, is sovereign. In fact, sovereignty is nothing but the exercise of the general will. "Just as nature gives each man absolute power over his members," Rousseau argues, "the social pact gives the body politic absolute power over all of its members, and it is this same power which, directed by the general will, bears, as I have said, the name of sovereignty."[5] The only plurality that Rousseau can accept within the political body of this representative public is pushed to the extreme of individualism, since individual voices can be nullified in the general will.[6]

Viewed in historical context and, in particular, the context of the social and economic conflicts of his times, Rousseau's conceptions of general will and public are complex, and even contradictory. Conflicting aspects of his theory, in fact, correspond to the contradictory phase of class struggle in eighteenth-century Europe. The general will brings together and negotiates between two poles. On one side, pointing in a revolutionary direction, it seeks to liberate the common from the dominion of the ancien régime and the hold of the aristocratic lords in order to give it back to the multitude. On the other side, pointing in a bourgeois direction, it makes representation into a form of command, a new form of transcendence, and constructs the public as an authority charged with defending the private. This latter position, which is at the base of not only Jacobin republicanism but also the dominant streams of modern political thought, must be demystified. In order to understand how the general will poses representation as a form of command we would have to unravel the different meanings of the term *public* and also the relationship between the public and the private, including the way theories of the public serve to mask and protect the power of private property. Let us set aside the historical question regarding Rousseau's theory in the eighteenth-century context and focus instead on how today his concepts designate a regime of representation that supports and protects private property against democracy and the common.

We will analyze in detail the nature of contemporary capitalist relations in parts II and III, but here we need to anticipate just a few aspects of the ways in which property and production are changing today. Those, including us, who speak of a new capitalism, cognitive capitalism, communicative capitalism, immaterial production, affective production, social cooperation, the circulation of knowledges, collective intelligence, and the like are trying to describe, on one hand, the new extension of the capitalist pillage of life, its investment and its modes of exploitation not only in the factory but throughout society and, on the other, the spread of the field of struggles, the transformation of the sites of resistance, and the way that today the metropolis has become a site of not only production but also possible resistances. In this context, capital cannot continue desubjectifying people—through processes of individualization and instrumentalization—and grinding their flesh to make a golem with two heads: the individual as the productive unit and the population as the object of mass management. Capital can no longer afford to do this because what most centrally creates economic value today is the common production of subjectivities. Saying that production is becoming common should not imply that workers are no longer exploited and worn down on the factory floor. It means simply that the principle of production, its center of gravity, has shifted, and creating value increasingly involves activating subjectivities in a network, capturing, siphoning off, and appropriating what they make in common. Capital today needs subjectivities; it depends on them. It is thus chained, paradoxically, to what undermines it, because resistance and the

affirmation of people's freedom rest squarely on the power of subjective invention, its singular multiplicity, its capacity (through differences) to produce
the common. Without the common, capital cannot exist, and yet with the
common the possibilities of conflict, resistance, and reappropriation are infi-
nitely increased. This is one delightful paradox of an era that has finally managed to shrug off the rags of modernity.

The mystification of contemporary capitalist relations rests on the almost
permanent re-proposition of two terms, the private and the public, which
function together as a kind of bait, but correspond to two ways of appropriating the common. In the first case, as Rousseau says, private property is an
appropriation of the common by an individual, expropriating it from others:
"The first man, who, having enclosed a piece of ground, to whom it occurred
to say *this is mine*, and found people sufficiently simple to believe him, was the
true founder of civil society. How many crimes, wars, murders, how many
miseries and horrors Mankind would have been spared by him who, pulling
up the stakes or filling in the ditch, had cried to his kind: Beware of listening
to this imposter; You are lost if you forget that the fruits are everyone's and
the Earth no one's."[7] Today private property negates people's right to share
and together care for not only the wealth of the earth and its ecosystems but
also the wealth that we are able to produce by cooperating with one another.
Rousseau's indignation at the injustice of private property remains today as
vital as it was over two hundred years ago.

Whereas Rousseau was so lucid and severe when identifying private property as the source of all kinds of corruption and cause of human suffering, he
stumbles when he confronts the public as a problem of the social contract.
Given that private property creates inequality, as Rousseau says, how can we
invent a political system in which everything belongs to everyone and to no
one? The trap closes in on Jean-Jacques—and on all of us. The public is meant
to answer that question: what belongs to everyone and to no one really belongs to the state. It was necessary to come up with something to dress up its
grip on the common, and to convince us that it represents us. It is legitimate
that the public assumes the rights to and makes decisions regarding what we
produce, the argument goes, because that "we" is really referred back to a
prior foundation, what allows us to exist. The common, the state tells us, does
not belong to us since we don't really create it: the common is our foundation, what we have under foot, our nature, our identity. And if it does not
really belong to us—being is not having—the grip of the state on the common

is not called appropriation but rather (economic) management and (political) representation. Don't worry. The action and expression of the public is really your will—a kind of antecedent expression and an infinite debt. QED: behold the implacable beauty of public pragmatism.

Conservative intellectuals have long dismissed democratic claims of political representation and romantic Rousseauianism and, although their arguments are often aimed against democracy itself, they do express a kernel of truth. Early in the twentieth century, for instance, Robert Michels famously theorized "the iron law of oligarchy" whereby political parties, even those that claim and attempt to represent their constituents, end up inevitably being ruled by a small clique. Michels's claims have strong resonances with a series of other analyses of modern organizations and their maladies, including the studies of bureaucracy of his teacher Max Weber and the theories of elites developed by Gaetano Mosca and Vilfredo Pareto. Michels targets the democratic claims of socialist parties (especially the German Social Democratic Party, the most prominent socialist party at the time) and strives explicitly to discredit Marxism, but his theory applies equally to all political parties and, more generally, all structures of representation. His primary aim is to dispel false claims: don't be fooled by parties that claim to represent you; all parties are ruled by oligarchies, even the socialists.[8] Indeed today, despite numerous attempted reforms, political parties and the coalitions that surround them still in substantial ways decide elections and other key questions of political life.[9]

Some of today's most influential conservatives effectively carry the banner that Michels raised, assuming at least implicitly that the democratic pretenses of representation are false. One complex but extraordinarily consequential example is the argument of US Supreme Court justices in the 2010 *Citizens United* decision that removes limits to how much individuals and corporations can spend to sway elections and policy. To even casual observers, unlimited contributions seem a clear corruption of the representative system, granting some vastly more influence than others—and, indeed, as Zephyr Teachout convincingly argues, the decision departs radically from the anticorruption traditions that characterized the first two hundred years of US constitutional thought. One could conclude that the justices in the majority simply believe that the rich (individuals and corporations) should rule, but the decision is more intellectually coherent when coupled with the assumption that the representative system is already corrupt and that democratic claims of the representative system are in large part invalid. Consider, for instance, the otherwise puzzling equation that Justice Anthony Kennedy, writing for the majority, makes between the responsiveness of a representative to a voter and to a contributor: "It is the nature of an elected representative to favor certain policies, and, by necessary corollary, to favor the voters and contributors who support those policies. It is well understood that a substantial and legitimate reason, if not the only reason, to cast a vote for, or to make a contribution to, one candidate over another is that the candidate will respond by producing those political outcomes the supporter favors. Democracy is premised on responsiveness."[10] We can read behind Kennedy's reasoning a tacit assumption, echoing Michels, that the democratic claims of political representation are substantially untrue. By equating the two types of "responsiveness," he is not really elevating contributions to the level of representation (or "democratic speech"), but effectively bringing representation down. All politicians, political parties, and political structures—equally on the left and right—are, despite their claims to representation, controlled by elites. There is thus no compelling reason, the argument seems to go, to favor one form of oligarchic control (tied to the representative and electoral system) and ban another (based on monetary contributions), no reason to favor the party and media elites over the wealthy elites.[11]

The kernel of truth contained in this purportedly realist and certainly cynical tradition of conservative thought is that the democratic claims of representation are false: political representatives and their electoral parties tend to limit decision-making to a small group, an elite, a kind of oligarchy. This is not merely a critique of the way that the political party system has been corrupted—think of the sham of "managed democracy" in Putin's Russia or numerous other examples—but an analysis of the fate of modern political representation itself. Politics ends up being controlled by elites, the conservative theorists seem to believe, and there is no reason to give advantage to the pious left-wing elites who feign democratic representation over the right-wing forces more honest about their elitism. Representation, to go back to our earlier discussion, is another form of sovereignty.

The rational kernel of this conservative line of thought, though, is thoroughly shrouded in a mystical shell, which maintains that democracy is incompatible with organization and institution and, ultimately, that creating a democratic society is unrealistic or undesirable. Instead, making democratic organization a reality is the aim of our first call. To do this we also need to question the "progressive" assumption that political representation is the royal road to democracy and recognize it instead as an enormous obstacle. Don't misunderstand us: we are not questioning representation in order secretly to support some vangardist (and thus nonrepresentative) solution or to refuse any participation in institutional structures that mix representation with democratic elements. Our base assumption instead is that those are not our only choices.

Frequently today social movements highlight the conflict between representation and democracy, and critique the insufficiencies of electoral schemas of representation in order to affirm the possibility of achieving a "real" democracy. In the 2001 uprising in Argentina against government austerity programs, for instance, protesters chanted, "Que se vayan todos," out with them all, opposing not a specific leader or party but the entire political system, and even more directly the Spanish indignados in May 2011 chanted, "no nos rapresentan," they don't represent us. These refusals are symptoms of an increasingly widespread and radical critique of the republican—or, better, Rousseauian—solutions to the problem of representation.[12]

Critique of constituent power

In the tradition of modern constitutional theory, constituent power—in contrast to established, constituted power—designates a revolutionary event, an exception to the legal order that expresses ex nihilo a new political order, with the US and French Revolutions as oft-cited examples. The sovereignty of constituent power in legal terms derives precisely from this exceptional character. And the act of "taking power" is distinguished by its evental nature, the social unity of the victorious revolutionary forces, and, for many commentators, its purely political (rather than social or economic) character.[13]

Several aspects of contemporary capitalist globalization, however, undermine the concept of constituent power defined in the modern legal tradition, as an originary and unconditioned power in a national frame.[14] The construction of the global market has weakened the powers of nation-states and lessened their constitutional autonomy. Nation-states retain important legal, economic, and administrative powers, of course, but increasingly these are subordinated to, on one hand, structures and institutions of global governance and, on the other, the demands of the capitalist world market. The national space can thus no longer serve, as it did most often in the modern tradition, as the theater of constituent power. Furthermore, the economic structures of global capital tend to condition—and increasingly absorb—legal and administrative apparatuses. Society as a whole is being subsumed within the circuits of neoliberal rationality and capitalist command, primarily through the workings of finance capital and the power of money. The conception of an autonomous political realm in which constituent power could act is thus ever more implausible.

Even more damaging for the concept of constituent power are the philosophical analyses that have thrown into question its revolutionary pretensions by demonstrating that it is not really separate from constituted power. Giorgio Agamben calls "the paradox of constituent power" the fact that, notwithstanding the insistence of legal theorists to the contrary, constituent power "remains inseparable from constituted power, with which it forms a system."[15] Jacques Derrida similarly highlights the problem that constituent violence cannot really be held distinct from state violence but instead repeats it: "the very violence of the foundation or position of law (*Rechtsetzende Gewalt*) must envelop the violence of conservation (*Rechtserhaltende Gewalt*) and cannot break with it."[16] Despite claims to exceptional status, Agamben and Derrida agree, constituent power cannot be conceived as a revolutionary force separate from constituted power.

One could conclude at this point that we should simply abandon the concept and stop talking about constituent power. That would deprive us, however, of an important means of understanding contemporary forms of resistance and revolt, and appreciating their potential for social transformation. It would be better to reconceive the concept by following how it is being rewritten in practice. In fact, the only reason we do not fully subscribe to Agamben's and Derrida's conclusions, even though they convincingly critique the notion of constituent power in the modern legal tradition, is that they do not grasp what constituent power really was in modern revolutionary struggles and what it is becoming in contemporary movements. We need to complement their critical positions with an appreciation of the materiality and plurality of revolutionary processes, and to pass from constituent power as a legal concept to constituent power as a political *dispositif* in action. There we can recognize it not as a unified event but rather in terms of social heterogeneity and temporal duration, a plural, replicating, continuous power. When constituent power abandons its unity, it gains rather than loses in revolutionary potential.

The most useful means to re-evaluate the concept of constituent power is to interpret and analyze the forms of struggle—which tend to become forms of life—that have blossomed since the end of the cold war and, in particular, those invented since 2011 in the experiences of encampment and occupation across the globe. In order to appreciate the significance of the cycle of struggles born in 2011, however, we need first to look back briefly at the extraordinary laboratory of political experimentation that developed in Latin America over the three previous decades: a back and forth trajectory, sometimes conflictual and sometimes reinforcing, between social movements and progressive governments—a development that today, in some respects, has come to an end.

One important characteristic of these Latin American experiences is that economic, social, and political action have proceeded together and are continuously mixed. In contrast to how the dominant modern forms of constituent power were based on a notion of "the autonomy of the political," that is, how they tended to isolate political dynamics from economic and social needs and translate them into jurisdictional powers of a formal constitution, the Latin American constituent processes at their best have subordinated any notion of the autonomy of the political to theories and practices of an ontology of social liberation—liberation from racism and coloniality, exploitation and ecological devastation, and the destructive imperialist legacies in the region, including military dictatorships, repeated coups d'état, death squads, and disappearances. The twin desires for economic participation and biopolitical decision-making give new definition to the concept of constituent power, which can be recognized, in part, by a shift from human rights as designated by the modern definition of constituent power to more substantial notions of social rights.

In Latin America we also witnessed a series of (partially successful) attempts to construct institutions of constituent power not as the result of a unitary political power and a centralized administration but as a product of a widespread plurality of political and social subjectivities. In the most successful experiences, constituent power has not taken the form of a unified revolt pursuing a linear sequence of uprising, insurrection, and the taking of power in order eventually to be transformed in formal constitutions. Instead it has developed through *continuous* operations of renewal prolonged in successive constitutional initiatives—a process that keeps open the collaborative and conflictual dynamic between social movements and progressive governments. These constituent processes still celebrate symbolic events in the narratives of their coming to power, but their essential core is really a series of short- and long-term dynamics that are more or less radical but in any case continuous. Where these developments have successfully taken place constituent power has revealed a new and deeper nature—that of being a widespread and multitudinous germination of the desire for freedom and equality. In short, the temporal and social unities of constituent power have become plural: the imagined punctual event has extended to a continuous process and the fantasy of a unified people has been expanded to a vast multitude.

In the powerful cycle of social movements that has developed since 2011, many of these elements not only reappeared but were also developed and deepened—subordinating notions of the autonomy of the political to projects that weave together political, economic, and social liberation; redefining constituent power as continuous processes of transformation; and promoting and constitutionalizing a plurality of diverse social subjectivities. A strong current running through these movements, first, weaves together the political, the economic, and the social through critiques of inequality, privatization, and the powers of finance. Consider, for instance, how a feeling of magic was created at the various urban encampments from Tahrir (Cairo) to Taksim (Istanbul), from Puerta del Sol (Madrid) to Zuccotti Park (New York), and from Ogawa Plaza (Oakland) to Cinelândia (Rio de Janeiro) when activists temporarily *made urban space common*, that is, no longer private or public but instead characterized by open access and experimental mechanisms of democratic management. Common urban space was experienced as a kind of antidote to the poisons of neoliberal privatization—and such experiences are symptomatic of a larger struggle that poses the common against the hegemony of private property and finance. Attacking private property and insisting on social cooperation and the common as motors of a new constituent process does not mean abandoning the desire to have access to social goods and to achieve security in life. On the contrary, as we will argue in chapter 6, private property is a central obstacle to security and access to the necessities of life for the vast majority. Moreover, today, given the increasingly social and cooperative nature of production, the right of property can no longer be a right to monopolize a good and hold individual decision-making powers—it can no longer be the right of a wolf that jealously defends its spoils from other wolves—but must instead be transformed into a right to the common, an exit from solitude through production in cooperation and a social existence in equality and solidarity.

   This cycle of struggle has also demonstrated, second, the plural temporalities of constituent power, beyond the brief event in the media limelight.
Constituent power is expressed not only as act but also as potential—indicating
both the power of future actions and the accumulated potential of the past. In
essence, the task of activists is to produce "constituency"—that is, create constituent potential—even during periods of seeming calm and then to ignite
the explosive charge of all that deposited potential when crisis erupts. Crises
can reveal in this way what was accumulated in the preceding period. One
could conclude that constituent power is not only (as Gilles Deleuze and Félix
Guattari say) a political "insistence" but an ontological "consistency." You should
not need a soothsayer, then, to see that the movements of 2011 are not fin-
ished. Their explosion was strong and the repression against them severe, but
their effects will continue. Even when out of view they are accumulating potential like a battery storing up an electric charge in wait for its next release.
And it is similarly obvious that the Greek referendum of July 2015 against neoliberal austerity was not an isolated event or a failure but the appearance in the
open of a subterranean river that will eventually—despite obstacles of renewed
nationalisms, racisms, and security apparatuses—spread across Europe. This is
an example of constituent consistency against the neoliberal regime of crisis.
   Finally, the transformation of constituent power into a plural, continuous
process has been deepened through its immersion in biopolitics: the content
of constituent power tends to become life itself. Protesters and activists not
only demand increased income and enhanced welfare services but also shine
a light on the fact that all life is subject to threat and exploitation. Black Lives
Matter has successfully highlighted the biopolitical nature of contemporary
struggles and the extent to which life itself is at stake, not only in the exercise
of excessive force by police but also in the everyday functioning of power in
its myriad forms.[17] The fact that black lives generally matter so little confirms
the necropolitical nature of the racial regime, which extends, of course, well
beyond the borders of the United States. It demonstrates too how any notion
of biopolitics must appreciate, as Alexander Weheliye argues, "how profoundly
race and racism shape the modern idea of the human."[18] The June 2013 protests in Brazil, which were ignited by a rise in urban transport costs, reveal
another face of biopolitics, posing the right to affordable transport as a critical
element of urban life. Such struggles demonstrate not only a temporal continuity but also a social extension of constituent action: an expansion of needs, desires, and social demands. Constituent power must become a composition of
diverse constituent singularities. (It could be useful in this regard to experiment

with the notion of "constituencies" understood now outside the standard electoral framework and instead as elements in a process of composition.) Conceiving of constituent power as a swarm concept, as a multitudinous pluralism means breaking with every fetishistic conception of political union and thus critiquing the concepts of the people and the nation for the ways they have traditionally been posed as unities.

At this point, in light of the forms of struggle that have emerged in recent years and the ways they are redefining constituent power as a continuous, radically plural, and biopolitical process, we are in a better position to recognize the distance from the modern legal concept, and especially how constituent power is no longer compatible with representation and sovereignty. As we saw earlier, the democratic claims of political representation are becoming ever more widely recognized as hollow and, similarly, speaking in the name of others is becoming ever more proscribed in social movements. In the place of representation, cooperation and composition arise as mechanisms by which a plurality of diverse political forces act in common. This shift away from representation occurs correspondingly in the economic field. When economic activity consists of wide networks of social cooperation aimed at producing and reproducing social life—subjectivating society—then the representative mandate no longer makes sense. In this context any recourse to notions of the general will seem completely out of place and illegitimate. The will of all can and must be organized in cooperation.

The exclusion of sovereignty from constituent power is especially significant. It is impossible to establish today a form of constituent power conceived in terms of transcendence or "exception." The sovereign requires unity, which is irremediably broken by the radical pluralism of the emerging, contemporary concept of constituent power. Whereas sovereign decisions are always *empty* insofar as the sovereign will stands separate from and above society and insofar as the sovereign rules over the exception, today's constituent power is always *full* of social contents to the point of overflowing. To reconceive constituent power, then, the exception of sovereign power must be replaced by the excess, that is, the overflowing nature of social production and cooperation.

Second call: Invent nonsovereign institutions

In modern political and legal thought, the institution is always posed as an instance of sovereignty. Despite their profound methodological and political differences, the German social scientists who from the eighteenth century to the twentieth founded and developed the theory of European public law—including Gustav Hugo and Friedrich Carl von Savigny, Paul Laband and Georg Jellinek, Carl Schmitt and Hans Kelsen—always maintain an indissoluble nexus between sovereignty and public institutions. It is certainly true that various developments in twentieth-century legal theory pry open the conventional understanding of the institution: the institutionalist theories of public law, for instance, represented in France by Maurice Hauriou and in Italy by Santi Romano, ground their understanding of institutions in the social powers of association; and, in a different way, the US pragmatists, with their insistence on context and practice, reject any foundational source of institutions. But even in these cases the essential link between institution and sovereignty is never broken. Only in the final decades of the twentieth century begin to appear the first cracks in this relationship. In particular, analyses of the emergence of legal institutions of global governance and, more generally, the passage from "government" to "governance" conceive legal institutions in relative autonomy from the sovereignty of nation-states. Günther Teubner, for example, who develops Niklas Luhmann's systems theory for legal thought, presents global governance in terms of autopoietic systems.[19] Even such innovative analyses, however, maintain the assumption of institutional sovereignty, albeit in a new, attenuated form.

We must go beyond the assumptions of institutional sovereignty in a really substantial way. As we said earlier, abandoning sovereignty does not mean relinquishing autonomy and self-determination. It means leaving behind, on one hand, the sovereign relationship of power and domination and, on the other, the mandate to unity. In this passage the multitude needs institutions more than ever—not institutions to rule over us but institutions to foster continuity and organization, institutions to help organize our practices, manage our relationships, and together make decisions.

Some decolonization projects from the mid-twentieth century provide inspiration for nonsovereign institutions. For example, Aimé Césaire and Léopold Senghor refused to accept, as Gary Wilder puts it, "the *doxa* that self-determination required state sovereignty." They were wary of the standard narrative that defines liberation as national independence and the establishment of a new sovereign state, and instead experimented with different forms of self-determination. Césaire's (ultimately failed) project of "departmentalization" for former French colonies, Wilder maintains, was one attempt to formulate a nonsovereign form of freedom.[20] The contemporary Kurdish Liberation Movement similarly poses decolonization in nonsovereign terms. In the 1990s Abdullah Öcalan advocated a shift in the goal of the movement from national liberation (and hence sovereignty) to "democratic autonomy." "Öcalan argues," according to Nazan Üstündağ, "that the three ills of contemporary civilization are nation states, capitalism and patriarchy, which together constitute what he calls 'capitalist modernity.' The aim of democratic autonomy is to recreate a political and moral society, which was destroyed by capitalist modernity."[21] The contemporary political experiments in Rojava (Kurdish Syria) give a clue to what a decolonial democratic autonomy might become.

The passage from property to the common, as we will see in chapter 6, also requires the creation of new institutions. Private property, which is characterized by a monopoly of access and decision-making, is at base an instance or derivative of sovereignty. Maintaining the common, that is, goods and forms of wealth to which we have equal access, requires that we create structures to manage democratically this wealth and our access to it. Sustaining the common requires networks of democratic governance and institutions of collective decision-making that are at once social and political. The encampments of the cycle of struggles that began in 2011, experimenting with the means to govern occupied urban territories outside the logic of private or public property, already give us a hint of the nature of these institutions of the common.

What would it mean, then, for a multitude to take power? Taking power remains for us a central objective and, as we have tried to explain, that does not mean simply reversing the relationship of domination, ruling over others, and, ultimately, maintaining the machinery of sovereign power while merely changing who sits at the controls. For a multitude to take power a first requirement is this: to invent new, nonsovereign institutions.

First response: Ground political projects in social life

Any attempt to respond to the first call to reverse the relationship between strategy and tactics or the second to compose new institutional forms from within the constituent movement of the multitude will invariably founder if we only look to the political terrain. With our eyes fixed on the political, assuming that people have the capacities necessary to organize and sustain long-term visions or to manage collectively lasting institutions—in short, that people are capable of democracy—will inevitably prove to be an illusion. If people were angels, you might be tempted to say, echoing James Madison's supposed realism, then and only then would a real democracy be possible. The only really effective and realistic way to respond today is to shift our perspective from the political to the social terrain or, better said, to wed the two. Only then will we be able to recognize and foster the existing, widespread circuits and capacities for cooperation and organization, and indeed to comprehend that the talents of social cooperation are a broad and solid basis for political organization.

Soviet society succeeded in the early 1920s—partially, temporarily—in connecting the radically democratic, constituent activity of the soviets to the institutional processes of social and economic transformation. For a brief period, the revolution became a real and proper "instituent" machine or, rather, a complex of constituent institutions. The formula that Lenin proclaimed in 1920, for instance, "communism = soviets + electrification," combines a form of political organization with a program of economic development.[22] The soviet project for industrial development quickly ran into insurmountable obstacles, in part due to the very low level of industrialization in Russia at the time and the narrow existing basis for industry in the social and educational resources of the population. What we might learn from Lenin's formula, nonetheless, is the need to couple revolutionary political organization with a project of social transformation.

It would be anachronistic, of course, to repropose any such plan of economic modernization (and in part II we will confront directly how the concept of economic development has to be rethought radically given contemporary social and ecological conditions). Today democratic organization must be coupled with a program of social and economic postmodernization or (post)modernization, a program that not only appreciates the destructiveness and tragedies of modernization but also grasps and organizes the contemporary capacities for social production and reproduction, that is, the potentials of existing forms of life. Such a program would have to present development not as simply producing more goods but instead as an ontological expansion of social being.

Today's challenge takes shape clearly when situated in the phases of capitalist development. Between the eighteenth and nineteenth centuries, as Marx explains, the center of gravity and the dominant mode of capitalist production passed from manufacture (which relies primarily on the division of labor to increase productivity) to large-scale industry (which increases productivity by introducing complex machinery as well as new schemes of cooperation). Carlo Vercellone extends Marx's periodization to the cusp of the twenty-first century, when capital's center of gravity shifts from large-scale industry to the phase of "general intellect," that is, production based in increasingly intense and widespread circuits of social cooperation as well as machinic algorithms as the basis to extract value from the production and reproduction of social life, a phase in which the distinction between the economic and the social is becoming increasingly blurred. This démarche is strictly linked to the analysis of the transformations of the mode of capitalist production from the phase of manufacture (with the formal subsumption of society under capital and the extraction of absolute surplus value) to the phase of large-scale industry (with the real subsumption of society and the extraction of relative surplus value) and finally to the phase of the productive organization of the general intellect (with what might be called the "cognitive" subsumption of society toward increasing cooperation and extractive, financial exploitation). *Socialized production and reproduction is biopolitical activity.* Noting this shift—or, really, this point of inflection in the curve of capitalist development—does not imply, of course, that large-scale industry has ceased to exist or even decreased in quantitative terms, just as agricultural production remained predominant in quantitative terms during the first period of industrialization. The shift instead redraws the lines of the global divisions of labor and power, and forces us to reorient our understandings of both the mechanisms of capitalist command and the forms of antagonism that challenge it.[23] We will return in more detail to all these concepts as well as this periodization in chapter 10.

Against alienated (that is, isolated, individualized, instrumentalized) labor arises a common resistance, which in the industrial regime was expressed most powerfully as a refusal of work and today is expressed in new forms of antagonism that are active across the entire social terrain. Constituent power can thus no longer be conceived in purely political terms and must be mixed with social behaviors and new technologies of subsistence, resistance, and transformation of life. The process of the construction of new institutions must be absorbed into this new materiality.

Our response is thus not yet a substantive proposal but rather a methodological guideline. A response, after all, should not be expected to offer a solution, and put the matter to rest. A good response, instead, catches the call and sends back a volley in the other direction creating a back-and-forth dynamic. Here, then, is our first response: when searching for the bases of new democratic forms of political and institutional organization, begin by investigating the cooperative networks that animate the production and reproduction of social life.

Against the autonomy of the political

The "autonomy of the political" is conceived by many today as a force of redemption for the Left, but in fact it is a curse from which we must escape. We use the phrase "autonomy of the political" to designate arguments that claim political decision-making can and should be shielded from the pressures of economic and social life, from the realm of social needs.

Some of the most intelligent contemporary proponents of the autonomy of the political conceive it as a means to rescue liberal political thought from the ideological dominance of neoliberalism, as an antidote to not so much neoliberalism's destructive economic policies, including privatization and deregulation, but rather the ways that neoliberalism transforms public and political discourse: the way it imposes economic rationality over political speech and effectively undermines all political reasoning that does not obey market logic. Whereas "liberal democracy," Wendy Brown argues, provided a "modest ethical gap between economy and polity," neoliberal political rationality closes this gap and "submits every aspect of political and social life to economic calculation."[24] Neoliberalism, according to this view, is the discursive and ideological face of the real subsumption of society under capital or, as Brown puts it, "the saturation of social and political realms by capital."[25] The ideological project to subordinate political reasoning to market logics, although now perhaps more intense, was not born with neoliberalism. The "methodological individualism" and "social choice" research models, which were key components of cold war ideology in the social sciences, particularly in the United States in the work of authors such as Kenneth Arrow, similarly insist that in order for research to be scientific it must base political rationality on economic logics of choice.[26] To argue for the autonomy of the political, in this context, is a way to refuse the dominance of market logic and to rescue political discourse from its demise, to restore not the economic liberalism of free markets but the liberal tradition of political thought, the liberal tradition of rights, freedom, and equality—

equaliberty, as Étienne Balibar says—that has strong resonances with the work of Hannah Arendt and stretches back at least to John Stuart Mill.[27]

The best of these liberal critiques of neoliberalism are honest and valuable endeavors but are inadequate for democratic projects. On the one hand, merely political notions of freedom and equality, which do not directly attack the social and economic sources of inequality and unfreedom, including the rule of property and the command over our productive and reproductive lives, will prove forever inadequate. On the other, as long as they are considered only in political terms, the capacities for people to rule themselves collectively will remain perpetually obscure, and thus real democracy sustained by a multitude able to make political decisions will appear a noble but unrealistic idea. Liberal theorists who ride the train of the autonomy of the political will never arrive at their destination.

A second group of left arguments—equally well intentioned but equally ineffective—is aimed at the economic face of neoliberalism, its projects of privatization and deregulation, and for them the autonomy of the political means primarily the return of some form of state and public control. In response to neoliberal globalization that has eroded the powers of national sovereignty, these authors seek to return to Keynesian or socialist mechanisms to reassert state powers over the economy and thereby to rein in the monstrous powers of finance and corporations. One can recognize both explicit and implicit calls for the "return of the state" as a force to thwart neoliberalism in the work of several progressive intellectuals, such as Paul Krugman, Álvaro García Linera, and Thomas Piketty. We regard the proponents of this version of the autonomy of the political as allies, and we are sympathetic to their aims, but—setting aside for the moment the desirability of state and public authority—we find contemporary appeals for Keynesian or socialist state control, although presented as eminently pragmatic, to be unrealistic and unrealizable: the social and political conditions on which these projects were based in the twentieth century no longer exist.[28] Under neoliberal rule, the traditional trade unions and organizations of the working classes have been utterly broken and corporatized, the social constitutions and welfare structures have been eviscerated, and the professional associations (and citizens themselves) scattered to the point of generating nostalgia even among right-wing elites. This is not to say that we should abandon all hope and resign ourselves to neoliberal rule, but instead that we must construct an alternative starting point, from the production and reproductive *lives of the multitudes as they are today, recognizing their capacities for organization and cooperation. This will be one of our tasks in part II.*

Finally, a small group of left intellectuals argues for the autonomy of the political in vanguard form, often presented in response to the inability of today's horizontal social movements to overthrow the existing capitalist structures and to take power themselves. Slavoj Žižek, for instance, following Alain Badiou, proclaims that "a new figure of the Master is needed...a Thatcher of the left: a leader who would repeat Thatcher's gesture in the opposite direction."[29] Knowing Žižek's work, we do not read these statements at face value, that is, as a proposal to elevate some leftist leader to the position of ultimate authority. His proclamations are better understood as provocative gestures animated, on the one hand, by understandable frustration at the demise of leaderless movements—he is writing in early 2013 when Zuccotti Park, Tahrir Square, and Puerta del Sol had all been swept clean by police—and, on the other, by dogmatic psychoanalytic assumptions about group formation, which we do not share. Jodi Dean, expressing similar frustrations at the defeat of Occupy but without Žižek's ability to hide behind the ambiguity of tongue-in-cheek provocations, extends the argument for vanguardist leadership.[30] As we argued earlier, given their highly developed immune systems, it would be impossible today—thankfully!—to impose central authority and traditional leadership over the dynamic and creative social movements.

These diverse affirmations of the autonomy of the political from the liberal to the radical Left share not only the fact of being fearful of and mesmerized by the authority of neoliberalism but also a faith in sovereignty as a recipe for restoring the power of the Left. It is true, as many of these authors maintain, that neoliberalism has undermined traditional political sovereign powers. There is no need to look further than the ways that in Europe the forces of global capital have managed the crisis since 2008 and how inelegantly the leaders of finance capital—going beyond all obstacles through the pressure of "markets"—have imposed their will not only on the debtor states but on all European countries. European societies have literally been reconstructed according to hierarchical criteria created by the power of money, the new coercive configurations of the division of labor (precarity, mass unemployment, etc.), the aleatory but systematic organization of productive infrastructures, the variable salary scales in the reordering of the norms of social reproduction, and the diverse designs and alternative measures rigidly established in the program for the supposed exit from the crisis but in reality for the deepening—through the crisis—of class divisions. Finance capital, under neoliberal command, is in this context unchained from the need to respond to the traditional political structures of representation and the functioning of national governments: electoral mechanisms, fundamental legal structures, and more are swept away.

This is all true—in Europe and throughout the world. We object, however, to the reasoning that, since neoliberalism undermines the political, the only means—let alone the only effective or desirable means—to combat neoliberalism is to restore the autonomy of the political, that this kind of play of opposites defines our political possibilities. We contend that we have other options, and, specifically, a nonsovereign and truly democratic organization of society is possible. Instead of resurrecting the autonomy of the political, the political must flow back into and be reclaimed by the social: political rationality and political action can no longer be considered autonomous but always completely embedded in the circuits of social and economic life.

We seem to be faced with a paradox: the more protests and social movements develop notions of democracy against the autonomy of the political, the more strongly some left intellectuals call for a "return to the political." This is not really a paradox from the perspective of these authors, though, because they generally conceive of sovereign political power as the necessary means to complete and consolidate democratic experiments and developments on the social terrain. We find ourselves thrust back to the double bind of the Communards: their "error" of dismantling the central committee and distributing decision-making power to all leads to defeat, and yet not dismantling the central committee would negate the democratic nature of their entire project. This double bind, however, does not (and perhaps never did) define our political alternatives. Sovereignty is not required for political projects to be effective, to win, to take power. Demonstrating the effectiveness of and existing conditions to support nonsovereign political institutions and democratic organization is a task we must address in subsequent chapters.

The concept of the Left may have been born in the seventeenth century with the vows of the New Model Army or at the end of the eighteenth century with the tennis court oaths at the Jeu de Paume. These were noble efforts to redistribute property and power and to configure a new freedom. But there is a gulf between those projects and those who claim the mantle of the Left today. Does it make sense to reopen once again the inquiry that the New Left launched fifty years ago? Can the Left become something *new based on today's social struggles, or instead, is the very concept of the Left something to be left behind? Whether or not we call it Left, contemporary movements have repeatedly affirmed the need to start over, to discover a radical new beginning: whether in the demand for distributive justice in the alterglobal struggles or the calls for real democracy in the Mediterranean springs—these are incitements to a radically innovative "what is to be done." It is clear to us, in any case, that the "autonomy of the political" in any of its forms cannot serve as a vehicle to foster new progressive or revolutionary projects but instead is a primary obstacle.*

CHAPTER 4

THE DARK MIRROR OF RIGHT-WING MOVEMENTS

Social movements, of course, are not all progressive. Right-wing movements, from the Nazis to religious fanatics, have animated some of the most destructive and barbaric political developments of the past century. Today right-wing movements, often in collaboration with right-wing governments, are once again on the rise. Understanding their nature and inner workings is an urgent task, but that would require a much longer study and is well beyond our aim in this chapter. Here we seek merely to individuate a few defining characteristics of right-wing movements to see what lessons progressive and liberation movements can derive from them.

The fact that social movements can be destructive and even that right-wing movements at times deploy some characteristics of liberation struggles should not lead us to distrust the politics of social movements in general or claim that somehow here the radical Left and radical Right meet. Right-wing movements do, in fact, reflect liberation movements but in a distorted mirror, inverting the primary elements such that identity becomes paramount and democracy deferred or negated. Efforts to restore or redeem the identity and unity of the people, in fact, emerge as a thread that runs through the diverse range of contemporary right-wing movements, both religious and secular, from European antimigrant movements to the Tea Party and from ISIS to anti-Muslim movements in India.

Right-wing thought and practice are in general not really conservative but reactionary: they seek not to preserve or protect what now exists but instead to restore a previous order. Those who have recently lost social power and prestige—such as white men in the United States, white working-class Europeans, or oligarchies in Latin America—constitute a core of right-wing mass mobilizations, with race, religion, and national identity most frequently the key unifying factors. Often, in fact, the goal to re-create the ancien régime is not even a restoration but instead the invention of an imagined, fictional past.[1]

Right-wing movements are reactionary also in the sense that they *react* or respond to left-wing movements: they seek not only to block movements for liberation but also to appropriate selectively, often in distorted forms, the protest repertoires, discourses, and even stated goals. The US antiabortion group Operation Rescue in the late 1980s, for example, staged sit-ins in front of abortion clinics on the model of civil rights struggles of the 1960s, and Latin American oligarchies and disgruntled middle classes in this century descend into the streets with pots and pans to protest progressive governments, mirroring the cacerolazos that brought those governments to power. Right-wing movements appropriate elements of the leadership, organizational structures, and protest repertoires of liberation movements of decades past. This is an example of our general hypothesis: *resistance is prior to power*. Revolutionary movements and struggles for liberation are the source of political innovation, whereas right-wing movements are able only to mimic some of their innovations, often with horribly destructive results.

To restore the unity of the people

Over the course of the twentieth century, two primary characteristics define right-wing movements: authority and identity, specifically, the exaltation of leadership and the defense or restoration of the unity of the people. Whereas the focus on authority has, in the twenty-first century, lessened somewhat or undergone variations, the sense that the people are under siege and need to be defended remains at the heart of right-wing movements.

Carl Schmitt's analysis of the Nazi movement is an extreme example to be sure but a lucid assessment that serves as a measuring stick for contemporary right-wing movements.[2] Schmitt's pamphlet *State, Movement, People*, which celebrates the 1933 "provisional constitution" of the German National-Socialist State, unsurprisingly identifies leadership as a top priority.[3] "The strength of the National-Socialist State resides in the fact that it is dominated and imbued from top to bottom and in every atom of its being by the idea of leadership [*Führung*]."[4] The primary effort of liberal democratic legal theory, he laments, is to eliminate leadership and substitute for it structures of supervision (*Aufsicht*).

Leadership in today's right-wing movements bears little resemblance to that in Schmitt's analysis. Even the most recognizable leaders of far-right European electoral parties in recent years—such as Marine Le Pen of the

Front National, Nigel Farage of the UK Independence Party, Jimmie Akesson of the Sweden Democrats, or Nikolaos Michaloliakos of Golden Dawn—serve roles that are closer to the liberal democratic structures that Schmitt abhors rather than absolute authority. Donald Trump, despite his capricious and autocratic tendencies, certainly has little of the leadership that Schmitt admires. In right-wing social movements leadership is an even less central factor: Lutz Bachmann, for instance, the founder of PEGIDA (Patriotic Europeans against the Islamization of the West), often speaks to the media in the name of the group but is a relatively insignificant figure. The absence of charismatic leaders in the Tea Party is even more pronounced. Some have cited as Tea Party leaders minor politicians such as Sarah Palin, media personalities such as Glenn Beck, or funders such as the Koch brothers, but really such authority figures are relatively inconsequential to the movement.

In military organizations such as ISIS or al-Qaeda in Iraq, authority figures—like Abu Bakr al-Baghdadi, named "caliph" of the imagined caliphate—are more prominent, and many right-wing political-religious movements maintain charismatic structures of religious authority, using the mosque, temple, and church as sites for the spread of political doctrine. But really these leaders are minor figures who are somewhat interchangeable. The shift away from traditional leadership structures and chain of command is exemplified most clearly by the anonymous nature of ISIS recruitment strategies in Europe and North America, which have proven horrifyingly effective. Sometimes ISIS operatives establish personal contact with potential recruits who are subsequently vetted and trained in a traditional way but in many cases those who have had no direct contact with the organization or leadership—who have been "recruited" by an open call to violence broadcast on social media—pledge allegiance to ISIS by committing barbaric acts of mass murder. Such leaderless and structureless forms of recruitment baffle traditional counterinsurgency strategies.

In contrast to leadership, identity continues to play a central role. Schmitt grasps the most enduring characteristic of right-wing movements, in fact, in the mandate to restore or redeem the identity of the people, which is constantly under threat from those alien to it.[5] Right-wing movements operate on the logic of a clash of civilizations defined primarily in terms of religion, race, or both. Such civilizational identity, Schmitt asserts, is the psychological and ontological basis for political interest and desire: "Down, inside, to the deepest and most instinctive stirrings of his emotions, and likewise, in the

tiniest fibre of his brain, man stands in the reality of this belongingness of
people and race." The primary political obligation, then, is to defend one's
own kind against aliens. Schmitt paints the alien with stereotypically Jewish
characteristics, but it takes little imagination to translate his vile portrait into
the Nigerian in South Africa, the Muslim in Europe or India, the person of
color in the United States, the Bolivian in Argentina, the Shiite in Saudi
Arabia, or any number of other "outsiders." "An alien wants to behave critically and also to apply himself shrewdly," Schmitt writes, "wants to read books
and to write books, he thinks and understands differently because he is differently disposed, and remains, in every crucial train of thought, in the existential
condition of his own kind."[6] The central point is that the unity of the people
is always characteristic of the (real or imagined—sometimes primordial) past
social order that the right-wing movements seek to defend against aliens, to
reclaim, and to redeem. These movements are populist in the strict sense that
they focus on the identity of the people and the exclusion of others.

Earlier we cast the Tea Party as "leaderless," but, in fact, when considered
in relation to President Barack Obama, it presents an interesting twist on
Schmitt's argument: the only legitimate leader is one who shares and can thus
defend the identity and sovereignty of the people. Tea Party supporters, according to Christopher Parker and Matt Barreto, should be considered not
"conventional conservatives" but "reactionary conservatives" because in addition to their libertarian economic arguments they seek to "turn back the
clock" and restore an imagined national identity that is primarily white,
Christian, and heterosexual.[7] They demonize those they perceive to threaten
the unity of the people—including the poor, migrants, welfare recipients, and
Muslims—and believe that President Obama represents (and even embodies)
all of them. He is, in effect, the Tea Party's antagonist in chief. He affirms, for
Tea Party supporters, the unity of their imagined national identity. The people
stand out all the more brightly against his blackness. The movement grew
after his 2008 election, founded in large part on the belief that Obama is alien
to the national identity (and the bizarrely persistent claims that he was born
outside the United States are only a symptom of this), and will likely fade
from view now that he is out of office. Schmitt's diagnosis explains remarkably clearly the rationale behind the Tea Party's incessant indictments of Obama's
"imperial presidency" and the "tyranny" of his administration: "Only ethnic
identity can prevent the power of the leader from becoming tyrannical and
arbitrary. It alone justifies the difference from any role of an alien-transmitted

will, however intelligent and advantageous it might be."[8] The Tea Party's core mission—and this is key to understanding contemporary right-wing movements in general—is to affirm the unity of the people and to defend or restore it against all who are alien. Sovereignty can be achieved only in those terms. Even when right-wing movements don't preach racist slogans openly, turn over the rock just a little and their core mission to defend the racial, national, or religious identity of an imagined people against aliens creeps out.

Populism and racialized property

Right-wing populist movements, particularly those in the dominant countries, pose a conundrum for analysis insofar as in the search for sovereignty they combine paradoxically antielitist politics with efforts to maintain social hierarchies. One way to disentangle this knot is to follow the line of property essential to right-wing populism, one that is entirely infused by racial identity. To say that populism is grounded in the love of identity (a horrible, destructive form of political love, in our view) is undoubtedly true, but behind identity lurks property. Sovereignty and racialized property are the stigmata that mark the body of right-wing populisms.

Right-wing movements, as we said earlier, are reactionary not only in that they seek to restore a past social order but also in that they borrow (often in distorted form) the protest repertoires, vocabularies, and even stated goals of the left resistance and liberation movements. This is especially evident in right-wing populist movements that mobilize the poor and subordinated segments of society to protest against elites in the name of the people, but nonetheless serve to maintain or restore social hierarchies. "That is the task," Corey Robin asserts, "of right wing populism: to appeal to the mass without disrupting the power of elites or, more precisely, to harness the energy of the mass in order to reinforce or restore the power of elites. Far from being a recent innovation of the Christian Right or the Tea Party movement, reactionary populism runs like a red thread throughout conservative discourse from the very beginning."[9] Robin is certainly correct that right-wing populisms serve to reinforce the power of some elites but to make sense of this we have to distinguish among different kinds of social hierarchies and, in fact, different forms of property.

On the one hand, the purported condescension or abandonment by liberal elites often fuels right-wing populist movements—and indeed it is not difficult to find evidence of ways in which liberal elites exploit and neglect the poor and working classes. We don't doubt the sincerity or intelligence of many right-wing activists' protest against the elites of finance, global institutions, and national government. (And indeed some populist elements could be re-cuperated by intelligent left-wing movements.) Populism's antielite politics often expresses indignation against the rule of property, a form that is disem-bodied, mobile, and unattached to identity. The power of money, global mar-kets, and even national central banks that "debase" currency are particular objects of criticism. On the other hand, populisms, in seeking to defend the people, especially defined in racial, religious, or civilizational terms, affirm another kind of property: immobile and embodied property, and ultimately property that is tied to identity. Land rights are thus a recurring theme as is the fixity of monetary values (for example, in gold).

This relationship between identity and property takes two primary forms. First, identity is meant to provide privileged rights and access to property. A primary appeal of populist movements is to restore the (even minimal) eco-nomic power and social prestige they imagine to have lost, most often con-ceived, explicitly or implicitly, in terms of racial identity. Conceptions of a superior race, as Hannah Arendt observes, take the aristocratic experience of "pride in privilege without individual effort and merit, simply by virtue of birth" and make it accessible to ordinary people said to share a common nature.[10] In the populist antimigrant movements that have expanded throughout Europe, the identity of the people—sometimes defined explicitly in terms of white-ness and Christianity and at other times in "civilizational" terms centered on liberal values—is strongly mixed with promises of property. For both the criminal movements that violently attack migrants, such as Golden Dawn in Greece and Casa Pound in Italy, and their more "respectable" counterparts, such as the Front National and the Sweden Democrats, the racist, antimigrant rhetoric is backed by the promise to restore the social position they believe they have lost, specifically the race privilege of working-class whites, and pay them their due "wages of whiteness" to borrow a notion developed by W. E. B. Du Bois and David Roediger.[11]

Identity, secondly, itself *is* a form of property, one in which the economic, the cultural, and the racial are inextricably intermingled. Identity connotes, to use the language of property theorists, the possession of something exclusively one's own, and it should not trouble us that identity is largely immaterial since many forms of property today comprise material and immaterial forms. The law accords "holders" of whiteness, Cheryl Harris asserts, the same kind of privileges and benefits that it grants holders of other types of property: "The exclusion of subordinated 'others' was and remains a central part of the property interest in whiteness and, indeed, is part of the protection that the court extends to whites' settled expectations of continued privilege."[12] Whiteness belongs to you—it is your possession to the exclusion of others and it offers the promise of your sovereignty. Property and sovereignty, we will argue in part II, are intimately mixed in the twinned operations of possession and exclusion.

This conception of racial property provides a useful frame for understanding the motivations of poor and working-class white populations who support right-wing political groups, even when those groups act against their economic interest. What Arendt calls "pride in privilege" does not always convey economic benefits, and lack of gains in monetary wealth is not necessarily a disappointment to the poor and working-class supporters of right-wing movements. The need to defend identity and its privileges—the restoration of its racialized property that they believe they have lost—sometimes eclipses all other goals. Identity and property thus have a double relation in right-wing populisms: identity serves as a privileged means to property and also as a form of property itself, which promises to maintain or restore the hierarchies of the social order.[13]

The violence of religious identities

Although some of today's most vicious right-wing movements are driven by religious fervor, one should not assume that faith dictates their political actions, at least not in any direct way. One key to understanding many religious movements today is the way they combine the defense of religious identity with resentment against alien powers. It is important, on the one hand, to recognize both the real causes for indignation and the reactionary projects in which these movements are mobilized and, on the other, to grasp the destructive nature of religious identities.

Not all religious movements, of course, are reactionary, and throughout history, the political directions of religious movements vary widely. This is not explained simply by what Ernst Troeltsch, who is undoubtedly among the greatest sociologists of religion, calls the relative autonomy of the religious idea.[14] It depends primarily instead on the specific historical situations from which religious movements emerge, even though the same situation can give rise to different and even contradictory political developments. During the times of the Crusades of Roman Catholicism against Islam and the consequent militarization of faith, for example, also arise great experiences of pacifist and charitable sects, such as Franciscanism. The same is true for the history of Islam, when in the same era are born both despotic military projects of conquest (which force conversion on the vanquished) and mystical forms of life. At the highest point of the Abbasid Caliphate and its rule as political and spiritual guide of the universal Islamic community developed various ascetic mendicant fraternities, "religions of the poor" that had an important role in the development of Arab Muslim civilization. In Judaism, similarly, the doctrinal and political endeavors to restore the temple to the chosen people coincided with prophetic, messianic, and revolutionary practices. The legends surrounding the life of Sabbatai Zevi contain this contradictory power of the religious experience of the Jewish people, and Gershom Sholem's wonderful book on the subject could be read as a classic analysis of this contradiction.[15] All of this is also true later, in the period of the primitive accumulation of capital, when religious movements served, on the one hand, as primary factors of capitalist development (according to authors such as Werner Sombart and Max Weber) and, on the other, as privileged forms of resistance to capital (as analyzed by Ernst Bloch, Vittorio Lanternari, and Ranajit Guha).[16]

The two qualities that most centrally characterize contemporary right-wing religious movements, as we said, are, on one hand, their aim to construct identity and defend its purity and, on the other, the resentment of wrongs at the hands of outside political forces. The focus on the purity and stability of identity is why religious movements often tend toward dogmatic closure, expressed both in theological and political terms, and why religious movements can communicate and mix so freely with movements based on racial or civilizational identity. Some claim that the depersonalizing and alienating effects of globalization have contributed to the resurgence of religion in the public sphere and the increased power of religious identities along lines of the long tradition of the politicization of faith. It is not surprising that such identities return in periods of instability and crisis. Such movements typically shift quickly from morality to politics, and soon—once they gain hegemony— transform faith into an *instrumentum regni*.

These identities are activated and consolidated by mobilizing resentment and indignation regarding the humiliations suffered or the poverty imposed by foreign powers. Sometimes the wrongs invoked are quasi-mythical events but often they are very real. Many contemporary religious movements focus the attention of believers on the misery created by the politics of neoliberalism and others highlight the legacies of and continuing forms of colonial domination by Europe, the United States, and the current supranational power structures. These are echoed, in effect, by the resentments regarding the racial forms of exclusion and subordination in European cities. "We are not facing a radicalization of Islam," writes Alain Bertho, with regard to the poor suburbs of Paris, "but an Islamization of the anger, disarray, and hopelessness of the lost children of a terrible era, who find in Jihad the meaning and weapons for their rage."[17] We have to recognize, on the one hand, that such resentment and indignation cannot be eradicated by fiat because there is some truth to it. On the other hand, however, this indignation, even in reaction to real injustices, even when it echoes the reasoning of liberation movements, is enlisted in projects of another form of enslavement. The cult of identity, religious fanaticism, and social conservatism are interwoven in a deadly and explosive mix of sad passions that nourish violence and totalitarian tendencies.

The military developments in Syria and Iraq from 2014 to 2015 organized by ISIS and factions of al-Qaeda represent an extreme example of this explosive mix of resistance and domination in the name of religion. Religious sectarianism intersects here with popular resentment against some real wrongs, including the territorial organization of the Middle East in the twentieth century established univocally (with long-term effects) by colonial powers and subsequently the twenty-first-century foreign interventions, especially the US war on terror and its occupations of Afghanistan and Iraq. The amalgam of religious extremism and anticolonial sentiments makes meaningless, in the abstract, political designation of these forces as belonging to the Left or Right (even though they do explicitly reject those powerful socialist and secular tendencies such as Nasserism that emerged in the region in the late twentieth century). Don't think that because we recognize that some of their resentment has a real foundation we are "sympathizing with terrorists" or justifying their actions. No, the only effective way to oppose them is to disentangle the strands of truth from falsity and separate the elements that at least ape projects of egalitarianism and emancipation from economic misery and colonial subjection from the barbaric and totalitarian framework of the movements as a whole. It is impossible to say at this point whether people's desires for freedom and autonomy can be extricated from the fanatical religious regimes that now dominate and can then be redirected toward projects of liberation—or whether such projects could be conducted on the religious terrain. Even if they were possible, there remains the strong possibility, we fear, if they still center on the construction and defense of identity, that they would only lead to the reconstruction of barbaric and fascistic states.

One striking element of many reactionary religious movements today, especially Islamic movements, is the exaltation of the martyr as the extreme figure built on resentment, identity, and fanaticism. We should remember that there are really two distinct traditions of martyrdom, which both span all the major religions. In one, martyrs are willing to defend their faith and testify to justice even unto death. Archbishop Óscar Romero, for example, assassinated by right-wing death squads while giving mass in San Salvador, had received threats and knew that his political pronouncements in favor of the poor endangered his life. In the other tradition, which is more prevalent today, martyrs attack and destroy their enemies along with themselves, celebrating extreme forms of terror and making martyrdom no longer a form of testimony but a religious expression of political identity. Religious movements thus line up with disastrous political projects: saintliness is offered to those who hate and destroy. The anonymous ISIS recruitment campaigns in Europe and North America we mentioned earlier rely strongly on appeals to such martyrdom, and ISIS's open invitation through social media to martyrdom in its name has proven appallingly effective. Such religious beliefs and practices should lead all of us, following Spinoza, to denounce superstition.[18]

Does every religious identity carry this message of barbarity and death in one form or another? Voltaire suspects as much: "Theology has only served to subvert minds, and sometimes states."[19] Erik Peterson also attempts to prove this suspicion regarding the monotheisms.[20] It would be naïve to hope that the diverse religions manage to find common ground or simply tolerate one another peacefully or, better, adopt love of the world and life as absolute values. Mahatma Gandhi on the eve of Indian independence, witnessing barbaric "intercommunal" violence between Hindus and Muslims and foreseeing clearly the greater bloodbaths and tragedies to come during partition and after, sought something like a nonsecular end to religious identity. Gandhi remained, of course, a religious man, but he recognized that even religious tolerance is insufficient for peace insofar as tolerance means maintaining the separate religious identities and merely advocating respect for the other. Instead Gandhi promoted "intercommunalism" and modeled that behavior by adopting Muslim and Christian texts and practices, effectively destroying religious identities from the inside by multiplying them. He didn't become less Hindu but, so to speak, more Muslim and more Christian. Gandhi's key insight, we think, which remains equally vital today, is that not religion per se but religious identity, the construction and defense of a religious people, leads inevitably to violence and barbarity, and must be destroyed.[21]

Finally, even though right-wing movements often are derivative of the structures and practices of liberation movements, they do offer a series of lessons. By gazing at these reflections in a dark mirror, liberation movements should recognize, first, that they must be antagonistic. Movements cannot simply serve to reinforce the ruling powers or to support the maintenance or restoration of the hierarchies of social order. They must instead be autonomous, disruptive, contestational actors. Second, movements must be democratic and maintain an attitude critical of centralized leadership without refusing the need for organization and institution. We will continue in the chapters ahead to articulate the necessary relation between horizontalism and verticality. Finally, movements must be nonidentitarian. Identity based on race and ethnicity, religion, sexuality, or any other social factor closes down the plurality of movements, which must be instead internally diverse, multitudinous. Liberation movements that do not learn these lessons risk (sooner or later) drifting to the right.[22]

Poverty as wealth

Since time immemorial religious authorities have tried to bind the multitude of the poor to the ruling powers. Dominant religious logics, which legitimate both political power and the possession of worldly wealth, generally pose poverty as a natural outcome, not even worthy of pity: God will forgive the poor and reward those who accept their condition. But in each religious tradition there are also minoritarian currents that affirm poverty and the practices of nonproperty against the sovereign powers.

At the dawn of the modern era, while the Catholic Church in league with the feudal order was denying that Christ counseled poverty and emphasizing explicitly Christ the King rather than the Christ born poor, the Franciscans affirmed that poverty is the highest form of spiritual life and that all should practice it. This proclamation was immediately translated into social and political practices—and the Franciscans maintained that their "ecclesial vow" dictates not only the renunciation of property but also the rigorous limitation of the use of goods.[23] This episode is one instance of the revolutionary discovery of the practices of poverty in (and against) the emerging modern world, making property a religious and political problem. The Franciscans (and before them the Cathars, the Waldensians, and many others) introduced a critique of property and proposed practices of nonproperty that disrupt and threaten to overthrow the ruling powers.[24] When the defense of property is stripped away, the alliance between religious life and sovereignty dissolves. Today, at the dusk of modernity, new social strata struggle against the "natural" order of feudality and coloniality, as well as the lordly organization of the various churches, renewing these early traditions, imbuing practices of nonproperty again with revolutionary potential.

The crucial point is that the affirmation of poverty and the critique of property are not conceived as deprivation or austerity but rather as abundance. The Franciscans propose usus pauper, a moderate, limited use of goods, and interpret radically a passage of scripture: "And the multitude of those who believed were of one heart and of one soul; neither did anyone say that any of the things he possessed was his own, but they had all things in common" (Acts 4:32).[25] In material terms the affirmation of poverty as plenitude and the mandate to subvert private property highlight the value and political power of our cooperative productive capacities. In the usus pauper there is an idea of the abundance of our shared wealth and the anticipation of a potential constitution of the common.[26] The refusal of property is thus not only essential to spiritual transformation, according to Franciscans, but also to a life of plenitude. Poverty is not the absence of wealth but, perhaps paradoxically, its fundamental precondition: "everything for everyone," to cite a Zapatista slogan, is the fundamental dictate of the life of poverty.

Once the church smashed this revolutionary, humanistic enterprise, the birth of modernity came to be defined, in many respects, by its successful domestication within capitalist relations. In the capitalist world, poverty became inextricably linked to exploitation. The poor tend to become no longer slaves, beasts of burden, untouchables at the margins of the human race, but instead integrated and subordinated as producers. After having been separated from the land and every other autonomous means of subsistence, workers become "free" insofar as, on the one hand, they are no longer sub-ordinated to relations of feudal servitude and, on the other, they no longer *have access to the means of production and subsistence. The capacity to work, Marx writes, "the purely subjective existence of labour, stripped of all objectivity" is thus "absolute poverty." And the worker, as a simple personification of that, is the poor.*[27] *The proletariat, a multitude of free sellers of labor-power who have nothing else to sell and no other means to survive, is cast in a "second nature" constructed by capital and reinforced by theological justifications of the work ethic and the hierarchies of the social order. The poor are invited to participate responsibly in their own exploitation, and that will be considered a dignity.* Ad majorem Dei gloriam. *Capitalist asceticism becomes the damnation of the poor and exploited.*

But this capitalist construction of poverty also reveals another truth: the production of wealth and the reproduction of social life are, in a real and profound sense, in the hands of workers. This fact potentially contradicts the "natural history" of capital that subordinates the poor and exploited workers. Marx, continuing the passage cited above, after denouncing the poverty of workers, links that poverty to their power, in the sense that in capitalist society the living labor of workers, although stripped of the means of production, is "the general possibility of material wealth." That explosive mix of poverty and potential represents a mortal threat to the private ownership of the means of production.

Today, in the postindustrial period of capitalist development, the mix of poverty and potential becomes even more volatile, and the intuitions of the Franciscans at the dawn of modernity come back with full force at its twilight. On the one hand, in the current neoliberal formation and under the rule of finance, the alienation of productive labor has reached extreme levels as the lives of the poor and the entire working population have become increasingly precarious, as we will see in more detail in part III. At the same time that labor insecurity—which has long been experienced by subordinated populations in the dominant countries and almost all populations in the subordinated countries—has become the rule, the structures and institutions of public support are being destroyed. Precarity has become something like a generalized existential condition. On the other hand, our cooperative productive capacities, engaged both inside and outside the world of waged work, increasingly develop and engage the terrain of the common, and the common has the potential to provide forms of security that the precarious need and demand (a claim we develop further in part II). Precarity and the common are the key terms for recognizing the poverty and potential of the multitude in the age of neoliberalism.

There are two primary ways by which the poor themselves can respond to this contemporary neoliberal condition. One involves viewing our increasingly precarious lives as redoubling the need to construct, defend, or restore the identity of the people, which would serve as a bulwark against the threats posed by global capital, finance, the dominant nation-states, the supranational powers, migrants, aliens, and other real or imagined sources of dispossession. The community of the faithful and its restored identity are imagined to furnish a refuge from precarious life. As we have seen, however, the affirmation and reinforcement of the identity of the religious community in this context generates perverse, destructive practices, including the martyr's deployment of death as a challenge to and a weapon against the oppressors and the dispossession of life.

A second response refuses the siren calls of identity and instead constructs, on the basis of our precarious condition, secure forms of life grounded in the common. Judith Butler, over the course of several books, has developed a notion of precarity not (or not only) in terms of victimization and suffering but primarily as a site of potential. The vulnerability of the poor, the disabled, and the subordinated in terms of gender, sexuality, and race forces us to recognize the ineluctable dependence on others that all of us share; the development of circuits of interdependence are the primary (perhaps only) path to a real security.[28] We read Butler's affirmation of interdependence in line with theories of the common that pose open and expanding networks of productive social cooperation, inside and outside the capitalist economy, as a powerful basis for generating free and autonomous forms of life. In these cases, the poor react to the torments of precarity not by retreating behind the walls of identity but instead by constructing new, mobile constellations of shared life.

This combination of precarity and possibility is expressed especially powerfully in the lives of migrants. Multitudes that cross over, around, and through national boundaries have the potential to undermine fixed identities and destabilize the material constitutions of the global order. When migrants must be included as active agents in global biopolitical production, when they cannot be merely subordinated as the poorest of the poor but when their multilingual and pluricultural capacities become essential for social production, then their presence and action inevitably undermine the hierarchies of traditional identities. These subjectivities, ever more mixed, are increasingly able to evade the fusional, identitarian powers of control. In the inferno of poverty and in the odyssey of migration resides a new power.

Here we encounter again the essence of the Franciscan project: poverty as not deprivation but a state of wealth and plenitude that threatens every sovereign and transcendent power. Practices of nonproperty like those of the Franciscans, which in their day in alliance with Ghibelline forces sought to subvert the feudal religious order, once again today have revolutionary potential in the struggles of the common against the financial power of capital. Even deeper: does poverty contain the seeds of a radical refusal of identity and the creation, instead, of an antagonistic, multitudinous subject grounded in the common? There is indeed a sacrilegious, corrosive element in poverty that dissolves all kinds of identity, including religious identity. Without strong identitarian concepts (nation, race, family, etc.), there is no way to project in God oneself and one's own eminence, which is the essence of religious identity, along with fanaticism and superstition.[29] *But would that still be religion?*

CHAPTER 5

THE REAL PROBLEM LIES ELSEWHERE

In order to resolve the dilemmas of leadership revealed by the history of revolutionary and liberation movements, which we posed earlier, we have to recognize, first, the extent to which the social conditions of political action have changed. The end of modernity and modernization has in some central respects rearranged the array of political possibilities. Second, and perhaps more important, the current political impasse cannot be addressed adequately in purely political terms, based on an assumption of the autonomy of the political. We must leave this noisy sphere of political discourse, as Marx might say, and descend into the hidden abode of social production and reproduction. Can we discover (beyond modernity) an "other" terrain, which lies on a path between the multitude and the common, a path on which the multitude produces and reproduces the common?[1]

Blow the dam!

Machiavelli instructs us that, in order to tame fortune and to weather the unforeseeable storms of political events, we must construct institutionalized virtue (*ordinata virtù*) as a line of defense. When the weather is calm, he counsels, we should build dikes and dams so that when the raging waters of the river rise up, the damage can be mitigated.[2] We subscribe wholeheartedly to Machiavelli's prudence. As we said earlier, movements need organization and institutions in order to last and to withstand all manners of adversity. No one should take the justified and necessary contemporary critiques of centralized leadership and authority to mean that political organization and institutions are no longer necessary. And yet there are times when destituent rather than constituent actions are needed, when the most pressing need is to break the consolidated institutions of domination to clear the way for new, different institutions. Sometimes, in other words, we must take the other course: blow the dam!

"Blowing the dam" entails, first of all, understanding the extreme point to which capitalist forces dominate today the totality of our social and political relations, mystify our desires, and yoke our productivity to its goals. It also requires, second, that we find the means to explode the cage of biopolitical domination, the monetary command that the central banks impose, the authority that the political structures collaboratively define, and the discipline that the economic compulsion imposes.

Let us sketch in broad strokes the genealogy of this contemporary condition, which we will analyze in more detail in subsequent chapters. Today's structures of capitalist rule came as a response to the diverse forms of resistance that marked the global event of 1968—anticolonial and anti-imperialist struggles, antiracist movements, feminist movements, worker revolts, various forms of refusal of capitalist discipline and control, and numerous others. One effect of those struggles can be recognized in the way that, especially in the dominant countries, public spending exceeded its limits and public debt became for a period the only key to development and to maintaining control over social unrest. Only through widespread social repression and the reorganization of the social order in the following years—the early 1970s were key—could the capitalist system be reorganized and maintained.[3] These are the years when neoliberalism was born. The 1973 coup d'état in Chile opened the way for a neoliberal experiment and the radical application of Chicago school economics. Margaret Thatcher and Ronald Reagan initiated neoliberal strategies in their countries, but Tony Blair and Bill Clinton (with Gerhard Schröder a bit later) really consolidated them through the destruction of welfare structures and labor protections and elevation of global finance to the position of rule. Blair, Clinton, and Schröder did the "dirty work" for the capitalist class and oversaw—in the guise of reformist centrism—the triumph of the neoliberal revolution [sic]. This "dirty work" marked the death of the official Left, and today that cadaver weighs heavily on all social-democratic parties and completely blocks their efforts to represent the popular classes.

Capitalist relations set in motion at that time, through political and economic forms of control and repression, a postindustrial, digital, and biopolitical reform of production processes. In the conflicts that emerged in this process between the social composition of the labor force and the new technological composition of capital, all correspondences that had existed between productive society and capitalist politics, between forms of resistance and figures of rule, were completely broken. Capitalist command functions today increasingly as a pure exercise of power, aimed at containing social unrest within strict limits, sometimes with violent means of pacification. As the sovereign exercise of power over social relations increases so, too, do various mechanisms of benefits and privileges for the financial and propertied elites—in other words, corruption. What else can we call a power that no longer maintains proportion in its schemes of exploitation and distribution?

That is the basic story of the interaction between the political composition of the working class and the political structures of capital from 1968 to 1989, but the social struggles, as we saw briefly earlier, certainly did not stand still—to the contrary, within this crisis they found ways to open new paths of resistance. One cycle, the cycle of alterglobalization struggles, which was born perhaps in Chiapas in 1995 or Seattle in 1999, was shut down in many respects after the September 11 attacks as a byproduct of the "war on terror," but its core elements were not lost. Another cycle was born after the 2008 crisis, the cycle of various "springs" characterized by encampments and the occupation of urban space. These struggles seemed to flash up and burn out rapidly, only to reappear in another place with even greater force. And yet these cycles have not managed to invent a new and effective organizational form that is adequate to today's needs. We will have to understand why such a wealth of struggles—across a long period and in a wide variety of national and political contexts—still demonstrates a poverty of organization.

In the past we have employed for pedagogical purposes a Hegelian conception of the dialectic between "in-itself" and "for-itself" to understand the needs of organization: the class in-itself, that is, the empirical existence of the class, would have to be transformed into a class for-itself, imbued with consciousness of its position and potential. This scheme, however, is today completely worn out. That dialectic has always been weighed down by the dualistic prejudice that sees in consciousness a reflective operation of a higher nature: consciousness, mind, reason, and individual will are human capacities, the theory goes, that dominate (and must dominate) life, the body, passions, and being itself. Turn another corner and we run back into the centaur of modern political thought, a perspective that the dominant strains of modern revolutionary thought bought into completely. Today and in the context of biopolitics a new type of reflection on organization is possible, one that might begin by inverting the two halves of the centaur but quickly ends up refusing its dualisms entirely. The regime of needs organizes sensation and consciousness, the imagination cuts across and reconfigures the relation between reason and passions, and reflection comes through performative processes and the construction of *dispositifs* open to the future.

Keep in mind that, as we said earlier, it is futile to maintain that the political composition of the struggles should correspond or grow directly out of the technical composition of the new forms of labor, either when this is imagined in industrial terms or when projected on network forms. Gone are the days—and thankfully so—when the working class or, more specifically, the segment of the class most central to capitalist production could claim to represent the others in struggle. Gone are the days when industrial workers could claim to represent peasants, when male workers could claim to represent women in the reproductive sphere, when white workers could claim to represent black workers, and so forth. The invention of political organization, even when cast in subversive form, by making it conform to the structures of capital is today an empty gesture, or worse. Only social cooperation, which extends across the spheres of social production and reproduction, can provide an adequate framework for organization.

We should emphasize that questioning the relationship between the technical composition and the political composition of the working class (or, better, of the multitudes that work and are exploited under the command of capitalist biopowers) undermines, too, the traditional definition (which might be more Engelsian than Marxian) of the way the cultural and political superstructure is determined by the economic base. Gramsci and Louis Althusser long ago critiqued this framework, recognizing it as an indirect product of a spiritualist philosophical conception and the residue of a crude materialism. It was born, in fact, as the simple reflection of a metaphysics of knowledge, society, and the human that separated spirit from matter. "If the notion of structure is conceived 'speculatively'," Gramsci argues, "it assuredly does become a 'hidden god' but for that reason it must be conceived not 'speculatively' but historically, as the ensemble of social relations in which real people move and act, as an ensemble of objective conditions which can and must be studied with the methods of 'philology'."[4] Althusser makes a similar point about ideology. "Ideologies," he writes, "are not pure illusions (Error), but bodies of representations existing in institutions and practices: they figure in the superstructure, and are rooted in class struggle."[5] Working through this passage again, beyond the metaphysical dualism (even when its two poles were infused with revolutionary theory), is one way of interpreting a long and suffering but victorious experience of contemporary Marxism—a refusal to let anything overdetermine the struggles, which are even more definitive when confronting the new characteristics of capitalist biopowers and the strategies of the multitude to overthrow it.

Second response: Seek the plural ontology of cooperative coalitions

At this point a solution to the problem of leadership can be found only within the movements of the multitude. Before addressing how to invent a leadership that is merely tactical—a difficult and even dangerous proposition, we admit—we thus need to investigate the ontology of the multitude, and descend into social reality to confirm how the contemporary transformations of social production are making possible a multitude capable of strategic projects. We do not mean to suggest that social movements are everything and sufficient in themselves, but they do present a powerful ontological substance, and this nature of the movements must be understood before we can properly frame our contemporary political problem. The movements that interest us often have a Carsic nature; that is, they flow sometimes in full view and then descend for periods into subterranean channels, but together they nonetheless generate an accumulation of practices and subjectivity. Their flows deposit geological layers of a sedimentary social being. We need to focus for a moment on these discontinuous and multiple flows that characterize a plural ontology of politics.

Our notion of ontology here refers to a historical account of being that is firmly planted and formed—*Da-sein*, being there—in our collective existence. But, one might object, how can you propose an ontological method that is rooted in history—being *in* history and being *of* history—when historicity implies relativism? Whereas being is necessary, according to this view, history is always contingent. This objection, however, implies a metaphysical standpoint that seeks certainty either in the (transcendental) foundation of consciousness or in the sublime plane of transcendence. Instead, our notion of historical ontology, beyond metaphysics, is completely immersed in experience and anchored by its historicity. The history and historicity of *Dasein* are not indifferent or accidental phenomena, which seen from above can be relativized by a presumption of absolute truth, but rather they create true expressions in and by human action. Their truth is determined by their constituent power—constituting new common being—and their falsity, in contrast, is defined by the extent to which they destroy or constrain common being. Wilhelm Dilthey proposed such a hermeneutical definition of truth when in response to Martin Heidegger's claim that the "historical" was impoverished and reduced to the "ontic" level—for Heidegger a mere "being present"—Dilthey contended that in the realm of experience, the *Erlebnis* of the ontic, an expressive operation, which goes beyond a relativism that effectively nullifies human action, can construct the truth of existence.[6]

To investigate this historical being, let us return to the experience of the movements often characterized by encampments and occupations of urban space in 2011, which exploded again in 2013 in Turkey and Brazil with strong echoes in Israel and Britain in the summer of 2011, Quebec in 2012, Hong Kong in 2014, and in the Black Lives Matter protests in the United States beginning in 2014. These struggles emerged in very different political contexts—whereas they overthrew authoritarian regimes in Tunisia and Egypt, for example, they confronted center-left governments in Spain, the United States, and Brazil—and their protagonists have very different forms of life. Why, then, do we consider them as part of the same cycle and as figures of the same lived reality? One obvious continuity among these movements is that they share a protest repertoire. They play, so to speak, off the same score, involving in many cases encampments and occupations that temporarily make public space common—openly accessible to all and managed collectively according to innovative rules that are often decided in assemblies or forums. Another shared aspect, which is more complex but nonetheless real, is the demand for a new democratic system, often thought to be prefigured in miniature in the governance of the encampments themselves.[7]

Behind these shared practices and aspirations is a more fundamental fact: the plural ontology that the movements express. Small groups and communities focused on specific neighborhood issues—police brutality, high rent, mortgage defaults, sexual violence—link together in powerful networks. These connections and the common languages that support them are essential. The movements (whether or not they are conscious of this) find support in federalist models—not, clearly, those in the federalist traditions of state sovereignty but instead the federalist modes of association and articulation. Without renouncing their own autonomy and difference, a wide plurality of groups and subjectivities are able to form coalitions and cooperate in common social and political projects. It should come as no surprise, then, that repressive forces have focused on breaking these associative logics. In North Africa religious fanaticism is often an effective wedge to create divisions; in Brazil and Britain racist campaigns often successfully split urban and suburban groups; in North America provocations to push some protesters toward violent acts creates rifts; and everywhere old-fashioned police repression and media campaigns are reliable tools for breaking connections.

These movements affirm a beating heart of plural ontology. A pluralism of subjectivities, multiple models of temporality, and a wide variety of modes of struggle, which emerge from different traditions and express different objectives, together form a powerful swarm held together by cooperative logics. Their aim is to create a model of constituent democracy in which differences are able to interact and together create new institutions: against global capital, against the dictatorship of finance, against the biopowers that destroy the earth, against racial hierarchies, and for access to and self-management of the common. The next step for the movements thus promises not only to confirm this will to animate and incarnate new human relations but also to participate from below in the construction of new institutions. Whereas up to this point the movements have primarily constructed a "politics of plurality," now they must set in motion an "ontological machine" of plurality.

We use the term *multitude* to name the agent of this plural ontology. We have emphasized elsewhere that *multitude* designates a radical diversity of social subjectivities that do not spontaneously form together but instead require a political project to organize.[8] Multitude, understood as a political project, is the hinge between the plural social ontology and the possibility of a real democracy. We cannot, however, fully understand this plural ontology or arrive at this political project if our vision remains fixed on the political terrain, even when we analyze the most powerful protests, rebellions, and uprisings. The movements themselves are only symptoms of a deeper social reality, embodied in the daily practices and capacities of the multitude, and its circuits of social production and reproduction.

Third call: Take power, but differently

We are not ones to shy away from the fact that in order to change the world we need to take power, and we have little sympathy with those who want to maintain their purity and keep their hands clean by refusing power. But we are equally aware that simply filling the existing offices of power with more honest, moral, or well-intentioned people, although better than the alternative, will never lead to the change we seek. It seems that we are caught in a double bind—we can't take power and we can't not take power—but really this is just a poorly posed problem. We need to look more closely at what it means to take power and, indeed, at what power itself means.

Most European languages have two words for power—*potestas* and *potentia* in Latin, *pouvoir* and *puissance* in French, *poder* and *potencia* in Spanish, *Macht* and *Vermögen* in German—whereas English has only one.[9] This might seem at first sight an example of the poverty of the English language, and in the past we have tried to remedy it rather inelegantly with capitalization, distinguishing between *Power* and *power*, using *Power* to name the vertical, centralized ruling powers, capitalist command, and biopower while employing *power* for the horizontal processes of resistance, the force of living labor, and the creative aspects of biopolitics. But perhaps, on closer examination, not marking such a distinction with different terms for power is paradoxically a strength of the English language insofar as it forces us to grapple with the relations between the two notions of power and to articulate the possible passage between them.

Let's begin with Machiavelli's definition of power—as decision and virtue, as cunning and fortune, in the construction and the legitimation of the relationship of government, which requires consent and demands obedience—in relation to that of Foucault, who defines "the exercise of power as a mode of action upon the actions of others," and thus emphasizes the margin of freedom of those subject to power.[10] The two definitions share the grounding of power in a *relationship* between or among agents. If these agents are conceived as qualitatively different and fixed in their positions—authority on one side and resistance on the other, domination on one side and submission or consent on the other—then perhaps one can be satisfied to maintain the distinction between Power (*potestas, pouvoir, Macht*) and power (*potentia, puissance, Vermögen*) and to focus analysis on how they interact with and oppose one another. This is the interpretive framework deployed, for example, when the economistic vulgate of dogmatic Marxism speaks of the relation of power between "constant capital" and "variable capital": in one corner is capital and in the other, in a subordinated and antagonistic position, is labor-power. The problem is that with the relationship fixed in this way the superiority of the one and subordination of the other can never be overcome. The subordination of variable to constant capital, to return to the example of dogmatic Marxism, cannot be challenged fundamentally within the terms of that relationship but only by introducing an exogenous element, that is, the development of political consciousness.

When we return to Machiavelli and Foucault, however, and look more closely, we can begin to see how the relation of force can be overturned and how "power" can recompose "Power," forcing us to reinterpret and relativize the distinction. The key is to recognize that Power on its own is weak and insufficient, that it can live only from the relationship, sucking the vital energies from those it seeks to rule. Whether conceived in terms of the lion or the fox, as force or cunning, beast or human, technique or machine, and so forth, all these images hide the fact that Power faces a living and indestructible adversary. And yet Power is not only a villainous reality. The struggle against Power, which takes place within the relationship that defines it, is not only an effort to unhinge the current characteristics of Power (command and domination), not only an effort to break the structural (economic and state) physiognomy of Power, and thus to set in motion strong processes of the subjectivation and liberation of labor. It is also a long march that destructures the relationship between Power and power, to the point of overturning the balance and posing the concept and the reality of power at the center of the relationship, thus giving it priority and hegemony.

We thus arrive at a third call. After the first call to give the responsibility for strategy in progressive and liberation struggles to the movements and limit leadership to a tactical position; after the second call to develop new institutions animated by the constitutive action of the movements beyond the traditional mechanisms of representation and regulation through which the dominant modern tradition has understood democracy; and keeping in mind the first and second responses, which rest on the cooperative networks of social production to read the coalitions of political organizing, which create a plural social ontology, we are ready for a third call: to take power, not simply by occupying the existing offices of domination with better leaders, but instead by altering fundamentally the relationships that power designates and thus transforming power itself. Identifying the means at our disposal to accomplish this will be a central task of part IV.

Before we can confront this problem directly, however, we will have to investigate how the crisis of the relationship of capitalist power must be read from a dual perspective. In part II we will consider, from below, from the standpoint of the subordinated, how today the multitude not only opposes the capitalist organization of command but also invents modes of life and forms of production and reproduction that go beyond the capitalist capacity to exercise power. In part III we will see how capital and its institutions have sought to respond to these developments, adjusting their mechanisms of exploitation and developing modes of financial command that constitute the basis of neoliberal governance. Analyzing how even at the center of these transformations are born resistances and struggles will also be part of our task. Part IV, finally, will have to close the circle and delineate the paths for resistance and subversive practices to lead to the construction of a new, sustainable, democratic organization of society, the Prince of the common.

Marxism against Das Kapital

In History and Class Consciousness, *Georg Lukács celebrates the way that Rosa Luxemburg returned to the young Marx and developed his capacity to engage the economic and legal categories of capitalist development through the construction of revolutionary subjectivity. As Lenin did in* State and Revolution, *Luxemburg resolved a central paradox of Marxist theory that, posing freedom and necessity in opposition, seemed to reduce the prospects of revolutionary action to some kind of nineteenth-century mechanicism and, in so doing, negate its potential. Whereas Lenin was subsequently embroiled in the tasks of constructing socialism in Russia, Lukács continues, Luxemburg was able to renew Marxist "orthodoxy" and thereby overcome the dominant modern conception of power, which is absolutist in the sense that it views power as one and indivisible—a conception that also infects much communist thought. In the wake of Luxemburg, according to Lukács, "Western Marxism" was able to break from the mechanistic ontology of the Second and Third Internationals, which was inevitably catastrophic. A new orthodoxy was thus formulated that posed, as Gramsci wanted, Marxism against* Das Kapital, *prying open the fetish of scientific objectivity to release the dynamics of class struggle as an ontological power and a* dispositif *of constituent subjectivation. The power of capital exists against the working class; the taking power of the working class must be posed against capital; the concept of power and the substance of capital are thus defined in a condition of duality and conflict. That puts an end to the modern (and theological—that goes without saying) conception of power as one and indivisible.*

Reading Marx and reinterpreting Hegel, Lukács positions philosophical action as the interpretation of the totality. After 1917, that totality was refigured by the revolutionary process of the soviets and the working class organized in the communist movement. This process transforms the totality in two ways: producing it and being its product, as subject and object. The proletarian subject is not simply the product of a historical process, a "thing" produced and dominated by capital, but also a mode of ethical and political conduct, liberating itself from within capitalist relations to go beyond capital. Revolutionary praxis reveals the coordinated power of the diverse singular modes of conduct of the struggle. This is how Western Marxism is born, and even though it was suffocated by Stalinist dogmatism, it was reborn stronger than ever after the Second World War and, especially, after 1968.[11]

Note that what is Western about Western Marxism is its contrast, conceived strictly in provincial European geography, to the Eastern dogmatism of Soviet scientific socialism. There are numerous other powerful and creative currents of twentieth-century Marxist theory that are located outside of this restrictive European map, equally non-Western and non-Eastern, including, just to give a few names to indicate the diversity, Roberto Schwartz in Brazil, Álvaro García Linera in Bolivia, Wang Hui in China, Ranajit Guha and Dipesh Chakrabarty in India, Cedric Robinson in the United States, and Walter Rodney in Guyana. Socialist feminist authors, even those in Europe and the United States, such as Christine Delphy, Mariarosa Dalla Costa, and Nancy Hartsock, should probably also be considered another "non-Western" territory of Marxism. The contributions of these various non-Wests to Marxism have been extraordinarily significant, but allow us to limit our view here to Western Marxism conventionally conceived to appreciate some of its theoretical riches as well as its limits.

There is no shortage of critiques of Lukács's ideas, and it is easy (and correct) to reproach him, on the one hand, for transforming the working class into a sort of Prometheus, the author of an ideal revolutionary process, and on the other, for seeing the working class as the only subject capable of liberation. And yet the realism of Lukács's reinvention of Marxism is also undeniable. He envisions a social subject, which restitutes the world to a free production, the totality of the desire of workers. "A political revolution," Lukács writes, "does no more than sanction a socio-economic situation that has been able to impose itself at least in part upon the economic reality.... Social revolutions, however, are concerned precisely to change [the social] *environment. Any such change violates the instincts of the average man so deeply that he regards it as a catastrophic threat to life as such, it appears to him to be a blind force of nature like a flood or an earthquake.*"[12] *This is where Lukács's Prometheus acts, defeating both assumptions that the current order is natural and necessary and idealistic conceptions of change. This is not an ideal subject but a mass reality, constituted by the power of revolutionized labor and driven by the spirit of a working class that seeks to revolutionize all of life, the totality, and that has seen in the Bolshevik Revolution the seeds of a new world.*

After 1968, Western Marxism was reborn by recuperating intensively the concept of totality and developing it in time: history as a process and continuous mutation of the capitalist mode of production; the action of the working class as a movement that implies the production of subjectivity between social revolution and political revolution. Maurice Merleau-Ponty anticipated 1968 in some respects by translating this new experience of historicity—as product and as productive—into language and into the pro-letarian practices of the second half of the twentieth century. With explicit reference to Lukács's History and Class Consciousness, *Merleau-Ponty incorporates the subjectivity of history and liberates subjectivation from Lukács's Prometheanism, while maintaining intact its power:*

> *We give a form to history according to our categories; but our categories, in contact with history, are themselves freed from their partiality. The old problem of the relations between subject and object is transformed, and relativism is surpassed as soon as one puts it in historical terms, since here the object is the vestige left by other subjects, and the subject— historical understanding—held in the fabric of history, is by this very fact capable of self-criticism....Lukács is trying to preserve—and his enemies are trying to attack—a Marxism which incorporates subjectivity into history without making it an epiphenomenon. He is trying to preserve the philosophical marrow of Marxism, its cultural value, and finally its revolutionary meaning.*[13]

Here again the two relationships—consciousness product and consciousness productivity—are held together.

Merleau-Ponty also transforms the concept of totality by extending and deepening Lukács's thought. Now the idealistic and totalizing perspective is presented as capital's mystification. It represents society as "subsumed" in command, "reified" in the market. Real subsumption = biopower.

But there is always resistance to command and a subversive drive against the hierarchies of the market—a rebellious class that shakes capitalist objectivity from the inside and seeks to open the field to revolutionary subjectivation.

Rather than reading the hypostases of the capitalist totality, which is typical of the authors of the Frankfurt school (which in this regard seems aimed, as Hans-Jürgen Krahl maintained, at neutralizing the work of Lukács), Merleau-Ponty highlights how class struggle shakes and reopens continually the total reality of power.[14] *He finds the reified totality in Lukács's discourse, paradoxically, to be open, precisely because it is totalized. This is no longer a dialectic of overcoming, an idealistic Aufhebung that restores order, but a "hyperdialectic" of rupture. Merleau-Ponty initiates a practice of thought that is predisposed to grasp the dialectical procedure of revolution not as pacification within the trinity but as irreducible and conflictual: a material, corporeal, living dialectic.*

In the long period that now separates us from that "short twentieth century," which ended in 1968, capitalism has not stood still. But neither have those who produce and reproduce society, who remain the antagonistic driving force of capitalist development. The transformations of labor and labor-power have led to an era of biopolitical production, in which the production of subjectivity plays a significant role in the creation of economic value. Capital understands this passage and develops its productivity through the further socializations of production. The capitalist practice of subjection through the reification of the lifeworld and the human itself, in a society subsumed within capital, puts labor-power in a straitjacket at the level of the totality. Look at capitalist management theories and you will find more or less explicit proposals to dominate the subjectivation of workers— imploring them, above all, to love their work, despite its odious reality.

One achievement of Western Marxism was to renew our understandings of the processes of social transformation. "Totality as truth" means the construction of the totality on the basis of singularities, giving priority to the emancipative dimensions of subjectivity. In Merleau-Ponty this epistemological model is framed by the critique of Soviet dictatorship, which is presented as totalitarianism against subjectivity. Through his notion of dialectic that breaks with modernity, communism becomes, as Merleau-Ponty says, "a society of permanent crisis and continual imbalance, replacing government with revolution."[15] *This communism has nothing to do with conventional notions of progress and progressivism.*

Another achievement, which is not often articulated explicitly in Western Marxism, is to renew our conception of power. Power is understood as completely immanent, without any transcendental unification or expression of theological continuity, without a global centralization of thought and government, and without the assumption that its elements are or can be unified. This resonates with how Deleuze interpreted, correctly in our view, Foucault's conception of power: "Power has no essence; it is simply operational. It is not an attribute but a relation."[16] Power "invests" the dominated, as Foucault says, and works through them and their practices, but in return the dominated also make use in their struggles against power of all the practices and behaviors that power has exercised over them. The final word on power is that resistance comes first: "In Foucault," he continues, "there is an echo of Mario Tronti's interpretation of Marxism as a 'workers' resistance existing prior to the strategies of capital."[17] The relations of power are completely closed within the diagram whereas resistances have a direct relationship with the "outside" from which diagrams derive. And it is no coincidence that resistances in Foucault affirm a completely transversal plurality.

Should Foucault be considered, then, the final representative of Western Marxism? What is important to us is certainly not to give him this label but to discover the continuity of resistance and struggle throughout this entire theoretical period, a period of explicit and implicit reinterpretations of Marxism. And most of all we want to grasp, in these analogies, a question we have addressed in other terms earlier in this book: where is leadership when an "essential" conception of power can no longer be proposed? When the totality appears as fractured? When the movements claim for themselves the strategy of revolution?

PART II

SOCIAL PRODUCTION

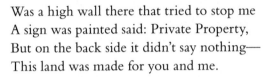

Was a high wall there that tried to stop me
A sign was painted said: Private Property,
But on the back side it didn't say nothing—
This land was made for you and me.

——WOODY GUTHRIE, "This Land Is Your Land" (1940 version)

For just as those who paint landscapes place themselves in a low
position on the plain in order to consider the nature of the
mountains and the heights, and place themselves high on top
of mountains in order to study the plains, in like manner,
to know well the nature of peoples one must be prince, and to
know well the nature of princes one must be of the people.

——MACHIAVELLI, *The Prince*

To discover the nature of our *political* problem we must investigate the
current forms of *social* domination, specifically the ways that neoliberal
governance and the power of finance today both extend and transform the
modes of capitalist exploitation and control. It is not just a matter of knowing
our adversaries in order to combat them. Some weapons for struggle are
invariably provided by the developments of capitalist society—if only we can
recognize how to use them. Although finance capital creates more brutal and
rigid mechanisms of capture and control, it also allows for new and more
powerful means of resistance and transformation. The investigation of the
contemporary forms of domination, in other words, can also reveal the real
(and increasing) productive powers and capacities for autonomy that multitudes
possess in their daily lives.

But a political realism that begins with power gives us an upside-down image of the world and masks the real movements of social development. If you begin with power, you will inevitably end up seeing only power. Today's forms of neoliberalism and financial command should really be understood as *reactions* to projects of freedom and liberation. In a kind of intellectual short-hand, in other words, resistance is prior to power. This methodological prin-ciple highlights not so much that struggles for freedom come before new struc-tures of power chronologically (although this is often also true), but rather that the struggles are the principal authors of social innovation and creativity, prior, so to speak, in an ontological sense.

First methodological principle of political realism: *begin with the multitude.* As Machiavelli says, and Spinoza after him, political realism requires reasoning not on the basis of people as we wish they were but on how they really are, here and now: "Many writers have imagined republics and principalities that have never been seen nor known to exist in reality. For there is such a distance between how one lives and how one ought to live, that anyone who abandons what is done for what ought to be done achieves his downfall rather than his preservation."[1] This means we must see the world from below, from where people are. What, today, can the multitude do? And what is it already doing? We need to begin with a materialist analysis of the passions of the multitude.

The key is to grasp the increasingly *social* nature of production in a double sense: both how and what the multitude produces. The multitude, first, both within and outside capitalist relations, produces socially, in expansive coop-erative networks. And, second, its products are not just material and immate-rial commodities: it produces and reproduces society itself. The social produc-tion of the multitude in this double sense is the foundation for not only rebellion but also the construction of alternative social relations.

What does "from below" mean?

Machiavelli's claim, cited in the epigraph above, expresses in just a few words a full conception of power. Only from below can one know the nature of those above; only from the standpoint of citizens can one know the nature of the prince, and only from that of workers can one know the nature of capital. This passage leaves no room for what some call "Machiavellianism," namely, the "autonomy of the political" or, really, state reason. On the contrary, power can be understood and judged only by those below, who can either obey or revolt against it. At the dawn of modernity, Machiavelli demystified the modern concept of power as a Leviathan. Many years were necessary before Machiavelli's intuition could be carried through in action and that organic conception of power—that is, its definition as autonomous and monolithic—could be effectively demolished. Merely articulating a concept of power in the form of a relationship, though, already constitutes an audacious intellectual enterprise.

Many scholars have followed in Machiavelli's footsteps, even without knowing it. E. P. Thompson, Howard Zinn, the Subaltern Studies Group, and many other historians have demonstrated how writing from below, from the standpoint of the subordinated, affords a clearer and more comprehensive understanding of historical development.[2] W. E. B. Du Bois similarly affirms that the standpoint of the subordinated offers the potential for a more complete knowledge of society. The double consciousness of black Americans, he maintains, is both an affliction and a mark of superiority: they are "gifted with a second-sight."[3] They see society more fully, with knowledge of both black culture and the dominant white culture, and they contain within themselves, written on their very bodies, the history of domination: "in every aspect of his living," writes James Baldwin, in line with Du Bois, the black American "betrays the memory of the auction block."[4] From below is indeed the standpoint of a wide range of projects for liberation, and that is the perspective we will try to develop in our analysis.[5]

*Let us step back, though, and trace how some of the great theorists of power in the modern tradition share much of Machiavelli's analysis but never fully draw its consequences. Max Weber, for instance, asserts that power (*Macht*) is in dialectical relation with domination (*Herrschaft*) such that whereas the former "is the probability that one actor within a social relationship will be in a position to carry out his own will despite resistance, regardless of the basis on which this probability rests," the latter "is the probability that a command with a given specific content will be obeyed by a given group of persons."[6] Thus arises the conception of legitimation or, really, the idea of how command must be bound by consent, the need for command to represent the interests of the obedient, which forms the very idea of the "autonomy of the political" and the "realist" version of Machiavellianism (which runs counter to Machiavelli's thought). Weber continues:*

To be more specific, domination *will thus mean the situation in which the manifested will* (command) *of the* ruler *or* rulers *is meant to influence the conduct of one or more others* (the ruled) *and actually does influence it in such a way that their conduct to a socially relevant degree occurs as if the ruled had made the content of the command the maxim of their conduct for its very own sake. Looked upon from the other end, this situation will be called* obedience.[7]

The concept of power, a dialectical synthesis of kratos *and* ethos, *thus finds its Machiavellian synthesis—not an ideal relation but rather an effective synthesis in which power and obedience act in consonance. In the end Weber thus undermines the definition of power as a relationship. Resistance fades from view when command,* Herrschaft, *is celebrated as the prefiguration of obedience.*

Hannah Arendt also attempts to counter the organic conception of power, to break up the Leviathan. And in her work, too, power is posed as a relationship but, in contrast to Weber, she does not close down that relationship. Machiavelli, for her, is a hero of change in the world, the mutatio rerum. *These mutations correspond, first of all, to a conception of legitimation that is open, in transformation, engaging not fixed ideal types but diverse political voices. This openness is what characterizes democracy. Arendt finds a seemingly predestined historical narrative in the Machiavellian "moment" that stretches from the revolt of the Ciompi in fourteenth-century Florence all the way to the early twentieth-century Saint Petersburg workers' soviets. Tyranny has no basis in Machiavelli's thought: he is a man of revolution, of constant mutation, of constituent power. State reason, in contrast, can be only a function and an interpretation of a closed, established authority. In the place of a fixed foundation of power is an expansive composition of political differences in interaction: "the spirit of foundation," she writes, "reveals its vitality through a virtue that it can increase—it can expand the foundations."[8] In this context Arendt makes repeated positive references to Machiavelli, and the concept of the "autonomy of the political," in its pessimistic form, seems to fall away. Power is put in the hands of the subjects and "authentic" praxis for Arendt must be public, political action. The* vita activa *is completely engaged in civil life, not flattened in this relationship but open toward the "inter-esse," toward human interactions.*

Neither Weber's analysis of power (and its legitimation of the relations of force) nor Arendt's developing conception (from the objective concept of legitimation in her early work to its democratic form in her later work) is able fully, however, to pull us out of the dominant modern definition of power. Ultimately, over the social relationships grasped by both Weber and Arendt triumphs always the One and over the immanence of antagonistic resistances prevails the transcendence of command. Arendt gives us a Machiavelli who is not so much "advisor to the Prince" but rather a "confidant of providence," to borrow a phrase from Raymond Aron. Weber presents the mechanisms of the legitimation of power without leaving any alternative possibility: the mechanical and objective character of the bureaucratic function has its own forms of the production of subjectivity, but Weber banishes affects, the passions, and even innovation, which all "escape from calculation."[9]

The essential point that defines Machiavelli's work is, on the contrary, recognizing power not only as a relationship (which breaks open the "autonomy of the political") but also seeing it born from below. Power always exceeds fixed relations; it overflows and wells up from the field of social conflict. The multitude frightens those in power, and the source of its fearsomeness is an uncontained, overflowing force. When Machiavelli says that only from the bottom of the mountain is its summit visible and describable, he is not posing the position of the humble servant of the Prince nor a rhetorical figure of those obsequious to the powerful. Moreover, this indicates not only an epistemological standpoint—seeing power more clearly—but also a political trajectory that constructs from below toward the top. This is the path of the multitude when, as Spinoza says in the Political Treatise, *it both interprets democracy as an instrument of freedom and also poses freedom as the product of democracy.*

Michel Foucault allows us to translate these challenges to the dominant modern conception of power into the conditions of our contemporary world. At the beginning of his course on biopolitics, in 1979, he explains a methodological decision: "I would like to point out straightaway that choosing to talk about or to start from governmental practice is obviously and explicitly a way of not taking as a primary, original, and already given object, notions such as the sovereign, sovereignty, the people, subjects, the state, and civil society.... How can you write history if you do not accept a priori the existence of things like the state, society, the sovereign, and subjects?"[10] This defines a very radical "path from below," and we can see where it leads. Truth is constructed on a poietic terrain that produces new being. Liberation struggles, for example, develop "intransitive" practices of freedom, a freedom that creates truth. In his debate with Noam Chomsky, when Chomsky poses the actions of the proletariat as being based on justice, Foucault inverts the relationship: "I would like to reply to you in the terms of Spinoza and say that the proletariat doesn't wage war against the ruling class because it considers that war to be just. The proletariat makes war with the ruling class because, for the first time in history, it wants to take power. And because it will overthrow the power of the ruling class, it considers such a war to be just."[11]

So many theorists, however, refuse to accept Foucault's proclamation of an epistemology of power from below! They pretend instead that he is proposing an autonomous and totalizing conception of power, echoing that of the Frankfurt school, which allows no subject to resist. That is not even true for his writings in the 1960s and '70s. Despite the strong structuralist framework of his work in that period, he managed gradually to break through structuralist constraints. First, he accomplished this by conducting a bitter polemic against every individualizing operation and every reprise of Cartesian subjectivity, and then through a "destitution" of the subject, which is presented as an excavation and exploration of the "we"—of the relationship between I and we—not only as a becoming but also as a practice of multiplicity. Foucault's development of the concept of micropowers in the 1970s opened a new dimension that certainly generalized the concept of power but in no way gave it an autonomous and totalitarian figure—on the contrary, it began to destroy that. The important thing is that it is a relational conception of power.

One should really situate Foucault's work in the major political tensions of the 1970s. His work followed the expansion of social antagonism from the factories to the wide social terrain and analyzed the new forms of the subjectivation of the struggles. Foucault was completely inside of this, and that is how he went "beyond" Marx. It was necessary, obviously, to go beyond the economistic versions of Marxism (as adopted by some activists) and to recuperate Marxist thought transfigured in the social. That is what the concept of "biopolitics" eventually represented: not the negation but the readoption of the economic in the modes of life—and thus in the subjective, in subjectivation. What developed in the movements of the 1970s was thus reflected in or parallel to Foucault's courses, which explicitly marked a break with structuralist and economistic frameworks of the conception of power.

What, then, does "from below" mean? It means, first, defining power from the standpoint of the subordinated, whose knowledge is transformed through resistance and struggles of liberation from the domination of those "above." Those below have a fuller knowledge of the social whole, a gift that can serve as the basis for a multitudinous enterprise of constructing the common. From below also designates a political trajectory: an institutional project that has not only the force to subvert command but also the capacity to construct politically an alternative society.

CHAPTER 6

HOW TO OPEN PROPERTY TO THE COMMON

For centuries the ruling powers have told us that private property is a sacred and inalienable right, the bulwark that defends society against chaos: without private property there is not only no freedom, justice, or economic development, but also no sense of self or bonds to those around us—no social life as we know it. The right to property is written into constitutions and, more important, embedded so deeply in the social fabric that it defines our common sense. Private property as we know it was invented with modernity and became for the modern era ineluctable, determining both the foundation and the ultimate horizon of political passions. Without property it seems impossible to understand ourselves and our world.

Today, however, as property is increasingly unable to support either our economic needs or our political passions, cracks begin to appear in those common sense understandings. Private property is not the foundation of freedom, justice, and development but just the opposite: an obstacle to economic life, the basis of unjust structures of social control, and the prime factor that creates and maintains social hierarchies and inequalities. The problem with property is not merely that some have it and some don't. Private property itself is the problem.

Social and political projects are now emerging that defy the rule of private property and pose instead the rights of the common, that is, open and equal access to wealth together with democratic decision-making procedures. And yet it remains extraordinarily difficult to imagine our social world and ourselves in terms not defined by private property. We have only meager intellectual resources to think outside property, let alone conceive of a world in which private property is abolished (and the socialist regimes that maintain the power of property and accumulate it in the hands of the state are a poor guide). Resources are available, paradoxically, in the tradition of property law itself. Some alternative legal traditions lead away from property and toward the common, but faced with the precipice, as we will see, fail to take the leap and end up mystifying the common.

A bundle of rights

Today's commonsense, popular understanding of property remains remarkably close to the eighteenth-century definitions of classical liberalism. "[O]wnership [*dominium*]," writes Hugo Grotius, "connotes possession of something peculiarly one's own" to the exclusion of other parties.[1] William Blackstone's definition echoes this view with added poetic flourish: "There is nothing which so generally strikes the imagination, and engages the affections of mankind, as the right of property; or that sole and despotic dominion which one man claims and exercises over the external things of the world, in total exclusion of the right of any other individual in the universe."[2] Property grants a monopoly of access and decision-making to an individual owner to the exclusion of others.

First-year law students are often taught, however, contrary to the classical definitions, that property denotes a plural set of social interests: a bundle of rights.[3] This line of reasoning, which is developed in the United States by the legal realists in the late nineteenth and early twentieth centuries, accepts fully the rule of property but, by undermining the grounds of exclusion and thus introducing plurality, transforms property from the inside. "[P]rivate property as we know it," writes Felix Cohen in explicit response to Blackstone's notion of exclusion, "is always subject to limitations based on the rights of other individuals in the universe."[4] The legal realists argue, in effect, that the exaggerated individualism and the focus on exclusion in the classical definitions of private property are profoundly antisocial, that is, they fail to account for the fact that we live in society and the actions and property of each have effects on others. The argument, in other words, effectively socializes property by, first, recognizing that property is always already social, affecting others in the universe, and, second, creating a basis for those others to express their rights. Being affected is a basis for having a right. Since a coal-burning factory, for example, affects both those living around it and the workers inside, they, in addition to the owner, have rights with regard to that property. This conception preserves the rights of individual property owners, as we said, but also embeds them in a larger, plural field of often-conflicting, unequal social rights. The rights that this notion of a bundle introduces are really counterrights empowered to operate as balances or challenges within property.

The legal realists' conception of property rights is particularly powerful because it combines the pluralism of the notion of a bundle with the claim that property implies sovereignty, a form of domination that is equally politi-cal and economic. "There can be no doubt," writes Morris Cohen, "that our property laws do confer sovereign power on our captains of industry and even more so on our captains of finance."[5] Today's captains of industry and finance, whose power has grown exponentially since 1927, the year in which Morris Cohen wrote, exert authority based on their property without even the thin-nest claims to representation. The legal realists' argument not only demon-strates how deeply economics and politics are interrelated but also blurs the traditional division of legal thought and practice between civil law and public law, bridging the gap, which stretches back to Roman law, between *dominium* (an individual's rule over things) and *imperium* (the sovereign's rule over soci-ety): "We must not overlook the actual fact," Cohen cautions, "that dominion over things is also *imperium* over our fellow beings. The extent of the power over the life of others which the legal order confers on those called owners is not fully appreciated by those who think of law as merely protecting men in their possessions."[6] Property is thus a sovereign power, not so much in the sense that it repeats the functions of sovereignty on an individual scale—I have sovereign authority over my things—but insofar as property has sover-eign effects on a social scale.[7]

For the legal realists one important political consequence of conceiving property as both a bundle of rights and a sovereign power is that it counters the liberal, laissez-faire arguments for property rights free from state interven-tion. Coercion is always mobilized by property rights in order to regulate and suppress the rights of others, even (and especially) when classical liberal, laissez-faire advocates sing the praises of freedom. On one hand, as a sovereign power, property owners exert political coercion over those around them that is equivalent to forms of state coercion. On the other hand, the protection of property rights and the "freedom" of laissez-faire liberals require the state to wield coercive force. "In protecting property," Robert Hale argues, "the gov-ernment is doing something quite apart from merely keeping the peace. It is exerting coercion wherever that is necessary to protect each owner, not merely from violence, but also from peaceful infringement of his sole right to employ the thing owned."[8] One might argue on the basis of the two primary elements of the legal realists' argument—the recognition that property always involves economic and political coercion and the affirmation of plural social rights—that property should be abolished and a more democratic, equal management of social wealth established, something like what we call the common. The legal realists, however, do not go that route. They mobilize the fact that coercion and state are always already involved in property rights, which undermines laissez-faire claims to freedom, in order to legitimate the actions of the state to address and protect the full plurality of other social actors whose rights are part of the bundle. It is easy to recognize how this line of reasoning paves the way a little later in the twentieth century for some of the basic tenets of the New Deal.

Beginning in the 1960s, the critical legal studies (CLS) movement revived the radical potential of the legal realists, extending both the plural, social notion of property rights and the recognition of its sovereign, coercive character. One of the core tenets of the CLS movement is that law is not autonomous from economics. Duncan Kennedy, following the legal realists, particularly Robert Hale, asserts that law dictates the "ground rules" of economic life in such a way as to empower some groups over others. In this context, the notion that property is a bundle of rights or, better, "a set of social relations"[9] highlights the social hierarchies that are created and supported by property. A second core tenet of CLS is that law is not autonomous from politics; law is itself a political weapon. Social hierarchies—race and gender hierarchies are a primary focus of the critical race theory and feminist legal scholars who followed on, often critical of, the work of CLS scholars—are created and maintained by the Constitution, the courts, and legal practice. The CLS recognition that law, especially property law, is a weapon of power but one that is internally plural opens law as a field of struggle, one in which hierarchies can be challenged effectively.

Like the legal realists, however, CLS scholars do not extend the implications of their arguments toward an abolition of property but instead strive to reform property from the inside: they use the pluralism of property law to affirm the rights of the subordinated. This strategy is clear in some of the practical projects CLS supports. Duncan Kennedy's proposal, for example, to create limited-equity co-ops as an alternative form of property that provides affordable housing for the poor puts the bundle of rights conception into practice by combining nonprofit ownership with limited decision-making participation by residents and attention to the interests of the larger community. In order to tame the pressures of the real estate market and gentrification, Kennedy advocates a system whereby residents who sell their property will receive only what they paid for it plus an adjustment for inflation and perhaps a fraction of the increase in equity. Affirming some rights over others in this way serves to combat social hierarchy and blunt the power of property owners. This legacy finds resonance with a variety of legal strategies not directly associated with the CLS movement, such as the Creative Commons project, which provides an alternative to copyright and gives authors options for limited control over their cultural products, thus reorganizing the bundle of rights to creative products, and Anna di Robilant's proposal for affordable housing cooperatives and community gardens that remix the bundle of rights to promote the "equality of autonomy." In these examples and the many like them one can recognize how the assertion of plural rights serves to combat the sovereign powers of owners while maintaining the paradigm of property.[10]

Keep in mind, however, that the pluralism of the bundle of rights conception, especially when not complemented by the recognition that property is sovereignty, is not necessarily progressive. Some uses, in fact, point in the opposite direction. Chicago school economists, such as Armen Alchien and Harold Demsetz, accept that property is a bundle of rights but quickly add that the primary function of these rights is to guide incentives to allocate resources for the greatest productivity, to reduce transaction costs, and to internalize externalities. Plural property rights, in other words, become instruments of economic "rationality."[11] The notion of a bundle can even be turned around so as paradoxically to reassert Blackstone's "sole and despotic dominion" of the owner to exclude others: "one of the most essential sticks in the bundle of rights that are commonly characterized as property," writes Justice William Rehnquist in a 1979 decision of the US Supreme Court, is "the right to exclude others."[12] In these cases the bundle of rights conception is used not to attenuate but to reinforce the political and economic coercion of property ownership and the social hierarchies it creates and maintains.

Other uses of the bundle of rights, although progressive, remain primarily ethical injunctions rather than politically effective projects. "Progressive property" theorists, for example, take up the notion of plural property rights to assert the political nature of property and, in so doing, counter neoliberal, "law and economics" arguments.[13] Property is not merely a law of things and property law is not merely a mechanism of coordination, Joseph William Singer asserts, "it is a quasi-constitutional framework of social life."[14] Property law, write the authors of the manifesto-like 2009 progressive property statement, "can render relationships within communities either exploitative and humiliating or liberating and ennobling."[15] In contrast to the legal realists and the CLS scholars, however, progressive property theorists give little attention to the economic effects of property, perhaps with the fear that any engagement with law and economics will end up in the camp of their neoliberal antagonists. More important, their political vision is not grounded in the recognition that property is a form of sovereignty. As a result, the politics of progressive property is most often expressed through pallid appeals to values and ethics.[16] This approach thus bears traces of the "autonomy of the political," which we analyzed in chapter 3. In any case, these authors, despite their recognition of the plural and political nature of property, offer little help to think beyond it.

One might assume that legal scholars working with immaterial forms of property, such as intellectual property, would be the best positioned to recognize the insufficiencies of property law and the political potential of the pluralism of rights. Every time something you used to take for granted as common is made into private property—will they find a way to make the air we breathe private property next?—it provides a critical standpoint to look back and recognize the incoherence and injustice of property in general. Today the center of gravity of the property world is shifting from material forms of property, which served as the classic reference for notions of possession and exclusion, toward immaterial forms. Rights to immaterial property, such as ideas, images, culture, and code, are in some respects immediately plural and social. Making immaterial property conform to the old systems of exclusion and scarcity that were created for material property is an increasingly difficult endeavor and, ultimately, bound to fail. Immaterial property, along with the forms of freedom and cooperation opened by network culture, helps us glimpse the potential for a nonproperty relation to social wealth, that is, how we could share and manage wealth with equal access and democratic decision-making—and this can even help us to see the potential for sharing material wealth through nonproperty relations. (These possibilities will become clearer in our discussion of new forms of labor in the next section.) Several theorists of intellectual property seem to peer over the edge of property and glimpse the common, pushed in that direction by the phenomena they study, and their work is very useful, but they ultimately pull back from the precipice and find ways to express their project within rather than against the property paradigm.[17]

The developments of property law across the last century can appear to be moving, despite the intentions of its theorists and practitioners, beyond property and toward a theory of the common. In the 1970s, for instance, Thomas

Grey thought he recognized that the acceptance of property as a bundle of rights not only undermined the classical liberal conception of ownership as the right of an individual over things but also introduced fragmentation such that property is disintegrating and thus becoming no longer a coherent category in legal and political theory. This process, which has taken place internal to capitalist development, Grey claims, ultimately erodes the foundation of capitalist rule. Marx was wrong, he concludes, because "private property need not be *abolished* by revolution if it tends to *dissolve* with the development of mature capitalism." We believe Grey's intuition of the historical tendency pointing beyond property (and ultimately beyond capital) is correct, but he is mistaken to think this will proceed on its own. History has led us to an abyss, and we need a little push to leap. The establishment of the rights of the common, if they are to be realized, will be the result of struggle on a wide variety of fronts. At the end of this chapter we will investigate the terrain of struggles and propose forms of social strike. Now, however, let us investigate another avenue within legal theory that opens property toward the common in a way complementary to bundle-of-rights arguments, a stream of thought that is more prominent in Europe than the United States, and proceeds from the basis of property rights in labor.

The social properties of labor

In capitalist society the possession of private property is legitimated (at least, in principle) by labor. If one were to follow the logic of capitalist ideology, then, contemporary forms of production should undermine private property. As labor and economic production are increasingly socialized, following this logic, the individual nature of ownership should gradually be undermined. The social nature of production should imply an equally social scope of the use of, access to, and decision-making over wealth. Capitalist legal structures do not follow this path, of course, but the transformations of labor create a constant tension and provide a resource for change, pointing toward the common.

John Locke expresses the argument for the legitimation of property based on labor in its classic and perhaps clearest form: what was common becomes private when individuals add their labor to it: "The labour of his body, and the work of his hands, we may say, are properly his. Whatsoever then he removes out of the state that nature hath provided, and left it in, he hath mixed his labour with, and joined to it something that is his own, and thereby makes it his property."[18] One key precondition for this claim is that in the state of nature individuals encounter vacant lands (terra nullius—devoid of sovereignty) that are open for ownership. Locke regarded the Americas with a colonialist imaginary, for instance, as being in such a state. The second assumption is that all (or, at least, all free male citizens) own their own bodies and, specifically, their own laboring capacity. Ownership of one's own labor is the building block. When it engages with and mixes with the common, then the common too becomes property through a logic of contagion. Labor sets in motion expansive waves of possession and property. The logic of property based on labor undergoes a series of modifications and qualifications (already in subsequent passages of Locke's treatise and then through the ensuing centuries of capitalist thought), but it remains a basic element of capitalist common sense. If you build a house, then it should be yours. Consider, for example, how labor logic also continues to animate portions of property law: one is eligible to apply for patents when one invents or discovers a new and useful process, machine, manufacture, or composition of matter.[19] Intellectual labor, at least in principle or rather at the level of ideology, legitimates intellectual property.

Despite the enduring capitalist ideology of individual property based on labor, capitalist property does not, of course, belong to those who produce it. Karl Marx was fond of remarking, especially in light of the propaganda that communism would take away what rightly belongs to people, that capital in its industrial form has already negated "individual private property, as founded on the labor of its proprietor."[20] Capitalist property accrues not to those who produce but to those who own the means of production. He takes seriously and adopts the equation between labor and property promoted by capitalist ideology, in other words, to show that capital undermines its own assumptions.

We should note in passing that whereas one could imagine on the basis of this recognition seeking to establish, beyond the limits of capital, the real foundation of property in labor, Marx moves in the opposite direction: the abolition of private property requires also the refusal of work.

> *"Labour"* is the living basis of private property, it is private property as the creative source of itself. Private property is nothing but *objectified* labour. If it is desired to strike a mortal blow at private property, one must attack it not only as a *material state of affairs*, but

also as *activity,* as *labour. It is one of the greatest misapprehensions to speak of free, human, social labour, of labour without private property. "Labour" by its very nature is unfree, unhuman, unsocial activity, determined* by private property and creating private property. Hence the abolition of private property will become a reality only when it is conceived as the abolition of *"labour"* (an abolition which, of course, has become possible only as a result of labour itself, that is to say, has become possible as a result of the material activity of society and which should on no account be conceived as the replacement of one category by another).[21]

The equation between private property and labor, in Marx's vision, effectively doubles the challenge: we must imagine and invent not only social bonds and social cohesion without property but also systems of cooperative social activity and creativity beyond work, that is, beyond the regime of waged labor.

Today, however, the nature and conditions of labor have changed radically from the industrial forms that Marx analyzed and even more so from the agricultural and colonial imagination of Locke. In order to investigate contemporary property relations we need first to look to today's forms of social production and reproduction. For now let us mention only two primary aspects. First, people work in ever more flexible, mobile, and precarious arrangements. Even Wall Street bankers have to be ready every day to clean out their desks by 5 p.m., but more important the vast majority work under the constant threat of unemployment and poverty. Second, labor is increasingly social and based on cooperation with others, embedded in a world of communicative networks and digital connections, which run throughout industrial arrangements, agricultural systems, and all other economic forms. Capital is valorized through cooperative flows in which language, affects, code, and images are subsumed in the material processes of production.

The fact that production in contemporary capitalist society is ever more cooperative and socialized strains to the breaking point the link between individual labor and private property promoted by capitalist ideology. It no longer makes sense to isolate the one whose labor created some thing or, as patent law imagines, some idea. The one never produces. We only produce together, socially. Wealth continues to be produced by labor, in other words, in increasingly social networks of laboring cooperation, but the concept of private property based on labor becomes merely an ideological remnant—and the modern conceptions of property (along with, in part, Marx's own) become obsolete.

This rupture leads to two radically different developments. First, as property seems to be "freed" from any even ideological grounding in labor, the logic of private property becomes all the more absolute, a power of pure command. We will analyze in part III the ways in which finance and money have come to redefine property and how, in the era of neoliberalism, private property in its financial and monetary forms rules ever more completely over production and society as a whole. But even at such extreme points, capitalist property and value still carry the sign of labor like a birthmark. Jean-Marie Harribey, in his dialogue with André Orléan, is right to insist that even when value no longer appears in substantial, material form it is not merely a fantasy of accounting. It is the sign of a productive social network, mystified but effective, that is continually developed more intensively and extensively.[22] Second, the ever more cooperative and socialized nature of production opens toward an understanding of the common. Rather than speaking of the social function of property, which seems to have flowed toward capital to the point of residing completely in finance, it would be better to speak of the social properties of labor. We are immersed in the common, cooperative circuits of production and reproduction that are both sustaining and chaotic. Try a thought experiment to follow the Lockean strain of capitalist ideology that bases property rights in production to its conclusion: if wealth today tends to be produced not by individuals but only in expansive cooperative social networks, then the results should be the property of the productive network as a whole, the entire society, which is to say the property of no one; that is, property should become nonproperty and wealth must become common.

We arrive at the same point—of the need today for a notion of right rooted in the common—if we go back and trace the developments of labor rights with respect to the state. It is sometimes difficult to remember today, when labor organizing is so brutally attacked in countries throughout the world, that in the twentieth century institutionalized labor movements, especially in the dominant countries, played a central role in stabilizing the functioning of capital and the state. The first article of Italy's 1948 Constitution declares, for example, "Italy is a democratic republic founded on labor." Labor is "constitutionalized" and made into a pillar of support. The creation and constitution of welfare policies not only served to tame markets and overcome the exclusive normative power of private property and contracts but also sought to domesticate radical labor militancy. The welfare state aimed to treat the causes of crisis, both the objective (economic) and subjective (worker).[23] Wages thus came to be supplemented by various "indirect" incomes provided by the welfare system, including pensions, healthcare, and various other social programs. State action, especially monetary action, had to maintain "effective demand," and economic development depended significantly on the development of the needs of workers and citizens. From these threads of public actions and social services through the course of the twentieth century was knit a tightly woven biopolitical fabric.

In recent decades, however, neoliberalism has violently attacked the social conditions of labor, reimposing the norms of the market and negating the notion that labor can have any autonomous right as the basis of the public regulation of economic development. Public law is thus ever more explicitly subordinated to private law, pulverized into thousands of subjective rights. And, similarly, all fiscal and social legislation is swept into the whirlpool of privatization, where instruments of progressive taxation are drowned; the savaging of public services becomes the rule, virtually prohibiting acts of solidarity among social groups; and the public functions of the state are subordinated to the market. The "rights of labor," which in the welfare state were raised up to the dignity of "public rights," with labor union bargaining supported and recognized by the state, are now degraded and translated once again into private and patrimonial law.[24]

In response to the depredations of neoliberalism, several European legal scholars have engaged in pragmatic efforts to tether private property to the public interest and public needs. Stefano Rodotà and Ugo Mattei, for example, seek tirelessly, in different ways, to use the means provided by the Italian Constitution and the Italian legal tradition to protect natural resources (such as the national water supply) against privatization and to defend popular occupations that seek to prevent national heritage sites, such as Teatro Valle in Rome, being handed over to private interests. Their primary aim is not just to reassert the powers of public law for the benefit of social solidarity, affirming the "social functions" and general interests of law, and thus posing a definition of the "common" that is really a form of the "public." Their aim is also to promote, from within private law, a proliferation of subjective, socially protected rights, wresting them away from a strict definition of property rights and casting them instead in the direction of social interests. Stefano Rodotà, for example, has spearheaded the promotion of the "right to have rights," and

Ugo Mattei has insisted on the other aspect of the crisis of private law, developing the social functions of the private toward a conception of "common goods," conceived as new categories of the "right to the common."[25]

These pragmatic legal projects are especially urgent as a line of defense in the context of global neoliberalism with its general ideological celebration of the rule of private property and the erosion of the powers of states. But those same conditions transform the conceptual and practical possibilities of these strategies. As the powers of states fade, in other words, efforts to pluralize and socialize the rights of property must look beyond the public to other means of support. In fact, when left legal theorists appeal to the public and state power as the centerpiece of strategies to combat the excessive rule of private property—when Rodotà, for example, speaks of "making the public public again" (*ripubblicizzazione del pubblico*)—this sounds to us, in contemporary conditions, neither feasible nor desirable.[26] Such state responses are even more prevalent in France and Germany, where the "institutionalist" line is still preeminent and the promotion of the "rights of the common" is generally conceived as an expansion and deepening of public law. Unfortunately, this spurious demand remains foundational for large segments of the socialist Left in Europe, whose imagination is fixed on state action and state power as the sole plausible defender of society.

This may be an instance, however, in which capitalist elites (or, really, their collective unconscious) have a more lucid analysis than "progressive" theorists. Above we noted that as part of the neoliberal project the institutionalized social rights and labor rights that supported capitalist rule throughout the twentieth century have been dramatically undermined. It is as if the capitalist political class, in its paranoia, were to have mistaken these "reasonable" rights, which in the past have protected it against crises, for a much more threatening right, the right of the common. This is something like the moment after the failed 1848 revolution when the French bourgeoisie saw in the rather tame calls for a "social republic" the specter of communism and went running in the opposite direction to embrace the empire of Louis Bonaparte.[27] Perhaps today's capitalist elites—in their hysteria—also divine the truth. The extravagant, excessive violence of the privatization of the welfare state, despite the dangers of crisis it risks, betrays the fact that, beyond the claims to restore the hegemony of the market and the primacy of private law, it is fundamentally driven by the fear that social rights are a slope that inevitably leads to an affirmation of the common. That is the possibility that capital must destroy!

In short, the social properties of labor, on one side, unmask the illegitimate rights of individual property, affirming the social, shared right to socially produced wealth, and, on the other, they illicit the terror of propertied classes, financial elites, and neoliberal governments because behind the assertion of social rights they perceive (correctly) the emergence of a right of the common.

Third response: The common is not property

Legal projects to reform property and limit its power have certainly had beneficial effects but now we need finally to take the leap beyond. Some work within property law, as we have seen, points in this direction but pulls back at the cliff and fails to take the decisive step, maintaining in one way or another the exclusion, hierarchy, and centralized decision-making that always ultimately characterize property. If the bundle of rights theorized by legal scholars were extended equally to society as a whole, for example, quantity would pass over into quality and the internal plurality would explode the hierarchies that property maintains. Similarly, when labor is socialized and the whole society becomes a terrain of valorization, when the intelligence, corporeal activity, cultural creativity, and inventive powers of all are engaged cooperatively and together produce and reproduce society, then the common becomes the key to productivity, whereas private property becomes a fetter that hinders productive capacities. It is becoming increasingly clear, in other words, that property can and must be stripped of its sovereign character and transformed into the common.

The common is defined first, then, in contrast to property, both private and public. It is not a new form of property but rather *nonproperty*, that is, a fundamentally different means of organizing the use and management of wealth. The common designates an equal and open structure for access to wealth together with democratic mechanisms of decision-making. More colloquially, one might say that the common is what we share or, rather, it is a social structure and a social technology for sharing.

The history of property and the common is useful for denaturalizing property relations. Private property is not intrinsic to human nature or necessary for civilized society, we should remember, but rather a historical phenomenon: it came into existence with capitalist modernity, and one day it will pass out of existence. Recognizing, however, that the violent and bloody construction of private property throughout the world involved the suppression of social forms of sharing wealth—land, most importantly—should not lead us to conceive the common in terms of precapitalist social forms or to yearn for their re-creation. In many cases the precapitalist forms of community and systems for sharing wealth were characterized by disgusting, patriarchal, hierarchical modes of division and control. Instead of gazing back prior to capitalist private property we need to look beyond it.[28]

Today we have the potential to establish modes of sharing wealth that are equal and open, to institute a right to decide together democratically about the access, use, management, and distribution of social wealth. (Keep in mind, to avoid confusion, that this conception of the common is aimed at social wealth, not individual possessions: there is no need to share your toothbrush or even give others say over most things you make yourself.) The objects of the common have varying characteristics and to some extent our reasoning about how to share them must take different forms. Some forms of wealth are limited and scarce, for instance, while others are indefinitely reproducible, and thus managing how we can share them will face different challenges. Here is a very rough schema that gives some initial guidelines for considering the different forms of the common:

—First, the earth and its ecosystems are ineluctably common in the sense that we are all affected (albeit in varying degrees) by their damage and destruction. But we cannot have faith that the logics of private property or national interest will preserve them, and instead we must treat the earth as common so as collectively to make decisions to care for and guarantee its and our future.
—Second, forms of wealth that are primarily immaterial, including ideas, code, images, and cultural products, already strain against the exclusions imposed by property relations and tend toward the common.
—Material commodities, third, produced or extracted by increasingly cooperative forms of social labor can and should be opened for common use— and, equally important, planning decisions (whether, for instance, to leave some resources in the ground) should be made as democratically as possible.
—Fourth, metropolitan and rural social territories, both built environments and established cultural circuits, which are the fruit of social interactions and cooperation, must be open to use and managed in common.
—Finally, social institutions and services aimed at health, education, housing, and welfare must be transformed so as to be used for the benefit of all and subject to democratic decision-making.[29]

Crucial to any understanding of the common, in all its forms, is that use of and access to wealth must be managed. Elinor Ostrom, in particular, whose work has been central in introducing so many to the contemporary relevance of the common, rightly focuses on the need for governance and institution. Ostrom convincingly reveals the fallacy of all the "tragedy of the commons" arguments, which maintain that in order to be used effectively and preserved against ruin all wealth must be either public property or private property. She agrees that "common-pool resources" must be managed but disagrees that the state and capitalist enterprise are the only means for doing so. There can be—and indeed already exist—collective forms of self-management: "a self-governed common property arrangement in which the rules have been devised and modified by the participants themselves and also are monitored and enforced by them."[30] We wholeheartedly endorse Ostrom's claim that the common must be managed through systems of democratic participation. We part ways with her, however, when she insists that the community that shares access and decision-making must be small and limited by clear boundaries to divide those inside from outside. We have greater ambitions and are interested instead in more expansive democratic experiences that are open to others, and we will have to demonstrate the feasibility of such a new, fuller form of democracy today in the following chapters.

We should emphasize that any eventual "rights of the common" must be distinguished not only from private and public law but also, as we have said, from what especially in Europe have been called "social law" and "social rights." Social law, in fact, which does develop some functions of the common, lives in a sort of chiaroscuro. Bringing it into the light allows us to define better other characteristics of the common that are emerging. First, whereas social law and social rights are fundamentally static—they register legal norms that have been affirmed within the market in the guise of regulating social relationships—the common instead is fundamentally productive and does not simply regulate existing social relationships but rather constructs new institutions of "being together." Second, whereas social law imposes a sort of "total mobilization" under public law in the service of the state, maintaining all the statist ambiguities (from the right and the left) of this tradition dating back to the 1930s, the common constructs a society of democratic cooperative relationships managed from below. Third, whereas social law assumes a mass of individuals as its object, the common lives from the cooperation of singularities, each of which is able to bring a specific contribution to the construction of institutions. Finally, whereas social law, even though it was born from labor

movements, has been transformed by neoliberalism to manage "human capital" and participate in the mechanisms of biopower that subordinate and
order human actions and relationships to the rule of money and finance, the
common advances without legal mediations and emerges as a multitude, that
is, as the capacities of subjects to bring together their singularities in productive institutions of wealth and freedom.

The common therefore is not really a *tertium genus*, beyond private property and public property, if that were to mean it is simply a third form of property. (Indeed Ostrom's formulation of "common-pool resources" and Ugo
Mattei's conception of "common goods" [*beni comuni*] often seem to name
merely another form of property.) The common stands in contrast to property in a more radical way, by eliminating the character of exclusion from the
rights of both use and decision-making, instituting instead schema of open,
shared use and democratic governance.

Fable of the bees; or, passions of the common

Albert O. Hirschman traces in early modern Europe the development of an
ideological support of capitalist accumulation based on the play of passions.
The story begins in the sixteenth and seventeenth centuries with the realistic
recognition by Machiavelli and others that humans as they really are (not as
we wish they were) are driven in large part by passions that can be destructive
to themselves and others. Sustainable political arrangements must tame the
passions, the thinking goes, not by moralizing or imploring people to be virtuous or rational, but rather by setting beneficial passions against detrimental
or dangerous ones. "It is fortunate for men," Montesquieu writes, in one of
Hirschman's favorite passages, "to be in a situation where, though their passions may prompt them to be wicked (*méchants*), they have nevertheless an
interest in not being so."[31] Interest, that is, the passion for acquisition, the passion for property, emerges in Hirschman's narrative as the key virtuous (or at
least benign) passion that is able to tame the dangerous ones. Interest is seen
to be constant and orderly, and thus governable. Moreover, it has the power to
transform traditional sins, such as greed, selfishness, and avarice, into virtues.

The theory of the subject that emerges with capitalist ideology is thus
grounded in possession. The word *property* itself undergoes a transformation
in the course of the early modern period from meaning nature or quality

(what is proper to a person or thing) to possession or thing owned. What it means to be human—and even what it means to be alive—comes to be imagined in terms of possessions of various types. Not only external material articles such as land or goods but also "internal" immaterial properties such as power and intelligence must become thinglike in order to obey the logic of possession. You are what you have.[32]

The intellectual framework that poses interests and acquisition as an antidote to the destructive passions fades from prominence, Hirschman notes, in the nineteenth and twentieth centuries, but it remains present in the background as an anchor of capitalist ideology: the pursuit of property and accumulation are the guarantors of security, prosperity, freedom, and more. Today, however, the virtuous passions of property—if they ever really existed—have all but crumbled, and in their void the passions of the common, truly sustainable virtues, are taking root. Let us look, just as an introduction, at a few key passions.

Security (against fear)

Private property promises to connect you in community but instead merely provides shelter by separating you from others, defending you from the hordes. It will protect you from hunger, homelessness, subordination, and economic crisis, and even protect your offspring via inheritance: because you have property, others will be first to go hungry, to be homeless, and so forth. Today it's easy to see, however, that your property can't even do that. Property won't save you.

Scratch the surface of private property's veneer of security and you will find its real foundation: fear. The society of private property manages and propagates fear. The racially segregated metropolis, for example, from Ferguson and Baltimore to São Paulo, London, and Paris, is a boiling cauldron of fear that periodically overflows in rage and revolt. Private property is only one weapon in the arsenal of racial subordination and violence, but it is a fundamental one that has been deployed constantly at least since slavery. Black and brown populations are afraid most immediately of the police but they fear too the prospects of poverty and destitution. The whiter populations hold to their property and hide behind its walls. But really no one is safe.

Austerity and debt show another face of how private property's promise of security is quickly revealed as fear. Across the globe national economies fall prey to crises that, through a cycle of debt and austerity, destroy the property and lay waste to the savings of the middle classes that thought they were pro-tected. All but the wealthiest face insecurity today and for the indefinite future, and even those who have been spared so far tremble in fear at news of bank crises and stock market collapses.

The socialist tradition has long critiqued the claims that property can pro-vide security on a social scale and has maintained instead that security can be provided only by the state. State powers to create security, however, to the extent that they ever existed, have in the era of neoliberal globalization been severely undermined. States, and socialist states in particular, wield their own weapons of fear.

Real security is something altogether different. Security, as Spinoza defines it, is hope from which uncertainty has been removed; it is confidence that our joy will continue in the future. Security is what defeats fear.[33]

Today security can derive only from the freedom and cooperation of sin-gularities in the common. We find a powerful foretaste of this real security, which neither private property nor the state can accomplish, in the forms of community and cooperation that emerge in the midst of social and ecological disaster. In recent years, for instance, from Brazil and Argentina to Spain, Greece, and Japan, people have emerged from poverty and crisis to develop solidarity economies and organize production, incomes, services, food, and housing on a local scale. Solidarity economies emphasize cooperation and self-management as an alternative to the regime of profit and capitalist control, which is not only more egalitarian but also more efficient and stable. The way people share and come together in the wake of ecological disasters also hints at the security provided by the common. "Disasters provide an extraordinary window into social desire and possibility," writes Rebecca Solnit, admiring the forms of social cooperation and solidarity, "and what manifests there matters elsewhere, in ordinary times and in other extraordinary times."[34] The ways that people develop security in the common in times of crisis provide a foretaste of what a society of the common could be.

Prosperity (against misery)

Prosperity is another fundamental rationale for private property's domination of society: we need to tolerate extreme social and economic inequality, we are told, because the rule of private property is the only way to ensure development. Today the shambles of this supposed development are all around us, from economic ruin to ecological disaster, but the failures of private property to generate economic development do not originate with neoliberalism. "The capitalist process," Joseph Schumpeter admits reluctantly in the early 1940s, "takes the life out of the idea of property.... Dematerialized, defunctionalized and absentee ownership does not impress and call forth moral allegiance as the vital form of property did. Eventually there will be nobody left who really cares to stand for it—nobody within and nobody without the precincts of the big concerns."[35] The economic benefits of private property were already becoming at that time a purely ideological façade, propped up in part by anticommunist ideology.

Private property also undermines prosperity in the sense that, despite the constant marketing of new commodities, private property actually narrows the world of needs. Political economy "is therefore—for all its worldly and debauched appearance—a truly moral science," Marx writes, "the most moral science of all. Self-denial, the denial of life and of all human needs, is its principal doctrine. The less you eat, drink, buy books, go to the theatre, go dancing, go drinking, think, love, theorize, sing, paint, fence, etc., the more you *save*— the *greater* will become that treasure which neither moths nor maggots can consume—your *capital*. The less you *are*, the less you express your own *life*, the more you *have*."[36] The ideology of private property leads to a poverty of needs that infects rich and poor alike: the pathological hypertrophy of the passion for acquisition blinds people to all other needs, specifically their social needs. Don't listen to the moralists of the Left who preach renunciation as cure to our social disease of too much enjoyment. The capacity for enjoyment, as Marx says, is itself a productive power, a measure of productivity.[37] There is a world of needs and desires to discover and invent—beyond private property.

Private property's false promise of prosperity intersects with its unrealized vow to create security. Once upon a time, capitalist ideology pledged secure employment and thus confidence in the future, although only to a select population even in the dominant countries. Secure labor contracts have now evaporated such that the precarity that has long been the experience of workers in the subordinated countries and among subordinated populations in the dominant countries is now becoming universal.[38] Life in contemporary society is becoming precarious not only in terms of work contracts, but in all phases of life. Some communities, including migrants, people of color, LGBTQ people, the disabled, and others, recognize this precarity first and suffer it most acutely, but their experiences are harbingers for others. A society of precarity is a form of misery.

Precarious life, however, also reveals a crucial resource of wealth. The vulnerabilities that we share, Judith Butler argues, are the basis for social bonds that can generate real security. To be vulnerable is not merely to be susceptible to injury but also and more important to be open to the social world. "To say that any of us are vulnerable beings," Butler asserts, "is to mark our radical dependency not only on others, but on a sustaining and sustainable world."[39] Vulnerability, she continues, can be a form of strength when it is mobilized with others. On the basis of our shared vulnerability we can begin to construct institutions of the common, social institutions that can provide real security and prosperity. This must be not merely the passive complement to neoliberalism that continually compensates for the damages and seeks to fill the holes left by the retreat of welfare structures, but instead an aggressive strategy that also destroys the noxious forms of precaritization and institutes in their stead secure social bonds.[40]

Freedom (against death)

"Without private property there is no freedom": this refrain was faithfully translated into laws that defend every type of property, including real estate, industrial capital, finance, and money capital. Whereas state regulation = coercion, according to the familiar catechism, the rule of private property = freedom. In the late nineteenth and early twentieth centuries, as we saw earlier, the legal realists pierced this ideological veil by arguing that the supposed freedom of classical laissez-faire market liberalism also involves strong state coercion. State action is always enlisted to protect private property and to exert coercion against all who are excluded from its use. Perhaps such state coercion is invisible to those whose property is defended, but to those who are excluded it is just as real and powerful as any other form of violence. For the legal realists, as Duncan Kennedy observes, "capitalism was as coercive in its way as socialism."[41] Each, in fact, undermines what it claims to provide: the private, egotistical and isolated in individualism, destroys freedom; the public, which is blind to the wealth of singularities, annihilates social solidarity.

Singularities, in contrast to self-interested individuals, are born only when freedom and cooperation are intrinsically linked. On the one hand, only the extension of freedom can construct cooperation, organize the common, and guarantee social security. On the other, only the rules of cooperation and the norms of democracy can construct free, active subjectivities. The common constructs free human conviviality beyond the archaic and destructive pair of the private and the public.

The modern theory of the subject, which emerged from capitalist ideology, is characterized by possessive individualism, to use C. B. Macpherson's formulation.[42] The individual subject is defined by what it *has*. The modern subject is something like a coat hanger that supports all its possessions: the individual has real estate and ideas just as it has the ability to work and the capacity to invent, and all are exchangeable on the market. Alexandra Kollontai argues that the logic of possession is so deeply ingrained that it infuses even the modern conception of love. People have no way to think of their bonds to each other except in terms of property: you are mine and I am yours.[43] In contrast, subjectivities in the common are grounded not in possessions but in their interactions with and openness to others. Subjectivity is defined not by having but being or, better, *being-with*, acting-with, creating-with. Subjectivity itself arises from social cooperation.

In all these respects, then, we should today recognize the virtue of the passions of the common. Even though we have reached a point in history when the rule of property is recognized ever more clearly as a fetter to social well-being and development, and when the common appears as a real alternative, private property, counter to what Thomas Grey thought, will not dissolve on its own. The common, as Ugo Mattei rightly says, "can only really be defended and governed with the physicality of a mass movement ready for a long and generous battle to retake its own spaces."[44] Humanity needs a push in order to leap over the precipice into the common.

CHAPTER 7

WE, MACHINIC SUBJECTS

The passions of the common, beyond private property, demand a new conception of the subject or, better, they require an adequate process of subjectivation. We need to verify here, moreover, that a multitude is formed capable of ruling and leading itself, able, as we said in part I, to conceive and carry out strategic goals. This potential emerges from below, from within the processes of cooperative social production and reproduction, but the value produced in these processes is constantly captured and extracted. This issue becomes all the more complex when we recognize that technologies, modes of production, and forms of life are increasingly woven together, and some of these technological developments are creating cataclysmic disasters for humanity and the earth. This is not a matter, however, merely of liberating ourselves from technology. Such a project makes little sense since our bodies and minds are (and always have been) mixed inextricably with various technologies. And just as labor is not passive with respect to capital, we have active relations to technology: we create technologies and suffer from them, renovate them and go beyond them. Instead of rejecting technology, then, we must start from within the technological and biopolitical fabric of our lives and chart from there a path of liberation.

The relation of human and machine

Before considering how new subjectivities of production and reproduction are being and can be configured, we need to dispel some prevalent illusions regarding the dehumanizing effects of machines and technology. Let us consider two influential philosophical propositions, which are really both sophisticated versions of assumptions about the opposition between humans and technology that too often function today as common sense.

Max Horkheimer and Theodor Adorno's *Dialectic of Enlightenment* (1947), written in the shadow of the crimes of the Nazi regime and with enormous influence in the second half of the twentieth century, is based on the claim that the Enlightenment quest for freedom and progress, along with its institutions and technologies, leads to an aporia: "the very concept of that [Enlightenment] thinking, no less than the concrete historical forms, the institutions of society with which it is intertwined, already contains the germ of the regression which is taking place everywhere today."[1] What can be done when all aspects of public life and even the masses themselves are constantly commodified and degraded, and thus when attempts at progress inevitably result in its opposite? Since the Odyssey of bourgeois civilization develops in secret (or open) complicity with domination, that question seems unanswerable. Indeed Horkheimer and Adorno's tragic assessment of modern humanity, its ideology, and its technologies can lead only to bitter resignation rather than to any active project.

Heidegger, in "The Question Concerning Technology," published just a few years later, agrees in effect with Horkheimer and Adorno on a central point: science and technology are not neutral. The essence of technology, he claims, is to reveal or "enframe" the truth, but today this relation to truth has been broken and instrumentalized. Whereas peasants working the earth made it reveal its truth, the enframing of modern technology does not reveal the truth but only an instrumental relation to resources. "The earth now reveals itself as a coal mining district," Heidegger writes, "the soil as a mineral deposit."[2] The primary threat to humanity, then, is not nuclear weapons or other lethal technologies. "The actual threat," he warns, "has already affected man in his essence. The rule of Enframing threatens man with the possibility that it could be denied to him to enter into a more original revealing and hence to experience the call of a more primal truth."[3] Heidegger thus responds to Horkheimer and Adorno from a metaphysical standpoint, upping the ante and radicalizing the catastrophe. This is no longer the product of a contradiction, the result of the lost hope for human liberation, and it is not a moment of a negative dialectics, but, on the contrary, it is a radical loss of the sense of being. Heidegger, as much as Horkheimer and Adorno, claims that theories of progress have reached the point of exhaustion, but now from a metaphysical rather than a historical perspective.[4]

Is modern technology, though, really responsible for this damage and this destiny of humanity? At first sight, there seems to be no denying it: technology's social and ecological disasters have not only created misery and disease but also have set human history and the ecosystems of the earth on a path to destruction. We should never forget this, but it is not really enough. We should not forget either that humanity and human civilization are incomprehensible without technology, mechanical and thinking machines that configure our world and our selves. It makes no sense to construct some sort of tribunal to pass judgment on technology as such or even modern technology. Instead we can only judge specific technologies and their social uses and control.

A first response to these verdicts on modern technology requires historicizing their arguments. The standpoint of Heidegger's analysis, as Günther Anders rightly noted, is preindustrial and even precapitalist.[5] Even Horkheimer and Adorno's analysis is limited to the phase of capitalist development dominated by large-scale industry, and in this regard their phenomenology does not really go much further than the fabulations of Ernst Jünger and his colleagues in the 1930s. The world of large-scale industry was effectively deposed from the pinnacle of the capitalist economy when forms of resistance, revolutionary movements, and class struggle made necessary the reorganization of the subjectivities at work. Today's reality is different, and the new conditions of production are continually transformed by "human machines" that are put to work.

A more profound response to these arguments requires that we recognize their mistake in posing an *ontological* division and even opposition between human life and machines. Human thought and action has always been interwoven with techniques and technologies. The human mind itself, as Spinoza explains, constructs intellectual tools, internal to its functioning, that allow it to increase its power of thought, and these are perfectly analogous to the material tools that humans develop to perform more complex tasks more efficiently.[6] Our intellectual and corporeal development are inseparable from the creation of machines internal and external to our minds and bodies. Machines constitute and are constituted by human reality.

This ontological fact does not change but is only revealed more clearly in the contemporary, postindustrial world. Many early theorists of cybernetics grasped the ontological relation between humans and machines but were confused about its implications: they conceived of the development of new technologies effectively in terms of *lowering* the human to the level of machines. At the historic Macy Conferences, which from 1943 to 1954 brought together prominent researchers such as Norbert Wiener, cybernetic theorists generally conceived human neural structures in terms of information processing and grasped subjectivity in disembodied form. Humans were thus seen primarily, Katherine Hayles explains, "as information-processing entities who are *essentially* similar to intelligent machines."[7] Later cybernetic theorists, however, such as Humberto Maturana and Francisco Varela, paved the way for recognizing machines and humans alike in terms of embodied and distributed cognition. The second and third waves of cybernetic theory, which emerged together with postindustrial production, no longer lowered the notion of the human but *elevated* machines to the ontological plane of the human, a common plane of embodied cognition. If our contemporary reality is posthuman, Hayles maintains, that signals not a coming apocalyptic rule of machines but instead the opening of new potentials for humans to cooperate intensively with machines and other living beings.[8]

Gilbert Simondon moves in the same direction when he criticizes the standard view that opposes human culture to technology. Like Spinoza, Simondon recognizes that humans and machines belong to the same ontological plane. "What resides in machines is human reality," he argues, "human actions [*du geste humain*] that are fixed and crystalized in machines."[9] Against those who celebrate human culture as a sort of barricade, then, a defensive barrier to protect us from the advance of supposedly inhuman technologies, Simondon calls for a technical culture, which recognizes, on the ontological plane, the fully human nature of machines. Deleuze and Guattari heed and build on Simondon's call: "The object is no longer to compare humans and the machine in order to evaluate the correspondences, the extensions, the possible or impossible substitutions of the ones for the other, but to bring them into communication in order to show how *humans are a component part* of the machine, or combine with something else to constitute a machine."[10] Humans and machines are part of a mutually constituted social reality.

The fact that machines are part of human reality and constituted by human intelligence does not mean, of course, that all machines are good or that technology solves all problems. They contain the potential for both servitude and liberation. The problem lies at not the ontological but the political level. We must recognize, specifically, how human actions, habits, and intelligence crystallized in technologies are separated from humans and controlled by those in power. *Fixed capital*, in Marx's terminology, is a kind of social repository in the banks of scientific knowledge and in machines, in software and hardware, of the accomplishments of living labor and living intelligence, that is, to use Marx's terms, of the social brain and general intellect. Think of your smartphone, just as much as the spinning jenny, a patented method to temper steel, or a pharmaceutical formula, as the concrete result of the intelligence of not only the corporate CEO or even just the paid employees but also and most important a wide social network of cooperating actors. Despite the fact that it is produced socially, however, fixed capital becomes a weapon that can be used antisocially, so to speak, for capitalist profit as well as for war and destruction. And through the successive periods of capitalist production, from manufacture to large-scale industry and now to the phase dominated by general intellect, the role of science and technology, the repositories of social intelligence, become ever more crucial. The curtain raises on the field of battle over the control of fixed capital.

Walter Benjamin, reflecting on the tragic experiences of the First World War, is rightly suspicious of those who use evidence of technological disasters to indict technology as a whole:

> This immense wooing of the cosmos was enacted for the first time on a planetary scale, that is, in the spirit of technology. But because the lust for profit of the ruling class sought satisfaction through it, technology betrayed man and turned the bridal bed into a bloodbath. The mastery of nature, so the imperialists teach, is the purpose of all technology. But who would trust a cane wielder who proclaimed the mastery of children by adults to be the purpose of education? Is not education above all the indispensable ordering of the relationship between generations and therefore mastery, if we are to use this term, of that relationship and not of children? And likewise technology is not the mastery of nature but of the relation between nature and man.[11]

Today we must immerse ourselves into the heart of technologies and attempt to make them our own against the forces of domination that deploy technologies against us.

The changing composition of capital

In the early 1970s, facing a cycle of struggles that had put in serious crisis the Fordist mode of industrial production in the dominant countries, capital struck back by using automation and robotics in the factories to replace rebellious workers, and using information networks to extend production socially, beyond the factory walls. Cybernetics and information technologies helped create a relation of force favorable to the owners against the workers and, at the same time, construct a society of obedient subjects, dedicated to the production of ever more abstract commodities in cooperative social networks. "Industrial *automation* and social *necromation*" is what we used to call this gigantic project to displace the industrial working class from its position as a central (and potentially revolutionary) actor in productive society and to impoverish almost everyone.

That project has become a reality. Over the course of a half century the spheres of capitalist production and society have been radically transformed, extending the primary site of production from the factory to society. Automation constituted the central point of transformation—not only from the political point of view (destroying the power of the working class and expelling workers from the factories in dominant parts of the world) but also from the technical point of view (intensifying the rhythms of production). In order to re-establish profits that could no longer be obtained in the factories, capital had to put the social terrain to work, and the mode of production had to be interwoven ever more tightly with forms of life. While the automated industrial processes produced more material goods, outside of the robotized factories grew productive and ever more complex and integrated "services," bringing together complex technologies and fundamental science, industrial services and human services. In this second phase, digitization became more important than automation: this, in fact, spreads throughout society a transformation of the technical composition of labor-power that has already taken place in the factory.

Here, then, at the end of this savage cavalcade, enter triumphantly computers and digital networks that bring together the automation of the factories and the digitization of society, modes of production and forms of life: the automaton administers and controls society through digital algorithms. Although the machines and the systems of machines depend on the intelligence and the very existence of humans, human action and the human psychic faculties, Heinrich Popitz asserts, must adapt increasingly to the needs of the machines.[12] At this point, in a dramatic reversal of the fundamentals of the industrial economy, society—an "artificial" society that is continually created and re-created—becomes central to the production of wealth.

Marx highlights how this entire process, although maximizing profits in the short term, can lead ultimately to the disadvantage and even crisis of capital. He characterizes the increasing implementation of machines and technologies in production, and the corresponding decrease in workers, in terms of the changing "organic composition" of capital, specifically the rising proportion of constant capital (raw materials, machines, etc.) and the decreasing proportion of variable capital (the sum of all the workers' wages). Marx claims that in capitalist development constant capital continually increases with respect to wages even though labor remains the essential element that creates value. This occurs because "whether condition or consequence, the growing extent of the means of production, as compared with the labour-power incorporated into them, is an expression of the growing productivity of labour. The increase of the latter appears, therefore, in the diminution of the mass of labour in proportion to the mass of means of production moved by it, or in the diminution of the subjective factor of the labour process as compared with the objective factor."[13] The changing composition of capital and the growth of "objective" factors in production lead directly to the concentration and the centralization of capital in enormous corporations that is typical of contemporary capitalist development.

Marx continues this analysis across the three volumes of *Capital* to emphasize the expansion and violence of the process. In volume 2, for instance, he explains that the relationship between accumulation and centralization affects not only production but also the circulation of commodities and capital. This centralization operates "with the violence of an elemental process of nature" on ever vaster scales: "[S]ince the scale of each individual production process grows with the progress of capitalist production, and with it the minimum size of the capital to be advanced, this circumstance is added to the other circumstances which increasingly turn the function of the industrial capitalist into a monopoly of large-scale money capitalists, either individual or associated."[14] In volume 3, Marx argues that as capitalist accumulation leads to ever greater concentration and monopoly, the power of capital acts increasingly against the actual producers: "Capital shows itself more and more to be a social power, with the capitalist as its functionary—a power that no longer stands in any possible kind of relationship to what the work of one particular individual can create, but an alienated social power which has gained an autonomous position and confronts society as a thing, and as the power that the capitalist has through this thing."[15] As a direct result of capitalist development and the search for greater productivity, the contradiction becomes ever more extreme between the social power that capital becomes and the private power of individual capitalists over the social circuits of production and reproduction.

One endpoint of this analysis of the changing composition and increasing concentration of capital is Marx's much criticized hypothesis of the law of the fall of the rate of profit. His reasoning is simply that since, even if both grow in absolute terms, there is a proportional rise of constant capital and diminution of variable capital—or, put more simply, more value invested in machines and less paid to workers—and since the generation of surplus value and profit rests fundamentally on capturing a portion of the value produced by labor, then as its basis narrows the rate of profit will fall.[16] Certainly this process is only "tendential" in the sense that some factors counteract or even negate the effects of the general law. For example, in the period of the crisis and demise of Fordism, when the relationship between constant and variable capital was irremediably thrown out of balance and then broken by workers' struggles over wages, what was the capitalist response? As part of the neoliberal project, capital imposed a rise of the level of exploitation, a reduction of salaries, the growth of "surplus" populations, and other aggressive actions disastrous for workers. Those were some ways in which capital has successfully counteracted the fall of profits.[17]

Although these "objective" arguments from *Capital* seem crucial to us, we are even more interested in his proposal in the *Grundrisse* that the changing composition of capital also contributes, subjectively, to strengthening the position of labor and that today the general intellect is becoming a protagonist of economic and social production. We should also recognize, perhaps now beyond Marx, as production is increasingly socialized, how fixed capital tends to be implanted into life itself, creating a machinic humanity. "Hence it is evident," Marx writes in a jagged sentence typical of the *Grundrisse*, "that the material productive power already present, already worked out, existing in the form of fixed capital, together with the population, etc., in short all conditions of wealth, i.e. the abundant development of the social individual—that the development of the productive forces brought about by the historical development of capital itself, when it reaches a certain point, suspends the self-realization of capital, instead of positing it."[18] Fixed capital, that is, the memory and storehouse of past physical and intellectual labor, is increasingly embedded in "the social individual," a fascinating concept in its own right. To the same degree that capital, as this process proceeds, loses the capacity for self-realization, the social individual gains autonomy.

Marx could only take this analysis so far, of course, given when he was writing. Today, in a "biopolitical" context, we can see more clearly how the transformations of the composition of capital and the fact that fixed capital is being incarnated in and by social production present new potentials for laboring subjects. "What comes to be called immaterial and intellectual capital," Carlo Vercellone argues, "is in reality essentially incorporated in humans and thus corresponds fundamentally to the intellectual and creative faculties of labor-power." This then poses a challenge or even a potential threat to capital because the primary role in the social organization of production tends to be played by the living knowledges embodied in and mobilized by labor rather than the dead knowledges deployed by management and management science.[19] Furthermore, Vercellone continues, this "mass intellectuality" or Marx's general intellect, which tends today to invest and configure the entire social field, derives from the appropriation of fixed capital and implies an anthropological transformation of working subjects, with capacities for production and valorization that are fundamentally collective and cooperative. The productive social cooperation of workers endowed with fixed capital, although it now yields the surplus it produces to capital, poses the potential for the autonomy of workers, inverting the relation for force between labor and capital.

Workers are no longer merely instruments that capital uses for transforming nature and producing commodities. Having incorporated the productive tools and knowledges into their own minds and bodies, they are transformed and have the potential to become increasingly foreign to and autonomous from capital. This process injects class struggle into productive life itself. In some of our previous works we analyzed the characteristics of biopower, not only how life has been instrumentalized and come under political command but also, following Foucault, how from life arise constellations of resistance and refusals to submit to command. This dynamic and antagonistic relation poses forms of class struggle that one can properly call biopolitical, but we will return to that in more detail later.

Fourth call: Take back fixed capital ("This fixed capital being man himself")

When Marx proclaims that fixed capital, which we normally conceive in terms of machines, has become "man himself," he manages to anticipate the developments of capital in our time.[20] Although fixed capital is the product of labor and nothing other than the labor of others appropriated by capital, although the accumulation of scientific activity and the productivity of what Marx calls the social brain are incorporated into machines under the control of capital, and finally, although capital appropriates all this for free, at a certain point in capitalist development living labor begins to have the power to invert this relationship. Living labor begins to demonstrate its priority with respect to capital and the capitalist management of social production, even though it cannot necessarily take hold of the process. In other words, as it becomes an increasingly social power, living labor (and life activity more generally) operates as an ever more independent activity, outside the structures of discipline that capital commands. On the one hand, past human activity and intelligence are accumulated and crystallized as fixed capital, but, on the other, reversing the flow, living humans are able to reabsorb fixed capital within themselves and their social life. Fixed capital is "man himself" in both senses.

The process of labor-power appropriating fixed capital, however, is no triumphal march, but instead it bleeds. It is physical and psychic suffering, and thus continues the long-standing experience of humanity "put to work" under command. As labor becomes increasingly cooperative, immaterial, and affective, and as workers become ever more responsible for their productive arrangements and even responsible for each other in cooperation, suffering is multiplied and becomes something like a political suffering. Consciousness of the dignity of one's own labor, the power of one's professional abilities, and the responsibilities one shoulders at work are met with a lack of recognition and a feeling of exhaustion.[21] Suffering at work, moreover, has multiplied further as both digital and affective labor have become central to the organization of production.[22] It is no coincidence that work-related pathologies are becoming increasingly social. Christophe Dejours, following the work of Georges Canguilhem, notes that in this situation health is no longer a normal condition or a stable state but becomes a goal one can sometimes aim for. Suffering, he continues, is "the field that separates illness from health."[23] Humans recognize themselves as more powerful as they appropriate fixed capital but are still filled with suffering—a profound reason for revolt.

At this point we should ask ourselves, who is the boss and who is the worker in this new situation? In part III we will concentrate on the boss, that is, the new figures of capitalist command, and analyze how in response to the new social productivity of labor, capital has proceeded in a dual operation of abstraction and extraction: the boss is ever more abstract from the terrain of social production and reproduction from which value emerges, and thus the capitalist tends to operate by extracting value, often through financial mechanisms. In support of the capitalist extraction of value are developed neoliberal structures of governance and administration, which not only provide the means to corral the autonomous energies of social productivity but also at times manage to make people participate in and feel co-responsible for their own domination.

Here instead we want to focus on the new figures of labor, especially those who create in social networks constructed by workers themselves. These are workers whose productive capacities are dramatically increased by their ever more intense cooperative relationships. Labor becomes in cooperation increasingly abstract from capital—that is, it has a greater ability to organize production itself, autonomously, particularly in relation to machines—but still remains subordinated to the mechanisms of the extraction of value by capital. Is this autonomy the same as the forms of worker autonomy we spoke of in earlier phases of capitalist production? Certainly not, because now there is a degree of autonomy not only in regard to the processes of production but also in an ontological sense—labor gains an ontological consistency, even when still completely subordinated to capitalist command. How can we understand a situation in which temporally continuous and spatially widespread workers' productive enterprises, collective and cooperating inventions, come to be fixed as value and extracted by capital? This is a situation in which the relationship between the production processes in the hands of workers and the capitalist mechanisms of valorization and command are increasingly separated. Labor has reached such a level of dignity and power that it can potentially refuse the form of valorization that is imposed on it and, thus, even under command, develop its own autonomy.

The increased powers of labor can be recognized not only in the expansion and increasing autonomy of cooperation but also in the greater importance given to the social and cognitive powers of labor in the structures of production. The first element, expanded cooperation, is due at times to increased physical contact of workers but more often to formations of "mass intellectuality," animated by linguistic and cultural competencies, affective capacities, and digital facilities. From this follows the second element, through which the abilities and creativity of labor increase productivity. Paolo Virno emphasizes the performative nature of social labor, forms of production that have no material result, which he calls "virtuosity."[24] Luc Boltanski and Eve Chiapello similarly highlight the "artistic" character of labor.[25] Do these seem like exaggerations when you are faced with deadening jobs in the convenience store or the call center or the factory? Such propositions have to be understood as indicative of a tendency, pointing toward those who are spread throughout society and active in production even when they are not paid at work. Consider, for example, in broad schematic terms how the role of knowledge has changed in the history of the relations between capital and labor. In the phase of manufacture, the artisan's knowledge was employed and absorbed in production but as a separate, isolated force, subordinated in a hierarchical and inhuman organizational structure. In the phase of large-scale industry, in contrast, workers were held to be incapable of the knowledge necessary for production, which instead was centralized in management. In the contemporary phase of general intellect, knowledge has a multitudinous form in the productive process, even though, according to the boss, it can be isolated, as was artisanal knowledge in manufacture. From the perspective of capital, the figure of self-organizing labor, which is increasingly the basis of production, remains an enigma.

One potent figure of labor, for example, is today masked in the functioning of algorithms. Along with today's unbridled propaganda affirming the necessity of the command of capital and the latest sermons regarding the effectiveness of capitalist power, we often hear praise for the rule of algorithms. But what is an algorithm? It is fixed capital, a machine that is born of social, cooperative intelligence, a product of "general intellect." Although the value of productive activity is extracted by capital, one should not forget the power of living labor at the base of this process, living labor that is virtually, and potentially, disposed to affirm its own autonomy: without living labor there is no algorithm. But algorithms also present several novel characteristics.

Consider Google's PageRank, perhaps the best-known and most profitable algorithm. The rank of a web page is determined by the number and quality of links to it, and high quality means a link from a page that itself has a high rank. PageRank is thus a mechanism for gathering and incorporating the judgment and attention value given by users to Internet objects: "[E]ach link and vector of attention," Matteo Pasquinelli remarks, is "a concentration of intelligence."[26] One difference of algorithms like Google's PageRank, then, is that whereas industrial machines crystallize past intelligence in a relatively fixed, static form, algorithms continually add social intelligence to the results of the past to create an open, expansive dynamic. It might appear that the algorithmic machine itself is intelligent, but that is not really true; instead, it is open to continuous modification by human intelligence. Most often when we say "intelligent machines" we are really referring to machines that are continuously able to absorb human intelligence. A second distinctive characteristic, which follows from the first, is that the processes of expropriating value established by such algorithms are also increasingly open and social in a way that blurs the boundaries between work and life. Google users, for instance, are driven by interest and enjoyment, but even without their knowing it, their intelligence, attention, and social relations create value that can be captured. Finally, another difference between the production processes studied by Marx and this kind of production of value consists of the fact that cooperation today tends no longer to be imposed by the boss but generated in the relationships among users-producers. Today we can really begin to think of a reappropriation of fixed capital by the workers and the integration of intelligent machines under autonomous social control into their lives, a process, for example, of the construction of algorithms disposed to the self-valorization of cooperative social production and reproduction in all of their articulations.

We should add that even when cybernetic and digital instruments are employed in the service of capitalist valorization, even when the social brain is put to work and called on to produce obedient subjectivities, fixed capital is integrated into workers' bodies and minds and becomes their second nature. Ever since industrial civilization was born, workers have had a much more intimate and internal knowledge of machines and machine systems than the capitalists and their managers ever could. Today this process of worker appropriation of knowledge can become decisive: it is not simply realized in the productive process but is intensified and concretized through productive cooperation and spreads throughout the life processes of circulation and socialization. Workers can appropriate fixed capital while they work and can develop this appropriation in their social, cooperative, and biopolitical relations with other workers. All this determines a new productive nature, that is, a new form of life that is at the base of a new mode of production.

If this is how things are, if the relations of force are tipping in this way, then capital can manage to maintain control only by increasingly abstracting itself from labor processes and the productive social terrain. Capital captures value not only through industrial exploitation and through the time management of the organization of labor but also and increasingly through the extraction of social cooperation, which we will investigate in part III. In this type of organization of labor and valorization, an ever greater and ever more complex role is played by the production of subjectivity, by which we mean, on the one hand, subjectivation, that is, the production of subjectivities through autonomous circuits of social cooperation, and, on the other hand, subjectification, that is, the continuous capitalist attempt to reduce expressive and cooperating singularities to a commanded subject. And, as Marx insists, this relationship has direct political implications: "[T]he direct relationship of the owners of the conditions of production to the immediate producers—a relationship whose particular form naturally corresponds always to a certain level of development of the type and manner of labour, and hence to its social productive power—[is one] in which we find the innermost secret, the hidden basis of the entire social edifice."[27] Today the various possible mixtures of the two processes of producing subjectivity reveal not only the diverse figures of living labor in its postindustrial situation but also how the terrain they populate becomes a central field of battle. The reappropriation of fixed capital, taking back control of the physical machines, intelligent machines, social machines, and scientific knowledges that were created by us in the first place, is one daring, powerful enterprise we could launch in that battle.

Machinic subjectivities

Young people today, according to a cultural commonplace, enter almost spontaneously into digital worlds, which for previous generations were unknown and only engaged later, with difficulty. Today's youth grow up in these worlds and find joy and community there. Often they are drafted into forms of work that seem like games; sometimes they think they are merely consumers when they are also producers—"prosumers," as Christian Fuchs and others say.[28] Certainly the characterizations of the new freedom of digital life promoted by corporate advertisers, product marketers, and management gurus are mystifications, but they can also help us recognize the nature of the machinic subjectivities and machinic assemblages that are forming.

We conceive the "machinic" in contrast not only to the mechanical but also to the notion of a technological realm separate from and even opposed to human society. Félix Guattari argues that, whereas traditionally the problem of machines has been seen as secondary to the question of techne and technology, we should instead recognize that the problem of machines is primary and technology is merely a subset. We can see this, he continues, once we understand the machine's social nature: "Since 'the machine' is opened out towards its machinic environment and maintains all sorts of relationships with social constituents and individual subjectivities, the concept of technological machine should therefore be broadened to that of *machinic assemblages [agencements machiniques]*."[29] The *machinic*, then, never refers to an individual, isolated machine but always an assemblage. To understand this, start by thinking of mechanical systems, that is, machines connected to and integrated with other machines. Then add human subjectivities and imagine humans integrated into machine relations and machines integrated into human bodies and human society. Finally, Guattari (and together with Deleuze) conceives machinic assemblages as going even further and incorporating all kinds of human and nonhuman elements or singularities.

In the context of twentieth-century French thought the concepts of the machinic, machinic consistency, and machinic assemblage respond effectively to philosophers, such as Louis Althusser, who, to combat the spiritualist ontologies that plagued theories of the subject, pose "a process without a subject." Deleuze and Guattari certainly appreciate the political importance of this polemic. Althusser asserts that "the individual *is interpellated as a (free) subject in order that he shall submit freely to the commandments of the Subject, i.e. in order that he shall (freely) accept his subjection*, i.e. in order that he shall make the gestures and actions of his subjection 'all by himself.' *There are no subjects except by and for their subjection*."[30] We seem to be caught, however, in a double bind: the "subject" functions as part of apparatuses of domination, but one cannot live or construct community on the basis of a pure and simple cancellation of the subject.[31] The concept of the machinic in Deleuze and Guattari—just as, in a different way, the concept of production in Foucault—addresses this need, adopting, without identity, subjectivities of knowledge and action, and demonstrating how their production emerges in material connections. These connections are also ontological connections. The machinic thus constitutes, stripping away every metaphysical illusion, a humanism of and in the present— a humanism after the critical adoption of the Nietzschean declaration of the "death of man."

A machinic assemblage, then, is a dynamic composition of heterogeneous elements that eschew identity but nonetheless function together, subjectively, socially, in cooperation. It thus shares characteristics with our concept of multitude, which attempts to pose political subjectivities as composed of heterogeneous singularities—one significant difference being that whereas we usually pose the multitude exclusively in terms of human singularities, a machinic assemblage is composed of a wider range of beings, human and nonhuman. Donna Haraway's conception of the cyborg and her various efforts to combat identity and essentialized subjects lead her further in this direction, recognizing the breach in our standard divisions between humans and machines and between humans and other animals.[32] But machinic assemblages extend the elements of subjective compositions even further to include all beings or elements that reside on the plane of immanence. All of this is based on the ontological claim that places humans, machines, and (now) other beings on the same ontological plane.

In economic terms, the machinic appears clearly in the subjectivities that emerge when fixed capital is reappropriated by labor-power, that is, when the material and immaterial machines and knowledges that crystallize past social production are reintegrated into the present cooperative and socially productive subjectivities. Machinic assemblages are thus grasped in part by the notion of "anthropogenetic production." Some of today's most intelligent Marxist economists, such as Robert Boyer and Christian Marazzi, characterize the novelty of contemporary economic production—and the passage from Fordism to post-Fordism—as centering on the production of humans by humans ("la production de l'homme par l'homme") in contrast to the traditional notion of the production of commodities by means of commodities.[33] The production of subjectivity and forms of life are increasingly central to capitalist valorization, and this logic leads directly to notions of cognitive and biopolitical production. The machinic extends this anthropogenetic model further to incorporate various nonhuman singularities into the assemblies that produce and are produced. Specifically, when we say fixed capital is reappropriated by laboring subjects we do not mean simply that it becomes their possession but instead that it is integrated into the machinic assemblages, as a constituent of subjectivity.

The machinic is always an assemblage, we said, a dynamic composition of human and other beings, but the power of these new machinic subjectivities is only virtual so long as it is not actualized and articulated in social cooperation and in the common. If, in fact, the reappropriation of fixed capital were to take place individually, transferring private ownership from one individual to another, it would just be a matter of robbing Peter to pay Paul, and have no real significance. When, in contrast, the wealth and productive power of fixed capital is appropriated socially and thus when it is transformed from private property to the common, then the power of machinic subjectivities and their cooperative networks can be fully actualized. The machinic notion of assemblages, the productive forms of cooperation, and the ontological basis of the common are here woven together ever more tightly.

When we look at young people today who are absorbed in machinic assemblages, we should recognize that their very existence is resistance. Whether they are aware or not, they produce in resistance. Capital is forced to recognize a hard truth. It must consolidate the development of that common that is produced by subjectivities, from which it extracts value, but the common is only constructed through forms of resistance and processes that reappropriate fixed capital. The contradiction becomes ever more clear. Exploit yourself, capital tells productive subjectivities, and they respond, we want to valorize ourselves, governing the common that we produce. Any obstacle in the process—and even the suspicion of virtual obstacles—can determine a deepening of the clash. If capital can expropriate value only from the cooperation of subjectivities but they resist that exploitation, then capital must raise the levels of command and attempt increasingly arbitrary and violent operations of the extraction of value from the common. But we will return to this in more detail in part III.

CHAPTER 8

WEBER IN REVERSE

The bureaucracy of the modern administrative state has gone into crisis. We need to read this process from below because viewing it from above, seeing like a state, to borrow James C. Scott's expression, fails to grasp its real motor.[1] From below we can see how the increasing capacities of the multitude, the essential activities of social production and reproduction as well as the abilities to organize society effectively, threw the administrative apparatuses into crisis. Modern administration has been forced to open itself to the multitude as the multitude has developed the potential to carry out the functions of social organization autonomously, in a different way.

Keep in mind that the modern state was forged as a weapon in a war on two fronts. On one side, the modern state served as a means to combat, manage, and channel the struggles of the poor, peasants, and other disenfranchised classes against the political and social customs of aristocratic rule and the legal structures of property. On the other, it contributed to the social and political emancipation of the bourgeoisie, which imagined itself to be the only social actor capable of generating social peace through mediation. This "reasonable mediation" consisted in the formation—guaranteed by the economic power of the bourgeoisie—of an administrative machine able to manage and regulate the interests of conflicting social forces. The modern political structures of representation are built on this mediatory function: the "will of all" becomes the "general will" of the nation, which stands not so much on "the sovereign people" [sic!] but rather on the mediatory apparatus that manages and constructs the people. The bourgeoisie is both intermediary and hegemonic, both administrative and political.[2]

The formation of the administrative machine of the modern state dovetails with the developments of capital, and modern administration increasingly takes on the mechanical qualities of industrial production. This is not to say that these administrative and legal apparatuses are merely superstructures that derive from or depend on or are determined by the economic base of society. The parallel developments of the modern state and the capitalist economy are due instead primarily to the fact that both are driven by class struggle. One cannot understand the modern formation of the administrative state or its contemporary crisis without grasping the nature and capacities of the antagonistic subjectivities in play.

Weber's dream and Kafka's nightmare

Max Weber envisions a rational, just, and efficient administration based on expert knowledge and legitimate institutional leadership. The roles of actors in Weber's administrative apparatus follow the modern military and political deployments that we analyzed in part I: the leader is responsible for strategic planning and long-term decision-making whereas the cadre that populates the bureaucracy has tactical duties and implements the plan. No organization exists, Weber insists, without a leader and thus modern administration is inseparable from *Herrschaft* (which Talcott Parsons translates as "leadership" but is more often rendered as "domination" or "authority"). The leader provides the will, and the army of administrators is the brain, arms, and legs that implement the will.[3] Weber's administrators are not mere cogs in a bureaucratic machine, but its thinking and rational core. The primary superiority of modern, bureaucratic administration, he claims, lies in the role of technical knowledge and technical competence. "Bureaucratic administration," he asserts, "means fundamentally domination through knowledge."[4] Modern bureaucracy is thus a form of domination, a form of authority, but one that is superior to previous administrative forms because it destroys their irrational structures and bases its legitimacy primarily in knowledge.

The modern bureaucratic administrator of Weber's vision is a curious animal characterized by a series of separations. First, administrative staff form a social body that is separated from the rest of the population: their knowledge separates them from the general (ignorant) population and, in order for them to act on the basis of reason and law rather than interests, he continues, they must also be completely separated from the ownership of the means of production or administration. He thus envisions modern bureaucratic administrators as a separate social body but not really a class—in fact, something like an anticlass: possessing knowledge without property sets administrators outside modern class struggle and thus, he imagines, in a purely mediatory position.

Second, administrators are defined by internal separations. Administration, Weber insists, must be a career, a vocation, a duty that lasts a lifetime, but the office must be separated from the spheres of life. The administrator thus lives a dual existence. Furthermore, the knowledge and technical competencies that characterize the administrator must be narrow and limited. Whereas older administrative forms sought "cultivated" administrators with wide social knowledges that were integrated with their lives, modern bureaucracy requires specialists and experts whose limited knowledges do not qualify them to make decisions but rather to carry out the duties of their office. The impersonal nature of bureaucratic knowledge and action is one basis of its claim to rationality and its ability to mediate social conflict.[5]

Weber's dream of a rational, just, and transparent bureaucracy based on expert knowledge is experienced by many, however, as a nightmare. According to a line of critique that reaches its apex in the work of Franz Kafka, modern bureaucracy is characterized fundamentally instead by irrationality and injustice. This is not the result, the argument goes, simply of the administrative project being incompletely or imperfectly realized; rather, any project of rational social administration carries within itself an irrational core. The "experts" don't know the true, the right, and the just—instead they institute an incomprehensible system of injustice and untruth. Kafka's tale of the man confronting the doorkeeper before the law and K.'s obsessive attempts to enter the castle are parables of the obscure and alienating forms of modern bureaucratic power.[6] Such critiques of modern bureaucracy based on the "pessimism of reason" are certainly persuasive, and the frustrations are well known in all countries throughout the world. You don't need to have had the misfortune to enter the criminal justice system to know firsthand the injustices and irrationalities of the modern administrative mentality. Who hasn't suffered through the seemingly interminable wait in a line to complete some absurd administrative task? We all every day experience the labyrinthine, opaque passages of bureaucracy.

The problem with Kafkaesque characterizations, however, is that they tend to portray modern administration as a behemoth, autonomous and inscrutable, when, in fact, like all forms of power, modern administration is a relationship, divided in two. On the one hand, we must grasp its mediatory function: in parallel to the bourgeoisie, as we said, the modern administrative state develops as a paradoxical mix of both hegemony and mediation. On the other hand, any critique of bureaucracy that doesn't recognize the power of those who struggle against it, affirming their own freedom, not only is trapped in a cycle of despair but also will never illuminate why modern administration has been thrown into crisis. Modern administration has not crumbled of its own accord, from some internal corruption, but was thrown into crisis by forces that not only attack its power but also have the potential to replace its essential functions.

We have already accumulated above several components for an analysis of the forces that challenge modern administration. One type of analysis focuses on how the dominant forms of labor in contemporary capitalist production are transforming such that intelligence, social knowledges, complex technological skills, and, most important, wide circuits of social cooperation are becoming central capacities both inside and outside the workplace. Another type charts how people have increasing access to digital tools and platforms, reappropriating fixed capital for their own purposes and, more important, integrating it into their social lives. Any sixteen-year-old (or twelve-year-old!) with a smartphone or a laptop has an extraordinary wealth of knowledges and tools, as well as the means to cooperate with others. Third, the access to information of all sorts and the inability of governments to protect data also plays a central role. Repressive governments are constantly thwarted in their attempts to limit Internet access, and as the continuing WikiLeaks revelations demonstrate, all states have less and less ability to control access to information. In effect, the "domination through knowledge" of Weber's modern administration begins to break down when the monopoly over knowledge, expertise, and information is pried open, when people have the competencies, the machines, and the information necessary to produce knowledges themselves. The widespread and alternative production of knowledges is an essential weapon in the arsenal of protest and liberation movements that recognize that knowledge corresponds not only to power but also to freedom. These are some of the forces that have forced open administrative apparatuses by demonstrating that they have the capacities that were once exclusive to administrators.

Sine ira et studio

The crisis of modern administration implies a transformation of administrative subjectivity. The modern administrator, according to Weber, must banish affects: *sine ira et studio* (without anger or partiality) is the motto that he uses, borrowing from Tacitus, to describe the subjective attitude of good administration.[7]

Like the dispassionate historian, Weber seeks to avoid affects that can distort administrative reason. The corps of career bureaucrats, separated from society, separated from property ownership, and separated in their work from their nonwork lives, thus occupy impersonal offices and marshal knowledge, information, and technical expertise without passion or prejudice.

The banishment of affects from the subjectivity of administrators echoes Weber's distinction between charismatic and rational forms of leadership. Charismatic authority plays on the passions of followers and changes people from the inside, through something akin to religious conversion. In contrast, rational authority, like bureaucratic administration, quells the passions and changes people from the outside, transforming social structures and their conditions of life. Weber's rational leader, like the bureaucratic administrator, is an ideal subject of pure and practical reason.[8]

One problem with affects, Weber argues, is that they cannot be measured. This is perhaps just another way of expressing the standard rationalist notion that affects are inconstant and unreliable, but it helps clarify an essential link between modern administration and capitalist production. Administration must take into consideration only social factors that can be calculated, excluding affects and other factors that are properly "human" because (presumably) they are beyond measure. "Bureaucracy develops the more perfectly," Weber continues, "the more it is 'dehumanized,' the more completely it succeeds in eliminating from official business love, hatred, and all purely personal, irrational, and emotional elements which escape calculation. This is appraised as its special virtue by capitalism."[9] Modern bureaucracy is a particularly adequate complement to the rule of capital, in other words, because capital, too, functions primarily through measure (the measure of value) and, like bureaucracy, capital is threatened by the immeasurable. One primary function of capitalist money, as we will see in chapter 11, is to fix the measure of values, and increasingly today, through complex financial instruments such as derivatives, to stamp measures on social values that threaten to escape calculation.

The machinic subjectivities that today have thrown modern administration into crisis, although they are endowed with intelligence, knowledge, information, and technical skills, do not banish the passions. It is tempting to label these subjectivities *cum ira et studio*, but they are not simply the specular image of Weber's rationality: irrational passion.[10] Instead these new subjectivities have to be understood, first, by the collapse of all those separations that for Weber defined modern administrators. Increasingly central to the contemporary capitalist economy, in fact, is the production not only of material goods but also of a range of immaterial goods, including ideas, images, code, cultural products, affects—in short, the production of subjectivity. The formation and life of the contemporary productive multitude, therefore, does not and cannot rely on a divide between reason and passion, but instead engages the production of subjectivity with all its affects, measurable and immeasurable. These productive capacities, engaged with immeasurable and subjective social phenomena, indicate a potential for politics: deciding the incalculable, the undecidable, is a properly political faculty.[11]

It is even more difficult and often impossible to maintain the Weberian separation of reason from passion in the context of contemporary economic and social crises. The passionless bureaucrat, who may be conceivable in periods of social calm, becomes unimaginable in the chaos of war and crisis. From this standpoint, Weber's thought appears as the product of a belle époque of relatively tranquil capitalist social rule. Today, however, crisis prevails. After German chancellor Angela Merkel, following the law, denied German citizenship to a Syrian child, she was obliged quickly to reverse her decision and open the doors to Syrian migrants, only then to close them again soon after. This is just one instance of the complex mixture of legal reasoning, compassion, fear, and callousness in play in governmental decisions. With regard to the migrating multitudes in particular it is impossible to see contemporary administration acting *sine ira et studio*.

The difficulty in normalizing and bringing back the management of affects under the rule of law is even clearer in the social emergencies following terrorist attacks in Europe and North America, such as September 11 in the United States, March 11 in Madrid, July 7 in London, November 13 in Paris, March 22 in Brussels, and June 12 in Orlando. The norms of legality and reason are quickly swept away following such tragedies by passions and proclamations of states of emergency. But even outside such dramatic circumstances, when the law cannot be executed—for example, when migrants cannot be controlled—the law is replaced by administrative behaviors that are functional to the new situation. In crisis situations, in other words, the bureaucratic rationality of the government of the people yields to passions that guide the governance of the multitude. *Ira et studio* once again permeate, but in a completely inverted way, the supposedly rational system of law and administration. Is the presumption to exclude *ira et studio* from rational administration from the beginning an illusory and hypocritical presumption that is necessary for the repressive management of the passions of the multitude? Administrative actions in periods of crisis and states of exception could certainly lead one to think so.

Digital Taylorism

The modern bureaucrat, blinkered to see only what is measurable and calculable, seems more machine than human. Indeed, Weber views the rational subjects of bureaucracy as analogous to industrial machines. "The fully developed bureaucratic apparatus," he explains, "compares with other organizations exactly as does the machine with the non-mechanical modes of production."[12] Pause for a moment to think about this rich analogy. Essential to the passage from nonmechanical to industrial modes of production is the inversion of subject and object. Whereas in handicrafts and manufacture, craftsmen and workers develop lifelong relationships with their tools, the cobbler's awl and the blacksmith's hammer, which became something like prosthetic limbs that extend their bodies, in large-scale industry the relationship is reversed and the workers are deployed by and become prostheses of the complex industrial machine. Machines are now subjects and workers their objects.[13] Charlie Chaplin, in the opening sequences of *Modern Times*, attempts (and fails comically) to become the mechanical worker that the industrial machine requires. Modern administration, Weber's analogy suggests, operates a similar inversion of subject and object: it does not pretend that all human and social phenomena are measurable, but it filters and accepts as inputs to the machine only the "objective" data. All the "subjective" phenomena that escape calculation are irrelevant for (or even harmful to) its work. In the machine of modern bureaucracy, as the saying goes, you become a number.

Just as modern, mechanical administration does not make human labor obsolete but instead forces humans to act more like machines, so too contemporary, machinic administration creates new realms of routine digital work and rote analytics. The Taylorist methods that were applied in both modern factories and modern bureaucracies, rationalizing activity by dividing all operations into simple and measurable tasks, have been translated into new digital forms of Taylorism. It sometimes seems as though computer systems, artificial intelligence, and algorithms are making human labor obsolete, but, in fact, there are innumerable digital tasks that machines cannot complete. Humans are left to accomplish the menial "clickwork" to support machinic administration and also to provide the interface with users through call centers or chat mechanisms. Every administrative unit, every banking division, every large business requires an army of workers who enter unstructured data in the appropriate form fields, answer standard questions, or perform some other routinized task in front of the screen. Sometimes this digital tedium is completed in-house but often it is outsourced to subordinated countries such as India or China. Paradoxically, although these tasks are "mindless" because so routinized, they require a relatively high level of education. The rising higher education rates in many parts of the world are creating not only "graduates with no future" but also armies of graduates with a future of digital tedium.[14]

Just as, according to Weber, the advent of modern bureaucratic organization compares to the passage from nonmechanical to industrial mechanization, so too the contemporary passage beyond modern administration moves from the mechanical to the machinic, from industrial gears to digital algorithms. More than one generation of science fiction writers has imagined how the dawn of intelligent machines represents an intensification of the objectification of the human: when machines think, humans will become their slaves. Machinic production, however, does not repeat the industrial subject-object relationship nor does it simply return to the preindustrial and nonmechanical arrangement, putting digital machines in the hands of individual human subjects. Instead the machinic scrambles the subject-object relationship itself. As much as our past collective intelligence is concretized in digital algorithms, intelligent machines become essential parts of our bodies and minds to compose machinic assemblages.

A paradox thus emerges in the contemporary phase of economic and social production between capital's requirements for objective calculation and the machinic subjectivities of producers. On the one hand, even as capitalist production becomes increasingly biopolitical, that is, as the production of human subjectivity becomes the centerpiece of the creation of value, capital still requires that the bodies and minds of workers be transformed into commodities: labor-power that can be bought and sold. The objective character of labor-power is an ineluctable element of the functioning of capital and its generation of profit, and the capitalist imaginary remains tethered in this sense to the subject-object relation of large-scale industry in which industrial machines employ workers. On the other hand, the machinic subjectivities that are necessary for biopolitical production resist calculation, measure, and objectification. The sale and purchase of their activity as labor-power strains increasingly against their real corporeal and intellectual productivity as living labor, and the value of subjectivity always overflows and exceeds the objective measures stamped on it in the processes of capitalist valorization. In contrast to the industrial workers whose productivity largely depends on being in the plant, machinic subjectivities often produce in social space, in circuits of co-operation, and thus realize certain limited margins of autonomy.

To the extent that workers reappropriate elements of fixed capital and present themselves, in a variable and often chaotic way, as cooperating actors in the processes of valorization, then, as they are precarious but nonetheless autonomous subjects in the valorization of capital, there tends to be an inversion of the function of labor with respect to capital. Workers are no longer instruments that capital deploys to transform nature and produce material commodities, but the workers, having incorporated the tools of production, having been metamorphosed anthropologically, act and produce machinically, separately and autonomously from capital. On this terrain opens a form of class struggle that we can properly call biopolitical.

The contradiction between biocapital and productive machinic subjectivities can be overcome only by eliminating one of the two poles. And capitalists cannot eliminate workers if they want to make profit. This is thus the terrain proper to politics, the terrain of the decision over undecidables, with all of its back and forth. For the productive subjectivities, politics means constructing the multitude "institutionally," that is, transforming the social experience of the multitude into political institutions. This operation must go beyond the modern bourgeois model of the relationship between constituent power and constituted power, as we saw in chapter 3, not because constituent action disappears but because it can no longer be closed in the construction of a unitary power. Revolts are not aimed at *taking power as it is* but rather at holding open a process of counterpowers, challenging the ever new apparatuses of capture that the capitalist machine creates, and discovering in the process what kind of society the new machinic subjectivities can create.

Fourth response: Smash the state

Some might greet the recognition of the crisis of the modern administrative state by enthusiastically affirming the end of administration as such. Let's bury Weber six feet under! Our view instead—just as in chapter 1 we affirmed that the critique of traditional forms of leadership should not be confused with a refusal of organization—is that the critique of modern administration must be accompanied by the creation of alternative administrative forms. The point is not to be done with Weber but to run Weber in reverse. This is why we have tried to highlight that the same subjectivities that throw modern bureaucracy into crisis also demonstrate the social and organizational capacities, the intelligence, knowledges, and access to information that are required for effective and autonomous social administration.[15]

What does it mean to smash the state? That is the heroic feat, according to Marx, accomplished by the Parisian Communards. When the bourgeois forces retreat to Versailles, the Communards dismantle the state apparatus, but they do not simply assume that in its absence social life will organize spontaneously: smashing the state does not mean ignoring the need for social organization. In the place of the bourgeois state they invent democratic political and administrative practices and institutions to govern the life of the Commune. The state is an instrument of class rule insofar as it stands above and rules over society, that is, insofar as it maintains separation between the rulers and the ruled. Smashing the state means destroying that gap and thus creating political and administrative institutions that immanently organize the collective, democratic decision-making of the entire population. The question for today's machinic subjectivities, then, so full of knowledge and intelligence, is how they can invent democratic practices and administrative institutions that organize effectively the life of the multitude.[16]

This task, enormously complicated on its own, is made even more difficult, as we will see in part III, by the fact that neoliberal governance is created as a response not only to the crisis of modern bureaucracy but also and more directly to the potentially autonomous cooperative subjectivities full of knowledge, talents, and capabilities. Neoliberalism interprets their freedom and their capacities for self-administration in ways that seek to close back the powers of administration. The terrain shifts once again, but the struggle continues.

The end of Mitteleuropa

We need to ask ourselves—everyone probably should—to what extent, even when we critique modernity, are we still prisoners of the modes and concepts of European bourgeois thought from which the dominant notion of modernity arose? Numerous authors have "provincialized" Europe and developed anticolonial, postcolonial, and decolonial critiques of modernity with great success and important results. We should remember, though, that powerful challenges to modernity and its modes of oppression have repeatedly arisen within Europe too.[17] Let us here limit our view on modernity and its crisis to Europe and, even more specifically, "Mitteleuropa," where we can both identify a critique of modernity that remains its prisoner but also glimpse the end of the bourgeois subject that is its basis. When we look to the bourgeois Europe of Mitteleuropa today, we cannot even hate it, as if we were rebellious children. Although in some sense we were born of Mitteleuropa, now it has repudiated us and we can take pride in a new innocence.

What was Mitteleuropa? It was a period, a place, an idea, a crisis. It was a period in which, roughly from 1870 to 1914 and 1917 to 1945, while European powers pursued imperialist projects in Africa, Asia, and Latin America, at home the conflict between labor and capital become a central element of public life, leading to war and dictatorship. A mass society was formed with crowds that were repugnant to the bourgeois sensibility and that, in turn, bridled at the "rational" administration of bourgeois power. The bourgeoisie, deploying its rich intellectual and moral armory, clashed with rebellious workers and tried to domesticate them, while exploiting their power. This drama took place throughout Europe, but here we are focusing on its extended midsection, from Germany and Austria to Poland and Hungary—especially Germany, where national unity was recently achieved. But above all Mitteleuropa was an idea or, rather, two conflicting ideas. On one hand, Mitteleuropa was the heroic idea of European modernity, together with the allied identity concepts such as the individual, property, the people, the nation, and sovereignty. The valiant, confident cadences of Beethoven's Third Symphony still resonated through these words. On the other hand, though, Mitteleuropa was the growing suspicion and then the clear recognition that the bourgeois mediation in social equilibrium of conflicting social forces, particularly capital and labor, was no longer possible. The bourgeoisie collapsed as a political class, although it still thrashed about, sometimes blindly, as if it still could maintain moral and cultural leadership. Mahler's tragic Sixth Symphony might serve as an adequate soundtrack.

Between Nietzsche (for the German spirit) and Robert Musil (for the Austro-Hungarian Empire he called "Kakania") we can recognize all the *elements of the tragedy: the struggle among larger-than-life subjects set on determining the destiny of civilization; the heroism of those destined to defeat who gradually measure the weight of the tragedy; and the disbanding, the coming apart of European modernity and progress. These were just presentiments for the bourgeoisie entering into the carnage and barbarity of its thirty years' war from 1914 to 1945, a conflagration in which Mitteleuropa was definitively dissolved. One still today hears talk of the "crisis of civilization," a theme that occupied the tormented soul of the bourgeoisie in Mitteleuropa. One still hears whispered the same names: Nietzsche, used in one way or another according to one's taste; Thomas Mann, but already back then Naphta and Settembrini beat their wings in the void; Benjamin, who cannot figure out if he is a rabbi or a communist; Heidegger, who implausibly has been cleaned of his collaboration with the Nazis; and so forth, in a confused chant of litanies. This kind of weak nostalgia only reinforces the status quo.*

Mitteleuropa thus initiated an odd bifurcation that has become ever more apparent today: the persistence of capitalist rule but the end of the bourgeoisie. Today capitalists abound, but the bourgeois is nowhere to be found. Already in 1932 Thomas Mann remarked that "the bourgeois is lost,"[18] and along with Mitteleuropa the bourgeois subsequently died. "What has evaporated," Franco Moretti writes, "is the sense of bourgeois legitimacy: the idea of a ruling class that doesn't just rule, but deserves to do so."[19] Moretti is certainly right but more than merely the legitimacy has died—also the bourgeois as a cultural and moral figure of social mediation, development, and progress.

Paradoxically, perhaps, some remnants of Mitteleuropa in the latter half of the twentieth century appeared clearly in the Soviet Union. Although the masses had won both the great revolutionary struggle and the battle against the Nazis, they found themselves faced with the same forms of power and thus the same effects of crisis as in western Europe. The bureaucratic elite was unable to manage internal social conflicts but intent on imperialist endeavors at the margins of the empire. The motto "the future has an ancient heart" could be applied to Soviet bureaucrats, perhaps with a touch of irony, where the ancient is not medieval, czarist, or Boyar, but rather Mitteleuropean. Class struggle defeated western European bourgeoisies and eventually destroyed also the bureaucratic elites of the East. Both were denied the stable mediation they sought of conflicting social forces: wages and profit, life and production, well-being and arms. Is that still even possible?

But we will never understand the end of Mitteleuropa if we look only at its own contradictions and crises, failing to recognize the emerging alternative subjectivities that were author of its demise. In 1848, 1871, 1905, and smaller events throughout Europe, rebellious populations refused capitalist command over their productive lives, were unwilling to act as a united people ordered in fixed social hierarchies, declined to serve the glory of the nation, and engaged in infinite other acts of defiance. Such refusals, however, powerful though they are, are only part of the explanation.

More important are the new social forms that are invented in rebellion, particularly along two axes we have tried to articulate in the course of part II. First is, accompanying rebellions against the rule of private property, the construction of the common, that is, forms of wealth that we share equally and manage democratically. In the face of the common both the bourgeois administrative routines and those of the Soviet party failed, and neither was able to give the common a political form: in the West because bourgeois leaders felt suffocated by the common and knew that it would put their cherished individualism in chains; in the East because Soviet leaders wanted to be the bosses of the common and transform it into state property. The common is what created an insurmountable abyss and opened a new world. One might say, then, that out of the ashes of Mitteleuropa emerged the "class of the common," but that is not right if by class here one understands a homogeneous or unified identity. Indeed the second axis of these new social forms is their irreducible multiplicity, which corrodes all identity formations. The social producers and reproducers refused to be reduced to a people, but could no longer be conceived either as a crowd or a mass. They had already entered the scene as a protagonist multitude, as machinic assemblages.

Here we can appreciate the unbridgeable distance from Mitteleuropa: a distance that allows for no nostalgia because in Berlin, Vienna, and Leningrad the old rationality on which bourgeois order rested has been liquidated and instead has been proposed a radical renewal of political rationality itself, oriented toward plural subjectivities in the common. This project is by no means accomplished. It is an open road, a path to be traveled, and here there is no need for heroism to resist our destiny but rather faithful dedication to construct it. The ghosts have now all vanished and Mitteleuropa, just like the ancients or the baroque, becomes for us at this point just an archive.

And yet in the last decades, there has been a kind of repetition of the Mitteleuropa syndrome. In Brussels a political apparatus unmoored from any social reality (the concept of class cannot even be whispered!) believed it was guiding the construction of a united Europe. It was a tragicomic experience: comedic in its caricature of a past bureaucracy that, even though it can no longer form common values, maintains the pretense of them; tragic in its leading the continent to the edge of a precipice. Only the struggles of the new generations of Europeans, born with the desire of the common, have prevented a catastrophic fall into the abyss. Will some demon arrive next, claiming to save Europe?

CHAPTER 9

ENTREPRENEURSHIP OF THE MULTITUDE

We live, we are told, in an entrepreneurial society in which everyone is called on to be an entrepreneur. The important thing is to incarnate the energy, responsibility, and virtue of the entrepreneurial spirit. You can go into business, launch your own start-up, or organize a project for the homeless. "Even fields commonly thought to exist outside of the sphere of business and labor," writes Imre Szeman, "such as artistic and cultural production, have been colonized by discourses of entrepreneurship. Entrepreneurship exists in the twenty-first century as a commonsense way of navigating the inevitable, irreproachable, and apparently unchangeable reality of global capitalism."[1] We will return in chapter 12 to analyze the entrepreneurial ideology of neo-liberalism, but here we want to insist that first and foremost entrepreneurship belongs to the multitude, and names the multitude's capacities for cooperative social production and reproduction. Like many other terms in our political vocabulary, entrepreneurship has been diverted and distorted. We need to take it back and claim it as our own.

We will try to uncover the entrepreneurship of the multitude through an indirect route and a direct one, that is, through a symptomatic reading and an ontological reading. For the former we will engage Joseph Schumpeter's theory of the entrepreneur against the grain to unmask, underneath the ideology of the capitalist entrepreneur, the continuous expropriation of the cooperative power of the multitude. The capitalist entrepreneur, from this perspective, is unjustly given credit for an entrepreneurial function accomplished elsewhere, but rather than such a moral claim we are much more interested in how capitalist entrepreneurship reveals the potential of the multitude. The latter route instead investigates directly the productive social power of the multitude, exploring how much its leadership can be developed and questioning what leadership means in this context.

How to become an entrepreneur

Joseph Schumpeter's classic theory goes against today's standard image of the entrepreneur in many respects. Entrepreneurial activity in his view, for instance, is not defined by risk taking. Neither does it involve scientific discoveries or inventing new technologies. Whereas "the inventor produces ideas," Schumpeter asserts, "the entrepreneur 'gets things done,' which may but need not embody anything that is scientifically new."[2] Entrepreneurs, he continues, are not managers and most often not owners of the means of production, only ones who have them at their disposal. The essence of entrepreneurship, instead, according to Schumpeter, is to create *new combinations* among already existing workers, ideas, technologies, resources, and machines. Entrepreneurs, in other words, create new machinic assemblages. Moreover, these assemblages must be dynamic over time. Whereas most capitalists merely pursue "adaptive responses to change," adjusting their existing arrangements, entrepreneurs carry out "creative responses" that grasp and set in motion what is new in their world.[3]

In order to enact these combinations, of course, the entrepreneur must not only bring together workers with resources and machines but must also impose on them a mode of cooperation and discipline by which they are to work together. *The essence of combination is cooperation.* It requires, in other words, the establishment and repetition of new social and productive relationships. Schumpeter is very close to Marx in his recognition that the key to increased productivity (and hence greater profits) is the cooperation of workers in coordination with systems of machines. Marx explains, in fact, that cooperation, while increasing productivity, also has a transformative effect on labor, creating a new social productive force: "the special productive power of the combined working day is, under all circumstances, the social productive power of labour, or the productive power of social labour. This power arises from co-operation itself. When the worker co-operates in a planned way with others, he strips off the fetters of his individuality, and develops the capabilities of his species."[4] The powers of humanity are realized in cooperation or, really, a new social being is forged in this process, a new machinic assemblage, a new composition of humans, machines, ideas, resources, and other beings.

Schumpeter is well aware, moreover, that in addition to the paid cooperation of the workers they employ, entrepreneurs also need the *unpaid* cooperation of a vast social field: "Just as a sovereign cannot place a policeman behind every citizen, the entrepreneur cannot pay everyone in social and political life whose cooperation he requires."[5] The analogy with the sovereign and its police emphasizes the threat of force or violence required by the entrepreneur. Marx similarly compares the capitalist overseeing cooperation as a general on the battlefield, dictating strategy for the troops under his command.[6] Cooperation in capitalist society is always accomplished under the threat of force. Schumpeter's analogy goes further, however, by recognizing that the cooperation imposed or required by entrepreneurs takes effect not only in their factories but across society, over populations paid and unpaid. Social labor, in addition to being unpaid, must also be functionally subordinated and ordered toward a specific productive goal. This is precisely the hypothesis that, during the years of the crisis of the Fordist industrial model, led to practices of externalization, along with the diffuse factories and construction of complex industrial zones that supported a new social organization of production. From Silicon Valley to software technology parks in India, from the innovative production centers in northern Italy and Bavaria to the free trade zones and export processing zones in Mexico and China, these entrepreneurial "combinations," administering the productive power of a vast social field, a wide variety of paid and unpaid social actors, have had great success.

Who, then, are these entrepreneurs? Schumpeter, in the original 1911 edition of *Theory of Economic Development*, in passages eliminated from later editions, provides an illuminating social vision—with weak echoes of Nietzsche or, really, foreshadowing Ayn Rand—that divides society into three groups on the basis of new combinations and entrepreneurship. The masses, he begins, who go about their lives in a habitual way and are in this sense "hedonistic," do not see the potential of new combinations. A minority of people, he continues, "with a sharper intelligence and a more agile imagination," can see the potential of new combinations but do not have the power or character to put them into action. "Then, there is an even smaller minority—and this one *acts*....It is this type that scorns the hedonistic equilibrium and faces risk without timidity....What matters is the disposition to act. It is the ability to subjugate others and to utilize them for his purposes, to order and to prevail that leads to 'successful deeds'—even without particularly brilliant intelligence."[7] It is interesting, but not really important, that he seems to contradict here his insistences elsewhere that entrepreneurship does not require risk. More important is his conception of the "Man of Action," the weight of whose personality demands obedience. If there is to be economic development, he maintains, there have to be such leaders.[8] And, correspondingly, Schumpeter presents "the masses" of workers, peasants, artisans, and others as hedonistic, passive, and resistant to the new.

Schumpeter's anthropology of the "Man of Action" is certainly crude, but it clearly resonates in the contemporary media-driven cult of the entrepreneur, especially in the digital world of dotcoms and start-ups. The bright white faces of men of action, distinguished by their energy and daring, confidently stare at us from the magazine racks of newsstands.

When he revises the *Theory of Economic Development* for the 1934 edition, however, Schumpeter abandons the heroic figure of the entrepreneur. He recognizes now that the entrepreneur creates new combinations "not by convincing people of the desirability of carrying out his plan or by creating confidence in his leading in the manner of a political leader—the only man he has to convince or impress is the banker who is to finance him—but by buying them or their services, and then using them as he sees fit."[9] The increasingly powerful rule of finance, Schumpeter realizes, reduces the entrepreneur from a leader whose force of personality or ideas gains the consent of the masses to a supplicant of the banker. The power of money, finance, and property, and the economic coercion they deploy, which we will study in more detail in part III, replaces the traditional modes of authority and consent required for leadership.

Finally, a decade later, in the 1940s, Schumpeter becomes convinced that even property and ownership, organized now in huge corporations, are no longer able to gain the consent of all those engaged in social production. This returns us to the passage we cited earlier. "The capitalist process," he laments, "takes the life out of the idea of property....Dematerialized, defunctionalized and absentee ownership does not impress and call forth moral allegiance as the vital form of property did. Eventually there will be nobody left who really cares to stand for it—nobody within and nobody without the precincts of the big concerns."[10] Schumpeter reluctantly admits, at this point, that the only path forward for capitalist production is centralized planning.

Schumpeter, however, is blind to the other side of the equation. Whereas he rightly cuts down to size the figure of the entrepreneur and recognizes the social limits posed by the power of money and property, he maintains a view of the "masses" as fundamentally passive. Instead, in the course of capitalist development, as productive cooperation extends ever more widely across the social field in diffuse, polycentric circuits, new combinations are increasingly organized and maintained by the producers themselves. With the potential to reappropriate fixed capital, as we indicated earlier, the multitude becomes increasingly autonomous in the generation and implementation of productive cooperation. No longer are generals needed to deploy them on the battlefield of social production; the troops, so to speak, can organize themselves and chart their own direction.

Faced with potentially autonomous cooperating forces of social production and reproduction, capitalist owners would seem to have two options. Either they can imprison them, reducing them to the dimensions of industrial discipline and forcing them to obey the supposedly scientific organization of labor, diminishing people's intelligence, creativity, and social capacities, for example, with "clickwork" and regimes of digital Taylorism. For this option capital must intervene at the level of subjectivity and produce workers who are happy (or at least willing) to put their lives in the service of the company. But then capital ends up reducing productive powers and thwarting its own thirst for profit. The other option (really capital's only feasible path) is to embrace the autonomous and cooperative potential of workers, recognizing that this is the key to valorization and increased productivity, and at the same time try to contain it. Capital does not pose the problem of disciplining labor and controlling it from the inside but instead seeks to rule it from the outside, from above. In line with this option, capital retreats from the traditional modes of imposing productive cooperation and instead tends, from outside the productive process and its circuits of cooperation, to *extract* value socially produced in relative autonomy.

Fifth call: Entrepreneurship of the multitude

We can begin to recognize emerging within the circuits of cooperation of social production and reproduction an altogether different notion of entrepreneurship, which was perhaps latent in Schumpeter's notion from the beginning: the entrepreneurship of the multitude, that is, the autonomous organization of social cooperation.

The emerging entrepreneurship of the multitude is closely related with the establishment of a new mode of production, a phase of capitalist development in which social cooperation, affective and cognitive labor, and digital and communicative technologies have become dominant. When we say a new mode of production we are not conceiving a historical passage through homogeneous stages, a conception that has had pernicious effects both in the workers' movement and in colonialist ideology. Conceiving the slave organization of labor, for example, as a distinct mode of production separate from capitalism led to both conceptual confusion and insidious political effects. We conceive the new mode of production instead as a heterogeneous formation in which labor processes remaining from the past mix with new ones, all of which nonetheless are (not so much ordered by but) cast in a new light by a dominant set of elements.[11] (We will return to this discussion in more detail in chapter 10 in relation to concepts of the real and formal subsumption.) Mode of production in this sense, then, is another way of saying form of life or rather the production of forms of life, and this is increasingly so since in social production, more than commodities, society and social relations are the direct objects of productive processes. Producing, in other words, means organizing social cooperation and reproducing forms of life. The mode of production of social labor, then, of general intellect and the common, is a field in which the entrepreneurship of the multitude appears.

Before we can see the entrepreneurship of the multitude growing, however, we have to clear away some of the weeds that block our view. After all, doesn't neoliberal ideology exhort us each to become entrepreneurs of ourselves, to wean ourselves of state assistance and construct an entrepreneurial society? Being entrepreneurs in this way means that each of us individually must be responsible for our own lives, our own welfare, our own reproduction, and so forth. What is missing and mystified by this neoliberal entrepreneurship, however, are the mechanisms and relations of cooperation that animate social production and reproduction. In fact, as we will argue in chapter 12, neoliberal practices and governance, including the neoliberal notion of entrepreneurship, attempt to interpret, contain, and respond to the movement toward autonomy that the multitude has already set in course. The neoliberal mandate to become the individual entrepreneur of your own life, in other words, is an attempt to recuperate and domesticate a threatening form of multitudinous entrepreneurship that is already emerging from below.

Another mystification to clear away is the notion of "social entrepreneurship" sometimes espoused by social democrats and center-left politicians. The rise of social entrepreneurship, in fact, coincides with the neoliberal destruction of the welfare state, as its flip side, its compensatory mechanism, its caring face, forming together a "social neoliberalism."[12] Charles Leadbeater, a former advisor to Tony Blair, who is credited as originator of the term, argues for social entrepreneurship to fill the gap left when state benefits and assistance disappear. (As we claimed earlier, the destruction of welfare policies, although initiated under Reagan and Thatcher, were predominantly carried out by their center-left successors, Clinton and Blair.) Social entrepreneurship, Leadbeater explains, involves a combination of volunteerism, charity, and philanthropy, which create nonstate, community-based systems of services "in which users and clients are encouraged to take more responsibility for their own lives."[13] Leadbeater points to examples such as a brave and tenacious woman who, instead of allowing a public hospital to close, transforms it into a Christian community hospital, and a dedicated black Briton who solicits corporate sponsors and celebrity athletes to create a sports center for poor youth. Social entrepreneurship, despite its rhetoric of empowerment, is really the translation into the field of charity of the traditional ideology of the heroic business entrepreneur, adopting something like the anthropology of Schumpeter's early writings (with its rare men of action and hedonistic masses). Furthermore, social entrepreneurship, true to its social democratic roots, does not question the rule of property and the sources of social inequality but instead seeks to alleviate the worst suffering and make capitalist society more humane. This is certainly a noble task in itself, but it makes social entrepreneurs blind to the potentially autonomous circuits of cooperation that emerge in the relationships of social production and reproduction.

The illusory claims of social entrepreneurship are even more damaging, as many scholars have shown, in the circuits of international aid, philanthropy, and NGO activity in the most subordinated countries. In the name of empowerment, recipients of aid are often required to orient social life toward commodity production and internalize neoliberal development culture and its market rationalities, thus abandoning local and indigenous community structures and values or mobilizing them as entrepreneurial assets. For example, although systems of microcredit—that is, the extension of very small loans to those, especially women, who lack the collateral to access standard lending structures—have been celebrated for opening access to the means of entrepreneurship for the world's poorest populations, results show that such loans have done little to alleviate poverty and have instead saddled populations with lasting debt burdens. Women who receive microloans generally

have to "entrepreneurialize" existing networks of social solidarity and cooperation in the service of a neoliberalism from below.[14] In similar ways, a
variety of projects of social entrepreneurship through international aid that
pronounce goals to eliminate the worst poverty and eradicate disease—from
the widely promoted "Millennial Villages" in Kenya to irrigation aid for indigenous communities in Ecuador—require the adoption of neoliberal rationalities. The nexus of social neoliberalism and social entrepreneurship destroy
community networks and autonomous modes of cooperation that support
social life.[15]

Once these neoliberal notions of entrepreneurship are cleared away, we
can begin to glimpse some characteristics of a potential (or even already existing) entrepreneurial multitude, that is, a multitude that is author of "new
combinations" that foster autonomous social production and reproduction.
First, this entrepreneurship follows directly from the forms of cooperation
that emerge from inside and outside capitalist production. Whereas previously
the capitalist was required to generate productive cooperation through disciplinary routines, today increasingly cooperation is generated socially, that is,
autonomously from capitalist command. Second, the multitude can become
entrepreneurial when it has access to the means of production, when it is able
to take back fixed capital and create its own machinic assemblages. The machines, knowledges, resources, and labor combined by the multitude, third,
must be pulled out of the realm of private property and made common. Only
when social wealth is shared and managed together can the productivity of
social cooperation realize its potential.

In our first call in chapter 2 we proposed that strategy and tactics should
be inverted such that leadership becomes merely tactical and strategy is entrusted to the multitude. At that point in our argument, however, that proposal could only appear as a wish because we were not in the position to
confirm the capacities of the multitude to accomplish the tasks of strategy,
that is, to understand the contours of the social field, to organize complex
social projects, to orchestrate and sustain long-term plans. The results of this
chapter allow us in part to fill in that gap and recognize that potential. The
networks of productive cooperation, the social nature of production and reproduction, and, moreover, the capacities of entrepreneurship of the multitude are the solid foundations of strategic powers. Ultimately, this entrepreneurship points toward the self-organization and self-governance of the
multitude, and in order to realize this potential there must be struggles.

Social production→social union→social strike

Production is today, as we have argued throughout part II, increasingly social in two senses. On the one side, the productive processes are social; that is, rather than individuals producing in isolation, production is accomplished in networks of cooperation. Furthermore, those rules and habits of how to cooperate, how to relate to each other productively, tend no longer to be imposed from above but generated from below, in the social relations among producers. On the other side, the results of production also tend to be social. Rather than conceiving material or immaterial commodities as the endpoint of production, we need to understand it as the production (often via commodities) of social relations and, ultimately, of human life itself. This is the sense in which one can call contemporary production anthropogenetic or biopolitical.

The social nature of production in both these senses points directly to the common. Private property appears increasingly as a fetter to social productivity both in the sense that it blocks the relationships of cooperation that generate production and that it undermines the social relations that are its result. The path from social production to the common, however, is not immediate or inevitable. The affirmation and defense of the right to the common, as we said earlier, needs activist projects to be sustained. The potentials created by social production, specifically, require a combination of social movements and labor struggles to be realized. This is a key form of the entrepreneurship of the multitude.

On one side, social movements that affirm the right to the common, such as struggles over resources like water or the numerous urban encampments and occupations that have been born since 2011 (and continue to spring up) in the attempt on small scales to open urban space to the common, generate new combinations and new forms of social cooperation.[16] Moreover, various struggles over housing, welfare services, education, transportation, and other institutions of our common social life, which often involve self-management or mutualistic experiments, such as the antieviction and housing campaign in Spain (PAH, or "platform of those affected by mortgages") and the solidary health clinics in Greece, constitute forms of entrepreneurship from below. On the other side, as the center of gravity of capitalist production shifts outside the factory, labor organizing has to follow it on the terrain of social production and reproduction, where the entrepreneurship of the multitude arises.

On this terrain trade unions and social movements must create alliances or hybrid structures in the form of social unions. "Aware of the extreme ambiguity of this definition," write Alberto De Nicola and Biagio Quattrocchi, "we use the term 'social unionism' [*sindacalismo sociale*] to group together various experiences of struggle that, within and outside trade union organizations, counteract the ways that traditional trade unions, due to weakness or by choice, serve to obstruct or pacify social conflict."[17] Social unionism, which constitutes the intersection or interweaving of labor struggles and social movements, offers the promise of, on the one hand, renewing the power of labor organizing and overcoming the conservative practices of some existing unions and, on the other, of bolstering the longevity and effectiveness of social movements.

Social unionism overturns the traditional relation between economic struggles and political struggles, which is another version of the relation between strategy and tactics. The standard view regards economic and trade union struggles (especially those over wages) as partial and tactical, and thus in need of an alliance with and guidance from the political struggles led by the party, which is thought to have a comprehensive and strategic scope. The alliance between economic and political struggles proposed by social unionism scrambles the assignments of tactics and strategy since economic movements link not with a constituted power but a constituent power, not a political party but a social movement. Such an alliance should benefit social movements by allowing them to stand on the stable, developed organizational structure of the union, giving the struggles of the poor, the precarious, and the unemployed a social reach and a continuity they would otherwise lack. In return, the alliance should not only enlarge the social sphere of trade unions, extending union struggles beyond wages and the workplace to address all aspects of the life of the working class, focusing the attention of union organizing on the form of life of the class, but also should renew the *methods* of unions, allowing the antagonistic dynamics of social movement activism to break the sclerotic structures of union hierarchies and their worn-out modes of struggle.[18]

The locus classicus of social unionism in the anglophone world is the antiapartheid alliance formed in South Africa: in 1990 the Congress of South African Trade Unions entered into a "tripartite alliance" with the African National Congress (ANC) and the South African Communist Party. The alliance served as an umbrella for a wide variety of antiapartheid social movements, and served as inspiration outside South Africa for how a trade union organization could foster the developments and actions of social movements.[19] The South African experiences resonate with sporadic developments throughout the world in recent decades. The 1997 alliance between the carnevalesque social movement Reclaim the Streets and the sacked Liverpool dockers and the brief cooperation between Teamsters and Turtles (that is, environmental groups) at the 1999 World Trade Organization protests in Seattle are two significant examples. Some of the most dynamic trade unions in Italy, such as the Federation of Metal Workers (FIOM) and the grassroots unions in education, health, and other sectors (COBAS), along with the Service Employees International Union in the United States, have repeatedly experimented with social movement alliances with varying degrees of success.[20]

The tradition of social unionism must today, however, undergo a significant shift. Rather than posing an *external* relation of alliance between trade unions and social movements, groups must now around social production and the common construct an *internal* relation that regards labor organizing and social movements as not only intimately tied but also mutually constitutive in the modes and objects of struggle, recognizing how the terrain of labor is increasingly too that of forms of life. In order to realize the potentials of this new conception of social unionism we must understand social production and reproduction in a wide frame, well beyond the factory and the workplace. The metropolis itself is an enormous factory of social production and reproduction, or more precisely, it is a space produced in common (looking backward) that serves (looking forward) as the means of production and reproduction for future instances of the common. In capitalist society today, *the common names both the means of production and the forms of life.*

In this frame, then, the current international cycles of struggles that affirm the right to the common, which we cited earlier, open new possibilities for social unionism. The centrality of the common in contemporary production and reproduction does not negate the distinction between economic and political struggles, but it does demonstrate that they are inextricably interwoven. The struggles pose equal and open access plus collective self-management of the common as a precondition for any possible construction of a new form of democracy—and necessary too for constructing postcapitalist economic relations. One can trace a clear line, for example, between Spain's 2013 "marea blanca" protests against health care budget cuts, which brought health workers and health system users into the streets, and the 2015 municipal election victories in large cities, including Barcelona and Madrid, of coalitions dedicated to making health care and other social services common.

The primary weapon of social unionism (and the expression of the power of social production) is the social strike. The labor union since its inception has based its power on the threat of the organized refusal of work: when labor is withheld, capitalist production grinds to a halt. Historic and heroic battles have been fought on this terrain. In this traditional frame, however, unemployed workers, unwaged domestic labor, the precarious, and the poor appear to be powerless: since withholding their labor does not directly threaten capitalist production and profit, the standard logic goes, they have no leverage. Social movements, however, long ago discovered that the strategy of refusal can be an effective weapon for a wide variety if not all social groups: "some of the poor," Frances Fox Piven and Richard Cloward explain, "are sometimes so isolated from significant institutional participation that the only 'contribution' they can withhold is that of quiescence in civil life: they can riot."[21] Everyone, even the poor, wields in the final instance the threat to withdraw their voluntary servitude and disrupt the social order.

In the contemporary age of biopolitical production, when the common becomes the basis of social production and reproduction, as it does increasingly today, and when the circuits of productive cooperation extend throughout the social fabric, well beyond the walls of the factory, then the power of refusal spreads across the social terrain. Disruption of the social order and suspension of capitalist production become indistinguishably linked. This is precisely the potential that social unionism opens: the two traditions—the labor movement's interruption of industrial production and the social movements' disruption of the social order, both now based in the common—come together and, like chemical reagents, create an explosive mixture. In this context, in fact, the traditional conceptions of a general strike in which workers in all sectors of production will stop simultaneously gains a new and even more powerful meaning.

The social strike, however, must be not only a refusal but also an affirmation. It must, in other words, also be an act of entrepreneurship that creates or, better, reveals the circuits of cooperation and the potentially autonomous relationships of social production that exist inside and outside waged labor, making use of social wealth shared in common.

Taking the word as translation

A central task of every social and political movement is to allow new subjectivities to take the floor or, as they say in French, to take the word (prendre la parole). The various encampments and occupations, for example, that have continually sprung up since 2011 have all, with difficulties and shortcomings but nonetheless effectively, constructed sites of "taking the word." Taking the word, however, is not just a matter of being allowed to express yourself, and it is much more than the freedom of speech. Taking the word means transforming words themselves, giving them new meanings, those that are bound to new social logics of action and behavior. Taking the word also means getting out of yourself, escaping from solitude, encountering others, and constructing community. In both of these senses taking the word is a process of translation.

Taking the word in this first sense treats the key terms in our political vocabulary as if they were a foreign language in need of translation in line with the ways that we live and act today. Sometimes this involves coining new terms but more often it is a matter of taking back and giving new significance to existing ones. What does democracy really mean now? What does it mean to be free? Think, for example, of how the term "republican" was transformed in eighteenth-century Europe and North America, or how the word Commune after 1871 was translated throughout Europe to mean "social revolution," or how the word soviet after 1905 and after 1917 became the name for a dense theory of revolution and democracy. The political translation of these terms is not invented in the abstract or in the void, but rather materializes in collective practices. In this way, then, taking the floor, taking the word, emerges in reality or, better, it produces a "taking of reality."

Note that many times this operation of translation has served strategically to confuse and falsify the political reality. For example, the 1997 Labour Party Manifesto revised the political vocabulary to support neoliberal policies: the term social was posed in a completely neutral way, socialism was confused with "social services," the concept of "freedom" was given as "liberty" without any link to social struggles, the notion of "party" lost any reference to the community of workers in struggle and became instead an association of individuals, the concept of class struggle became an opposition between the few and the many, and so forth.[22] Tony Blair and the leaders of New Labour *understood that the language of the socialist tradition had to be undermined to establish political objectives.*

Today we have to break with the standard usage of some crucial terms in the dominant lexicon. We have attempted to redefine entrepreneurship *in this chapter, for example. And we also have to translate the concepts in the socialist vocabulary, but moving in an opposite direction than New Labour, giving terms like* class struggle, reform, welfare, party, *and* revolution *meaning in our contemporary reality. Some terms that were once subversive have certainly been misused, obscured, and emptied of meaning—but we may be able to uncover their former vitality. More significant and useful are efforts to translate traditional concepts into our new realities, bringing words into a constitutive relation with social practices as a key to activating passions and movements, oriented forward. Every radical enterprise in political thought has to redefine our political vocabulary.*

Taking the word also means translation in a second sense, since it must always involve plural speaking subjectivities. No one should hope or imagine to take the word today in order to speak the party line, which all must repeat ad nauseam. That would be a completely dead language, a wooden language. Instead taking the word in a living way must empower heterogeneous voices and "heterolingual" communities, to use Naoki Sakai's term, who, although each speaks as in a foreign tongue, are nonetheless able to translate one another and communicate.[23] This is the world of Zomia rather than Zamenhof, that is, the region of mixed cultures of the Southeast Asia highlands that James C. Scott sees as providing a counternarrative to modernity rather than the realm of Esperanto, invented by Ludwig Zamenhof.[24] The process of translation required here—which is at once linguistic, cultural, social, and political—is able to situate singularities in the common; it is a kind of commoning. But note here, as we have repeated before, the common does not mean "the same" and does not imply uniformity. On the contrary! The common is a platform for heterogeneity, defined by the shared relations among its constitutive differences.

Migrants, for example, who play such a fundamental role in shaping the contemporary world, who cross borders and nations, deserts and seas, who are forced to live precariously in ghettos and take the most humiliating work in order to survive, who risk the violence of police and anti-immigrant mobs, demonstrate the central connections between the processes of translation and the experience of "commoning": multitudes of strangers, in transit and staying put, invent new means of communicating with others, new modes of acting together, new sites of encounter and assembly—in short, they constitute a new common without ever losing their singularities. Through processes of translation, the singularities together form a multitude. Migrants are a coming community, poor but rich in languages, pushed down by fatigue but open to physical, linguistic, and social cooperation. Any political subjectivities seeking to take the word with legitimacy today must learn how to speak (and to act, live, and create) like migrants.

The image in the original frontispiece of Leviathan, which Hobbes himself commissioned, shows the body of the king as constituted by the bodies of all the male subjects of the English nation—an elegant and ingenious depiction of the unity among the people, the nation, and the sovereign. Imagine if we could re-create that image now with radically heterogeneous raced and gendered bodies in all their singularity, moreover bodies in motion, encountering one another, speaking different tongues, but nonetheless able to cooperate in both shared and conflicting relations. The image of such a multitude would depict how the processes of translation— taking the word—subvert the structures of sovereignty and construct the common.[25]

PART III

FINANCIAL COMMAND AND NEOLIBERAL GOVERNANCE

This is salvage accumulation: the creation of capitalist value
from noncapitalist value regimes.

— ANNA TSING, *Mushroom at the End of the World*

Above all things, good policy is to be used that the treasure and
monies in a state be not gathered into few hands. . . . And money
is like muck, not good except it be spread.

— FRANCIS BACON, "Essays or Counsels, Civil and Moral"

Mine, yours. "This dog is mine," say these poor children.
"This is my place in the sun." That is the beginning and the
image of the usurpation of all the earth.

— BLAISE PASCAL, *Pensées*

To understand neoliberalism you have to start with the multitude. The
"genius" of capital and its neoliberal "innovations" cannot be comprehend-
ed on their own terms, as if they were endogenous developments; instead they
must be grasped as reactions to resistance and revolt, as attempts to contain the
growing powers of social production and reproduction. Neoliberalism is
reactionary, as were many of the movements that followed the revolutionary
processes of the nineteenth and twentieth centuries: some strains of Roman-
ticism and nationalism responded to the revolutionary streams of the

Enlightenment and its universalism, fascisms rose up against revolutionary movements, state socialisms countered communist internationalism, and authoritarian regimes answered popular uprisings. Neoliberalism is similarly a reaction, but it functions primarily through ideology and economic action rather than philosophy and politics: it is a "science" rather than a "creed," mobilizing the command of capital rather than the authority of a "church," the force of the market rather than the identity of a nation. And neoliberalism accomplishes all this through a plural and varied deployment that seeks not so much to defeat but to appropriate the powers of its enemies. On the other side, the multitude that neoliberalism confronts has its own resources, wealth, and intelligence, which it has begun to develop on a completely new social and productive terrain. This sets the terms of battle.

One standard neoliberal tactic is to invent new economic instruments of exploitation and repression in order to de-democratize the state. It is no coincidence that Keynesianism—with its state structures of welfare, economic regulation, and public control—is consistently proclaimed enemy number one by neoliberal ideologues, from the most vulgar to the most sophisticated, from Ronald Reagan and Milton Friedman to Friedrich Hayek and Jeffrey Sachs.[1] Neoliberal hatred of Keynesianism, however, is due not only to its progressive character but also to the fact that its compromise aimed at containing and blocking social forces is no longer effective. By the late 1960s social movements powerfully challenged and undermined the disciplinary regimes of the welfare state. Samuel Huntington, one of the most lucid (and honest!) interpreters of the new emerging threat, feared that the resistances and liberation movements of "marginal social groups" of the 1960s and '70s—which comprised the vast majority of the population, including workers, women, and all people of color—would overload the Keynesian state: "The expansion of participation throughout society was reflected in the markedly higher levels of self-consciousness on the part of blacks, Indians, Chicanos, white ethnic groups, students, and women, all of whom became mobilized and organized in new ways to achieve what they considered to be their appropriate share of 'the action' and its rewards."[2] Huntington's diagnosis was that the political system suffered from a "democratic distemper" and the only cure was to de-democratize the state, retaining power in the hands of experts and reducing the participation and power of the multitude—in other words, returning the "marginal" to their marginal status. Huntington recognized what many other neoliberal ideologues only sense instinctively: the Keynesian state must be destroyed because in the face of the flood of social demands it is a weak defense, a defective levy, that leaves capital and its disciplinary regime vulnerable.[3]

One task of neoliberalism, then, is to dismantle the structures on which social struggles arise, breaking the mediations between capitalist command and social demands. Economic crisis has become a fundamental weapon in this battle—weakening investments and negating political faith in Keynesian government policies. In collaboration with the political crises that neoliberalism has wrought, this project is able to generalize—through new uses of money and financial power—an economy of dispossession, in which processes of extraction and mechanisms of debt spread exploitation across society. The "great transformation" of the economy in the socialist direction, foreseen by illustrious economists of the twentieth century, from Schumpeter to Karl Polanyi,[4] has thus been reversed—not by a new theory but by state sanction accompanied by a strong dose of violence.

Neoliberalism is best understood as a reaction to and attempt to contain exactly those resistance and liberation movements that Huntington recognized as the pallbearers of the Keynesian state and its strategies of capitalist control. Nancy Fraser argues, for instance, that there are disturbing resonances between neoliberalism and second wave feminism (along with the other liberation struggles of the 1960s and '70s), including feminist critiques of welfare state paternalism and social-democratic state policies. These resonances lead her to conclude, "second-wave feminism contributed something indispensable to neoliberalism's construction of hegemony."[5] We read this phenomenon as evidence not of the failure of feminism (or liberation struggles in general) but rather of how neoliberalism both responds to struggles and appropriates in distorted form some of the primary claims and concepts expressed in them. The new powers that we analyzed in part II must now be taken as the foundation of the developments of capital and the contemporary social mechanisms of control. And keep in mind that the neoliberal reaction, in all its forms, employs violence in unending wars, even when it dons peaceful garb, as in the case of financial modes of extraction and other mechanisms of dispossession.[6]

Neoliberalism usually shows its economic face, but has a political heart. It has not restored the freedom of markets but instead reinvented the state, attempting to extricate it from class struggle and social demands, pulling the theory and practice of capitalist development away from the dangers of social conflict—subordinating democracy to such an extent that it becomes completely unrecognizable. This "political" form of neoliberalism prevails over every other part of the system.

It is impossible today to return to Keynesianism and the other solutions that previously sought to create an equilibrium with social demands and class struggle through state action. That social model of the state, which both provided welfare and repressed social conflict, has been mothballed by the transformations of the mode of production. The only possibility of countering and overthrowing neoliberalism and its forms of rule resides in the same social forces that neoliberalism is designed to contain: the multitude and its projects of liberation.

CHAPTER 10

FINANCE CAPTURES SOCIAL VALUE

When finance emerged as a significant component of the capitalist mode of production in the late nineteenth and early twentieth centuries, it provided a powerful supplement to industrial capital, which held the dominant role in the economy and the entire social formation. Finance offered instruments of abstraction and centralization that not only facilitated the passage from manufacture to the rule of large corporations and their monopolies but also furnished a weapon in the arsenal of the imperialist projects. In the course of the twentieth century, however, the relationship between industry and finance was inverted so that finance now predominates, shifting some of the fundamental conditions of production and exploitation.

Under the rule of finance and its increasingly complex instruments, we will see, capital accumulates primarily through the capture and extraction of value that appears to be found, a natural gift, *terra nullius*. Finance capital extracts value from the common, both the values of materials buried in the earth and those embedded in society, but these values, of course, are actually produced historically and their extraction has enormous social costs. We have to track capital's extractive processes from below to recognize the destruction they bring as well as the potential for resistance and revolt.

Finance from above and from below

In order to understand how the power of finance capital has been consolidated and, indeed, how finance functions, we would do well to look at what changed around the 1970s, when finance began to have a dominant role in the economy and society as a whole. Our hypothesis is that in this case too when we adopt a standpoint from below, that is, from the perspective of social production and resistance, we understand better the forces at play and the potentials for liberation. Let us sketch briefly what this hypothesis looks like at the macro level before delving into it more deeply with regard to the workings of finance capital and extraction.

One account of the rise of finance, which certainly has some explanatory power, highlights the increasing role of global markets and, correspondingly, the decline of nationally organized industrial economies. In concert with the long economic crisis that began in the 1970s and the collapse (or demolition) of the Bretton Woods international monetary system, monetary control was shifted away from the nation-state toward global standards, and control over public debt was progressively stripped from sovereign national entities and submitted to mechanisms of value determined on the global market by the holders of finance capital. With the shift from public debt to stock markets, Christian Marazzi explains, "the financial markets have assumed a role that in the past was the responsibility of the Keynesian state, that is, the creation of the effective demand that is indispensable for insuring the continuity of growth."[1] Confronted with globalization and the increasing powers of global markets, the organization of industrial production in the dominant countries lost a central element of its legitimacy and functioning, that is, the nation-state as its sovereign basis. The declining importance of industry—and, especially, the geographical shift of industrial production from the dominant to the subordinated parts of the world—corresponds closely with the rising importance of finance.

Considered from this perspective, however, the rise of finance, although it corresponds with globalization, is understood better as a result of—and response to—forces of social resistance and revolt. Verifying this hypothesis requires much more detailed analysis but allows us here to give the general outlines of the argument.[2] The "reformist" system of capital in the dominant countries that emerged from the Second World War with its welfare structures, institutional labor unions, and imperialist regimes was designed to contain the workers' movements, liberation movements, and other social struggles. It disciplined social behaviors according to supposedly democratic rules. Revolts against this system culminated around 1968 with a global cycle of movements against capitalist disciplinary and imperialist regimes. As colonized countries won independence in the global South, workers and subordinated populations in the dominant countries made increasingly powerful demands. State debt, which was enlisted to respond to the revolts, quickly led to fiscal crises. The only "solution" to fiscal crisis, repeated in states throughout the world over the last decades of the twentieth century, was to shift public debt to private banks, and in the process transfer public governance mechanisms to the rule of financial markets. As the structure of debt shifts from public to private, then, both economic development and social justice are submitted to the rule of global markets and finance. Neoliberal administration, finally, reorganizes the state using financial mechanisms to manage the dual crisis of public debt and state governance. The general sequence goes something like this: resistance and revolt → government spending → fiscal crisis → financialization.

A smaller-scale version of this sequence of revolt → public debt → fiscal crisis was particularly clear and pronounced in major US cities. The multiple forms of social resistance and urban revolt of the 1960s culminated, in some respects, in the race rebellions, especially the 1967 Newark and Detroit riots and the widespread 1968 riots after the assassination of Martin Luther King Jr. This cycle of revolts was followed in the subsequent decade by dramatic urban fiscal crises. In the cities, though, the fiscal crises were due primarily not to increased spending but instead to a shift of public resources away from metropolitan centers and a rapid decrease of the tax base caused by wealthier white populations moving out of the cities, resulting in dramatic decreases in social services of all sorts, from health and housing to safety and water supply. These crises were "resolved" only with the intervention of private banks and financial funds, which took advantage of the "emergency" to appropriate large portions of public goods and to undermine the democratic functioning of public institutions. New York was a classic example of this process in the 1970s: "The management of the New York fiscal crisis," writes David Harvey, "pioneered the way for neoliberal processes both domestically under Reagan and internationally through the IMF in the 1980s."[3] The "resolution" of the fiscal crises of Detroit and Flint by financial institutions continues these processes today, with tragic social results.[4]

The creation of neoliberal administration and financial rule is understood better, however, when we focus not on large-scale processes but on how finance functions with respect to the generation of value. Standard critiques of finance generally assume that it has nothing to do with the production of value, but that it simply shifts the possession of existing values. Such critiques are often accompanied by the lament that the dominant countries don't produce anything anymore—all the "real" production is now in China. Most popular depictions of finance present it as a form of gambling or casino capitalism: high-stakes betting on stocks or commodities futures or housing markets or currencies or anything else. There is certainly some truth to this view. And there is even more truth to the more scholarly arguments that portray finance not as gambling but rather as an apparatus of dispossession. Finance does indeed function in the processes of the transfer to private hands of public property, such as railway or telephone systems, industries, or the cultural patrimony of the nation. It also facilitates the private accumulation from natural wealth, such as metals, coal, or oil. We will return below to these processes of "primitive accumulation," in which finance certainly plays a part. Each of these explanations, from gambling to dispossession, focus merely on the *transfer* of wealth, not its generation.

Viewed from below, however, we can see that, in addition to its gambling speculations, finance functions as an apparatus to capture from social and natural worlds values, which are often hidden. We will have to investigate, then, how the mode of production of finance capital is based, on one hand, on the control of social cooperation and the extraction of value produced in the innumerable circuits of social life and, on the other, on the extraction of value from the earth and the various forms of natural wealth we share in common. The center of gravity of the capitalist mode of production is today becoming— this is our general definition—the extraction of the common. Finance can only play a hegemonic role, then, because the common is emerging as an eminent productive power and the predominant form of value.

Abstraction/extraction

The first great analyses of finance capital highlighted its fundamentally *abstract* nature and thus the increased distance between those who produce and those who control production. In the early twentieth century, Rudolf Hilferding and Vladimir Lenin grasped the novelties of finance capital in relation to the shift of control from industrialists to bankers. Compared to the industrialist, who is relatively close to and engaged in the productive process and who, specifically, dictates the arrangements of productive cooperation, the banker is distant, abstract from production.[5] This increased distance is manifest in a shift from profit, generated from the direct organization and exploitation of workers, to rent, obtained at a distance. "[M]oney capital," Lenin explains, "is separated from industrial or productive capital, and…the rentier, who lives entirely on income obtained from money capital, is separated from the entrepreneur and from all who are directly concerned in the management of capital."[6] Finance, like all rent-generating activities, is characterized by its abstraction from production and its capacity to rule at a distance.

Finance capital, furthermore, with the increasingly dense web of relations between banks and industry and as capital became available to industrial capitalists exclusively through the banks, facilitated the centralized control over production. Abstraction implies centralization. And even more, Hilferding and Lenin continue, centralization creates a tendency to eliminate competition and concentrate control in a few enormous banks. Finance breeds monopolies, monopolies of money that rule over production. The monopolies of finance capital, Lenin continues, served as a central pillar of the European imperialist regimes.[7]

The concentration of money and the control over production in banks also create a general tendency toward the equalization of the rate of profit among economic sectors and across the world market. Equalization is accomplished in part through the mobility of firms in search of higher profits and, to a lesser extent, through the migrations of workers from one sphere of production to another and from one country to another in search of work and higher wages. But the mobility of capitalist firms and even more so the mobility of labor are severely limited by geographical, cultural, and political factors—"practical frictions," as Marx calls them, "that produce more or less significant local differences."[8] Finance and the credit system are much more effective in the equalization process since the mobility of money is less restricted than that of workers or firms. As finance capital flows to where it can receive the greatest returns, it tends to create a level surface, like water flowing across uneven terrain. The concentration and centralization of control over production in a few banks and the tendency toward the comparison and equalization of profits are instrumental factors in the creation of the world market. The establishment of a general rate of surplus value and the equalization of exploitation across the world market, Marx explains, is only a tendency, and like all economic laws, it is a theoretical simplification, but not for that any less real.[9]

The abstraction and centralization of control over production, monopolized in the hands of banks and money, and the spread of this power across the world market, tending to equalize rates of profit and exploitation, are all primary characteristics of finance still today. If one were to regard finance only in this light, however, one could assume that it is merely parasitical to "real" industrial production and thus finance's increasing centrality represents a decaying, precarious foundation of capital as a whole. Finance capital and the production over which it rules, though, are just as real as industrial capital. The primary difference is that production and, specifically, productive cooperation now tend to be organized outside capital's direct engagement. The key to finance—and capitalist accumulation as a whole—is how value is extracted from wealth that resides elsewhere, both the wealth of the earth and the wealth that results from social cooperation and interaction. This is the link between abstraction and extraction.

One window into the way that finance and social production rose to prominence hand in hand from the 1970s is provided by the operation of derivatives and, specifically, how they create mechanisms of measure and commensuration. A derivative in its most basic form is simply a contract that derives its value from some underlying asset, index, or security; derivatives typically refer to an unknown future and thus can be used either to hedge against risk or as vehicles of speculation. For example, imagine a Japanese company that contracts to buy a quantity of Brazilian soybeans at a certain price in Brazilian reis six months later, after the next harvest. The Japanese could use a derivative to fix the exchange rate and thus hedge against the rising value of the real against the yen, which would make the cost of the soybeans higher for them. The Brazilians, in contrast, might use a derivative to guarantee the value of soybeans and protect against a weak harvest, which would make the contract a loss. And for each of these companies to hedge their risks, of course, others must be willing to speculate that the value of the real will fall or that the soybean harvest will be plentiful.

Derivatives have existed for centuries, but until the 1960s they were mainly confined to futures markets on commodities, such as rice, pigs, and wheat. Since the 1970s, however, just as the disciplinary industrial order and the fiscal state were collapsing, and just as social production and the production of the common started to become predominant in the economy, derivatives markets have grown exponentially and included an ever wider range of underlying assets.[10]

Derivatives have become so extraordinarily complex and esoteric that an adequate analysis of their operations is well beyond our scope, but our argument here is focused on a specific function: the measurement role of derivatives. We have argued elsewhere that when confronting social production, capital is no longer able to measure value adequately, at least not in the way it had previously. Clearly value can no longer be measured, as David Ricardo and Karl Marx theorized, in terms of the quantities of labor time. This is not to say that labor is no longer the source of wealth in capitalist society. It is. But the wealth it creates is not (or is no longer) measurable. How do you measure the value of knowledge, or information, or a relationship of care or trust, or the basic results of education or health services? And yet the measure of social productivity and value are still required for capitalist markets.[11]

Derivatives are part of finance's response to the problem of measure. Their abstract position with respect to the actual fabric of productive activity— derivatives are by definition abstract from the assets that underlie them—allows derivatives to form a complex web of conversions among a wide range of forms of wealth. Many forms of derivatives, for example, grasp unknown and volatile assets—the future value of a currency or the result of a harvest in our example—and make them into tradable commodities. By virtue of establishing such trades, write Dick Bryan and Michael Rafferty, "derivatives provide a market benchmark for an unknown value."[12] Every derivative product, Bryan and Rafferty explain, "is a package of conversion of one form of capital to another—whether this is a simple commodity futures contract or a complex conversion of a particular currency index to a particular stock market index. When all these products are taken together, they form a complex web of conversions, a *system of derivatives*, in which any 'bit' of capital, anywhere and with any time or spatial profile, can be measured against any other 'bit' of capital, and on an on-going basis."[13] Derivatives and the derivative markets thus operate a continual process of calculation and establish commensurability, making an extraordinarily wide range of existing and future assets measurable against one another in the market. "The core operation of derivatives," writes Randy Martin, "is to bind the future to the present through a range of contractual opportunities and to make all manner of capitals across disparate spheres of place, sector, and characteristic commensurate with one another."[14] But are those values accurate, you might ask? That may not be the right question. The important fact in this context is that measures are precise and effective. The values of social production today may be unknown, immeasurable, and unquantifiable, but financial markets nonetheless manage to stamp quantities on them, quantities that are in some sense arbitrary but still quite real and effective.

Critics disparage finance—and derivatives even more so—as fictional and parasitical. Go ahead, respond ironically the captains of finance and princes of arbitrage, who are the only ones who can still measure (or pretend to measure) capitalist values over the totality of social wealth and across the entire world market. They can laugh as they accumulate vast wealth through extraction from the common. But we should be clear: such financial mechanisms do not prevent crises but instead intensify them. The volatility of finance, as we will see, is one element that makes permanent crisis the primary mode of neoliberal governance.

The many faces of extraction

With the growing importance of extraction, especially the large-scale exploitation of natural resources, such as oil, natural gas, metals, and minerals, capital seems to have turned back the clock. Today's land grabs and reckless chasing after resources can easily conjure up brutal scenes of exploitation in the silver mines of Potosí and the gold mines of Johannesburg along with the ruthless theft of land from native populations. Indeed the histories of conquest, colonialism, and imperialism were driven by a thirst to extract wealth in various forms, wealth that was "found" and free for the taking from across the globe, with, of course, the constant backing of armies and ideology. Humans, just as much as material resources, could be extracted as chattel, and through the Atlantic slave trade their value entered into the colonizers' ledgers. Land, precious metals, animal furs, spices, opium, and "lesser humans" were thus all found by colonizers, gifts that they happily accepted and proclaimed as the just desserts for their daring efforts.

The growing centrality of extraction today, however, although it too is brutally destructive, is not a remnant of the past or indication of a cyclical historical return. The best guide to understanding contemporary extraction, in fact, is to follow the forms of the common on which it depends, since the common is what is extracted and transformed into private property. One can say that the common is divided into two general categories: on the one hand, the wealth of the earth and its ecosystems, which generally is translated into the economic vocabulary as natural resources or raw materials, and on the other, the social wealth that results from circuits of cooperation, ranging from cultural products to traditional knowledges, and from urban territories and scientific knowledges.[15] These two forms of the common serve as a first guide to understanding the different faces of extractivism.

The earth and its ecosystems—the soil, forests, rivers, seas, and atmosphere—are (or should be) common to us all, not in the sense that humans should "have dominion...over all the earth" (Genesis 1:26) but rather in that we must together establish relationships of care and sustainable use. The extraction of generally nonrenewable resources from the surface and depths of the earth raises not only issues of injustice (as always when something that was common becomes private property) but also the prospect of large-scale and even catastrophic destruction. Capitalist industry and commodification have long had destructive effects, but in some respects extractivism today brings that process to a head and a point of no return. *Capital against the earth*—one or the other may survive, but not both.

The environmental and social destructiveness of extractive industries, especially energy industries, is nothing new. Large spills from drilling and transport accidents have been a constant byproduct of the oil industry since its beginning, and their size and frequency are only increasing, dotting the globe: Galicia, the Gulf of Mexico, Uzbekistan, Kuwait, Angola, and on and on. Coal-mining methods continue to destroy the health of miners and the environment around the mines—as do mines for metals. In some respects there has thus been what Maristella Svampa calls a "reprimarization" of the economy as extraction has come to play a more central role and many countries (such as the Gulf states, Russia, and Venezuela) act like fossil-fuel companies whose prospects rise and fall with oil prices.[16]

What is new is the dramatic expansion of the frontiers of extractivism. No corner of the earth is free from it. Metals important for technology industries send capital scrambling across the earth, developing lithium mines for lightweight batteries in Bolivia's salt flats and rare earth mines in China for a wide range of digital and high-tech devices. Moreover, technological developments (and temporarily high oil prices) opened new terrains for oil and gas extraction, such as tar sands fields in Alberta, Canada, and fracking (or hydraulic fracturing) in the United States, which are even more dangerous and destructive than traditional methods, creating new seismic zones, polluting the air, and contaminating groundwater. Large-scale agriculture has also, in many respects, become an extractive industry. When corn and soybeans grown in enormous plantations are not destined for human consumption or livestock feed but directly for the production of ethanol and plastics, then the fields become no different than oil wells or mines: they suck wealth from the earth as energy and industrial resources. And their level of environmental destruction, from deforestation to pesticide use, rivals that of other extractive processes.

The destructive effects of extractivism are raised to another power by the prospect of climate change. In the past the pollution and destruction from accidents and from oil wells and coal mines have been considered as relatively localized and potentially reversible phenomena. But now the prospect of general and irreversible destruction is immanent. In order not to raise global temperatures more than two degrees Celsius, explains Bill McKibben with now well-known figures, 80 percent of the proven coal and oil reserves must remain in the ground and not be exploited. "Given this hard math," he continues, "we need to view the fossil-fuel industry in a new light. It has become a rogue industry, reckless like no other force on Earth. It is Public Enemy Number One to the survival of our planetary civilization."[17] Climate change raises to a new level the stakes of extractivism and heightens the urgency of resisting it.

In order to understand contemporary extractivism, however, one needs to recognize not only the value stripped from the earth but also, as we said, the value captured from the other broad category of the common: the many forms of social production and social life. Consider, first, how corporations treat the human body itself as a repository of wealth open for extraction. "At stake here," Sandro Mezzadra and Brett Neilson write, "is not only the extraction of tissues and other biological substances from the human body but also the generation and patenting of knowledge derived from genomic manipulations that break down and recast genetic materials according to logics of risk and speculation."[18] Even the genetic information contained in our bodies can be extracted and patented as property. Furthermore, through various forms of what Vandana Shiva and others call "biopiracy," corporations extract value from traditional knowledges, for instance, by patenting knowledge of medicinal properties of a plant, which was long ago developed by a traditional community and held in common.[19]

Another face of extraction takes the form of data. The metaphors of "data mining" and "data extraction" paint an image of unstructured fields of social data that are available for capture by intrepid prospectors, just like oil or minerals in the earth—and indeed there is today a digital gold rush to rival California and the Yukon. The mining and extraction of data means capturing value by searching for patterns in large data pools and structuring data so that it can be stored and sold.[20] The concept of data, however, may be too thin and inert to account adequately for the way value is produced and captured. Earlier we described how the algorithms of search engine platforms, like Google's PageRank, capture value produced by the knowledge and intelligence of users by tracking and consolidating the decisions and links they make. Social media too have discovered mechanisms to extract value from the social relationships and connections among users. Behind the value of data, in other words, stands the wealth of social relationships, social intelligence, and social production.

A third face of extraction regards social territory itself. The metropolis, for example, much more than its built environment, is a cauldron of the production of the common, including cultural dynamics, patterns of social relationships, innovative languages, affective sensibilities, and the like.[21] One way of conceiving gentrification, then, is as a process of the extraction of the common embedded in the urban territory itself—perfectly analogous to pulling oil from shale, and sometimes with just as destructive effects. Real estate markets, dominated by finance, should be understood as vast fields for the extraction of social values across urban and rural territories.

The many forms of cooperative social production constitute another face of extraction, a face that helps compose together many of the others. Anna Tsing, for example, following the trails of wild mushrooms from the pickers in Oregon to the sale in Japan, recognizes the ability of capital to capture value that is produced autonomously: "This is what I call 'salvage,' that is, taking advantage of value produced without capitalist control."[22] "Salvage" is indeed an excellent description of how capital captures and extracts value produced in the relationships of social production and social life.

Extraction, in these and its many other faces, follows the trails of the common. In contrast to industry, extraction relies on forms of wealth that to a large extent *preexist* the engagement of capital. Whereas the automobile is produced in the factory, oil and coal already exist in the ground (although, of course, extraction is itself a production process and once extracted materials have to be refined and distributed). The distinction is even clearer with regard to social intelligence, social relations, and social territory. Whereas in the factory workers cooperate according to schemes and discipline dictated by the capitalist, here value is produced through social cooperation not directly organized by capital—social cooperation that is, in that sense, relatively autonomous. The renewed centrality of extraction is thus situated in the historical passage from profit to rent. Whereas industrial capitalists discipline and exploit labor for profit, the rentier extracts the common and accumulates existing wealth with little involvement in its production. The renewed centrality of the rentier, like that of extractivism, we repeat, is not simply a remnant of the past or indication of a cyclical historical return. Revealing the many faces of extractivism gives us a better understanding of capitalist development and historical progression, which is neither simply linear nor cyclical but characterized, through various geographical and cultural differences, by a complex, hybrid temporality.

Finance, then, has a double relation to contemporary extractivism. On the one hand, finance (and financial speculation) has always held an important role in extractive operations, in part because of the need for enormous initial expenditures for land and equipment. Finance's control increases further as extractive firms (whether private or state-backed, from Rio Tinto to Gazprom and from Glencore to Saudi Aramco) and their projects become ever larger. Finance also backs and controls the various enterprises of "mining" the social and biological fields we mentioned above, including data, genetic information, traditional knowledges, social intelligence, and social relationships. On the other hand, though, finance also extracts directly; it manages in various ways to extract value from the results of social production.[23]

Debt provides one mechanism to extract value from social life. Home mortgages and rental practices (along with foreclosures and evictions), for example, form one apparatus for capturing and extracting wealth from the poor and middle classes. Matthew Desmond, studying populations evicted from their homes in Milwaukee, presents a web of financial practices of extraction that surround the economic relations of housing. "Payday loans," he writes, "are but one of many financial techniques—from overdraft fees to student loans for for-profit colleges—specifically designed to pull money from the pockets of the poor."[24] It is essential to understand, however, that the social value extracted through such apparatuses is not inert but instead the result of circuits of social cooperation. Verónica Gago, studying migrant communities in the urban peripheries of Buenos Aires, emphasizes the social production of value and its relative autonomy, which is revealed when finance extracts value from popular life, sometimes through microloans in poor communities aimed at consumption: "financialization driven from above operates as a way of reading, appropriating, and reinterpreting popular forms linked to certain practices of productive and reproductive autonomy."[25] *Finance is itself an extractive industry.* It is not only a power of abstraction and centralization but also an apparatus that directly captures and extracts value from social production. From below such processes point toward the common constituted by innumerable interactions and forms of cooperation across society.

If you want to understand extraction from above, then, *follow the money*; but if you want to grasp it from below, you need to *follow the common*.

From social production to finance

When we look from below at finance, then, we can recognize social production in the double sense that we proposed earlier: it results from social interaction and it produces society. We can also see that the contemporary predominance of finance comes about as a *reaction* to the growing centrality of social production and ultimately it responds to the accumulation of resistances and revolts that destroyed the bases of the industrial and disciplinary regime. This passage is thus characterized by a new relationship between capital and labor: from Fordism to post-Fordism. Whereas in the Fordist period capitalist production was structured by disciplinary regimes and accumulation was driven by profits generated in the planned cooperation of industrial labor, in post-Fordism, as productive knowledges and social capacities of cooperation spread increasingly widely through society, finance serves both to control social production and to extract the value it generates in the form of rent.[26]

This new predominance of extraction—specifically, extracting the social wealth produced in common—changes the nature of exploitation, which must now be analyzed with new criteria. In particular, the "temporal" analytic of Marx's concept of exploitation no longer applies. Marx explains, pedagogically, that under wage labor workers are paid the value produced during the first hours of the working day and the capitalist expropriates the value produced in the remaining hours. This explanation has the virtue of revealing an intimate connection between exploitation and the organization of production, but today the mechanisms of exploitation and productive organization tend to diverge. Capitalist entrepreneurs, who extract value at a distance and only see productive subjects abstractly as a mass, tend to regard the results of social production as a natural gift, manna from heaven.[27] With their eyes fixed on derivatives markets and arbitrage strategies, they are no longer the central protagonists who organize production, forge new combinations, and generate labor cooperation, as Schumpeter theorized. Instead, those who produce value increasingly are able autonomously to cooperate and to plan production.

One key, then, is to recognize the generality of social production and the figures of labor that animate it. Contemporary labor is often characterized in terms of the power of knowledge, intelligence, and cognitive capacities.[28] But social production takes place throughout the economy, not just at the pinnacle of the digital world, in the rarefied air of "cognitive workshops" like Google's Alphabet. We need to dispel the idea that different strata of labor are entirely separate and fit neatly within each other like a Russian doll—no collars at their keyboards inside white collars in their office cubicles inside blue collars of the factory inside pink collars of health, education, and home care. Moreover, there is no time lag as if industry today were to function as it did in 1930 or agriculture as it did in 1830. Instead labor conditions and processes, which certainly vary in each country and across the global market, intersect and mix irregularly in ways that are coeval and equally contemporary: metalworkers throughout the world today perform highly specialized industrial crafts with digital instruments; cognitive workers enter and manipulate data in assembly-line arrangements; and health and education workers employ knowledge and care, intellect and affect together with advanced digital technologies, even when they are unpaid or paid wages barely above poverty rates. Carla Freeman provides an excellent example of such intersections in her investigation of an offshore data-processing facility in Barbados that employs women to perform routine digital tasks such as entering data in medical claims forms for a US insurance company. The facility has some characteristics of the blue-collar factory with the numbing repetition of the work; like white-collar workers, however, the women dress professionally in high heels; the digital work that, although routinized, requires knowledge and intelligence, is part of a global no-collar apparatus; and finally, the work is explicitly feminized as pink collar.[29] Work today across the spectrum—from law offices in Delhi to convenience stores in Stockholm, and from auto plants in São Paulo to semiconductor fabrication plants in Oregon—is characterized by the intersection of all these labor regimes. Most important for our argument is that throughout the economy social production is becoming more central both in the activity of producing (employing, for example, social and scientific knowledges or schemes of cooperation or relations of care) and in the product (which correspondingly contains social, shared components).

Another key is to recognize that the same characteristics of social production that allow finance to extract and amass wealth also provide the seeds and
the foundation for resistance and revolt. We conceive this double-edged character, drawing on Marx's arguments, as developing through a three-stage logical process: from abstraction to social production to subjectivity. First, abstraction. The economic relation between capital and labor, Marx writes,
"develops more purely and adequately in proportion as labour loses all the
characteristics of art; as its particular skill becomes something more and more
abstract and irrelevant, and as it becomes more and more a *purely abstract activity*."[30] In many respects abstraction increases dramatically in social production:
when workers interiorize knowledges, for example, and develop them socially in cooperation, their labor and the value they produce are ever more
abstract.[31] But Marx does not regard the loss of "art," such as the craftsman's
lifelong performance of his métier, with any nostalgia. The loss of a specific
art or craft is also a gain. "[L]abour is not this or another labour," he continues,
"but *labour pure and simple*, abstract labour; absolutely indifferent to its particular *specificity* [*Bestimmtheit*], but capable of all specificities."[32] The abstraction
of labor, then, is not empty but completely full—full, specifically, with the
social character of production. And the greater abstraction of productive processes and value—today in the implementation of languages, code, immaterial
articulations of being together, cooperation, affective elements, and the like—
presents extraordinary potential for resistance to and autonomy from capital.

The increasingly general capabilities of labor, the second step, presuppose
the social, communal nature of production: individual, specific labor is pos-
ited from the outset as social labor. "*[T]he social character of production* is presup-
posed," Marx asserts, "and the participation in the world of products, in
consumption, is not mediated by the exchange of mutually independent la-
bours or products of labour. It is mediated, rather, by the social conditions of
production within which the individual is active."[33] The increasing abstraction of productive processes, then, rests upon the web of social relations, the
social conditions that make production possible. It relies, in other words, on a
foundation of the common, including the shared knowledges, cultural forms,
and circuits of cooperation that constitute our collective existence.

The third step for Marx is to set this social basis in motion, subjectively.
Against the totality of capital stands labor, which is equally total and abstract. "Of course, the particularity of labour must correspond to the particular substance of which a given capital consists," Marx continues, "but

since capital *as such* is indifferent to every particularity of its substance, and exists not only as the totality of the same but also as the abstraction from all its particularities, the labour which confronts it likewise subjectively has the same totality and abstraction in itself."[34] The fact of labor being abstract and social contains the (often unrealized) potential of subjectivation. Neither Marx's mention of totality here nor his theory of the "social individual" should lead us to assume a homogeneous or unified subjectivity at play here. The social nature of production instead implies an open field of differences in which subjectivities cooperate and conflict in volatile compositions. The common is constituted by these myriad heterogeneous subjectivities of social production.

There is, obviously, a fundamental divergence between capital's approaches to the common and the autonomous organization of the common from below. This divergence is particularly evident, for example, in the sectors of social welfare conceived broadly, such as education, housing, health, infant and elder care, and scientific and medical research. All these activities imply a human value that cannot be reduced to capitalist measure, and in these sectors we can recognize a stark and growing gap between capitalist and social conceptions of productivity, which, in turn, signal divergent approaches to the common: on one hand, a common from which maximum profit can be extracted and, on the other, a common open to be used by and put at the service of the population. This divergence, moreover, constitutes subjectively a line of antagonism. Marx asserts:

> On the one side, then, it calls to life all the powers of science and of nature, as of social combination and social intercourse, in order to make the creation of wealth independent (relatively) of the labour time employed on it. On the other side, it wants to use labour time as the measuring rod for the giant social forces thereby created, and to confine them within the limits required to maintain the already created value as value. Forces of production and social relations—two different sides of the development of the social individual—appear to capital as mere means, and are merely means for it to produce on its limited foundation. In fact, however, they are the material conditions to blow this foundation sky-high.[35]

And the situation is even more volatile when we emphasize the plurality and heterogeneity of subjectivities in play.

Insofar as the plural dimensions of this immaterial, cognitive, cooperative, and social mode of production imply a certain volatility, and insofar as these forms of labor-power, spreading across the social terrain, tend to become hegemonic in production, and insofar as the abstraction of these productive processes implies the emergence of forms of the common, which on the capitalist side requires the subjection of producers and, on the other side, opens the potential for subjectivation—if all this is true, then capital is faced with a dilemma. If capital were to dive into society and engage intimately in the life of social production, it would completely block the productive processes; and therefore capital is forced to impose its command "at a distance," in the extreme and violent forms of money, which incarnates the financial abstraction of value. This development, if seen from the perspective of the struggles of subversive subjects, describes a rather stark class division and is a source of class antagonism. On one side are all those who live on the interest generated by the financial markets and seek to preserve exclusive access to the private property they accumulate. On the other side are those who produce social wealth through their collective knowledges, their intelligence, and their social capacities to communicate, care for, and cooperate with each other, who seek security through free and open access to the common they have produced. These are battle lines.

Logistics and infrastructure in the social factory

The capitalist production of value, as we have said repeatedly, no longer takes place primarily within the walls of the factory. Value is produced in the social factory that stretches across the entire social terrain and throughout the sites of production and reproduction. But even that is not enough. Too often economic analyses, by focusing on production, leave out or subordinate considerations of circulation and consumption and, by concentrating on the individual firm, fail to grasp the total cycle of capital. We need an expansive view that is able to integrate production, circulation, and consumption at the level of the social whole.

Business theory and practice have in recent decades partially addressed this mandate through increased focus on logistics, that is, control over the flow of materials and commodities from the point of origin to the point of consumption. Business thinkers adopt the notion of logistics primarily from the military:

just as without logistical support, without weapons and food reaching the front, troops cannot fight, so too, without logistics, without the commodity reaching the consumer, economic value cannot be realized. The "revolution in logistics" in business and management studies has brought an expansive notion of production that views the culmination of the process not when the commodity rolls out on the assembly line but when the consumer uses it. Adopting this perspective, then, businesses seek not only to maximize the creation of surplus value in production but also to limit costs, minimize waste, and maximize value added in transport and throughout the entire economic cycle.[36]

Marx theorizes logistics, without using that term, when he proposes the concept of total social capital. In volume 2 of *Capital*, after having limited his perspective in volume 1 to the production process of the individual capitalist, he opens his view to the entire economic cycle, including circulation and consumption. The transport of commodities and the transport of information, for instance, are inseparable from the production process. In the transport industries, "it is the production process itself, and not the product separable from it, that is paid for and consumed."[37] The transport industries, in other words, constitute on one hand a separate branch of reproduction and thus a specific sphere for the investment of productive capital; but, on the other hand, they represent the continuation of productive processes in circulation.[38] The spatial movement of commodities, which constitute also a shift in their social mediation, their social interactions, becomes itself a productive power.

Marx takes the theory of logistics one step further through his development of the concept of total social capital. On one axis, like today's business theorists of logistics, he highlights the continuous metamorphosis of value through the circuits of production, circulation, and consumption, the social process of capital. He adds to this a second axis along which we must expand our view: since the circuits of individual capitals are linked and presuppose one another, we must shift our view from the individual firm to the sum of all capitals, total capital. Embracing these two arms or axes is necessary to analyze the movements of total social capital.[39]

We need one more element to complete this analysis. "[L]ogistics," maintain Brett Neilson and Ned Rossiter, "is something more than a system for searching out and connecting diverse firms and labour forces on the basis of cost or other parameters. Logistics also actively produces environments and subjectivities."[40] Infrastructure, that is, the built environment and the legal structures that facilitate the flows of labor, capital, and commodities, complements logistics and the movements of total social capital through production, circulation, and consumption. Since the late twentieth century a series of "zones" has characterized global economic geography: export-processing zones, special economic zones, free-trade zones, industrial parks, transport hubs, border industrial programs, and the like. Just as logistics is not neutral, infrastructures are not apolitical: they facilitate some flows and prohibit others, and serve as instruments to influence competition among capitals and to be used against labor. Zones are generally conceived in terms of legal exceptions, but really their status is exceptional only from the perspective of the nation-state. These zones are symptoms of the formation of Empire and its emerging global governance that rules over the constellation of varied legal and economic structures. "While extolled as an instrument of economic liberalism," Keller Easterling writes, the zone "trades state bureaucracy for even more complex layers of extrastate governance, market manipulation, and regulation."[41] Question: does the nation-state rule over the zone or does the zone rule the nation-state? Answer: neither. Empire is emerging as a variegated and interconnected web of legal and economic forms. In any case, without infrastructure and without the archipelago of special zones, capital's projects in the realm of logistics would fall flat.

The shift in perspective along the two axes of total social capital and, specifically, the recognition that capital is a social relation means also recognizing all of society as a terrain of class conflict. When capital puts the revolution in logistics into practice, it effectively extends the terrain of class conflict beyond the sphere of production to distribution and circulation. Deborah Cowen recounts, for instance, how in the 1970s transport corporations adopted the standard shipping container, a technology developed and refined by the US military for logistical support of its troops in Vietnam, and, together with the mechanization of the ports and the deregulation of the transport sector, this logistical innovation allowed for mass firings of dockworkers and undermined once powerful and rebellious labor unions as part of a "domestic social war on transport workers."[42] Through logistics, expanding their vision and engagement beyond the terrain of production, businesses both increase their profits and expand the field of class warfare.

It would be a mistake, however, to view the class warfare of logistics as an independent innovation of capitalists focused on realizing profits. Capitalist developments in logistics are always a response to the rebellious, uncontrollable forces of production. Stefano Harney and Fred Moten trace this response back to the birth of modernity. "Modern logistics is founded," they write, "with the first great movement of commodities, the ones that could speak. It was founded in the Atlantic slave trade, founded against the Atlantic slave....Logistics could not contain what it had relegated to the hold."[43] Beneath every revolution in logistics reside unruly subjects and new forms of rebellion.

Labor struggles continually appear in the sphere of logistics in old and new forms. The labor revolts in Oakland and across the West Coast of the United States conducted in part by the International Longshore and Warehouse Union continue a long history of port struggles. But the multinational labor forces employed by logistics industries, such as DHL, Amazon, and IKEA, usually composed of migrants and disproportionately women, are generally not represented by trade unions. And yet these workers continuously find creative means to rebel.[44] Logistics poses a challenge today of understanding how workers can organize to act effectively and how they can link with workers in other sectors of production and reproduction.

Marxist debates 1: Primitive accumulation

Extractivism derails simple historical narratives of economic development in terms of either linear progress or cyclical return. Today's extractivist practices present something like a historical archive that contains all the pasts of capital, from the oldest to the newest forms of producing and accumulating value, ancient and postmodern methods of exploitation and control, with wide geographical and cultural differences. Contemporary Marxist scholars develop two concepts—primitive accumulation and formal subsumption— to investigate the complex temporalities of capitalist development in the age of extractivism, highlighting its nonlinear and nonsynchronous trajectory. These analyses also serve to pry Marx's thought away from Eurocentrism. "Deprovincializing Marx," writes Harry Harootunian, "entails not simply an expanded geographic inclusion but a broadening of temporal possibilities unchained from a hegemonic unilinearism."[45] Indeed, recognizing the geographical and temporal differences must go hand in hand.

Marx uses primitive accumulation to name the violent processes that take place prior to the capitalist mode of production and are necessary for it to begin, processes that create the two classes. He details, on one hand, how in England, through the "enclosures" that transformed land into private property, peasants were separated from the soil and transformed into a class of workers who are free in a double sense: they do not belong to the means of production as do serfs and slaves but they do not themselves have access to the means of production. On the other hand, colonialism, conquest, and the slave trade were some of the key moments in the formation of the English capitalist class.[46] Several contemporary Marxists rightly criticize Marx for asserting (or at least strongly implying) in this theory both a linear historical development and a global geographical hierarchy: primitive accumulation appears in Marx as a phase that, once capitalist accumulation begins, is complete and done; and all other nations will eventually have to go through primitive accumulation following the model of England, the most advanced capitalist economy of the time. Contemporary Marxists emphasize instead that primitive accumulation continues alongside capitalist accumulation throughout the world, constantly renewing its violent mechanisms of enclosing the common, creating class divisions, and generating global hierarchies. David Harvey's analysis of neoliberalism as "accumulation by dispossession" is one of the most influential translations and repropositions of the continuing mechanisms of primitive accumulation.[47]

One risk of proposing a continuing process of primitive accumulation as a means to grasp the contemporary modes of extractivism, however, is that it tends to confuse the nature of the "outside" whose value is being extracted and accumulated and to eclipse, in particular, the extraction of forms of the common that result from social interaction and cooperation. In other words, if we are to recognize primitive accumulation as a continuing historical process, we have to articulate also how it changes radically: today's processes of enclosure and extraction are different than those of the past, and today's rentier of finance is nothing like the rentier of old. Condemnations of primitive accumulation, furthermore, must not create a mythic utopia of the precapitalist era, as if then the common, equality, and freedom defined social reality. That is certainly not Marx's view. On the contrary, he is quick to condemn the brutal forms of domination of precapitalist societies throughout the world, maintaining that liberation cannot be achieved by a return to the past but only by pushing forward through the historical process. Marx's *story about primitive accumulation should be read as a kind of parable, written in the style of political pamphlets, for which the precapitalist condition serves merely as an origin to emphasize the dramatic violence of capitalist development.*[48]

Another risk of interpreting neoliberalism and its processes of extraction in terms of primitive accumulation is that this focuses exclusively on the mode of accumulation, whereas we must grasp also changes of the mode of production. Although the common may appear, especially from the standpoint of those who extract it, as wealth that is simply there, preexisting, and thus available for accumulation, the common (even in its "natural" forms) is always in some measure a product of social cooperation, and it is continually redefined by the pressures of class struggle. Just as important as or even more important than revealing how the common is expropriated and accumulated is to investigate how, socially, it is produced, because there is where the most powerful forces of resistance and antagonism arise.

Marx's concept of "formal subsumption" provides a richer framework than primitive accumulation insofar as it reveals geographical and temporal differences and discontinuities by focusing on changes in production processes. Marx explains that as part of its development capital engages local, existing, noncapitalist labor practices (such as a traditional method of cutting sugar cane) and brings them into the capitalist production process while transforming them only "formally" (for instance, by paying workers a wage). The formal subsumption of labor under capital thus corresponds in part with primitive accumulation. At a certain point of capitalist development, Marx continues, traditional labor practices are destroyed and new practices created that are proper to capitalist production, often through the introduction of new technologies. This shift marks the passage from the formal subsumption to the real subsumption of labor under capital, which he calls the properly capitalist mode of production.[49]

The concept of formal subsumption has been particularly useful to emphasize how much the capitalist economy always contains elements of previous economic formations, and thus it helps avoid some of the political dead ends created by considering the development of capital in uniform, unilinear stages. In India, for example, in passionate debates beginning in the 1960s, the dominant line of communist theoreticians maintained that Indian agriculture remained semifeudal and semicolonial because peasants continued to produce under share-cropping relationships, perpetual indebtedness, and other conditions typical of precapitalist formations. Conceiving the remnants of feudalism as the primary obstacle to progress—and maintaining a linear conception of capitalist development—led communist party theorists to affirm that India had to become more fully capitalist before struggling against capital. "The orthodox Left parties," argues Praful Bidwai, "have thus ended up by supporting the emergent forces of agrarian capitalism to the hilt in the name of fighting feudalism."[50] To counter such analyses Jairus Banaji argued that Indian agriculture is defined by not semifeudalism but formal subsumption. The significance of this conceptual shift, he explains, is that "in the absence of a specifically capitalist mode of production on a national scale, capitalist relations of exploitation may nonetheless be widespread and dominant."[51] In India, in other words, the struggles of peasants against capitalist exploitation are already fully active and have no need to wait for the establishment of a more completely capitalist society. The concept of formal subsumption thus allows us to see both the plural nature of capitalist rule, which incorporates various productive relations from the past, and the plural forms of resistance within and against it.[52] All of these passages—from primitive accumulation to formal subsumption to real subsumption and from the accumulation of absolute surplus value to that of relative surplus value—are accompanied by not only a new social organization of exploitation but also new forms of struggle against exploitation, corresponding to the creation of a system of institutions predisposed to the struggle against "subsumed" labor.

Marx's concepts of formal and real subsumption—and, specifically, the passage between them—are rightly criticized by some contemporary Marxists for their linear notion of historical stages that assumes all regions of the globe will eventually follow the model of the dominant regions, casting their differences as mere remnants. First, like the critics of primitive accumulation, they argue we should disrupt any teleological historical trajectory from formal to real subsumption. Álvaro García Linera, for example, describes contemporary processes of globalization from the perspective of indigenous politics as a "perpetual primitive accumulation" driven by practices of formal subsumption.[53] Second, these authors raise the concern that real subsumption implies a homogeneous capitalist society, indifferent to geographical and cultural differences, whereas formal subsumption, since it constantly relies on the "outside" of capital and thus local practices and cultures, grasps and engages both cultural and historical differences. Formal subsumption, Harry Harootunian maintains, is the general rule for all capitalist development, which exists alongside processes of real subsumption. Formal subsumption functions as a hinge between the present and various pasts, revealing the different paths of capitalist development in different societies.[54]

Part of the richness of the category of formal subsumption is indeed that it reveals the economic and cultural differences of labor, land, society, and community that have been subsumed within capitalist production but maintain their connection to the territory and the past, especially to colonial histories. Recognition of continuing formal subsumption, however, should not blind us to really existing processes of real subsumption. The passage from formal to real does take place, but in a way that never exhausts the formal. Seeing them together, side-by-side, copresent in contemporary society, in fact, should reveal how real subsumption is not homogenous but shot through with differences created and re-created within the capitalist system.

Primitive accumulation and formal and real subsumption help us articulate, then, how today's centrality of extraction in its various faces—from the extraction of oil and minerals to the financial capture of value produced through social cooperation and popular forms of life—does not indicate either a further step in a linear history or a cyclical return to the past. Contemporary Marxist debates make clear instead that capitalist development is defined by multiple temporalities, mixing precapitalist and older capitalist methods with the newest technologies of production and control. Recognizing these multiple temporalities, furthermore, helps reveal the geographical, social, and cultural differences and hierarchies that constitute and perpetuate capitalist rule in a global frame. The challenge at this point will be to grasp how resistance and revolt can and does already emerge on this complex terrain.

CHAPTER 11

MONEY INSTITUTIONALIZES A SOCIAL RELATION

Money is one of the most ubiquitous features of our daily existence and yet it is among the least understood. It is difficult to comprehend not only what money is but also how it rules over us. Standard theories present money as an instrument that facilitates the exchange of goods and the storage of value, and thus a *neutral* instrument. Money may be wielded by the powerful and money may even be the expression of their power, according to this view, but money itself does not dictate or even favor any social arrangement or class structure. Money is power only in the sense that those who have it can use it to accomplish their will.

Many social and cultural analyses of money complicate the presumed neutrality of money by explaining the ways in which money is affected by social or cultural relations, dependent on relations of trust, accepted by convention, and so forth. All that is true, but when we look deeper we see that money is not just affected by social relations; money is itself a social relation. The dynamic between money and social relations, in other words, is not external but internal. It is more accurate and more useful, in fact, to define money by not what it *is* but what it *does*. Money designates and reproduces a specific social structure. Money *institutionalizes* a social relation—or, rather, a set of relations of social production and reproduction.[1]

To say that money is defined by how it institutionalizes a social relation is already implicit in Keynes's claim that "Money-of-Account, namely that in which Debts and Prices and General Purchasing Power are *expressed*, is the primary concept of a Theory of Money."[2] "Money-of-account" emphasizes money's determination of a schema of measure of the value in an entire social field. If measure were a simple matter of honest accounting, assigning everything its true value, then money could plausibly be considered a neutral instrument. But since value has no intrinsic, natural, or necessary measure, since a standard and a schema of measure express and reproduce an entire set of social relations and a mode of production, then money-of-account, through its function as measure, opens the theory of money onto the social and political terrain. The instability and its social and political determinants become increasingly clear, as we saw earlier, in the current period when various financial instruments serve to measure capitalist values.

We will only get so far, however, by trying to define what money is or even what it does in general. Money can be understood only by grasping how it is embedded in a determinate social formation and, in particular, a specific mode of production and exploitation.[3] The many treatises on money that sidestep the question of money's essential nature and instead begin by recounting the history of money are working on a correct intuition. In contrast to them, however, we will not look back to coins in the ancient world or medieval banks, but instead to the history of money within the capitalist mode of production, that is, how money institutionalizes and thus reproduces capitalist social relations and economic hierarchies through its different phases. Marx conceives of a direct relation in capitalist societies between the production of wealth and accumulation in the form of money. This is true in general because "the elementary precondition of bourgeois society [is] that labor should directly produce exchange value, i.e., money."[4] But the specific relationship that links modes of production to monetary production shifts significantly in the different phases or periods of capitalist production.

What is money and how does it rule?

The only way to get a clear view of what money is (and, more important, what money does) is to map the correspondences that link it to the social and productive relations that surround it. And since those correspondences change in line with shifts in the mode of production we should approach the contemporary role of money historically by sketching three broad phases of capital: the phase of so-called primitive accumulation, by which we mean here simply the period in which capital was accumulated primarily through the expropriation and enclosures of the commons in Europe and elsewhere through the various forms of theft that accompanied European conquest and colonization; the phase that stretches from the birth of manufacture through the dominance of large-scale industry over the global economy; and, finally, the contemporary, post-Fordist phase characterized by the realization of the world market and the forms of extraction typical of finance. Carlo Vercellone calls this the "phase of general intellect," assuming that the production of wealth is now characterized, within the capitalist system, by the hegemony of cognitive labor, laboring cooperation, digitization, and the biopolitical socialization of producing. We view this phase more generally as defined by social production. These are just the first coordinates of a map (or, really, three maps) that could be extended indefinitely.

The different forms of money correspond in each period to specific temporalities of production, consumption, and exploitation. In the phase of primitive accumulation, (1a) labor time was linked to the rhythms of the earth and the natural world: the work of fishermen and agriculturalists was measured with the tides, the light of day, the cycles of seasons, the time of tasks—the time it takes to milk the cows, the time to weave a blanket, and so forth. The passage to the dominance of industry creates, as E. P. Thompson explains, (2a) a new inner sense of time, dictated by the precision and homogeneous units of the clock and divided by the working day into periods of production and reproduction.[5] A new sense of time emerges in the current phase (3a), a continuous, undulating time that sheds the solid boundaries of both industrial time and primitive accumulation. Today the divisions of the working day are breaking down as work time and life time are increasingly mixed and we are called on to be productive throughout all times of life.[6] With your smartphone in hand, you are never really away from work or off the clock, and for a growing number of people, constant access not only confuses the boundaries between work and leisure but also eats into the night and sleep. At all hours you can check your e-mail or shop for shoes, read news updates or visit porn sites. The capture of value tends to extend to envelop all the time of life. We produce and consume in a global system that never sleeps. In the nonstop rhythms of neoliberalism we are, as Jonathan Crary says, progressively "dispossessed of time."[7] In correspondence with these shifting temporalities money today becomes ever more fluid and its measures less distinct, beginning perhaps with the "floating" exchange rates initiated by the decoupling of the US dollar from the gold standard in 1971. "Perhaps it is money," writes Gilles Deleuze, analyzing this shift, "that expresses the distinction between the two societies [disciplinary society and the society of control] best, since discipline always referred back to minted money that locks gold as numerical standard, while control relates to floating rates of exchange, modulated according to a rate established by a set of standard currencies."[8] The guarantees and solid pillars that support money in the phase of industrial discipline are progressively dissolved and money is unmoored in the phase of financial control.

Money corresponds in each phase to different forms of the extraction of value, which is to say, different means of exploitation. In the phase of primitive accumulation, (1b) exploitation is accumulated in absolute surplus value through the dispossession and extraction of the common; and, at the monetary level, as a standard money, adequate to an accumulation based on possession, a fixed and strong measure in the guarantee of power. In the phase from the birth of manufacture until industrial capital becomes the protagonist of the economy, we have (2b) an exploitation exercised primarily through the extraction of relative surplus value from a stable working class centered on large-scale industry, whose reproduction was guaranteed by the family wage and welfare structures. The corresponding money was formatted for the investment and credit needs of industrial management and industrial society. By the time of the New Deal in the United States, a series of state guarantees of investments and credit, such as federal deposit insurance, were emblematic of the ways that this money constituted an industrial-class compromise. When the productive forms of post-Fordism emerge, dominated by finance capital, we have (3b) a social, cognitive, biopolitical exploitation addressed to biopolitical surplus value extracted from a precarious class of workers as well as from reproductive activities and the terrains defined by the new commons. The money created by the financial conventions links biopolitical surplus value and rent (financial rent, property rent, and so forth) and also removes all the guarantees of the previous period. Melinda Cooper calls this "shadow money," that is, money whose value is not formally underwritten or backstopped by the state. Whereas monetary guarantees previously corresponded to guarantees of employment, now the monetary instability of finance and speculation correspond to the precarity of labor.[9]

The figure of money in each of these phases also corresponds to distinct modes and spheres of the extraction of value. We thus can add to our map (1c) processes in which extraction involves the localized, immediate, and violent capture—the dispossession of labor and the commons; (2c) forms of extraction that correspond to industrial exploitation, an extraction measured by the portions of the working day; and (3c) the extraction of value from the circulation of commodities, created by banks, taken from the common wealth of productive social cooperation. The intensification of exploitation increases in parallel with its spatial extension—up to the point that value is extracted throughout the entire society. Here finance capital represents the material fabric of the constitution of value. But to the same extent that the formation of value implies an entire social system, here the form of value implies a form of life. In the contemporary phase, Christian Marazzi writes, money is "a *form of value*, a sedimentation in time of the forms of social activity that contribute to the production and the distribution of wealth....Money as a form of value is thus the set of relations, institutions, symbols, ideas, products of economic life, 'culture' in both its linguistic and material forms, in which is fixed the incessant flow of life."[10]

The relationship of money to property—money as a form of property—emerges here: the shifts in the dominant figure of capitalist property determine and correspond to distinct forms of money. Capitalist money, as many authors emphasize, is credit that has become impersonal and transferable. We have to look beyond the particular instances of the credit-debt relation, however, as Gunnar Heinsohn and Otto Steiger claim, to recognize the general nature of money as property; specifically, in their terms, money is "anonymized title to property."[11] This definition illuminates well the contours of the passage from the money of primitive accumulation to that of the era of industry. The dominant figure prior to large-scale industry (1d) was immobile property, land most importantly, which in the final instance is grounded in a personal relation to the sovereign. With legal transformations such as the Enclosure Acts in England, land became transferable in this period, but with a series of drags or resistances. Mobile property (2d), such as the innumerable commodities flowing out of the factories, is the characteristic property of the next period, and with it money takes ever more impersonal and mobile forms. The passage to the present era has brought a new dominant figure of property (3d), which intensifies the characteristics of anonymity and mobility. In contrast to the materiality of industrial commodities and the physical restrictions of use (that is, the logic of scarcity), the dominant figures of property in the contemporary era—including code, images, cultural products, patents, knowledge, and the like—are largely immaterial and, more important, indefinitely reproducible. The floating, liquid nature of money, correspondingly, is embodied increasingly in digital and anonymized platforms (sometimes also through decentralized experiments such as bitcoin and etherium).

The considerations of money as a form of property lead us to rethink the modes of exploitation and appropriation of mental energies and the appropriation of cognitive labor-power, that is, the brains of workers. But this form of labor-power should be situated in a historical series of the shifts of the composition of labor-power. In a first phase (1e), concurrent with primitive accumulation, a generic labor-power was pushed toward manufacture and the factories, after having been expropriated of the common resources of survival. Labor-power is absorbed into the productive machines of nascent capitalism and submitted to a massive *dressage*. The intelligence of the worker is considered at this point simply a natural quality of the "human biped" that substitutes for the quadruped in giving energy and being exploited, such that the *dressage* of bodies and that of brains functions together. One should not forget, of course, that in this form of exploitation the working day of artisanal workers is still in many respects managed in an independent way and characterized by the pride of their profession. Only with growing industrialization is their professional independence eliminated, to the point that the knowledge of the worker becomes totally subjugated to the mechanical processes of valorization. In the next phase (2e), characterized by the first massification of labor-power in manufacture and developing toward a more complete industrial massification (creating a mass worker), the capitalist system imposes a more complete subjugation of the bodies of workers. Taylorist methods and the scientific organization of work more generally absorb cognitive labor. And yet here exploited labor begins to appear as a mass opposed to command, and within this subjugated mass are liberated new technical knowledges; within this intimate relationship between fixed capital and variable capital, as we saw in part II, the efforts of the class of capitalists to discipline the mass worker begin to break down, specifically with regard to the cognitive capacities of workers. The social crisis of Fordism and, more generally, factory production in the dominant countries thus reveals the upheaval resulting from (3e) the emergence of cognitive labor. "In this mutation," writes Carlo Vercellone,

> the organization of productive activities situated at the center of the process of the creation of surplus value depends always less on the technical decomposition of the production of labor in elementary and repetitive tasks prescribed by management. It is founded instead more and more on the cognitive organization of labor based on the polyvalence and the complementarity of diverse *blocs of knowledge* that the workers mobilize collectively to realize a productive project and to adapt to a dynamic of continuous change.[12]

Here money, as the institutionalization of a social relation, as a social technology, must bend to the abstraction and maximum volatility that the mode of cognitive labor presents. Social "informationalization" and industrial automation (in addition to the centrality of research and development) make cognitive labor "eponymous" with the contemporary productive era.

Money can also be described in reference to different temporalities of realization, which imply a process that moves from (1f) an initial, "synchronic" relation (in which valorization is realized in the immediate transformation of possession into money) up to figures in which money is valorized in increasingly extended time periods, in the circulation and the progressive extraction of the new commons. Gradually, (2f) synchrony is replaced by the temporality of credit of financial investments and, finally, (3f) that of the future-oriented projects of financial agreements. In other words, with respect to the passage from Fordism to post-Fordism, one should add that, whereas (Fordist) credit capital is predicated on the capital-labor relationship—and thus obligated, so to speak, to follow closely the material relationship of exploitation—finance capital is a machine predisposed to future investment. It anticipates every industrial and monetary realization, and it is thus exposed to a higher level of risk that it can control only through state power. This verifies Marx's dictum regarding money: "Its functional existence so to speak absorbs its material existence."[13]

Since this process or flow of monetary value, linked to the relationship of capital, is an antagonistic relationship, class struggle too is formed differently in this relationship. In a regime of primitive accumulation (1g), popular struggles oppose the theft of the commons and the proletariat seeks the means of subsistence and survival. The old forms, either in mass *jacqueries* or small acts of sabotage, that emerge from peasant and plebeian cultures are introduced into the world of capitalist labor. In the wage regime of industrial production (2g), the working class is presented as an "independent variable" that seeks the stability of the direct wage and the indirect wage (that is, welfare). The strike becomes here an essential instrument of struggle, and its force, as a means of resistance and making demands, takes on a political form, directed by the working class. Money assumes here a (Keynesian) function of mediating class struggle. Finally, in the regime of finance capital (3g), class struggle is born from the recognition of the unity of capitalist command, which being socialized is abstract to the point that its mediation cannot but be a power (and thus the opposite of a form of mediation). The proletariat—all those who produce and reproduce social wealth—reduced to a purely precarious role, engages struggles around a social wage of citizenship. Class struggle, therefore, extending beyond the factory, permeates all of society. The social strike thus becomes the form of mobilization of large social sectors to maintain or enlarge welfare, and class struggle becomes completely political or, better, biopolitical.[14]

The political figures of work, whether in syndicalist form and whether immediately political or not, contribute to defining monetary relations also in another way. In the phase of primitive accumulation, (1h) the authorities that presided over monetary policy began to settle accounts with workers' guilds and with the mutualistic structures (which no longer simply distributed the surpluses of lordly luxury as acts of charity and philanthropy), the presence of which affected the domestic market, weakening mercantilist policies and those of physiocratic liberalism. Emblematic, in this regard, was the law proposed by Louis-Michel Le Peletier against any form of labor organizing during the French Revolution. Such disturbance of monetary relations expanded in the period of manufacture and large-scale industry (2h). Trade union action, now structurally tied to political and party organizations acting on the parliamentary level, was able to affect the structure of industrial salaries—both direct wages of workers and indirect, social incomes—and thus the organic composition of capital itself, that is, the relation between constant and variable capital. Money cannot be indifferent to the institutional movements and the Keynesian monetary policies born as attempts to regulate these relationships. Finally (3h), as the value of money is being determined on the global terrain, it undergoes conflicts with the restless movements of the multitude and diverse social coalitions.

One set of theories of money focuses on the institutions that have the power to create money, and in each of the three phases of the capitalist mode of production the combination and priority of those institutions shift. Class rule is supported and reproduced, from this perspective, not only because the ruling class possesses most of the money but also and primarily because its institutions have the power to create it. In the period of primitive accumulation, (1i) states and banks maintain a monopoly over the creation of money. States create money through control over the currency and, most important, by declaring what it will accept for the discharge of tax debt; banks create money primarily in the form of credit by making loans of greater value than their reserves. There is competition at times but also a profound collaboration between states and banks in the creation and management of money. Whereas in the phase of primitive accumulation, states maintain relative control over banks, in the phase of large-scale industry (2i), this priority tends to be reversed. As Hilferding and Lenin recognized, the birth of finance capital corresponds to the predominance of banks in the direction and coordination of production. In this period industrial firms are also sources of the creation of money. Bernard Schmitt, for example, explains how, through the circulation of money in the production process, industry creates money. Money is "enriched" in the industrial process like blood is enriched in circulation: "blood does not circulate always the same, identical to itself: it is enriched by oxygen and then depleted. In the same way, money in circulation in the body of society is enriched with objective power to purchase the current products, and then it loses its power with the final purchase of these goods."[15] In the phase of industrial hegemony, the creation of money is thus accomplished by the state-bank-corporation nexus. Finally, in the contemporary phase (3i), the creation of money is determined primarily by financial instruments. Finance summarizes all the previous modes (banks and businesses backed by state guarantees) and adds to them a further, "extractive" means of creating money. To some extent, financial instruments generate money in the manner of lending banks, that is, by lending more money than they have. In a less obvious way, but perhaps more importantly, finance generates money in the manner of business, that is, through the capture of value socially produced. The generation of money by rent-bearing capital stands in relation to that of industrial capital as the apparatus of capture in relation to profit. Finance has today achieved dominance over the other capitalist institutions of the power to create money: state, bank, and business.

Finally, one can also pose with respect to monetary forms (if we allow ourselves rather broad analogies) different forms of government. In sections h and i above we concentrated primarily on the "internal" dynamics, and now we should move, as much as possible, to a global perspective. The monarchies of conquest and colonization designated the form of government (1j) that best suited the state guarantee and the faith of the capitalist class in a money of violent accumulation, the dispossession of the commons, and the definition of private property in terms of standard measure. The money of the great European powers of this phase stood firmly on not only the gold and silver stolen from the mines of Guinea and Potosí but also the slave trade, slave production, the expropriation of lands through the exterminations of native peoples, and so many other brutal methods. The ingots that supported the money of this phase were mixed with equal parts of gold and blood. In the phase of manufacturing and industrial accumulation (2j), oligarchic capitalist governments wedded with imperialist regimes corresponded to the control of credit money or investment money in the function of the production construction of political and social mediations. The governments of this phase are no less brutal and bloody than those of primitive accumulation but their violence tends to take different forms. The slave plantations in the Americas coexist for a long period with the creation of factories in Europe: the plantation in many ways provides a testing ground and a blueprint for the industrial organization of labor and its disciplinary *dispositifs*. Imperialist regimes created myriad such divisions and correspondences between industrial exploitation in the dominant parts of the world and a wide variety of brutal methods of disciplining in the subordinated. The "sound money" and monetary guarantees of the dominant nation-states rested not so much on gold reserves but on value extracted by the intertwined disciplinary regimes of industry and imperialism. Finally, a global form of governance, a distributed and multilevel Empire (3j) is emerging today to organize money as a form of life and biopolitical institution of labor and exploitation (and to establish the political control necessary for the reproduction of a class society). Nation-states, especially the dominant ones, fulfill essential functions in this emerging form of governance but they are not able, even together in multilateral collaboration, to exert sovereign control. Financial markets, instead, are key to the creation today of something approaching a world money, which is based on the abstraction and extraction, the biopolitical exploitation, of the value produced by social life in its entirety.

The following table summarizes the social relations that the changing forms of money institutionalize.

The Social Relations of Capitalist Money

	1. Primitive accumulation	2. Manufacture and large-scale industry	3. Social production
a. Temporalities of production	Labor time of tasks and natural rhythms	Clock time and the division of the working day	24/7 time of the nonstop global system
b. Forms of value	Absolute surplus value	Relative surplus value	Biopolitical surplus value

	1. Primitive accumulation	2. Manufacture and large-scale industry	3. Social production
c. Modes of extraction	Extraction as conquest and dispossession	Industrial exploitation and colonial extraction	Extraction as appropriation of the common
d. Forms of property	Immobile property	Mobile property	Reproducible property
e. Compositions of labor-power	Artisanal labor and *dressage* of generic labor	Manufacturing and the scientific organization of industrial labor	Social and cognitive labor
f. Temporalities of realization	Synchronic realization of value	Temporality of the Fordist credit regime	Financial realization projected to the future
g. Forms of class struggle	Popular struggles or *jacqueries*	Working-class struggles and strikes	Biopolitical class struggles and social strikes
h. Forms of antagonistic political organization	Guilds and mutualistic structures	Trade unions and parties	Social coalitions
i. Sources of monetary creation	State-bank creation of money	State-bank-corporation creation of money	Financial creation of money
j. Forms of governance	Colonial monarchies and sovereignty	Imperialist oligarchies of discipline	Empire and biopolitical control

Objektiver Geist

Georg Simmel, in his sociological analysis of money, emphasizes both its impersonal (that is, objective) character and its social generality: money is objektiver Geist, objective spirit. Stripped of its Hegelian clothing, this formula means that money institutionalizes the structure of social relations: Geist indicates the social structure; and objective rather than subjective Geist refers to the institutional, structural social formation. Simmel's formula is thus in line with and condenses brilliantly a tradition that interprets money in the era of industrial capital as an institution that structures the entire social terrain.[16]

Simmel is perhaps the first philosopher to develop his research within a completely "reified" world, that is, reduced to a horizon of commodities, and he does so in materialist terms. Neither Bergson, who evokes social flows that are ever more spiritual, nor Heidegger, who links reification to a being that cannot be saved, does that. Simmel recognizes a contemporary condition in which money has become the horizon of life, the lived experience of human interchange. He then defines its objective figure as measure of the social division of labor and of society in its entirety. Some of the authors who followed after him, such as Lukács and Adorno, develop this image, enlarging and deepening the concept of reification well beyond the shadow that money casts over society, analyzing the reification of both nature and civilization. We will return to these problems shortly, linking this specific determination of money, as a complex function, to the analysis of the social reality, of the factory and the metropolis, of the market and its state organization.

One wonderful aspect of Simmel's sociology of money is the way that, by grasping the flow of value and its transformations as dynamics of subjectivity, he manages to anticipate central aspects of the passage from large-scale industry to the new biopolitical forms of accumulation. Many authors living in the heart of Paris and Berlin in the early twentieth century, including Lukács, Benjamin, and Kracauer, were able, in different ways, to interpret the social forms of finance capital, but Simmel was able also to read the seeds of its future transformations. He anticipates the power of money in a society tragically commodified, but a society that is also pervaded by the production of subjectivity: "The process by which labour becomes a commodity is thus only one side of the far-reaching process of differentiation by which specific contents of the personality are detached in order for them to confront the personality as objects with an independent character and dynamics."[17] Simmel emphasizes the growing social role of the intellect and cognitive production as parallel to the expansion of the money economy. "This form of life not only presupposes a remarkable expansion of mental processes . . . but also their intensification, a fundamental re-orientation of culture towards intellectuality. The idea that life is essentially based on intellect, and that intellect is accepted in practical life as the most valuable of our mental energies, goes hand in hand with the growth of a money economy." Economic value thus reflects and transforms the social world of subjective and intellectual development: it objectifies subjective values. Money is "a reification of the general form of existence according to which things derive their significance from their relationship to each other."[18]

These processes of objectification and reification, however, do not flatten the social field. Instead society is characterized by a constant play between economic, commodity, and monetary pressures and the emergence of singular subjectivities and forms of life. When recognizing the city as a zone of reification, Simmel (like Henri Lefebvre and David Harvey, two other authors who study the city in similar ways) recognizes it is not a pale, devitalized, or inexpressive context but a fabric on which, under the weight of domination, life does not stop. The reified city is a world of living, plural, dialectical relationships and effects, on whose monstrous surface act resistant forms of life. This would be more Terry Gilliam's Brazil than Fritz Lang's Metropolis.

Simmel does at times sing the praises of finance capital and its styles of life. Money payment, he claims, is "the form most congruent with personal freedom," and money establishes a general relation "between a money economy and the principle of individualism."[19] Is Simmel spinning mystifications? Probably. He cannot manage to transform his analytical and critical standpoint into a praxis of liberation. Lukács calls him a "real philosopher of impressionism" and attacks him, precisely, for his allusive views on money.[20] But Simmel's occasional mystifications regarding money and finance should not blind us to the real power of his analysis. The impressionistic analytic is exemplary as an intuition or, better, an anticipation of the future in which money and finance extract value biopolitically from the production of subjectivity.

For Simmel money retains an ontological character, which means, in part, that money is not merely for counting or storing value. Money instead is the reality of a social relationship, indicating, variously, the division of labor, the separation of the social classes, the synthesis of physicality and intellectuality, or the superposition of subjection and freedom. There is always an ontological level, that is, a historically determinate social relationship, from which money cannot be freed. There is no money stripped of social relationships; it is always clothed with social being, and thus always a biopolitical figure.

It is thus difficult to square Simmel's notion of money with the claims of various contemporary digital currencies, which are presented as mere vehicles of value, outside of social life. Digital currencies, even when autonomous from states and generated by algorithmic machines, will be no different at heart than other contemporary forms of money as long as they continue to reinforce the dominant social relations. A new money, to use *our earlier formulation, must institutionalize a new social relation. Even if the current digital currencies cannot do this, however, we should read in the enthusiasm that they often generate, in addition to the dreams of some to get rich quick, the utopian desire of a money that could indicate and express a fundamentally new society.*[21]

One should ask, at this point, whether for Simmel money is free of relations of power. He does not really pose this question, perhaps deluded by the supposed neutrality of sociological research. But for one who has so deeply studied the worldly reality of money and who allows us to consolidate (from an ontological standpoint) the efforts of comprehension and classification, it is easy to recognize in him an untamed critical spirit that, having grasped with such lucidity the money-reification relationship, does not shy away from this question.

Like Simmel, David Harvey understands money in terms of social value conceived most generally.[22] Whereas Simmel's analysis stops with the fact that *objektiver Geist* is a structured, institutionalized world in which the relationships interpreted by money have replaced nature with the metropolis, that is, the objective spirit of the productive machine of the being together of subjects, Harvey goes one step further, drawing the consequences of the power relationships that Simmel does not manage to confront. Money, he asserts, claims to represent the value of social labor but in many respects distorts or even falsifies it: "This gap between money and the value it represents constitutes a foundational contradiction of capital."[23] And the contradiction, for him, is a potential point of departure for struggling against capitalist social relations and, eventually, creating an alternative.

On private property and its dematerialization

The dominant figures of property today—such as code, images, information, knowledges, and cultural products, often protected by copyrights and patents—are largely immaterial and reproducible. This dematerialization of property seems to proceed hand in hand with the dematerialization of money. And yet what appears dematerialized with regard to *form* is much less so (or not at all) with regard to *relationships*. These, in fact, are the substance that defines the social order.

Gunnar Heinsohn and Otto Steiger emphasize how the system of property relations remains central in the transformation of monetary forms. Money, they claim, cannot be understood only in terms of credit: "money is created in a credit contract but is not itself a credit"; instead, they argue, as we noted earlier, money itself is "anonymized title to property."[24] Recognizing money as title to property is important because that is how money is materialized, despite its appearing dematerialized when considering only its form. Here instead, for Heinsohn and Steiger the form is absorbed in the relationship: the history of money is stripped from its merely formal existence and seen instead as an interpretation and guarantee of value. At the same time, money and property cannot be separated from the market and its fluctuations—as when some consider property the refuge in the final instance for the possessor of money. In fact, money is not title to any specific property—it is anonymized title, and in this way money refers to (and reproduces) the entire system of property relations. Money reproduces not so much the material figure of property but the set of conditions that permit the existence of a society of private law (or private property, contract, credit, and individual rights), understood as the interindividual fabric and institutional structure of the social order.

Ordoliberal and neoliberal economists generally take the opposing view and contest the possibility of a passage from property as title to property as relationship (thus maintaining a substantialist conception of the property-institution-money relationship). This ordoliberal position dominated German economics after the Second World War and was central in the constitution of the European Union. It presented conflicting claims, however, affirming the absolute pre-eminence of the market, active property, and *homo economicus*, but also insisting that the state ultimately underwrite and support property relations. Whereas property appears as a title of citizenship, property relations and market order are made independent of the social relations and relations of force among the classes. An "independent" central bank guarantees the monetary measures of this order. This is, obviously, a debatable ideological claim, but it is politically potent and, as we said, was realized both in Europe and elsewhere in the latter half of the twentieth century. In this context, property—and here ordoliberalism reveals its profound kinship with neoliberalism—is not only a "right" but also a "sphere of rights," a general rule of value and the organization of social life.[25] In ordoliberalism this ideological proposition is legitimated by a political project to support property and business, with some reactionary inflections regarding small agricultural property, for example, "the peasant node of political economy" in Wilhelm Röpke's work.[26] This materialization (or in Röpke even naturalization) of money today sounds so antiquated!

Much more effective and contemporary is the vision of property of Walter Euken, founder of the ordoliberal school in Freiburg, whose philosophical thought is grounded in Edmund Husserl's intentional logic. Euken's institutionalism is based on the assumption that property and market spring from nature and are constituted in an "ontological" dimension, balancing needs for security and trust in institutions. (Another characteristic element of ordoliberalism—the Freiburg school, in particular—is that it brings together the work of philosophers, economics, and legal scholars to form a coherent theoretical complex.) The constitutional order of property and the market becomes an insuperable horizon, and the state becomes the "guardian of a competitive order." Ordoliberalism thus becomes a theory of private property institutionally supported by the state and an independent central bank that guarantees the value of money. This last point creates the break between Euken and Hayek, effectively dividing ordoliberalism and neoliberalism (after they together flirted with the Mont Pellerin Society). But, despite this break, they still share a common dogma: the absolute defense of private property. The difference is merely in the means to realize that goal.[27]

A central historical moment in the gradual "dematerialization" of money was the 1971 US decision to decouple the dollar from the gold standard, the so-called Nixon Shock, which demonstrated how much free-market liberalism and the international monetary order had been an illusion. The dollar had become the global standard and its increased power aided the imperial materialization of US monetary command. There was no longer pretense in this framework of any "real" relationship between property and money and no longer any basis for maintaining an equilibrium between them, no fixed or "natural" rule, independent from the historical development of political command.

It was inevitable that monetary crises would proliferate in this new era, and we will return to them in the next section. There appeared to be a flight of money not only from private property but also from the very equilibriums that the nation-states established between the value of money and social relationships (including property relations). When the equilibriums are gone, command is all that remains. The financialization of the economy, in which this command is incarnated today, is increasingly global: monetary engineering imposes a fluid mechanics on the banking system. On this basis arise perverse phenomena, such as the securitization of debt that led, in the first decade of this century, to the explosion of the subprime bubble. These events, driven by a tireless financialization, have become so widespread and continuous that they undermine every attempt to rearrange and reestablish a stable relationship between money and value, creating an infernal circle with no exit. Financialization, Christian Marazzi argues, is no longer a parasitical deviation of the economy but instead its dominant form, coordinated with the new processes of the production of value. Financialization and the financial crises that follow from it have become, in fact, the primary form of the accumulation of capital.[28]

The dematerialization of property can also be recognized in the shift, which scholars have analyzed for more than a century, from the "property enterprise" to the "managerial enterprise." Whether ownership is maintained in the hands of a single family or spread widely among many shareholders, the manager increasingly assumes the position of control. The entrepreneurial function gains autonomy with respect to property and the manager is transformed into an "entrepreneur without property," which emerges as the dominant figure in business. Financial globalization further accelerates this process. The world of neoliberal production and accumulation requires financial management, rather than the old functions of the business owner. Entrepreneurship thus loses the characteristics that used to make the relationship between property and enterprise the center of development, and the fable of the heroic business owner evaporates, along with all the ideological claims that from Locke onward linked property and enterprise to labor. On the financial horizon, where money is king, the dematerialization of property is, in the end, celebrated by the new managerial figures of business command.

These consequences of the neoliberal (and, even more, ordoliberal) Geist of private property demonstrate the extent to which private property has been emptied of material bases. And as private property is dematerialized, the nature of money is revealed to be ever more purely political. This is why to understand how money functions today we must focus on no longer a stable *form* of money but instead the changing *relationships* among property owners and political forces. We should not be surprised, then, when right-wing voices in the United States, including politicians and "respectable" economists, indignantly demand the abolition of the Federal Reserve. Such calls to defend "sound money" are merely political attempts to return to the social order (with its hierarchies and forms of command) that money previously institutionalized while claiming those social relations are natural and necessary.

Crises arise from below

Up to this point we have analyzed the capitalist transformation and management of social production (and exploitation) under the hegemony of money and finance as a relatively linear process. But, in fact, this process is composed of cycles punctuated by spectacular crises. The onset of crisis may be sudden and unexpected, but capital always manages quickly to govern it politically and set in motion a machine of restructuring. After crisis strikes, capital transforms the social and political horizon so as to make workers and the poor pay the bill. Capital introduces new automation, raising both productivity and unemployment; it increases poverty and threatens the survival of the poor, lowering the (direct and indirect forms of) relative wage; it abolishes legislation that had protected workers; and, perhaps most important, capital uses crisis as an opportunity to further privatize public and common services and goods. Disaster capitalism: capital uses crises to leap forward in its project of social transformation.[29]

The neoliberal view of cycle and crisis preserves some elements of previous capitalist theories but adds a new inflection. Whereas Keynes considered the business cycle a process that progressively gathers together the factors of social production, and whereas in Schumpeter that gathering can take place only on condition that periodically the structures of production and its technologies are (creatively) destroyed and reconstructed, the neoliberal approach seeks opportunities to increase the distance (and thus the abstraction) of capitalist command from productive and reproductive processes. The relationships of production, which mark the terrain of inevitable and continuous social conflicts, have always been a nightmare for capitalists, who would wish them away if they could. They pretend that production refers only to stock market values and that the relationships of production and reproduction are configured only through money and its control by the collective capitalist— ultimately by "independent" central banks! It is easy to see how ridiculous this idea is, like the ideology of the end of history. But that does not necessarily make it any less effective.

We need to recognize, despite neoliberal ideology that obscures the terrain of social production, that crisis, although governed from above, always *arises from below*, from the antagonisms, resistances, and demands that course through capitalist society. The current crisis is one demonstration, among many, of how this comes about. Thus far we have analyzed the development of neoliberalism only in single frames and scenes. Now the film can be assembled and completed. For the origins of the current crisis we need to look back not to 2007 but the 1970s, the height of the long cycle of struggles that threatened the capitalist order, when the Keynesian equilibrium of postwar growth was falling apart. That is when capital's frantic search for a response began.

Already in the 1970s many radical economists—including Joachim Hirsch, Claus Offe, James O'Connor, Nicos Poulantzas, the French authors of the regulation school, and the Italian *operaisti*—developed critical analyses of the emerging neoliberal uses of and responses to crisis.[30] They examined the series of capitalist policies intended to go beyond Keynesianism and the (futile) attempts to maintain a link between economic development and representative democracy. And, most important, they highlighted the state regulatory mechanisms designed to respond to the social and class struggles of the 1960s and '70s, offering a powerful framework for understanding both how the crisis was born and how capitalist forces were weathering and managing it. It was obvious to them that crisis had welled up *from below*, driven by the accumulation of demands for social justice, including pressure for increased wages and welfare—and, ultimately, that any solution would have to be grounded in the power of the struggles.

These authors focused in particular on the monetary regime because that is mainly where the capitalist response was centered. The strategy of inflation in the 1970s, for instance, had two primary effects: from one side, the impoverishment of social sectors that relied on fixed incomes, effectively reducing wages, and, from the other, favoring business and corporate borrowers. "[I]nflation," wrote Lapo Berti at the time, "was revealed to be not a contingent disturbance or an abnormal phenomenon of the process of development, but rather a necessary mode of the entire process of the production and reproduction of capital, once it had reached a certain level of development."[31] Crisis, then, which came from below, from the struggles, from the antagonistic dynamic, drove capitalist development—and it was controlled from above primarily through inflation first and financialization later.

Wolfgang Streeck, who builds on the work of these authors, analyzes the current crisis similarly as arising from below. He understands the capitalist response as a *Zeit-kaufe*, an attempt to buy time and to defer the most violent effects of crisis, but even though today's processes of financialization were initiated to defuse the power of class and social struggles, in the end instead of righting the capitalist ship they further deepened its crisis.[32] Streeck understands the development of the current crisis and responses to it in three stages. When the 1970s policies of inflation became unsustainable and ineffective, and when the so-called fiscal state became unable to meet with tax revenues the spending imposed on it by the demands of workers' movements and other social movements, that first stage passed into a second in which state debt progressively became the prime mechanism to guarantee the regulation and reproduction of the capitalist system. The "tax state," Streeck claims, was transformed into a "debt state."[33] As nation-states became ever more indebted to financial markets, their sovereignty declined and they became increasingly subject to international pressures of creditors and international organs of control. The global markets imposed a sort of international "justice" on nation-states. Finally, beginning in the 1990s, with the increasingly unsustainable indebtedness of states, public debt was shifted to private hands primarily through processes of financialization, which at first seemed to calm but soon greatly exacerbated the crisis. Finance capital, now organized globally, is able to impose its own sovereignty directly over populations—a sovereignty that is not legitimate or legal in any traditional sense but nonetheless effective, a sovereignty that increasingly enacts the depoliticization of the economy and the de-democratization of politics.

We are in broad agreement with Streeck's analysis up to this point: inflation, public debt, and private debt are so many mechanisms to "buy time" and defer the crisis, although none of them can address its foundations. But after having magisterially analyzed the role of resistance and revolt in initiating the crisis—recognizing the "revolutionary" responsibility of the working class and social struggles of the 1960s and '70s—Streeck then drops them completely: in his estimation, in fact, all antagonistic subjects capable of challenging capitalist rule have now disappeared.[34] Certainly, if you are looking for a working class with the political composition it had in the twentieth century, you will not find it here. But you have to recognize that living labor, even when disorganized, even when reduced to precarity, is still there and, moreover, that production has taken increasingly social forms, in intellectual, cognitive, affective, and cooperative relationships. Moreover, even though neoliberalism seeks to produce docile subjects compatible with its rule, there continually arise new subjectivities that are social and intelligent—capable of spawning new crises and, ultimately, challenging capitalist rule. The current situation is constituted by a new relationship of power: between a capitalist command organized through finance that accumulates through the extraction of value generated in social production and ever more socialized productive forces, which are sometimes difficult to recognize but whose power is real.

Analyzing the ways that capital uses and manages crisis from above and how it profits from disasters is certainly important—and the indignation it generates is often satisfying. But it is crucial also to read crisis from below and recognize the power of the social forces that give rise to it. Throughout the periods of the current crisis, from the 1970s to today, while capital has invented new tactics to combat or accommodate mass social and worker struggles, the forces of resistance have adapted too. Despite all the mechanisms that extract the value they produce, they have been enriched by widespread knowledges, social capacities, and potentials for subjectification. The same forces that gave rise to crisis, from below, now must be able to move beyond the capitalist crisis machine. They will have to write the next chapter in this story.

Marxist debates 2: Crisis

Marxist authors have long debated the nature and causes of capitalist crises, and, moreover, the regularity and inevitability of crises is central to their condemnation of the rule of capital. Contemporary capitalist crises, however, do not fit well in the primary models that Marx himself formulated, at least those most often cited. Other aspects of Marx's work, in fact, are more useful for interpreting capitalist crisis in the age of social production and financial extraction.

Marx's most widespread views about crisis focus on the anarchic nature of capitalist production and circulation, and thus the periodic imbalances that interrupt the process.[35] A first group of his observations regards "horizontal" coordination failures among parts of the cycle, for example, among sectors of production and circulation. Blockage at any stage can throw the entire system into crisis. A second set of analyses focuses on the "vertical" disproportions between production and consumption, that is, crises that result from overproduction or underconsumption. The ultimate cause of capitalist crisis, from this perspective, is the poverty (and hence the limited potential for consumption) of the population coupled with the drive of capital constantly to increase production. Analysis of such horizontal and vertical breakdowns is certainly still important today, but that is not enough to explain crises of recent decades. A contemporary theory of crisis (Marxist or other) must address the expanding socialization of labor-power and the growing command of finance and money.

Perhaps paradoxically, Marx's much maligned theory of the tendency of the rate of profit to fall helps us better understand crisis in the contemporary world. It is true that relating crises to the falling rate of profit presupposes too many intermediate steps to be a particularly useful theory when seen in crude objective terms, as economists generally understand it. But when we see the law from the standpoint of the working class and as a result of social antagonism, then things look somewhat different. The law says, in essence, that in the course of development the average social rate of profit tends to fall in proportion to the progressive concentration of capital: value invested in fixed capital, such as machinery, increases with respect to that invested in labor both in order to increase productivity and to minimize exposure to worker antagonism. Capital is forced to ever higher levels of concentration, which exacerbate the conditions for crisis. When Marx claims that the real limit to capitalist production is capital itself, then, he means that capitalist crisis is neither pathological nor accidental, but is part and parcel of its development's inner essence and tendency.

Even though he conceives it as a law, Marx does not burden this theory with catastrophist implications—in fact, he proceeds immediately to consider all the countervailing tendencies. One particularly useful observation is that the centralization of capital dictated by the law brings with it an increasing socialization of production: "production loses its private character," he asserts, "and becomes a social process, not formally—in the sense that all production subject to exchange is social because of the dependence of the producers on one another and the necessity for presenting their labour as abstract social labour— but in actual fact. For the means of production are employed as communal, social means of production, and therefore are not determined by the fact that they are the property of an individual, but by their relation to production, and the labour likewise performed on a social scale."[36] The centralization of capital, then, in addition to fostering crises, increases the socialization of production, and thus raises the specter of the powers of social labor— which, of course, portends further crises.

When we adopt Marx's theory of the falling rate of profit as a motor of crises today, however, we are faced with at least two important difficulties. The first is the totalizing relationship he assumes between capital (which as it accumulates creates a general rate of profit) and the entire mass of labor-power, that is, the multitude exploited on a social scale. This perspective tends to mask and obscure the plural forms of exploitation and domination across society, as well as the diverse figures of resistance that rise up against those forms. That said, it is important to recognize that finance capital and its extractive structures of accumulation do cast a totalizing net over all of society, tending to pose in direct confrontation the rich and the poor, the exploiters and the exploited, configuring every form of governance as a command over the exception, spawning endless wars and dictatorships. Recognizing the totalizing effects of finance capital, however, should not lead to catastrophic or apocalyptic prophecies, and hence to extremist forms of resistance. Moreover, we should not meet one process of totalization with another: rather than creating a unified subject of resistance, in other words, we need to recognize how the contemporary situation poses the potential for coalition among the diverse social subjectivities that resist the rule of finance capital.

The second difficulty has to do with the reappropriation of fixed capital by the multitude, which we analyzed and called for above. Such reappropriation, to the extent it can be carried forward, constitutes a real countertendency, distributing rather than concentrating accumulated productive wealth. This does not contradict the law of the falling rate of profit but shows instead how within capitalist development (especially in the phase of financial command) the potential for resistance and alternative politics continue and increase. As the composition of labor changes and it gains the capacity to appropriate technologies and organize social cooperation autonomously, it gains too the potential to act immediately at an ethical and political level, posing the dignity of social creation and the constituent joy of producing the common. This countertendency, in other words, touches on the plural realities of social and class struggle.

The intersection of financial totalization and social reappropriation casts in new light the material relationship between formal subsumption and real subsumption that we spoke of earlier. Formal subsumption is a widespread phenomenon that acts within and beyond the terrain of the real subsumption, not only a "before" but also a "during" and "after." The complete domination of society by capital, that is, the real subsumption, is

CHAPTER 12

NEOLIBERAL ADMINISTRATION OUT OF JOINT

To say that money institutionalizes and reproduces social relations and relations of property (and thus class hierarchy) is a kind of shorthand. Money and finance do not rule on their own. Neoliberal social relations and relations of production must be administered and managed by institutions spread throughout society.

Standard narratives see the emergence of neoliberal administration from the crisis of modern bureaucracy. According to one accepted view, globalization, or more specifically the increasingly global circuits of capital, undermines the sovereignty of nation-states and thus also destabilizes and weakens the institutions and practices of administration in its modern, bureaucratic, state-based form. The powers of finance, processes of privatization, and institutions of neoliberal administration move in to fill the void. A complementary narrative maintains that national sovereignties and modern administration were not only attacked from the outside but also hollowed out from within by various forms of corruption. In what Sheldon Wolin calls "inverted totalitarianism," corporations exert increasing control over the government through lobbying and other forms of legalized corruption. Governments are unable not only effectively to regulate the banks and finance but also to take even the most basic actions of administration, such as budgeting, maintaining infrastructure, and providing social services. In short, modern administration and national sovereignties may have been attacked from without but they were already crumbling from within.[1]

Such narratives about the passage from modern to neoliberal administration are useful, but because they see the development only from above their vision is partial and they miss the essential elements of the process. We argued in chapter 8 that the real, living motor that threw modern administration into crisis emerged from below: the creative and cooperating circuits of the productive multitude; its increasing capacities, knowledges, and access to information; and its reappropriation of fixed capital. People began to develop, in other words, the social and organizational capacities to administer together their own lives. The key to understanding neoliberal administrative institutions and practices, then, is to see them as a response to the resistances, the revolts, the projects of freedom, and the capacities for autonomy of the multitude. Neoliberal administration is a weapon designed to contain and absorb the energies and abilities that made modern bureaucracy no longer tenable.

Neoliberal freedom

Neoliberal ideology sings the praises of freedom, and in this respect, it is the pinnacle of the modern conservative and libertarian traditions that put individual liberties at the center of the political agenda, including the freedom of property ownership, freedom from government control, the freedom of individual entrepreneurial initiative, and so forth. Some of these notions of freedom are simple mystifications. When you hear someone celebrating private property as the basis of freedom you should remember Robert Hale's argument that when governments protect property rights they are exerting coercion against all those excluded from access to and control of that property. Seen at a social rather than individual level, in a kind of Orwellian reversal, freedom means servitude.[2] Similarly, when neoliberals preach small government they most often mean larger budgets to fund the protection of property, the myriad security apparatuses, border fences, military programs, and so on. Neoliberalism, in other words, is not laissez-faire and does not involve a decline of governmental activity or coercion. "[N]eo-liberal governmental intervention," writes Michel Foucault, "is no less dense, frequent, active, and continuous than in any other system."[3] Neoliberal freedom understood as the lack or decline of governmental action and coercion, then, is largely an illusion. It means not less but a different kind of governmental action and coercion.

Beneath neoliberalism's mystified notions of freedom, however, we can sometimes discern the heartbeat of real instances of social autonomy. Keep in mind that neoliberalism does not rule over a desert or even a sea of victims. Instead, it must control a dynamic realm of cooperating subjectivities, and it lives on the back of their increasingly autonomous social production, capturing value through the various forms of extraction we discussed in chapter 10. To understand neoliberalism, then, we need to keep our eyes on both levels.

Neoliberal figures of entrepreneurship, for example, have to be understood both as mystification and as symptom of real forces of freedom. Under neoliberalism, Foucault maintains, the traditional liberal figure of a *homo economicus* returns, no longer as partner of exchange, as in classical liberalism, but instead as entrepreneur: *homo economicus* is an entrepreneur of himself. This means, Foucault continues, "generalizing the 'enterprise' form within the social body or social fabric" such that individuals are not really isolated entrepreneurs but instead "the individual's life itself—with his relationships to his private property, for example, with his family, household, insurance, and retirement—must make him into a sort of permanent and multiple enterprise."[4] This entrepreneurial figure, however, in our view, is not really an invention of neoliberal ideologues but instead an interpretation and appropriation in distorted form of the increasingly autonomous forms of social production. (Can't you hear throughout Foucault's lectures, sometimes sotto voce, a critical recognition of the resistances and struggles for liberation across society?) The generalization of the enterprise form in the social fabric also points in the opposite direction to neoliberalism, toward the freedom and autonomy of cooperative social subjectivities. Before and beneath the neoliberal *homo economicus*, in other words, we find the entrepreneurship of the multitude. Recognizing this connection should not in any way validate the neoliberal claims to freedom. Instead it should highlight the power of the resistant subjectivities that are subjected to neoliberalism and emphasize how neoliberal administration attempts to mold them into subjects that are, as Foucault says, "eminently governable."[5]

In practical terms, the freedom to be an entrepreneur of yourself and administer your own life translates for most into precarity and poverty. The most vicious aspect of neoliberal ideology, in fact, is not the discourse on the freedom of the property owner or the capitalist entrepreneur, but the celebration of the freedom of workers and the lowest members of society. Peter Drucker, a neoliberal enthusiast, encouraged by the first years of the Reagan administration, sounds as if he attended Foucault's lectures and mistook Foucault's critical voice for affirmation. Drucker maintains that the primary obstacle for workers to become entrepreneurs of themselves is the stable, guaranteed job for life. To create an entrepreneurial society, therefore, the power of trade unions must be broken because the employment stability they offer discourages workers from innovating in their lives and continuously refashioning themselves. Similarly, he continues, the permanence of public institutions, such as universities and government agencies, must be destroyed because the social stability they offer similarly discourages self-innovation. "One implication of this is that individuals will increasingly have to take responsibility for their own continuous learning, and relearning, for their own self-development and their own careers.... The assumption from now on has to be that individuals on their own will have to find, determine, and develop a number of 'careers' during their working lives."[6] Workers in a neoliberal entrepreneurial society are essentially bird free, that is, free from stable employment, welfare services, state assistance—free to manage their own precarious lives as best they can and survive. What lovely hypocrisy!

The Japanese term used to refer to the growing population of precarious youth, "freeter" (*furita*—a combination of "free" and "arbeiter"), contains all the bitter irony of the neoliberal freedom of individual workers made entrepreneurs of themselves. Japanese media and politicians pin the blame for ever greater levels of labor and social precarity not on the neoliberal transformations but on the victims themselves: youth have bad attitudes toward work, they maintain, and are too lazy to commit to the hard work of a stable job. In the inverted reality of neoliberal ideology the only freedom imaginable is that of the freeter, a freedom of poverty and insecurity.[7]

And yet you should not let your indignation at the crass mystifications of neoliberal ideology and the cruelties of neoliberal policy blind you to the dynamics of social cooperation that reside beneath them. Don't let the empty neoliberal exhortations to become an entrepreneur of yourself make you overlook the entrepreneurship of the multitude.

The characteristics of neoliberal entrepreneurship are repeated in various forms of compulsory individual self-management and self-administration. In the minutest practices of daily life, neoliberal administration provides and imposes the means for self-management: self-service, self-checkout, self-check-in, and so forth. In many instances new technologies allow companies to make entire categories of workers redundant by outsourcing services to consumers. You pump your own gas, buy your own plane ticket, and check yourself out of the grocery store—and you can do it all with an app on your smartphone. Even simple digital interactions can require hours of tedium—deleting spam from your inbox, installing software updates, inventing and remembering innumerable passwords. "The rhythms of technological consumption," writes Jonathan Crary, "are inseparable from the requirement of continual self-administration. Every new product or service presents itself as essential for the bureaucratic organization of one's life, and there is an ever-growing number of routines and needs that constitute this life that no one has actually chosen."[8] And the key is that you want all this—it's easier and faster to do it yourself.

Neoliberalism creates, at its lowest level, a bureaucracy of one, a structure of individual self-management in which it is difficult to distinguish freedom from constraint. It appears to be "liquid" and open to more decentered and participatory mechanisms that function from below, but that apparent participation and fluidity are really captured from above. Finance and the forms of capital that extract value from social production rely on the self-management and self-organization of production and cooperation. "What finance reads or attempts to capture," Verónica Gago writes, "is the dynamic of subjects linked to the structuring of new entrepreneurial, self-managed labor forms arising from the poor sectors in parallel with their condemnation to excess or surplus populations."[9] Is neoliberal freedom, then, merely freedom from social responsibilities for the wealthy and the corporations while the rest are convinced that their enslavement is actually their freedom? Yes, in part, but something more substantial is going on too, which can be recognized only from below. Beneath neoliberalism, as Gago suggests, are social forms of self-management and cooperation, whose value it seeks to extract.

We should remember, of course, that self-management was one of the core demands of the struggles throughout the world of colonized peoples, feminists, the racially subordinated, organized workers, and others that reached a peak in the 1960s and '70s. Those struggles not only made society ungovernable and threw modern administration into crisis but they also developed widespread alternative capacities of social organization and institution. It should be enough to cite some of the familiar examples of successful experiments of community self-management of social production and reproduction: the Black Panther Party's liberation schools and Free Breakfast for Children programs; the Lycée experimental de Sainte-Nazaire, founded by Gabriel Cohn-Bendit, an educational structure managed by students and teachers together; the Bauen Hotel in Buenos Aires, which after being abandoned by owners during the 2001 economic crisis, was recuperated and run by the workers themselves; the Boston Women's Health Collective, which published *Our Bodies, Ourselves*; and the list could continue with worker-managed factories, community-organized clinics, and innumerable other examples of self-management and the community organization of social life across the globe over the last many decades. In each country, in each community, there are rich experiences of such entrepreneurship of the multitude.

Projects for autonomy, some modest and others audacious, are not only directly attacked by neoliberalism but also, in certain respects, their principles are absorbed and redeployed in perverse form. The neoliberal appropriation takes place by reducing notions of freedom and self-management from the collective to the individual scale and by capturing and appropriating the knowledges and competences of the multitude. In this regard too neoliberalism operates by extraction. Neoliberal freedom is thus not only a cipher that remains of past freedom struggles, like some ancient word we repeat but whose meaning has been lost, perverted; it is also indexical, that is, it points toward really existing forms of knowledge, autonomy, and collective self-management that it captures and redeploys. Keep in mind, as Foucault says, that "power is exercised only over free subjects, and only insofar as they are free."[10] The key is to find that freedom and build on it.

Crisis points of neoliberal administration

Neoliberal administration is riven by internal contradictions. As we argued in chapter 8, modern administration was thrown into crisis when knowledges, competencies, and access to information became generalized in the population and overflowed the bounds of administrative control; it was also undermined as the social factors that it calculates became increasingly immeasurable. Administrative action must now engage not only strictly rational social factors but also the production of affects and subjectivity as well as a capture of the wealth of the common. Administrative and legal apparatuses, at national and supranational levels, are increasingly fragmented. "Legal fragmentation," write Andreas Fischer-Lescano and Günther Teubner, "is merely an ephemeral reflection of a more fundamental, multi-dimensional fragmentation of global society itself."[11] Neoliberal administration, as a mode of governance, does not negate overflowing, immeasurable, and fragmented characteristics, and so it does not really put an end to the crisis. In contrast to government, neoliberal governance generates and maintains a plural, flexible network form of control, which relies on a weak compatibility among the fragments. The key to neoliberal administration is how it is able to function in a state of permanent crisis and to exert command and extract value even when it cannot ultimately control or even comprehend the productive social field beneath it.

One crisis point of neoliberal administration centers on the measure of value, especially regarding social and immaterial products, which are becoming central to the capitalist economy. Whereas capitalist firms and modern administrations managed (however imperfectly) to measure the values of industrial and agricultural products, social products generally resist calculation. How do you quantify the value of the care provided by a nurse, or the intelligence of a call center worker solving computer problems, or the cultural product of an arts collective, or the idea generated by a scientific team? The value of the common in general resists calculation, and all of these results of social production bear the primary characteristics of the common: images and ideas, knowledges and code, music and affects tend to be open for others to share, and only with difficulty are they closed off as private property; they all instead constitute forms of social life. Although one can certainly count products of social production, their value overflows any quantities assigned to them. That's why you feel a kind of revulsion when a monetary value is assigned to an act of care or an idea, just as you do when insurance companies designate the monetary compensation for the loss of a limb at work or when climate skeptics calculate cost-benefit relations of the extinction of an animal species or the rise of the sea level. The value of the common is, by its nature, beyond measure.

This is not to say, of course, that overflowing productive forces and the immeasurable values of the common sound the death knell of capital. Various technologies are deployed to domesticate immeasurability. Derivatives, for example, as we argued earlier, provide benchmarks for unknown values and create conversion mechanisms from one form of capital to another. They stamp values on the immeasurable and allow such products to be traded in markets.

But even the technologies to domesticate immeasurability, although they may facilitate the extraction and trade of social values, do not successfully stabilize the foundations of the global economy; if anything, they make it more volatile. Every morning the business pages are full of exposés of faulty valuations, fears over housing bubbles, accounting scandals, and credit ratings controversies. The instability is due in part, of course, to criminal behavior by bankers, insurers, politicians, and financiers, but it also is a symptom of systemic fault lines. "The new economy," Christian Marazzi writes, "reveals the crisis of the commensurability that was the key to its own success."[12] Economic and financial crisis is becoming not the exception but the rule, and the instability of value is a contributing factor. Under the rule of finance capital, in fact, governance and crisis are not contradictory. Finance permits (or forces) state administrations to become more elastic and variable, leading to forms of administrative action unknown to the old modes of government. Capital, in effect, adopts crisis as a mode of governance.

Access to information and communication is a second crisis point of neoliberal administration. Authoritarian regimes still believe they can maintain control over access to Internet sites and social media. The Chinese government's attempts to block the content of websites and monitor the Internet access and activities of individuals are probably the most extensive, but many other countries, including Iran and Saudi Arabia, try to block access deemed dangerous to the government, and threaten journalists and bloggers with jail time or worse.[13] The United States also attempts to keep secret vast realms of government information, and its ongoing and multipronged programs of digital surveillance (tracking phone records and Web searches, for instance) are the most extreme: go ahead and communicate, but know that you are being watched. Secrecy and surveillance are justified with claims of security.

No matter how well they fortify their dams, however, the Internet police will always be faced with new leaks. Some teenager with a laptop will always find a way to work around obstacles to gain access to censored sites. Moreover, the cycle of struggles from Iran in 2009 to Ferguson in 2014 taught us that activists will always find new ways to use information and communication tools. Paul Mason, for example, enumerates some of the different uses: "Facebook is used to form groups, covert and overt—in order to establish those strong but flexible connections. Twitter is used for real-time *organisation* and news dissemination, bypassing the cumbersome 'newsgathering' operations of the mainstream media. YouTube and the Twitter-linked photographic sites—Yfrog, Flickr and Twitpic—are used to provide instant evidence of the claims being made. Link-shorteners like bit.ly are used to disseminate key articles via Twitter."[14] This list is already out of date, of course, and we can be sure that activists will continue experimenting with new platforms to overcome controls and find ways to communicate and organize.

State secrets are also increasingly difficult to control, even for the most powerful governments. The revelation of classified National Security Agency documents by Edward Snowden in 2013 along with the documents leaked by Chelsea Manning demonstrate that even the US military and security apparatuses are incapable of controlling the most secret information. And the ferocity of the US government persecution of both Snowden and Manning give an indication of how those in control feel their hold on information to be tenuous. One should not assume, of course, that the subversion of censorship or leaks of information will defeat the government structures that oppose the freedom of information and communication. Neoliberal administration is built to weather such storms; in this respect, too, it functions as a form of crisis management.

Migrations constitute a third crisis point of neoliberal administration. The statistics are staggering. In 2014 nearly 60 million people—a population roughly the size of Italy or Great Britain—were forcibly displaced worldwide due to violence, persecution, and war.[15] According to then UN high commissioner for refugees António Guterres, "the scale of global forced displacement as well as the response required is now clearly dwarfing anything seen before."[16] For many migrants, of course, the direct cause of flight is not to avoid war but to seek better economic and social conditions. Including these populations makes the number almost incomprehensible: today well over 200 million people live outside their country of origin.[17] This does not even include the enormous number of internal migrants. In China alone migrant workers are estimated to number almost 230 million.[18] It is reasonable to estimate that one in ten of all inhabitants of the earth are migrants.

The mind-boggling numbers of migrants and their suffering certainly condemn national governments and the structures of global governance. They demonstrate the extent to which people's lives are made unlivable by war, economic hardships, and political persecution. The dangerous and painful journeys of most migrants testify to just how dire their situations must be. The numbers of migrants serve also to indict the dominant countries and the global institutions, which consistently fail to aid those in need sufficiently. The cruelty of the US Border Patrol that allows migrants to die of thirst in the desert is rivaled by the criminal inaction of the European Union and member states regarding migrant deaths in the Mediterranean.

The stream of migrants to Europe, which became a flood in 2015 with more than a million new arrivals, mostly from Syria and Afghanistan, threatens the political contours of the continent. Desperate migrants follow risky paths across land and sea, and the repeated preventable tragedies—over one thousand died in shipwrecks in the Mediterranean only in the month of April 2015—testify to the cruel indifference of the individual states and the European Union as a whole, unable to mount effective rescue missions. The squalor of migrant camps at Calais, Lesbos, and various other transit points across Europe and the travails migrants suffer at border crossings in Macedonia, Slovenia, and Hungary are blights on the conscience of the continent. Even before the Brexit vote, Europe was coming apart at the seams, due both to external pressure and internal conflicts among states and within each state.[19]

In this context, one must admire the courage and perseverance of those who aid migrants at the various points of their trajectories, often against hostile social forces. No More Deaths/No Más Muertes, for example, provides direct humanitarian assistance to migrants in southern Arizona, such as leaving water along paths in the desert, and documents the abuses of the US Border Patrol. Throughout Europe since 2015 there have been extraordinary mobilizations to settle migrants, find them food, shelter, and employment; such efforts are often led by churches but are also sustained by both experienced political activists and those never before engaged. The heroic efforts of such activists, even when unable to meet even a fraction of the needs of migrants, stand as a further indictment of the inaction and incapacities of national governments and the supranational governance structures.

If we view migrations only from the standpoint of demographics and populations, however, we will be blind to the wealth and resources of those in flight. The suffering of migrants is real and their situations often tragic, but regardless of the many constraints they face, migrants are free and mobile subjects. Even those who seek to aid migrants and demonstrate solidarity with them, Sandro Mezzadra maintains, in a dialogue with Brett Neilson, too often treat them only "as victims, as people in need of assistance, care, or protection. Doubtless this work has been inspired by noble motives, but it also has a certain ambiguity. By exploring the subjective aspect of migration, one is able to move beyond this paternalistic vision and to see migrants as the central protagonists of current processes of global transformation."[20] Recognizing migrants as protagonists often requires an ethnographic approach to reveal their linguistic capacities, cultural knowledges, and survival skills, as well as their courage and fortitude in the decisions they have made. The challenge is to hold together a paradox of poverty and wealth. On the one hand, migrants are stripped of the scaffolding that supports stable and productive lives, including family and community, familiar cultural contexts, and achieved employment status (think of all those trained as doctors and nurses who end up working as taxi drivers and housecleaners). Migrants certainly do, in this regard, need assistance. On the other hand, flight is an act of freedom and an expression of strength. This is true equally in noble cases, such as those fleeing persecution, and banal cases, such as even those trying to cope with a mother's death or a failed romance.

The crisis posed by migrations is not only that they overflow borders and cannot be contained from a demographic perspective, then, but also that in terms of subjectivity migrants exceed all administrative and capitalist logics of measure. Here too neoliberal administration takes the form of a permanent apparatus of crisis management. Don't be surprised when each year you hear reports from the exasperated head of a UN agency or the burnt-out spokesperson of a humanitarian NGO of a new migration crisis.

Freedom and subjectivity characterize production, access to information, and migration—together with the many other crisis points of neoliberal administration. The production of subjectivity always exceeds the boundaries and the technologies of measure required for the functioning of administration. Even multiple crises, however, do not signal imminent collapse. Crisis management, instead, is the mode of operation of neoliberal governance, with innumerable fingers to plug every leak that springs in the dike. Or, better, rather than a dike intended to be a complete barrier, neoliberal administration is more like a sieve with an adjustable mesh designed to regulate and respond continuously to flows and leaks.

Crisis may be the norm of neoliberal administration, but this does not mean smooth and successful functioning. It results instead in a normative crisis: some rules enforced by neoliberal administration are effective but many administrative acts, rather than producing positive norms of governance, are reduced to arbitrary and sometimes desperate actions. The failures of neoliberal management in the cases we cite here, for instance, the incommensurability of the results of social production, the uncontrollability of information and communication, and the uncontainability of migrations, in addition to demonstrating the ineffectiveness of administration, also can determine chaotic and even disastrous consequences. In the coming years world events will continue to show, we fear, that the violence that results from such failures of administration can lead both to empowering emergency authorities to rule over a state of exception and to the outbreak of wars. Neoliberal administration's functioning with crisis as the norm carries within itself a host of pathologies.

Emptying the public powers

Although neoliberal administration appears to be a kind of liquid governance that moves fluidly from one crisis point to the next, it is not really liquid at all. It is more like a durable fabric woven of disparate and disordered connections that are effectively aligned toward a unified project: to empty out the public powers and impose economic logics over administrative functions. The subjectivities that animate neoliberal society, however, are not all functional to its rule. When we analyze neoliberal administration, then, our task, in addition to articulating its primary functions, is to reveal how from below emerge potentials for resistance and revolt that point beyond neoliberalism.

Neoliberal administration's emptying out of the public should be recognized first, materially, in the transfer of wealth from the public to the private. Neoliberal regimes privatize primary industries and services, including oil companies, train systems, urban transport networks, and even prisons, all of which had been central elements of modern state bureaucracies. State debt is one means to funnel public wealth to private hands, and that is an element of the continuing functioning of primitive accumulation we spoke of earlier. Costs of projects that enrich the few—the construction of railroads is a classic example—are entered into the national ledger as state debt.[21] Sovereign debt is today not only a direct means to privatize public wealth but also subsequently serves as a cudgel to privatize further other forms of public wealth in order to pay the debt. Austerity policies in countries throughout the world, for example, dictate the sale of the public patrimony of the nation—not only railways and communications systems but also historic museums and theaters—to raise funds. The Greek debt drama of 2015, with vicious attacks from European creditors, was one of the most extreme examples of the neoliberal project to empty the public coffers, privatize public goods, and, at the same time, drastically diminish public decision-making powers.

The transfer of public wealth to private hands is also frequently accomplished through illegal means: scandals regarding the misappropriation of public funds, inappropriate sales of public assets, awarding public works contracts under false pretenses, bribes, and the like are so frequent that it becomes hard to view them as exceptions to neoliberal administration. Scandals, though, are only the tip of the iceberg: the corruption of neoliberal administration submerged from view is continuous and structural, so widespread and deep that it has become part of normal administrative activity. When corruption

is periodically interrupted by crusading judges or politicians, grabbing headlines for a few days, one should note that the very politicians, administrators,
and magistrates who conduct these inquiries, preening themselves virtuously
for the cameras, also operate in this same system, even when they are on the
opposite side of the accused. "I'm shocked," they say, like Captain Renault in
Casablanca, "shocked to find that corruption is going on here!" Corruption
has become a constitutive element of the governance and normative structures of neoliberal administration. The revelation of scandals, of course, usually has political motivations and shortly after the spectacle dies down the
administrative system returns to normal.

The project to empty the public is aimed, second, at transforming the core
functioning of the state administrative apparatus through various external and
internal pressures. From the outside, for example, the movements of capital,
aided by various processes of globalization, evade many traditional national
structures of control in search of low labor costs or fiscal advantages or prox-
imity to resources. The evasion of government regulation is often accompanied by an injection of competition or blackmail on the part of multinational
corporations, which routinely strip away every pretense of democratic political decision-making: local and national governments routinely proclaim
themselves powerless in the face of corporate threats to move jobs elsewhere.
The logics of global finance (most often in the form of speculation) thus rule
over political decision-making, distancing the entire framework from national
governments and all other political bodies.

From the inside, too, neoliberal administration hollows out the core government structures of individual states and fills them with economic command. It is not unusual to hear career bureaucrats in the diplomatic corps
complain when research and policy analysis is outsourced to private think
tanks; it has become common for lobbyists to provide detailed legislative
blueprints that politicians enact directly; and legal campaign contributions (as
well as illegal government bribes) exert increasingly strong influence over
government decision-making, thus shifting administrative capacities to private hands (in line with the corruption of representation we analyzed in
chapter 3).

The phenomenon, however, is more general. As the sites of administrative
power are privatized, as the measures of the market become the benchmarks
of administrative performance, and as administrative decision-making is permeated by economic criteria, the political itself is emptied. Neoliberalism,

according to Wendy Brown, is a governing rationality defined by the super-imposition of economic rationalities over the political, as well as the creation of new subjects that are thoroughly constituted by economic logics: this is "the neoliberal vanquishing of *homo politicus* by *homo economicus*."[22] Neoliberal administration, in effect, injects economic rationality into social spheres and practices that previously were primarily free of economic logics and pressures. Legal practice and legal theory, for example, are some of the weapons at the disposal of neoliberal administration. "Law and legal reasoning," Brown continues, "not only give form to the economic, but economize new spheres and practices."[23] Keep in mind that political rationalities are used to regulate and rule over the economic terrain. Under neoliberal administration, however, the political powers that previously governed the mediation between the production and distribution, between the creation and appropriation, of social wealth are being dissolved. It remains to be seen how much violence will arise on the site of this dissolution.

We need to step back, though, from the standard laments about how neoliberalism is emptying the public powers, however just they are, because we have no desire to restore the public and the political to their previous positions in administrative power. Instead, for us the critique of neoliberal administration must reveal the productive social subjectivities that have the power to resist and create alternatives. Viewing neoliberalism from above, as we said earlier, gives only a partial understanding of its functions and, more important, eclipses the productivity and powers of the social world. Seeing it from below, instead, allows us to recognize how thoroughly neoliberalism is permeated by both acts of contestation and productive activity. Although neoliberal administration has proven relatively adaptable and flexible and although it succeeds in many respects to make the political subordinate to economic rationalities, its rule is by no means smooth and secure. In part because it is born and functions as a response and because beneath its surface reside swarms of productive subjectivities living in and creating the common, neoliberalism always remains the scene of resistance and struggle.

Three interlinked battlefronts give an initial indication of such scenes of struggle: transparency, access, and decision-making. The struggle over transparency is aimed in part at disarming the dominant powers. Secrecy is a weapon always at the ready for those in power and neoliberal administration employs strategic opacity to cover its unresolvable contradictions.[24] Shining a light on administrative and corporate activity can serve not only to prevent wrongdoing but also to make available productive knowledges and information for general social use. Struggles over access continue along these same lines and focus even more clearly on the common and the ability of all to make use freely of the means of social production. Issues over decision-making integrate the other two and situate us firmly on the political terrain. But this cannot be a matter of rescuing the autonomy of the political from economic rationalities, as we said. Battles over transparency, access, and decision-making, which all straddle the political and the economic, point us toward a potential production of subjectivities against neoliberal subjection.

The world of digital technologies is a primary front in all these battles. Digital surveillance is an increasingly central weapon in the neoliberal administrative apparatus, monitoring communications and activity to detect potential threats through complex algorithms. In addition, digital algorithms to track online activity, as we saw earlier, are a core instrument used by search platforms and social media to extract value from the various forms of social production of users. Your digital devices track the websites you visit, the connections you make online, and your movements around the city, catalogue your shopping and entertainment choices, trace your friendship networks and your political views, and more. And there is a strong continuum between the neoliberal security apparatuses and the extraction of the common by social media corporations. But we need to recognize that these same digital technologies actually play a dual role: as they create the conditions both for the capture of social production and for neoliberal administration, they also allow the multitude access to knowledges, communication, and capacities for self-administration. The reappropriation of fixed capital that we called for in chapter 7 is one means to harness these powers for projects of liberation.[25]

There is, of course, a hard and violent dimension underlying the neoliberal armory that cannot be ignored. The fact that the multitude is embedded in the common and necessary for its production and reproduction does not guarantee its advantage in any of these battles. On the contrary, the powerful weapons at the disposal of capital and neoliberal administration often seem to leave us utterly defenseless. Nonetheless, we recognize (without any optimism or despair) that our situation offers potential for the production of subjectivity and social life that can break with and provide alternatives to the dictates of neoliberalism. The challenge and task, then, which we will address in part IV, are how to articulate and organize revolutionary activity on this terrain.

Fifth response: Produce powerful subjectivities

Neoliberal governance, as we argued earlier together with Foucault and Brown, is a governing rationality that cannot be understood merely in terms of its general economic policies: the privatization of public services and industries, the deregulation of markets and firms, the destruction of labor unions, and so forth. Neoliberalism must be grasped also in terms of the production of subjectivity, that is, the creation at all levels of society of individual entrepreneurial subjects, *homines economici*, who, in turn, continually reproduce the neoliberal world. This recognition could easily lead to despair: how can we resist neoliberalism, let alone create alternatives to it, if our own subjectivity is produced by it and permeated by its rationality? There seems to be nowhere outside neoliberalism we can stand.

Power, however—and neoliberal power is no exception—is not organic or unitary but is always defined by relationship and antagonism. Foucault himself explains that power is a structure of "actions brought to bear upon possible actions; it incites, it induces, it seduces, it makes easier or more difficult; in the extreme it constrains or forbids absolutely; it is nevertheless always a way of acting upon an acting subject or acting subjects by virtue of their acting or being capable of action. A set of actions upon other actions."[26] Resistance is always present in power from the beginning, as is the potential for rupture. The processes of subjection, then, and the production of subjectivities that are functional to power are themselves both precarious and shot through with resistances and alternative potentials. *Subjectivity, in other words, is not a given but a terrain of struggle.*

The potential for resistances and alternatives to neoliberalism emerged in our analyses above perhaps most clearly in the context of social production. The fact that capital functions increasingly through processes of the extraction of the common, that instead of directly organizing productive cooperation as it does in the factory it captures value produced on the social terrain through processes from which it is distant, indicates that the circuits of social production and, in particular, the organization of productive cooperation are relatively autonomous from capital. That is one factor that has allowed finance, which is always distant from the scene of production, to become the predominant apparatus of capture. This migration of capital away from the scene of social production, moreover, is irreversible. Capital is not able to organize directly the plural field of subjectivities who produce socially in cooperation and communication in part because those subjectivities and the values they produce overflow capitalist systems of measure. Faced with this reality, the abilities of capital and neoliberal administration to measure, codify, and reproduce subjectivities and values in a hierarchical schema become tenuous. But any attempt by capital to dictate directly the cooperation of social subjectivities, just like its attempts to enclose the common as private property, risks reducing productivity and diminishing profits. Capital cannot get too close or it will strangle the life force on which its own survival depends. We do not mean for this analysis of the capitalist extraction of the common and the relatively autonomous processes of cooperation in social production to suggest that antineoliberal and non-neoliberal subjectivities already exist and are simply waiting to be emancipated. We mean for it simply to confirm that *a battle over the production of subjectivity is possible*—an asymmetrical combat between the capitalist technologies of measure and the immeasurable, overflowing forces of enlarged social production and reproduction, which reside in and produce the common.

To combat neoliberalism requires first a destituent project. We must not only challenge the processes of emptying the public and the capitalist right to extract and privatize the common but also demystify and combat the neoliberal processes of subjection. How can we sabotage and block the gears of the machines that produce and reproduce neoliberal subjectivity? This battle is possible because we are inside the productive project dominated by capital. It is not paradoxical for us to take what is power for capital—subjection—as an occasion for destituent subjectivation. In line with the Marxist tradition of subversion, this means, on one hand, that capitalist subjection is always forced to individualize productive subjects and, on the other, that the subjects put to work can discover in their own activities that they are not merely individuals but also have the potential to act together. To make sense of this being-together one must sabotage the capitalist project, not only blocking capitalist machines but also destroying ideological and material mechanisms of the organization of labor and society, along with their individualist subjection.

To this destituent endeavor needs to be added a constituent project of subjectivation, that is, in the language we used earlier, the construction of machinic assemblages to produce alternative subjectivities. How can the common be reappropriated by the multitudes that produce it? How can plural subjectivities construct and manage autonomously their own cooperative social relations? The struggle opens here to unhinge social cooperation from not only its direct exploitation but also the mechanisms of financial extraction. It is a matter of stripping cooperation from command—simple to say, difficult to do. Control and resistance, commodity production and capacities for innovation: these are some of the terms of the asymmetry between subjection and subjectivation, and the passage from destituent to constituent action.

One way forward at this point is to adopt the standpoint of existing subjects, specifically to take guidance from the agents of social production who, subjected to the command of finance capital, nonetheless manage to organize resistance and even projects of liberation. From the social struggles we need to learn, argues Pedro Biscay, former director of the Central Bank of Argentina, "a capacity of political invention able to transform the financial dynamic in the field of battle against capital."[27] That power of political invention, we should add, has its foundation in the cooperative terrain of social production and in the overflowing productive nature of the common. And, furthermore, that battle *against* capital must be also a battle for new social relations. At the end of chapter 9 we traced a progression, which is already in action today, from social production to social unionism to social strike. Social unionism, we argued, by combining the organizational structures and innovations of labor unions and social movements, is able to give form to the entrepreneurship of the multitude and the potential for revolt that is inherent in social production. Struggles valorize existing subjectivities but also create new ones; subjectivities are radically transformed by their participation in political organizing and political action. Struggle too is a terrain of the production of subjectivity.

Social struggles, however, even organized as social unionism and social strike, are not enough. They are not the endpoint but a point of departure, a launch pad for the production of powerful subjectivities. An alternative production of subjectivity and alternative social relations must be sustained and institutionalized. Earlier we claimed that money is a social technology that institutionalizes social relations, and we traced various ways that money sustains capitalist social relations through their different phases of the mode of production. In chapter 15 we will argue that this critique should lead us not to oppose money as such but instead to invent an alternative to capitalist money, that is, an alternative social technology for institutionalizing new social relations—a money of the common.

When we advocate for a money of the common we are not imagining any storming of the Winter Palace (or the Federal Reserve or the European

Central Bank), nor are we thinking of those (however noble) local or digital currencies that seek to escape from the totalizing power of the dominant currencies. Our analysis of money is not concerned primarily, as we said, with its function as a means of exchange. We are interested instead in deconstructing the social relations that capitalist money imposes and institutionalizes, and institutionalizing new social relations through a new money. A money of the common must first be a subversive money: it must transform the capacity of struggles over social production and forms of life into weapons that block (to use old terms) capital's power to coin money and (in newer terms) the increasing domination over the common through the financialization of society. Along with those destituent effects, a money of the common must also consolidate and extend the autonomous relations of social cooperation, confirming the values of the common and generalizing its principles of open access and democratic decision-making. A money of the common, then, must be a social technology to crown the processes of subjectivation, making lasting and socially expansive a production of powerful subjectivities. In part IV we will need to investigate this and other pillars of a potential project of transformation and liberation.

PART IV

NEW PRINCE

Learn, because we will need all our intelligence. Agitate, because we will need all our enthusiasm. Organize, because we will need all our force.

—Antonio Gramsci, *L'ordine nuovo*, 1919

My heart is moved by all I cannot save:
so much has been destroyed

I have to cast my lot with those
who age after age, perversely,

with no extraordinary power,
reconstitute the world.

—Adrienne Rich, "Natural Resources"

To be black in the Baltimore of my youth was to be naked before the elements of the world, before all the guns, fists, knives, crack, rape, and disease. The nakedness is not an error, nor pathology. The nakedness is the correct and intended result of policy, the predictable upshot of people forced for centuries to live under fear.

—Ta-Nehisi Coates, *Between the World and Me*

Social and political movements today do not need to choose, as we said at the outset, between ineffective horizontality and undesirable leadership; nor do they need to pick among traditional political models that balance spontaneity and centralism, democracy and authority. They must instead invert strategy and tactics: a strategy that expresses the emerging autonomy of social forces and a tactics of engaging (antagonistically) with existing institutions and deploying leadership structures for specific occasions.

The fact that the power of the multitude is constituted on the social terrain does not limit its political capacities. On the contrary, only when grounded firmly in social production and reproduction—that is, in the maintenance and furthering of the forms of life we share, in the common—can we properly speak and act politically today. The multitude must take power, but differently, through a radical innovation of democratic institutions and a development of capacities to administer together the common in which social life is written. This is not the program of a vanguard but that of a coalition that expresses in subversive, antagonistic form the plural ontology of society. The power of the multitude calls for a new Prince.

Throughout this book we have drawn inspiration from Machiavelli. A *new* Prince, though, will not be an individual or a central committee or a party. A Prince of the multitude is something like a chemical precipitate that already exists in suspension, dispersed throughout society, and under the right conditions, it will coalesce in solid form. It is also something like a musical composition: the plural ontology of the multitude does not merge into one but instead the singularities (that is, the different social forces that continue to express their differences) discover harmonies and dissonances, common rhythms and syncopations. They compose a Prince. It is also something like the center of gravity of a dancing body. Heinrich von Kleist, enchanted by marionettes that seemingly take on a life of their own, explains that they have freed themselves from the earth's gravity and dance instead around their own center of gravity: "They know nothing of the inertia of matter, the factor that most works against the dancer: for the force that lifts them into the air is greater than the one that chains them to the earth."[1] The Prince both frees us from the inertia of the life of today, negating our voluntary servitude, and creates a new gravitational field, a force of liberation. Or, finally, a new Prince is something like the multitude of worms that Margaret Atwood imagines, the downtrodden who suffer under the soles of boots that kick and keep them down but who will soon rise and silently invade everywhere from below:

Meanwhile we eat dirt
and sleep; we are waiting
under your feet.

When we say Attack
you will hear nothing
at first.[2]

When the time comes, the army of worms will topple the world of boots. A new Prince is also a threat.

CHAPTER 13

POLITICAL REALISM

The basis of political realism, as we said earlier, must be the existing and potential capacities of the multitude. Power comes second, as a response to the resistances and struggles for liberation. In part III we analyzed some of the material, ideological, and institutional forces and structures that maintain contemporary relations of domination and production, including money and other means by which neoliberal governance and administration structure social life. Now is the time for us to return to and build on the results of part II: to explain how the passage from property to the common results in the creation of new social relations; how by taking back fixed capital and establishing a new relation between humans and machines we can generate new machinic subjectivities; and how the entrepreneurship of the multitude, its self-organization and self-administration, is able to invent lasting democratic institutions. It is time to gather together weapons, in other words, in the armory of a new Prince.

Power comes second

Many of the processes and concepts that we developed in previous chapters indicate how the emergence of a new composition of labor-power has shifted the relations of force among classes. When it produces in cooperative networks, first, labor-power has the potential to appropriate the means of production. When it operates in structures of production that become ever more relational and that increase productivity the more relational they become, labor-power is able to take possession of those structures, incarnating and incorporating the instruments of production into its own body. The figure of producers becomes machinic, their formation (within the structures of capital) becomes social, and their products become common. Many authors read this passage to a new stage of capitalist society as the deepening of the commodification of labor and social life as a whole, and there are indeed strong elements of commodification in this transition. It seems to us, nonetheless, that these elements can be transformed into a new power and that, by reappropriating the instruments of production and taking control of the relations of cooperation, labor-power can emerge stronger.

The new power of labor, second, is demonstrated by the increasingly social nature of work. Its social nature takes the form of cognitive capacities: abilities to create, employ, and manipulate languages, code, symbolic systems, algorithms, and the like; affective capacities, including the power to care for others, work with social and cultural differences, and manage relationships; cultural capacities such as aesthetic and conceptual production; educational capacities; and more. The social nature of labor thus reveals how economic production is ever more oriented toward the production and reproduction of forms of life, both the generation of bodies and the production of subjectivity. In this case, too, some authors argue that the social qualities of labor, especially when submitted to new Taylorist rationalization, organized in assembly lines, create new and deeper forms of alienation and subjection. There is also some truth to these claims. But we should not let the suffering of workers and the new serfdom of social, caring, and intellectual production blind us to the dignity and potential of their cooperative capacities and mass intellectuality. When capitalist production becomes anthropogenetic—focused on the generation and reproduction of human life and subjectivity—then labor-power has ever greater potential for autonomy. Moreover, under certain conditions, the resistances and antagonisms of the social and cognitive producers can be more effective (directly attacking profits) and subversive (undermining capitalist command). The hegemonic appearance in capitalist production of the social and cognitive power of labor has the potential to push capitalist development to the limit.

A third motif that signals the new potential of today's productive subjectivities is their entrepreneurial character. We described earlier the rise of the entrepreneurship of the multitude as forming a chiasmus with the decline of the capitalist entrepreneur. As capitalists, under the rule of finance, lose their innovative capacities and are gradually excluded from the knowledge of productive socialization, the multitude increasingly generates its own forms of cooperation and gains capacities for innovation. Capital is constrained to transfer capacity for the creation of value and the organization of productive cooperation to the entrepreneurial multitude. But the multitude does not merely take over and repeat the tasks of the capitalist entrepreneur. It shifts social production and reproduction away from property and toward the common. The entrepreneurship of the multitude is a process of commoning. The sad image of selfish individuals accumulating what they can thus becomes obsolete, the vulgar remains of a defunct modernity. It is no coincidence, then, that the sites of capitalist command are distanced ever further from the sites of production, to banks and global financial markets. Capital, of course, still wields repressive weapons, some more severe than before, but it does not dare confront in direct terms the entrepreneurship that comes from below, for fear of destroying the forces of cooperation and reducing productivity. Here, the powerful monster that the multitudinous labor force has become chases away every Saint George who wants to slay it.

These emerging social powers of production serve as the basis for our conception of political realism. Political realism means treating power as a set of social relationships and basing the potential of political action on the intelligence and capacities of the existing social forces, which resist and create, composing and conflicting with each other. Saying political realism involves grounding political thought in the networks of social relationships means also that the social becomes political or, better, that social processes are already political. This first definition of political realism already implies a passage of the multitude of the poor, the multitude of producers and reproducers, toward organization. There is no political realism without organization—moreover, organization toward a definite goal. Political realism must reject every transcendent, ideological, theological proposition of a telos, every goal imposed from the outside, and instead embrace a telos constructed from below, from within the desires of the multitude: an immanent teleology. Finally, realist political analysis must engage institutions. Fundamental in this regard are Foucault's efforts to construct a genealogy of institutions that moves from a critique of the present toward (in his final lectures) the invention of new practices, the constitution of the power of life against biopower. The decisive problem here, just as important as dismantling the ruling institutions, is to develop the constructive function of political realism. This constitutive project can be legitimate only when it grows out of "being together," the ontological condition of the multitude, with all of its knowledges, desires, habits, and practices.

Too many communist movements have run aground on this point, operating on the false presumption of being able to *represent* the majority and thus make self-consciousness and totality coincide. This (idealistic?) illusion extends from the European "left communism" of the 1920s and '30s, including

Georg Lukács and Karl Korsch, to some Maoist vanguards of the 1970s. But rather than theorizing "as if" the majority were the author of concepts and actions, the multitude must actually be engaged in the constituent process aimed at creating new institutions. Communist movements can be defeated, of course, or reduced to shadows, but they will always be reborn as long as they are planted in the ontology of the present, the "being together" of the multitude.

This possible passage dictated by political realism from resistance and organization to institutions thus entails both being *inside*, that is, effectively immersed in social reality, and being *against* capitalist reality and the forms of command that block the potential of the multitude. Biopolitics is the field in which this relationship is most developed: inside the reality of life, shaking from it the sad figures of subjection, and against biopower, which is the motor of the capitalist invasion of reality. This conflict would never be resolved if the forces in the biopolitical field were not to produce an excess, an overflowing of being and creativity that unbalances the relationship of force. This overflowing results from a composition of resistances, an organizational decision. The subjective aspect of political realism is the capacity for political decision-making, strategic thinking, and constituent initiative. Earlier we critiqued the concepts of general will, constituent power, and taking power for the ways they repeat the figures of sovereignty, reduce the plurality of the multitude, and take power away from the multitude. And yet each of these concepts, when confronted with reality, can indicate aspects of the path forward: the initiative that produces subjectivity, the event that creates organization, the power that puts reality back into subversive hands.

This brings us back to the notion that "power comes second," because there are resistances, social struggles, and political movements. This means, as we said earlier, that power is not a substance but a relationship. Weber recognized this fact, and Foucault subjectivated the relationship. Posing the relationship in subjective terms reveals the asymmetry of the forces in play. The institutions of power are always asymmetrical: creativity and invention reside on the side of resistance, whereas power is fundamentally conservative, trying to contain and appropriate the innovations of the forces against it. Today we are living through a period of the growing hegemony of the forces of resistance. To them will be entrusted the capacity to produce a new measure, which, we hope, will be a measure of organization and institution and provide a model of justice.

The common comes first

Social and political movements today, seeking the key to decision-making and constructing lasting structures, seem to be faced with two opposing paths. The temptation, on one side, is an exodus from the existing social institutions, conceived sometimes as a project to create a separate community and other times as a form of *foquismo*, forming a small action group. The pull, on the other side, is to embark on a long march through the existing institutions with the aim of reforming them from within, nourished by the illusion that the public can lead to the common. We maintain, however, that both of these paths lead to dead ends. There can be no radiant "outside" to the biopolitics of the struggles nor a liberated "inside" within the structures of biopower. We must invent new institutions "within and against" the developments of bio-politics and biopower. We should thus adopt a double strategy that brings together antagonistic engagements with the existing institutions and projects to create new ones.[1]

Some readers will remember failed, utopian proposals of such a double strategy that were ineffective solutions to an old problem, that of the differ-ence between the social field and political action in the construction of insti-tutions. Indeed many projects emerging from the movements of 1968 failed to pass from action to institution. Cornelius Castoriadis, among others, argued that only by adopting a materialist (and, for him, Marxist) conception in-herited from the past can we cast the problem in a constructive way—an imaginary, analytical (psychoanalytical) perspective, he argued, in which the self-institution of society and the revolutionary ontology of the struggles reveal democracy "beyond the state." Castoriadis thus affirmed the work of the imaginary against a realistic conception of progressive political action. "The imaginary I am speaking of," he wrote, "is not an image of something. It is an incessant creation and essentially indeterminate (in social-historic and psy-chic terms) of figures/forms/images, and only on the basis of them can it be a question of 'something.' What we call 'reality' and 'rationality' are produced by them."[2] But doesn't this position adopt naively at its base precisely that equivalence of subject and command, biopolitics and biopower, that consti-tutes the problem? Castoriadis's solution seems insufficient to us because it poses the solution before the problem. Instead one has to live within the con-tradiction, discovering how ontology (our historical inheritance, what has been deposited and accumulated in social being) is the antagonistic basis on which interpretation and action are possible. Certainly, as in other moments, in 1968 the problem was not resolved. But every time it is posed in a new way, not as a repetition, and today the primary conditions of the problem are different than in 1968. We will explore our current problem from two points of view: the institutional and the political.

Regarding the institutional question, our assumption is that today *the common comes first*, prior to every other configuration of social action. In order to recognize the common, however, we must see that the alternative between private and public property, between market and state, which is continually repeated by modern political philosophy and legal thought, is not really an alternative. The US legal realists, whom we studied in chapter 6, share this argument, perhaps paradoxically, with Evgeny Pashukanis, the great Soviet legal theorist: civil law and public law, property and sovereignty are not really separate. They approach this connection, however, from opposite sides. Whereas the legal realist Morris Cohen explains how private property has the qualities of sovereignty, Pashukanis maintains that sovereignty is based on and expresses private property—that modern public and constitutional law derives from capitalist property and the commodity form.[3] The preconditions of the legal structure are rooted not in state power but in the material relationships of production, and thus the public is nothing but the projection and guarantee of private property. Hans Kelsen is not far off the mark, then, when he accuses Pashukanis of treating all law as private law.[4]

We can thus see how the two positions we cited earlier, exodus from the institutions and attempts to transform them from within, both treat the public as the exclusive institutional referent, rejecting it in the first case and privileging it in the second. These positions share a substantialist conception of power and a monocratic vision of institutions. These are old ideas, based on the modern tradition that can only conceive law and institution as sovereign prerogatives. Conditions, however, have profoundly changed. Already in the twentieth century socialist movements, trade unionism, and the revolutionary portions of the workers' movements imposed new relations of force on capitalist power and the state. They redefined the public and demonstrated that it is no longer a sovereign prerogative but a scene of struggle and agreement, a terrain of collective bargaining. The substantive eminence of power and the very definition of public power were thus reduced and flattened. When Walter Benjamin notes that "organized labor is, apart from the state, probably today the only legal subject entitled to exercise violence,"[5] he poses the two antagonistic powers as equivalent, emphasizing implicitly the "public" function of the workers' movement that breaks the *unicum* of capitalist state sovereignty.

The neoliberal attacks in the last decades of the twentieth century struck back against both workers' movements and the figure of a "democratic public," which decades of welfare policies and Keynesian governance had created. The private now rules over the public and empties it of its contents. The public can no longer serve as a lever to consolidate new social relationships of force and new figures of the distribution of wealth that favor the subordinated classes. Capital and labor-power, neoliberal capitalism and—how should we call them—the "common bodies" of social production thus confront each other directly and antagonistically. While on one side the march of privatization continues and the dominance of the corporations and finance over government is affirmed, while the remaining public powers are made functional to the "good life" of capital, on the other side social forces—tacitly or openly—try to break every institutional relationship of subjection, posing the need for a new constructive logic of "being together," of cooperating in production, of constructing new institutions. This is what "the common comes first" means in institutional terms.

Also from the political point of view, the common comes first. We alluded to that argument in the abstract when we mentioned briefly at the end of chapter 12 some mechanisms to construct a "money of the common." We should situate this also in historical terms, going back to the struggles that in 1968 across the surface of a globalizing world marked not only the striation of indomitable resistances but also lines of new institutionality, constructed from below, on common bases. There are emerging in contemporary society new social relations that attempt (and sometimes succeed) to configure institutionally the equality and freedom of the multitude in the common.

The Zapatista experiences in the Lacandon Jungle of Chiapas, the alterglobalization movements of the first years of the century, and the cycle of movements that were launched in 2011, for example, all operate according to a logic of new institutionality, even when they do not succeed in establishing lasting institutions. One could summarize their actions, paradoxically, by following the fundamental categories of social economic ordering prescribed by the Nazi theorist Carl Schmitt, with, however, a conceptually significant semantic inversion. According to Schmitt, the movements that constitute the social economic order have to "appropriate, divide, and produce" (*Nehmen, Teilen, Weiden*) social space.[6] Today's movements of the subordinated do appropriate the spaces in which they live and they do produce the wealth they want, but—and this is really a new characteristic of social and class struggle— they have no propensity to divide either in terms of individual or corporatist interests; instead they accumulate diverse collective desires. Through this accumulation of desire a new institutionality appears and a new notion of right is expressed. The movements of the Arab Spring, the Spanish Indignados, Occupy Wall Street, Gezi Park, and innumerable others have experimented, often naively but always on a multitudinous scale, with these elements.

We should note, first, that in these movements what used to be called the technical composition of labor-power and now we should name rather the technical composition of the young generations is defined by its profoundly social and cooperative nature, as well as its precarity. This technical composition, far from the traditional asymmetry with its political composition, which we spoke of earlier, approximates political experiences by proposing directly and explicitly the common (lived in social, productive, and reproductive cooperation) as the political model of new institutions. Paradoxically, such experiences of cooperation, such direct expressions of the common, which are often cast as "apolitical," are in fact eminently political. The new technical composition and political composition are able to approach one another by throwing overboard all the ballast of modern sovereignty and representation, and thus discovering the common as basis for the construction of society.

We should also note, second, that the rejection of Schmitt's "division," and thus the going beyond both individualism and corporatism, is not merely ideological but corresponds for these new generations to a collective desire expressed by the common as the only legitimate basis of institutions. This is a communitary anthropogenesis, which moves from the recognition of the ontology of the common to a project of its political affirmation. It is thus not a matter of "dividing" but, once the common is recognized and interiorized, of "distributing" it. We could say, revising Augustine's famous phrase, *in interiore homine habitat comuni*, inside humans resides the common. The common becomes, in the struggles, a joyful democratic passion, something like a new natural right.

Producing, too, third, tends toward the common. We argued above that the "production of humans by humans" is becoming the most widespread and the most productive factor in the capitalist economy. And we have seen how, as contemporary production and reproduction increasingly invest social life itself, the activities of care, affect, and communication become central, especially in growing sectors like health, education, and various forms of service. As Félix Guattari remarked, spontaneity and production come together in this new era of humanity in a developed ecological consciousness or, rather, a consciousness of care and interaction among humans and with the earth.[7]

These three observations together demonstrate how we must construct institutions of the common from within the multitude. This process, of course, is not automatic and its success is not assured. We should reject the old notions of the unstoppable transition "from socialism to communism," with which we have a long and painful experience, and which has too often stalled in the phase of socialist state power. We must recognize clearly instead all the weapons of power amassed against us and understand, in fact, that any such project has to confront a fundamental dualism between power and resistance, biopower and biopolitics. Institutions are formed in the struggles and express their antagonism. Lenin and Trotsky argued this point, not only when they analyzed the long history of class struggle but also, and above all, when they tactically insisted on the "dualism of power" in the short term, during the Bolshevik fight for power. That is just an example, but one that is very useful for interpreting our political situation. Simply adopting the standpoint of the struggles will not immediately eliminate the presence of the capitalist state that looms over us. But recognizing the dualism and situating ourselves on the side of resistance can help us to organize our knowledge of the world and position ourselves politically, allowing us to "be in the world" with the certainty of discovering its rules, measures, and mystifications. Only by immersing ourselves in the experience of the present, on the side of resistance, can our standpoint express an alternative—and, relying on the common, produce subversion.

Although we have not yet treated sufficiently the question of organization, which we raised at the beginning of this chapter, some elements have come to light: first, organization is born of the struggles, accentuating resistance and antagonism; second, organization must adopt the common as its foundation (and we will return to this later); third, organization also regards the common as its telos or, really, as a project and a program; fourth, organization is from the beginning both political and productive, and thus it interprets and lives within the entrepreneurship of the multitude; and, fifth, a radical dualism with respect to the capitalist institutions of production and political command defines the terms of organization. Productive autonomy and political independence are presuppositions of the organization of the multitude.

General strike

A "social strike" is always a general strike, which, like general strikes of the past, attacks immediately the structures of power. It is general in the sense that it generalizes or spreads the refusal of capitalist power across society and transforms economic, cultural, and political resistances into a demand for power. In a social strike, then, destituent and constituent moments cannot really be separated. A strike is born against exploitation and domination but contains in itself the urgency to create new social relations. Sometimes, of course, a social strike is primarily destituent, focused on attacking the structures of power, but even then constituent elements are implicit. Other times social strikes have utopian visions and seem not to take into account the destituent task, but in these cases, too, passion and suffering emerge to illuminate the need for antagonism. The young Hegel, for example, described well such a struggle of life and death in the context of the French Revolution.[8] One might say, following Hegel, that in the social strike the "tragedy of the spirit" is made concrete, incarnated in this dialectic. Or as the old anarchists used to say, "death to capital, freedom to the peoples!"

We should emphasize, for those who have any doubts, that our notions of social strike and general strike have little in common with the *grève générale* theorized by Georges Sorel.[9] For Sorel, proletarian violence is essentially and structurally different than capitalist and state violence. The working class must not repeat the bourgeois path to taking power, he maintains, which eventually shifts from creative instances of constituent power to repressive acts of constituted power. The concept of power itself is thus broken in two since the proletariat's taking possession of power is radically different from the bourgeois state form of power. All of that might be useful if not for the fact that in Sorel proletarian violence and communist insurrection lose their material contents and are defined by individualism and anti-intellectualism. Sorel's *grève générale* is not really about class struggle. In fact, the main problem with Sorel (and the anarchists who follow him) is that he believes that from violence and destruction will spontaneously arise a new society. It may be true that proletarians have wings, but they are wings weighed down by subordination and misery. To fly they need to free themselves and constitute together the bases of a new society. We, in any case, understand general strike completely differently than Sorel, seeing it instead as an instrument of the multitude's struggle for the construction of the common.

But Sorel was certainly not the only author in the late nineteenth and early twentieth centuries to see in the concept of strike a radical desire for social transformation. W. E. B. Du Bois interprets the revolts, mutinies, resistances, refusals, and flight of slaves during the US Civil War as a "general strike against the slave system" (and a determining factor in the outcome of the war).[10] In Europe, strikes and social uprisings often blended together in popular understandings after the Paris Commune. Victor Hugo, Gustave Flaubert, Emile Zola, and William Morris all write about the insurrectional *souffle* when they describe radical social movements and workers' strikes—strikes to put an end to hunger wages and unbearable abuses, struggles that communicate and bring everyone together, uprisings that give the bosses a taste of the pain and suffering that the poor and working classes know all too well. A destructive force is part of every strike, an ancient violence that can be transformed into a desire for liberation from the chains of servitude. Strikes change over time, of course, but these elements remain. And in fact we find these elements in all forms of social struggles throughout the twentieth century, from the Algerian Revolution to Black Power movements and from feminist struggles to student rebellions. That might explain the fascination with the Paris Commune and the Industrial Workers of the World that coursed through so many movements in the 1960s.

The history of general strikes is animated by an insurrectional and constituent passion: not passion in the sense of a charismatic or thaumaturgic event, but passion that lives in the highest moments of political ethics, in the intersection of resistance and solidarity, when spontaneity and organization, insurrection and constituent power are most closely tied together. It is an act, to use the language of ethical philosophy, when rationality and love triumph together. In the "strike" passion, reason creates a dynamic of common freedom and love generates an expansive action of equality. Calls for coalition, *tous ensemble*, speak the language of reason and freedom; expressions of camaraderie, compañer@s, sisters and brothers, are the language of love and equality. The general strike thus gives flesh to the bare skeleton of the language of human rights.

Today, however, if the concept of general strike can be still relevant, it must take a new form. In the past, labor strikes primarily developed in limited and repressive spaces of the factory and were strongly tied to the industrial working classes. Today, of course, that form of strike is relatively weak. In order to renew the general strike as a weapon for subversion and constitution, we need to confront, first, the extractive powers of capital and its new forms of exploitation that we investigated in part III and, second, the potential autonomy of forces of social production and reproduction that we explored in part II.

Capital functions today, as we argued earlier, primarily by *extracting* value both from the earth and from the cooperative dynamics of social life. Complementing this extractive power is a neoliberal administration that mixes elements of pure command—often operated by financial markets but in collaboration with state force—with plural and fragmented forms of governmentality, "participatory" forms of command that function through networks of micropowers able to register and engage social needs and desires. This neoliberal capitalist constitution thus not only extracts value from social production and reproduction but also manages to organize consumption and enjoyment, making them functional to the reproduction of capital. Money, finance, and debt serve as primary mediations between production and consumption, between social needs and the demands of capitalist reproduction. What can it mean to strike today against this complex capitalist machine? How can we conceive practices of refusal that block the processes of extraction and interrupt the flow of capitalist valorization, "doing damage to the bosses" and wielding against them an effective, material power? These questions recall the disruptive practices of all the traditions of workers' struggle: refusing the disciplines of work, abstention, sabotage, exodus, and more.

To recognize how these practices of refusal and subversion can be translated into contemporary conditions, we need to understand, first of all, that the increasingly social nature of production is a double-edged phenomenon. When cooperative production comes to invest all of social life, when the working day expands to include all waking (and even sleeping) hours, and when the productive capacities of all workers seem to be caught in the networks of command, on the one hand, it seems impossible to carve a space for independent action, which is required to "go on strike"; and yet, on the other, those engaged in social production and reproduction have their hands directly on the entire apparatus. Think of projects to occupy and block the metropolis (which has itself become part of the productive system) or to interrupt the productive flows of social networks and overload websites. We need to understand, second, that in this social matrix the borders separating production from reproduction are breaking down.

Too often in the past Marxist parties, unions, and theorists have maintained the centrality of "productive" labor, insisting that struggles within and against the processes of social reproduction are not able to strike at the heart of capitalist power. Such arguments often served as alibis for excluding from the "primary" struggle all except white male factory workers: women and students, the poor and migrants, people of color and peasants have all been victims of political strategies based on this view. To the extent that today the centrality of industrial production has been replaced by that of social production, struggles over production and over reproduction immediately implicate one another and are inextricably tied. *Any labor struggle today must include a critique of the (sexual, racial, global) divisions of labor and, in turn, the critique of the divisions of labor must include a refusal of the extraction of value in its various forms.* The social nature of production also implies that the conventional division between production and consumption is breaking down. Certainly the capitalist relationship between production and consumption, which is often governed by debt, must be broken, and the terrain of welfare (including health, education, housing, services, and the various forms of consumption) must be transformed into a terrain of struggle, through resistances and alternative projects. But consumption itself is not the problem: consumption is a social good when posed in relation to reproduction considered most broadly, that is, the sustainability of society, humanity, other species, the planet. Here we can see both the destituent function and the constituent work of the social strike. And by making this *social* definition concrete we can recognize the dismantling of capitalist command over consumption and the construction of a human production of humanity, not for profit, on the social terrain.

A social strike must thus be able to engage and transform the abstraction and the extraction operated by capital. It must, in other words, be able to encompass the wide social expanse ruled over by finance, transforming abstraction into generality, that is, embracing in coalition the wide range of forces extending across the whole society. It must also be able to transform extraction into autonomy, blocking the capitalist apparatuses to capture value while fortifying the cooperative relationships of social production and reproduction. These two terrains are, in any case, continuous and overlapping. Although the struggle against abstraction is horizontal (gaining social extension) and that against extraction is vertical (increasing the intensity of social cooperation), together they form a powerful machine for the construction of the common.

When Marx at the beginning of the industrial era analyzed how workers' struggles forced "total capital" to reduce the length of the working day, he recognized how workers were able to impose on capital a new relation of force and also to re-create themselves. "It must be acknowledged," he writes, "that our worker emerges from the process of production looking different from when he entered it."[11] The relationship of struggle that today is posed between "total capital" (primarily in financial form) and a "total living labor" that is socially exploited repeats Marx's conception: analogous to the factory strike to reorganize the working day is a social strike that addresses the configuration of what might be called the social working day. This could take the form, for instance, of fighting for a guaranteed basic income, unconditional and equal for all, which would to some extent address the precarity of contemporary society and provide an autonomous space of creation. Struggle today can become decisive only when it is able to break capitalist rule over social life and create autonomous alternatives.

Our analysis has thus arrived at a strange and in certain respects paradoxical point. On one side is a long history of the general strike, on whose basis was constructed the power of the workers' movement and the Left more generally. The strike was central to the definition of the political for more than a century of socialist struggles. On the other side are social struggles, which have now transformed the face of class struggle, as production and exploitation have become social, but which often have no real interlocutor on the Left. The institutions of the "official Left" or the "historic Left" have abandoned this terrain, and chosen the parliamentary arena as the exclusive space of bargaining (no longer between subaltern classes and power but instead) between groups of power that blend into one another behind an ideological screen. So when we hear some, who criticize neoliberalism with rectitude and courage, say "let's reconstruct the Left" it seems to us that this will be impossible until the social strike becomes central in the reasoning and the practice of what was once called the political forces of the Left.

Our brief analysis here leads to three points. First, every subversive action and every social struggle must be immersed in the biopolitical terrain, the terrain of social life, and oriented toward the common. The question of power comes second. The path we must travel requires, for example, reappropriating the fixed capital employed in productive social processes and thus blocking the multiplication of operations of valorization-capture-privatization developed by finance capital. The reappropriation of fixed capital means constructing the common—a common organized against the capitalist appropriation of social life, against private property and its markets, a common defined as the capacity of democratic management and autonomous administration *from below*. This is a process analogous to the struggle a century ago against the reduction of relative wages for industrial workers. That required, according to Rosa Luxemburg, "struggle against the commodity character of labor-power," that is, against capitalist production in its fundamental core. "The struggle against a decline in relative wages," she continues, "is thus no longer a struggle on the basis of the commodity economy, but rather a revolutionary, subversive initiative against the existence of this economy, it is the socialist movement of the proletariat."[12] For us, this is a process of commoning.

To construct the common, second, the social strike must also become political. It must produce a "dualism of power," breaking away from neoliberal governance and developing practices of counterpower. It must create institutions of being and producing together, becoming "multitudinous enterprises." The lived passion of all the great multitudinous movements of the end of the twentieth and beginning of the twenty-first centuries, including the occupations and encampments, demonstrates not only what the social strike can mean today but also how it can serve immediately as an instrument to create organization and institution. Even when they have lasted only briefly these movements have produced an institutional desire and have set in motion a constituent machine that will be hard to stop.

Posing this political terrain at center stage leads to a third point, because the very idea of the political must be renewed. The common comes first, as we said, before the political, because only the common and entrepreneurship on the terrain of the common can materially transform the world and take control of the production and reproduction of free subjectivities. The entrepreneurship of the multitude is forming historically the ontological basis of our existence. Don't be worried that the discussion is raised up to the question of being: there is no other way to construct freedom and equality except on the basis of historical being, produced and continually reproduced in the common. Around this entrepreneurship everything can be recomposed.

Extremism of the center

Among the sciences, perhaps no other more than political science holds strongly to its "realism." Thucydides, Machiavelli, Montesquieu, and many other luminaries in the European tradition give substance to this claim. The dominant streams of political analysis as they have developed over the last few centuries, however, have accumulated mountains of data and innumerable descriptions of political processes and developed statistical methods and predictive models, employing behaviorist and sociological approaches, but they do not deserve to be called either scientific or even realistic. Political science instead has primarily become a handservant to the ruling powers. We are thinking not primarily of the academic discipline, but rather the wide array of journalists, politicians, and analysts of various stripes (including, of course, many academics) who daily pronounce the supposed common sense of political reason.

The teachings of these vulgar and influential political scientists revolve essentially around three elements. First, most of them, explicitly or not, affirm the "autonomy of the political," which we discussed in chapter 3, offering apologies for state action, which is assumed to be the exclusive and indisputable center of political life. Second, they generally claim to provide value-free knowledge. Since claims to objective knowledge and practice even in the natural sciences should be challenged, as gender and race scholars have demonstrated most convincingly, claims to objectivity in the study of political systems and behaviors can have little basis—except perhaps to cloud or mask one's own political values.

We are most interested, however, in a third point: political scientists claim to identify a "center," a point of equilibrium and moderation, around which all reasonable political discussion should revolve. The elites and the people, the Right and the Left, they continually tell us, must move to the center because only the center can save democratic politics and its institutions from radical and irrational challenges. If we pose on the y axis the relationship between the summit and the base of the political system and on the x axis the conflict between Left and Right, then only at the origin, where the two axes meet, can we find equilibrium and stability, justice and moderation. Aristotle and Polybius maintained that only by knitting together the three forms of government (monarchy, aristocracy, and democracy) can the politeia, the just political society, be guaranteed, and Weber conceived power animated by three forms of legitimation (traditional, rational-legal, and charismatic) woven together. But those ancient and modern definitions of the political (and "democratic" politics in particular) had the virtue of being dynamic. They are replaced by the perfidious affirmation of politics reduced to a center, fixed in time and immobilized in space. The latest wave of political experts has thus produced this *wonderful result, eliminating the space for democratic conflict in the figure of "centrist populism." The affirmation that "we are neither Left nor Right" is followed by "we are both elites and the people"!*[13]

This result is due, first, to a completely ideological effect, far removed from the value-free analysis that political scientists claim. The "center" makes politics immobile not in the sense that the center does not move but in that every transformation can remain dominated by the center. Note, for example, how much today is in fashion among journalists, politicians, and bureaucrats an inflated usage of the word revolution. This serves not only to empty the meaning of the term and, they hope, eliminate its real possibility in the present but also to erase the memory of the historical developments of past centuries. At the base of all this, as Paolo Prodi, among others, has noted, is also a much broader phenomenon. Today historical time seems to be compressed and the future temporality of desires deleted: the present is eternal, unchangeable, and necessary. All this is registered and overdetermined by the sovereign ruling powers. Therefore the modern history that had previously been depicted as the continuous emergence of social conflicts and the repeated modification of constitutional structures must be paralyzed around a political center celebrated as the Eden of equilibrium.[14]

The insistence on the "center" has similar effects on space. The general idea is that political systems, centering themselves, settle around consolidated values and immutable hierarchies. Partisans of the center sound the alarm, inciting fear of change and terror at the new, insisting on the need for stability. "Today, in crisis-ridden Europe," write Giorgos Katsambekis and Yannis Stavrakakis, for instance, in the midst of the Greek crisis, "it is the institutional defenders of 'moderate politics' that construct a Manichean view of society, dismissing virtually any disagreement as irrational and populist, and thus becoming more and more radicalized and exclusionary."[15] Legitimation is not constructed around elements of consensus and participation but entrusted to authority charged with holding off the danger that surrounds us all, renewing a long tradition of the political uses of fear, from Thomas Hobbes to Carl Schmitt.

The insistence on the political "center" becomes all the more powerful when combined with the equilibrium prescribed by neoliberal economic theory. The reactionary idea of equilibrium and stability applied to the relation between state and populations also has a long history. The German administrative notion of cameralism, for example, celebrated it, *as did Friedrich Hayek. But today the force of the center and equilibrium has become more unyielding. Economics and politics are mixed in a sort of anarchic transvaluation of individualism, which paradoxically produces an image of social order, which is in large measure deterministic. The "center" thus loses every remaining possibility of being opened on any side, above or below, to the right or the left. It is the product and the brand of a necessary economic process. It would be a disaster if things went differently!*

We should be clear that this process of the legitimation of a stable and "moderate" center holds at arm's length those images of fear and violence that give rise to it, even while it uses them. What can appear more "central" and peace loving than having experienced fear and terror and now being calm and balanced? The cynicism that animates centrist political realism, in this dance between terror and tranquility, offers us perhaps the best key to interpreting the neoliberal "center" and the measure of its "extremism." All political positions must be brought together in the government of the center: "there is no alternative." What is more cynical than this dictum? Every value that is not reduced to the "center" must be excluded, outlawed.

This "nonviolent" center is far from that idea of stability and equilibrium guaranteed by God or by the princely order that had to be established, often with terrible violence. It is far from the bloody repression of revolting peasants in the name of Protestantism. To those who asked for the reasons of the massacre, Martin Luther responded, "It is pitiful that we have to be so cruel to the poor people, but what can we do? It is necessary and God wills it that fear may be brought on the people." Today fear is brought on people in ways different than at the beginnings of modernity, with money often replacing mercenaries. But so it is, and, as Luther continues, "Otherwise Satan brings forth mischief."[16]

Is it still possible today for political knowledge, beyond any "extremism of the center," to move within history and take up the project to transform it? Roughly in the period when Luther incited his mercenaries to massacre peasants, Machiavelli made the political into a passion and imagination of the common. The political is constituted, he teaches, by the desire of the multitude, for example, in the revolt of the Ciompi, the Florentine wool workers who struggled against the owners of the market.[17] It might be better to say they "appropriate" the political because this really involves laying claim to the space of politics by those who have no part, putting their lives at risk, struggling for liberation from misery and subjection, without fear and dread.[18] *That means posing desire within the struggles and facing the risks of struggle, within the relationship of force and its uncertainties, with the conviction that freedom and the common are always materially tested and constructed in struggle. Only this politics can be wrested from the hands of the Satan that Luther threated us with.*

CHAPTER 14

IMPOSSIBLE REFORMISM

For well over a century now reformism is posed as the only reasonable and effective path according to the supposed political realism of the official and socialist Left. Realism dictates, according to them, accommodating to capitalist rule, that is, participating in government, respecting capitalist discipline, and creating structures for labor and business to collaborate so that wages, work conditions, and social well-being can be slowly but surely improved. This realism has turned out to be entirely unrealistic. Reformism in this form has proven to be impossible and the social benefits it promises are an illusion.

Today the terrain of reform seems completely lost to the Left. One reason is that "reform" is one of the most frequently evoked terms in the neoliberal political lexicon and, in fact, it has become a pillar of the neoliberal obsession with the "center." In neoliberal hands, reform has come to mean, primarily, a shift of control from states to financial markets accompanied by sometimes hidden but often overt forms of violence. The market reform in postsocialist eastern Europe advocated by the likes of Jeffrey Sachs, for instance, took the form of "shock therapy." Certainly, this has little relation to what reform meant among progressive forces in the nineteenth and twentieth centuries. The term has been usurped, and its outcomes are sometimes almost the exact opposite of what socialist reformism sought in the past.

Another reason that progressive reformism seems impossible today is that the subject supporting reform in old socialist conceptions, the organized industrial working class, has withered. As we will argue below, once separated from working-class subjectivities, socialist reformism became merely a mechanism for managing capitalist development, almost indistinguishable from neoliberalism.

There is no need, however, for the critique of reformism to lead anyone to repeat the old reform-or-revolution debates that so inflamed our grandparents. We need to take measure of how much the conditions of social production and thus the potential for political action have changed. Those "radicals" who still rail against any type of reformism are dedicated to a notion of revolution just as impossible (and undesirable) as the old notions of reform. Our argument is that, based on the subjectivities of contemporary social production and reproduction, the concepts of both reform and revolution must be rethought, and that the two processes not only can but must march forward together. That is the course of political realism.

Fixing the system

Before exploring what reform can mean today, we should sketch briefly some key aspects in the history of socialist reformism. Already in the second half of the nineteenth century socialist revisionists chose, against Marxist and revolutionary forces, a "realist" path of negotiations for economic reforms. Since that time social democratic strategies have proven to be an utter failure and have brought on the terminal illness of socialism. Let's consider three scenes of failed twentieth-century reformism.

Scene one: Early twentieth-century nationalist revisionism. Blinded by the economic advantages of participating in and even championing the industrial destiny of the nation, social democrats in Germany, France, England, and Italy supported the military engagements of the First World War. This went well beyond the actions of trade unions defending corporatist interests and involved confusing the interests of labor with the presumed national interest. These social democrats mothballed the internationalist spirit of the workers' struggle and enthusiastically cheered on the imperialist and colonial adventures of their nations. They turned their backs on the inheritance of solidarity and struggle to embrace militarist discipline and the mantle of the oppressor. Whether their side won or lost the war, it was criminal to betray the previous half century of struggles of the workers' movement. In this case the concept of nation and dedication to its identity made socialist reformism fail.

Scene two: Post–Second World War social democratic reformism. The 1959 Bad Godesberg Conference, in which the German Social Democratic Party abandoned opposition to capital and adopted policies of collaboration, is one symbol of the reformist view that the only "realistic" route possible is to collaborate fully in the capitalist management of economic production. The trade unions of social democratic parties offered themselves as reliable partners in the economic and political world of capitalism.

This reformism raised the level of subjection and exploitation of the working class in the factories and in society while social democratic leaders praised exaggerated gains in the productivity of labor (which brought even more unbearable suffering) and the increasing discipline of the lives of workers. In the process, social democrats were also participants in the aggressive imperialisms and the defense of colonial powers (from Algeria to Vietnam), betraying signs of continuity with old conservative and fascist cultures. Anticolonial and anti-imperialist struggles were finally victorious in this period, but without the aid of the European and North American social democratic parties, which immediately opened the offices of neocolonialism.

Scene three: Post–cold war neoliberalism. After 1989, social democrats, beginning with Britain's Labour Party and the US Democratic Leadership Council, legitimated the most ferocious neoliberal policies and rode the coattails of global finance capital. The dismantling of welfare structures at home and the imposition of the Washington Consensus abroad were hallmarks of the new social democrats. The gravity of their decision to underwrite and guarantee the neoliberal model is still today in clear view. Social democracy became a direct instrument of neoliberal governance and condemned workers to infernal labor conditions and austerity wages. By entrusting society to a cruel and corrupting market, they not only destroyed welfare institutions and spread labor and social precarity but also renounced even the pretense of representing the interests of workers.

The twentieth-century failure of reformism, however, was not only the responsibility of social democracy. It was also due to the disasters of what might be called "revolutionary reformism." The Bolshevik revolution, for instance, eventually entrusted the enactment of reforms to a state that claimed to be socialist, but these failed just as dramatically as those of western European social democracies; or, rather, they functioned as a motor of modernization that yielded, in the final instance, to a "planned control" of capitalist development, which was first industrial and then financial. A successful revolution bequeathed to us a failed reformism. And that is because their reforms merely repeated the western European refrain of the accumulation of capital. In this case, we can see that a process of reform claiming to benefit the working classes failed and that a system of dictatorial command took its place. Socialist revolution crumbled, paradoxically, in its attempt to reform capitalism.

The disastrous outcome of socialist reformism (along with what we called "revolutionary reformism") is confirmed also by the path that Chinese

socialism has taken in the post-Mao era. At Tiananmen in 1989 the democratic students and workers demanded that the revolutionary path be taken
up again, not in an ideological form but in the form of a multitudinous democracy. The response of those in power, of course, was not only repression
but also to embark on a further phase of capitalist development, one that
mixed industrial development with the control of finance capital. As the students and workers were defeated the Chinese socialist regime entered into
the great game of neoliberal globalization.[1]

Various socialist reformisms have thus sought, often in partnership with
the political and economic forces of capital, to fix the system from the inside,
ameliorating gradually the lives of workers, blunting the worst forms of domination, and raising the social prospects of all. These experiences have demonstrated instead that capital cannot reform itself: the system is fixed, that is, like
the roulette table in the casino. The house always wins.

Instituting counterpowers

Is reform, then, impossible? Our selective initial sketch of twentieth-century
socialist reformisms certainly makes it seem so. It appears, in fact, that reform,
like a series of other political concepts such as democracy, freedom, and class
struggle, has been emptied of meaning. We need to return to some successful,
realist experiences in that history to find that a true reformism (both in revolutionary and social democratic contexts) requires the institution of counterpowers.

The outcomes of the Soviet and Chinese socialist experiences in state dictatorship to manage capitalist development certainly do not characterize the
revolutionary experiences from the beginning. Lenin, for instance, imagined
a system of governance organized around counterpowers—soviets against the
state and workers against capital—that would set in motion a real transformation of both the state and capital. A dualism of power or, better, a plurality of
powers, would initiate a process of liberation of the working masses from
subjection and misery. In various periods during the Chinese experience, especially during the Cultural Revolution, the establishment and institutionalization of counterpowers, antagonistic formations within and against the state,
pushed forward real processes of social and political reform. Subsequent socialist development in both countries, of course, crushed the hopes of democratic

reform under the heels of increasingly extensive dictatorships, but that does not negate the real effectiveness of counterpowers in earlier periods.[2]

Active counterpowers are also responsible for the few successes of social democratic reformism. One might consider, for instance, the New Deal period in the United States and the twentieth-century development of welfare policies in Europe as successful reformist experiments (even though in limited and ambiguous terms) insofar as they brought a measure of political participation and increased levels of social well-being. The New Deal was not so much a response to the crisis of circulation that exploded on Wall Street in 1929, or the imbalances of supply and demand, or any other objective criteria. It was rather a response to a political crisis created by the power of organized labor, especially the most militant unions, the threat of which was cast in a new light by the victory of the Russian Revolution. Labor militancy created (in certain respects and for a limited time) a "dualism of power" that threatened not only the production of profits but also the maintenance of the primary conditions of capitalist social reproduction. The establishment of counterpowers thus dictated a process that transformed the material constitution in economic, social, and political terms, enlarging political participation, revising some social hierarchies, and shifting the terms of the distribution of social wealth—all in limited and temporary but nonetheless real ways. The processes to form welfare states in Europe and other parts of the world later in the twentieth century were also driven in large part by the formation of militant, organized labor as counterpowers. Capitalism can, in fact, these examples show, be reformed, not by itself but when it is pushed and threatened from within by counterpowers.

We should note that although these examples illustrate the reformist effects of counterpowers, they also present distorting mirrors: in these experiences all that was democratic and common in the new forms of life and the new modes of production and all that was experienced as resistance and revolution came to be represented generally as the *public*, that is, primarily, as state action. But where there was real reformism, as we have seen, there was not only antagonism to the private but also struggle against the public, the guarantor of the private power of capital, and resistance against the state. Both "really existing socialism" and "liberal" politics were embroiled, and could not escape, from the public-private dialectic and thus replicated the "tragedy of the public," that is, the continuation of the public to be a sovereign prerogative, often misrepresented as the common or confused as representative and as interpreter of the social subjectivities of production and reproduction.

When we emphasize the institution of counterpowers we should recognize that this is characteristic of a much longer history of resistance and liberation that defines an altermodernity against the dominant modern history.[3] The long arc of European humanism, for example, from the Italian cities against the German emperor in the thirteenth and fourteenth centuries to the Dutch cities against the Catholic king in the seventeenth century, demonstrates the effectiveness of reformisms that bring power back to society. And this trajectory is continued, in certain respects, in the modern revolutions from the revolt of Haitian slaves against France and the rebellion of the American colonies against the English Crown to the English and French Revolutions.[4] In victories and defeats, the key feature is that they each create institutions of counterpower.

Closer to our time we should add to the history of altermodernity Polish Solidarność, the Zapatistas of Chiapas, the Bolivian cocaleros, the movements of 2011 (from Tahrir Square to Puerta del sol to Zuccotti Park), and numerous other initiatives that follow the path of instituting counterpowers. One crucial element added by the contemporary struggles is the insistence that counterpowers must always be plural and linked in coalition. The institutions of counterpowers, in the terms we articulated in chapter 3, make a *nonsovereign* claim on power. This does not mean, of course, that the sovereign, ruling power is left intact and the counterpowers occupy a separate social terrain but instead that sovereignty itself is rendered inoperative or destroyed. And, moreover, in this long history the creation of counterpowers goes hand in hand with the invention of new, nonsovereign institutions.

The potential of a nonsovereign power is what allows us most effectively to dismiss the old debates about reform versus revolution. We have already argued, on one side, that the old, supposedly realist notion of reform that accommodates to capitalist rule is an illusion and the only effective reform results from the institution of counterpowers that can threaten the ruling powers and force them to transform. We need now to look at the other side. The concept of revolution standing opposed to reform is most often grounded in an assumption of sovereign power: only a new sovereign power can challenge the ruling order, the thinking goes, sovereignty against sovereignty, and moreover, only a sovereign power can break with the present and introduce the new. It is fashionable today, in fact, to pose this argument in theological terms: we have never been secular, many scholars claim, and modern political thought itself has a theological basis.[5] We concur that many modern political concepts—sovereignty most important among them—have a theological basis, but authors who insist on political theology too often confuse *is* with *ought*, description with prescription. We recognize, in other words, that sovereignty is a theological concept, and that is precisely why we need to destroy it! A concept of revolution based on sovereignty, to return to our point, is an empty notion of revolution that is opposed to an equally empty notion of reform.

We need to construct instead a nonsovereign revolution, which overlaps and mixes with reformist action—when reform means instituting counterpowers. Defining *constitution* as a play of plural counterpowers means destroying the transcendent, monarchic, indivisible nature of power and stripping from any sovereign the possibility of acting "in the final instance" over society and the state. It opens instead toward the terrain of social production and reproduction, and its dynamic of counterpowers is matched with the composition of society and productive activity. It should thus be clear that we are not reformists in the neoliberal sense, nor in the late-socialist sense, nor are we trying merely to blunt the worst excesses of capitalism or to make politicians more representative of their constituencies or refound the traditional parties, or anything like that. Our reform is aimed instead at a revolutionary process that makes the existing social subjectivities, in all their differences, into a new Prince, the authors of strategy that sets in motion initiatives and practices of reform.

After affirming that the constitution of the multitude will consist of a construction of counterpowers, then, we have to return to the present state of the struggles. In this situation, the play among counterpowers cannot be conceived as harmonious or linear, but instead they must always function antagonistically, in an effort to subvert capitalist sovereignty—a subversion that transfers the struggle and the perspective of transformation from the horizontal axis of social struggles to the vertical axis of the struggle for power. The counterpowers expressed by the multitude of producers and reproducers (who eventually act as a new Prince) thus develop projects and express their force within and against sites of domination, which extend horizontally across society and protrude vertically as forms of command. A new Prince must (1) attack the vertical axis and empty its repressive power; and (2) construct against it counterpowers formed in the horizontal axis of social production and reproduction; (3) only then, when the construction of counterpowers is achieved, can a new Prince initiate a process of constituent power.

It might seem utopian to project a process of transformation or, really, a tendency toward the constitution of new social relations, grounded on exist-ing and emerging social subjectivities. Indeed there is nothing assured about this process. We see it rather as a *parie*, as Blaise Pascal puts it, a wager, which Pierre Bourdieu translates into a process of political decision-making based on the accumulation of resistances, struggles, and desires for liberation we have witnessed in the contemporary world.[6] This is the sense in which we propose a subversive reformism today as an instance of political realism.

Indignation in the fog of war

One task of any reformism is to limit the violence and destruction wrought by the ruling powers and to create effective mechanisms for social protection. But before constructing weapons of self-defense and effective counterpowers, before any call to arms, we need to bring out into daylight the contemporary forms of violence and recognize how people are already struggling against them.

When Carl von Clausewitz writes about the fog of war he is trying to cap-ture the uncertainty of military enterprises and the inability of commanders and combatants in the field of battle to gauge clearly the relations of force.[7] There is another fog of war, though, an ideological fog that clouds myriad forms of violence, making them all but invisible to external observers, and even sometimes to those who suffer them. Some extreme forms of violence, spectacular acts of brutality, of course, rise high above the fog, and no doubt, we must denounce them. But don't focus too much on exceptional events. We need to confront all forms of violence: civil wars, imperial wars, race wars, the violence of armies and militias, abuses of the police, rapists and wars on women, attacks on LGBTQ people, terroristic attacks of white supremacy and Islamic fundamentalisms, violence of capitalist finance, incarceration, ecological degradation, and the list goes on. We need to train our vision to see also and, especially, down in the fog, to reveal the daily, systematic and sys-temic, unspectacular forms of violence, what Slavoj Žižek calls the objective violence of the dominant systems of power, which sometimes appears as perpetrator-less crimes.[8] Down in the fog is where the real battles must be fought.[9]

Indignation is a first step toward finding adequate modes of resistance. Art and activism often go hand in hand to reveal and protest violence and war.

In the center of Picasso's *Guernica* a woman cranes her neck out the window and holds a lamp to illuminate the destruction and suffering. In some respects documentary film has today become the central art form of indignation. Indignation, however, is not merely a victim's cry, a weapon of the weak. Our hypothesis that power always comes second means that power acts to block the development of free subjectivities: the violence of power is aimed at containing and undermining the potential of those who resist and struggle for their own freedom. Indignation is a first expression of strength.[10]

But indignation is not enough. To disarm the perpetrators we need to forge new weapons. The critique of violence requires, in other words, creating new counterpowers. And even that is not enough. Resistance must contribute to the constitution of new subjectivities, to the project of their liberation. We will take up this argument in chapter 15 but here let us attempt a (admittedly partial and schematic) catalogue of some of the axes of violence seen and unseen that plague our societies, along with some of the emerging struggles against them.[11] From the standpoint of these struggles begin to emerge the transversal lines of coalition that we can construct across these different domains and across national boundaries. Building coalitions in an intersectional and international framework is the first step toward creating counterpowers.[12]

Criminal acts of police brutality against black people in the United States, including Michael Brown, Eric Garner, Freddie Gray, Tamir Rice, Philando Castile, and so many others, have recently taken center stage. But police brutality against black men and women in the United States, of course, is not new; what is new are the widespread technologies, such as video cameras in phones, that allow it to be seen and the outcry that has made it the object of mass indignation. And police violence against people of color is not by any means limited to North America. "We have a Ferguson every day," claims Ignacio Cano, referring to police killings of black men in Brazil's favelas.[13] Certainly the perpetrators of all these deaths should be held to account. But equally important battles are further down in the fog. We need to train our eyes not only and maybe not even primarily on police brutality (as an exceptional event) or even on the police culture of impunity that makes such acts of brutality possible but also on the normal and daily violence of the police together with the courts and carceral systems.[14] Traffic stops, drug arrests, unequal sentencing, the routine violence of the prison, housing policies, racially divided education systems—these are some of the scenes of racial violence from which we need to clear away the fog. Generating indignation against the silent institutionalized racism is one important aim of contemporary forms of antiracist activism. Black Lives Matter, the BlackOUT Collective, and the Movement for Black Lives are some of the activist organizations in the United States already constructing paths in this direction.[15]

Sexual violence similarly is most often seen in cases of spectacular brutality, such as the globally publicized 2012 rape of Jyoti Singh Pandey on a bus in New Delhi. The perpetrators of such crimes must be prosecuted and sometimes the horror can urge legislators to pass stronger laws. But most sexual violence takes place down in the fog, even when it involves mass deaths such as the femicide of hundreds of poor women and girls in Juárez, Mexico. "No one pays attention to these killings," writes Roberto Bolaño in his fictionalized account, "but the secret of the world is hidden in them."[16] Indeed the visibility of spectacular cases can lead women to "associate danger with public places," Kristin Bumiller writes, "despite the fact that most physical and sexual assaults take place in private," committed by known perpetrators.[17] Combating the daily and routine sexual violence—including rape on college campuses, abuse by husbands and fathers in the home, threatening environments for girls, as well, of course, as limits on reproductive rights—is just as important as protesting the spectacular cases of brutality. We can trace the lines of an emerging international cycle of struggles: the October 2016 demonstration for reproductive rights in Poland and the NiUnaMenos protests in Argentina against sexual violence in the same month are extending to other countries, including Italy, and they have strong resonances with the January 2017 Women's March on Washington.[18]

Ecological violence, suffered disproportionately by the poor, almost always takes place silently, unseen in the fog. It forms "a shadow," Rachel Carson writes, "that is no less ominous because it is formless and obscure."[19] For every Union Carbide Bhopal gas leak or BP Deepwater Horizon oil spill that monopolizes the attention of the global media there are millions of largely unseen industrial disasters, which little by little pollute and destroy the fabric of the earth and its ecosystems, leaving toxic rivers and lakes, flotillas of discarded plastic in the oceans, unbreathable air, and cancerous soils. The challenge of making visible these myriad forms of unseen ecological violence is doubled because their effects are most often delayed and only felt gradually. This is, to use Rob Nixon's phrase, a slow violence that is no less dangerous (and maybe more so) for its temporal delays.[20] Climate change is emblematic of the complex temporality of ecological violence because once its effects are finally visible the options for combatting it are (almost entirely) closed. And as many authors argue, the violence of ecological degradation and change affects first and most strongly the poor and the indigenous, in part because they rely most directly on the earth and have the fewest defenses. The 2016 Standing Rock protests to block construction of the Dakota Access Pipeline are one inspiring moment in recent environmental activism. In addition to being a historic gathering of North American tribes, it has been significant for the fact that environmental activists have followed the lead of indigenous activists in the direction and organization of the movement.[21]

The systemic violence of capitalist relations against working classes and the poor also leaves wounds that are often hidden. In 2010, global indignation was aroused when it was publicized that eighteen employees of Foxconn in China, the company that provides components for Apple computers, attempted suicide. In Japan the phenomenon of *hikikomori*, youth who withdraw to a solitary existence, sometimes refusing to come out of their rooms at home, is a symptom of the violences of precarity and unemployment in a society where social value has been so strongly associated with work.[22] The weapons of finance leave wounds that cripple just as other weapons do: indebtedness creates stunted forms of life that exclude all manners of social development and flourishing. The strategy of social unionism that we discussed in chapter 9, bringing together trade union and social movement traditions to address issues of full-time workers, the unemployed, the indebted, and the growing strata of precarious workers, is one of the most promising developments for addressing these forms of violence.[23]

The catalogue we have begun here is obviously an inadequate accounting. We have said too little to do justice to the few axes of violence we have mentioned, and still nothing yet about homophobic and transphobic violence, violence against the disabled, religious-based violence, and much more. These partial considerations should already make apparent, though, that where there is violence there will also be resistance, which will eventually emerge in organized and powerful movements. That is the key understanding we need to make in the next step in our argument.

Before leaving the question of violence, however, we need to turn our attention briefly to war. Military campaigns too, despite their spectacular, lethal effect, can hide their violence, at least from the view of certain observers. That is one intended consequence, for instance, of the restructuring of US military

strategy known as "revolution in military affairs" and "defense transformation," among other names. Those efforts, which use new technologies to
make the fighting forces more mobile and flexible, further earlier techniques
of killing at a distance, thus reducing the numbers of US troops at risk and
ultimately lowering the number of US fatalities. The dream behind these
changes is to create a mode of warfare that (from the standpoint of those
waging it) is virtual in the technological terms and bodiless in military terms,
while being very real and corporeal for those who suffer it. The semblance of
the virtual and the incorporeal allow for the violence to be (at least partially)
clouded. The emblem of this military mindset is the drone. Unmanned,
guided lethal projectiles are in many respects the continuation of long-range
missiles and bombers in that they allow those who are killing not to see those
who die.[24]

Although the strategic plans and the weapons technologies were already in
place beforehand, the Bush administration's war on terror along with the invasions of Afghanistan and Iraq were in many respects a proving ground. Over
a decade later, however, it is widely recognized that these wars were dramatic
failures, but remarkably the military logics behind them continue to be deployed. As US forces began to withdraw from Iraq and Afghanistan under
President Obama, for example, the military use of drones only increased. Just
like the bombing campaigns in Vietnam, drone warfare has quickly proven to
be a failure—drones sometimes succeed in killing targeted enemies but, especially given the wide collateral deaths and damages, they reinforce the will
and recruitment of those they intend to defeat—but that failure does not
mean they will cease to be employed. The organized indignation of antiwar
movements is necessary to make visible the systematic violence of drones and
bombing campaigns to the populations of the United States, Europe, and
Russia (those who suffer these attacks see them very well).[25]

Migrants can testify to the violence of war together with many other
forms: through warfare and economic destitution enormous populations are
forced to flee, who then suffer racist subordination along their journey and
when they arrive at their destination. Innumerable scenes of violence, for
example, followed Syrians fleeing war in 2015: the refugee centers set on fire
in Sweden; US politicians seeking to ban their entry; Hungary building a wall
on its Serbian border; the French riot police attacking the refugee camp at
Calais; and the list goes on. And yet there have also been extraordinary, heroic
mobilizations in countries throughout Europe and the world to welcome

migrants, to provide housing, clothing, and food, and to counter the toxic atmosphere of antimigrant violence.

Our catalogue of contemporary violence makes us sick even though, as we said, we only scratched the surface! May the gods, wherever they are, curse and plague the sad perpetrators of violence in all these hidden and overt forms! The racists, misogynists, homophobes, transphobes, destroyers of the earth, warmongers—may the putrid rot of their souls gnaw at them from within!

Invective and indignation are vital, of course, especially when organized as movements of resistance, and fortunately such movements arise all around us. But such movements are merely the first building block. We need to link the movements to create transversal coalitions in an intersectional and international frame. Furthermore, these connections have to transform identities and produce the kinds of subjective transformation that we spoke of earlier in the processes of translation in order to create effective counterpowers. Finally, then, counterpowers need to be formed into a project for liberation and the constitution of a real social alternative. In chapter 15 we will turn to the needs of that constituent process.

Empire today

Faced with a globalizing world out of control, many politicians, analysts, and scholars, on the Right and the Left, claim that the nation-state is back—or, rather, they wish it would come back. Some cite the need for sovereign national control over the economy, especially in light of the continuing crisis, to hold at bay the threat of a "secular stagnation" spreading across the globe or to protect workers and citizens against the depredations of financial markets. Others point to the need for secure national borders to defend the dominant countries against migrations of the poor and thus to preserve national identities. Finally, in the rush to respond to terrorist threats, the national security apparatuses are often posed as the primary or only defense. Given the renewed calls for the nation-state, globalization seems to have for many reaped more disasters than advantages.[26]

In these terms, however, the problem is poorly posed: arguing about the virtues of globalization versus the control of nation-states will lead only to dead ends. And, furthermore, the faith that national sovereignty can solve any of these contemporary problems is completely illusory. We need to formulate the problem better before we can see clearly the challenges we really face today.

Almost twenty years ago we proposed that there was forming an Empire that is reorganizing global political relations and shifting priority away from the sovereignty of nation-states. One guiding hypothesis was that, at the same time as the collapse of the Soviet Union and the transformations of Chinese socialism, the position of the United States as superpower was also changing. US imperialism, we claimed, is being displaced such that the United States can no longer successfully dictate global relations in unilateral fashion. In Giovanni Arrighi's terms, US global hegemony has suffered a terminal crisis.[27] In the formation of Empire, furthermore, no sovereign national power will be able to exert control in the manner of the old imperialisms. Another hypothesis we forwarded was that the increasingly global capitalist markets require a global power to give them order and coherent rules. As the circuits of capitalist production and accumulation achieve properly global reach, nation-states are no longer sufficient to guarantee and regulate the interests of capital. Consequently we foresaw the formation of a mixed imperial constitution, that is, an Empire composed of a changing cast of unequal powers, including nation-states, supranational institutions (such as the International Monetary Fund and the World Bank), the dominant corporations, nonstate powers, and others.

Empire, one might say, is incomplete. Indeed it is incomplete in the same way that capitalist society is incomplete, containing within itself a diverse array of previously existing social and economic forms. One should never expect either, in fact, to arrive at completion in some pure state. And yet their incompletion or mixed constitution is no obstacle to attacking them right now, in their present form.

Numerous authors working along the same lines in recent years have helped us see the problem of Empire even more clearly. Saskia Sassen, for example, puts to rest useless arguments that pose nation-states and globalization as opposed and mutually exclusive. She argues instead that nation-states and the interstate system maintain important roles, but they are being transformed from within by forces of the emerging global political and institutional order. Empire is an assemblage, one might say, of various state and nonstate authorities in concord and conflict.[28] Sandro Mezzadra and Brett Neilson, to give another example, make clear that globalization is not bringing about a borderless world but instead the geographies of Empire are defined by proliferating and fluctuating borders at all levels, which cut across the territory of each city and across continental divides. In fact, they argue that the standpoint of the border, the point of inclusion and exclusion, is the privileged site for bringing into clear view the dynamics of global power.[29] Finally, Keller Easterling, as we saw in chapter 10, demonstrates that rather than a homogeneous globe or one divided along national lines, the space of the world market should be understood as a myriad of varied "zones" subject to both state and extrastate governance: industrial zones, free trade zones, export processing zones, and so forth.[30] The problem, these authors and many more make clear, is not one of deciding whether to submit to globalization or return to the nation-state, but rather understanding the mixed constitution of this emerging Empire and inventing adequate political means to intervene in and combat its rule.

The proclamations of the return of the state, on the Right and the Left, have nonetheless been frequent in recent decades. The most dramatic and hubristic example of the renewed power of the nation-state on the Right was proclaimed by the United States in its "war on terror" and its occupations of Afghanistan and Iraq. The Bush administration believed it could unilaterally remake the global environment, starting with the Middle East, acting in the style of the old imperialist powers. In 2003, some viewed US forces rolling into Baghdad as evidence of the centrality of nation-states—the dominant nation-states, of course—in global affairs, but only a few years later it was clear to all that the utter failure of US unilateral adventures in military, economic, and political terms proved just the opposite: neither the United States nor any other nation-state can successfully dominate in imperialist terms.[31] On the Left, arguments about the "return of the state" and of national sovereignty have been especially prominent in Latin America, where progressive governments came to power as part of political projects to counter the policies of neoliberalism and the rule of global markets.[32] These experiences were extremely important and had enormously beneficial effects, in varying degrees and in various ways, for the populations of Brazil, Argentina, Venezuela, Ecuador, Bolivia, and elsewhere in the continent. The temporary successes of holding neoliberalism at bay were primarily due, however, not to the individual sovereign states but rather to the continental coalitions of states and the interdependence among them. Indeed as that interdependence is now falling apart the incapacity for individual states to achieve a "postneoliberal" economic and political order or to protect against the spread of the global crisis or even to slow the worst misdeeds of capitalist globalization is becoming increasingly clear.

The return of the state is an illusion. The dignity of the nation-state today would hinge on its provision of social welfare, the quality of services, education, health, housing, the levels of wages, and the potential for social mobility. But the crisis of social and political reformism goes hand in hand with the economic crisis, and the nation-state has proven unable on its own to reconstruct prospects of social well-being and development. Moreover, even when nation-states lavish spending on military and security apparatuses, these quickly prove unable to provide anything resembling real security to their citizens. We are convinced, in fact, that if the rebirth of the nation-state were not an illusion, if it were to come to pass, it would bring only tragedy, deepening crises, exacerbating poverty, and setting off wars, awakening demons that were thought to have been exorcized. "Those who sneer at history," declares Henry Kissinger, the brilliant reactionary stalwart of Empire, "obviously do not recall that the legal doctrine of national sovereignty and the principle of noninterference—enshrined, by the way, in the U.N. Charter—emerged at the end of the devastating Thirty Years War," referring to the two world wars from 1914 to 1945. The new discipline of international law sought, he continues, "to inhibit a repetition of the depredations of the seventeenth century, during which perhaps 40 percent of the population of Central Europe perished in the name of competing versions of universal truth. Once the doctrine of universal intervention spreads and competing truths contest, we risk entering a world in which, in G. K. Chesterton's phrase, virtue runs amok."[33] We are not saying, of course, that since the return of national sovereignty is illusory and undesirable, we need to content ourselves with neoliberal globalization and the devastating rule of finance capital. That is not the choice. We need, as we said earlier, to pose the problem properly.

The first task is to interpret Empire from above, that is, to track its shifting internal hierarchies. The mixed constitution of Empire is a constantly changing composition of numerous unequal powers. In part this still involves the old-fashioned realist analysis of international relations, gauging, for instance, the extent to which Russia has succeeded in shuffling the powers at play in the Middle East or eastern Europe, or evaluating the prospects of the BRIC countries (Brazil, Russia, India, and China). Similarly, one would have to understand if and how significantly the United States' "pivot to Asia" has shifted the primary axis of imperial power from the Atlantic to the Pacific. Imperial analysis, however, also has to consider many nonstate actors. The notion of a clash of civilizations, although purely hollow and false, animates equally those fighting to establish a new caliphate in the Middle East and the conservative ideologues in North America and Europe. Furthermore, material and digital infrastructures, mediascapes, production chains, international and global legal conventions, finance markets, and much more are structures of imperial power that must be illuminated by an analysis from above.

The second and crucial task, however, is to interpret Empire from below, that is, to grasp and nurture the existing powers of resistance and revolt. Resistance, of course, is expressed in specific locations, but it can also extend to the national scale and beyond. In part, this perspective carries on the tradition of proletarian internationalism, which seeks to carry class struggle beyond the limits of national capital and the national state. But we must also analyze all the other struggles endowed with the powers of social production and reproduction that we have investigated at different points in this book. Ultimately, against the power of money and the social relation it institutionalizes, against the power of property, stand the struggles for the common in their many diverse forms. In the next chapter we sketch some of the elements of a platform for an effective struggle for the common within and against Empire.

CHAPTER 15

AND NOW WHAT?

A new Prince, author of strategy, is already emerging in the actions of today's productive and reproductive subjects. It often seems, however, that one needs powers of synesthesia to register it: to smell it in their voices, hear it in their images, feel it in their desire. As a result of our investigations in parts II and III we are now in the position to identify at least the outlines of the emerging powers of the multitude. Specifically we are ready to articulate how the multitude is capable of generating strategy in today's political field—how it is able to see far, to construct counterpowers able to combat the existing forms of rule, to deploy social forces in lasting institutions, to create new forms of life. This is the key, as we concluded in part I, to solving the puzzle of horizontalism and verticality. The aim is not to dispense with leadership but rather—inverting the roles of strategy and tactics—to relegate leadership to a tactical role, employed and dismissed according to the occasion. This tactical position of leadership can be achieved and guaranteed, however, only by the establishment of the multitude's strategic capacities.

A Hephaestus to arm the multitude

Consider two classic scenes of armed self-defense. In March 1871 women and men of Paris refuse to allow the French army to take away the artillery on Montmartre and declare instead they will use it to defend the Commune. "Paris armed," as Marx writes from London, "is revolution armed."[1] Almost a century later, in May 1967, twenty-six members of the Black Panther Party enter the California State House in Sacramento with loaded weapons and declare their right and intention to defend the black community against police violence.

What arms does the multitude need to protect itself? Today it's clear to almost everyone that bullets and bombs, in most situations and especially in the dominant countries, will not protect you. In fact, using those weapons is most often self-defeating, even suicidal. What arms, then, can we use to defend ourselves? That turns out, however, to be the wrong question. If you begin by posing the question of defensive arms, you won't get far before running into dead ends. We have seen many political militants who were transformed by their arms into mere delinquents. By posing that conundrum we don't mean to advocate renouncing the use of arms—on the contrary. We don't want any more Guernicas, those scandalous defeats, horrific atrocities whose representations tug at the heartstrings of high-minded individuals everywhere. We want security. We want victories. Rather than renouncing their use we merely insist that the question of arms must be posed differently.

The use of arms always points in two directions: outward and inward, against the enemy and for the transformation of ourselves. Yes, defensively, our weapons must counter the forms of violence—both the "macroviolence" of wars and the "microviolence" of finance, poverty, racisms, gender oppressions, and environmental degradation. We must protect ourselves and disarm the perpetrators. But our weapons must also serve, inwardly, to build autonomy, invent new forms of life, and create new social relations.

The key is to reverse the order of these two functions. The productive use of arms must have priority and the defense application will follow. Real defense depends on not only the effectiveness of arms but also and primarily the power of the community. The famous dictum "political power grows out of the barrel of a gun" gets the order and priority wrong.[2] Real weapons grow out of social and political power, the power of our collective subjectivity.

This inversion gives a different view of the two examples we cited earlier. The real power of the Commune resided not in its artillery but in its daily workings, its democratic governance. The political innovations were prepared, as Kristin Ross brilliantly documents, in the popular reunions and club meetings of the Paris neighborhoods in the years preceding the Commune's establishment.[3] The power of the Black Panthers, similarly, was not in the display of guns but in its construction of social programs, such as free breakfast programs and free health clinics.[4] The Zapatistas are explicit about this: their power resides not in the weapons and military command structure of the Ejército Zapatista de Liberación Nacional (EZLN) but rather in the community councils and their experiments in justice and democracy. It is a question of priority. One cannot say we need first to engage the battle to defend ourselves and then, once we establish peace and security, we will have the free space to construct a new society. No, if you begin with war, you will end with it. We must build in the ruins, in the chaos and violence of our present, not ignoring our defense but subordinating it. The efficacy of the weapons of self-defense, then, should be judged first and foremost for how they serve the constructive struggle. Historians might go back and evaluate the artillery of Montmartre, the guns of the Black Panther Party, and even the defensive weapons of the EZLN with this criterion—whether these weapons served or obstructed the construction of a new society—but that is not our interest. Our point is that the search for weapons for today's multitude should focus on their subjective capacities and the effects of weapons in creating and maintaining (or destroying) new forms of life.

One might object that in some extreme contexts arms and military action must be given priority. This is only partially true, and the most inspiring examples of armed struggle, even in dire circumstances, manage simultaneously to invent democratic forms. For the defense of Kobane in Rojava (Kurdish Syria) in 2014 against the advances of Islamic State fighters, for example, the Kurdish movement needed guns and bombs. With sporadic and limited aid from the United States, and frequent obstruction from Turkey, the Kurds slowly won the battle with traditional military weapons. We have only admiration for the military prowess and the courage of the Kurdish fighters in this battle. But even in this example, it would be a mistake to view victory only from the battlefield. Kurdish communities in Rojava are also, in the midst of war, creating new social relations, inventing a form of "democratic autonomy," establishing governance councils with, for example, two representatives for each post, one male and one female. Even in this extreme case of chaos and violence, the real power resides in the ability of the community to transform the old social order, to create new, democratic forms of life.[5] The production of subjectivity in these cases is not merely a matter of consciousness-raising but also a kind of ontological deposit that builds up social being geologically, in a sedimentary way, layer after layer. This is a biopolitical transformation.

The Kurdish example recalls many instances of antifascist resistance that integrated armed struggle and the construction of democratic social organization—often of direct democracy—in liberated zones. The poet René Char, nom de guerre Capitaine Alexandre, who led a group of proletarians that held in check the Nazi armada and the forces of Fascist French collaborators, explains how a motley crew of partisans, in their differences, created a democratic dynamic. "The wonderful thing," he writes, "is that this disparate cohort of pampered and untrained children, workers raised up by tradition, naïve believers, boys terrified to have been exiled from their native soil, peasants acting with an obscure imagined patriotism of precocious adventures on horseback with the Foreign Legion, and those lured by the Spanish Civil War: this conglomerate was about to become one of the four or five most extraordinarily fertile political hotbeds that France has ever known."[6] Another poet, Franco Fortini, recalls how Italian partisans in August 1943 similarly constituted in the Val d'Ossola a republic that democratically organized the territory while serving as a base of armed struggle.[7] They succeeded only for a brief time and quickly the republic surrendered to the overwhelming enemy forces, but that experience was a fantastic crucible of invention. Fortini writes:

> There are no words for that atrocious and true aspect of the Resistance, which was upsetting but had deep effects. The only words for it were those of poetry that, from Dante on, is made from "what you cannot have understood."…History allows those most atrocious but also most human aspects of that struggle. It omits that the only real partisan song that grabbed you in the guts went, "There is no lieutenant, no captain, no colonel, no general." It was a violent cry of anarchy, which in those moments was completely true.[8]

That song founded a republic. Both in the lower French Alps and the Val d'Ossola, between Italy and Switzerland, in liberated zones, partisans constituted with arms a democratic experience. In retrospect we might call these "Kobane experiences."

The resistance of immigrant Algerian workers in France during the Algerian war of independence provides an analogous example. Among the conspiratorial activities and the resistance to the terrorism of the French state (in October 1961 protesting Algerian civilians were massacred in Paris, leaving hundreds dead) were constructed political communities that for a time constituted the ethical and political heart of liberated Algeria. Here too the two vectors—the resistance of the multitude that produces armed vanguards and armed vanguards that inspire multitudes—intersect and blend together, so to speak, on par, creating a solid and effective relationship between the constitution of a democratic multitude and the production of combative subjectivities, which nourish and feed off one another.[9]

Don't get too wrapped up, though, in the heroism of antifascist resistance! Yes, as these examples demonstrate, even in extreme conditions one can manage to invent new democratic forms. But most of us are not facing fascist regimes and, clearly, recourse to traditional weapons in our circumstances is counterproductive and suicidal. That does not imply renouncing arms, as we said, but rather posing the problem of force and weapons in a new way.

Our focus on the "inward" effects of weapons and their production of subjectivity, in other words, should lead us to revise the traditional understanding of arms. Just as in the previous chapter we found it was necessary to broaden the standard understanding of violence—to recognize also objective forms of violence and the deep wounds of microaggression—here we need to broaden the understanding of what constitutes a weapon. For example, fixed capital, such as the knowledge, intelligence, and information consolidated in a machine, has long served capital as an effective weapon. "It would be possible to write a whole history of the inventions made since 1830," Marx writes, "for the sole purpose of providing capital with weapons against working-class revolt."[10] Think, for example, of how the standard shipping container, introduced in the 1970s, as we noted earlier, fundamentally undermined the power of organized dockworkers, one of the traditionally most rebellious sectors of labor.[11] Or for a more challenging example, consider how computer algorithms employed by giant corporations like Google and Facebook exact a kind of violence on all users through the expropriation of intelligence and social connection. The Google PageRank algorithm, as we saw in chapter 7, tracks the links that users construct and on that basis creates hierarchies for web searches. Each link is a small expression of intelligence, and the algorithm, even without users being aware, extracts and accumulates that intelligence in the form of fixed capital. Machinic fixed capital, however, is not just a neutral force: it is wielded by the owners of property as a means to control and command living labor. If we were to reappropriate fixed capital, to take back what was taken from us, we could put the machines that have accumulated knowledge and intelligence in the hands of living labor and free them from the command of dead capital. In this way we can take hold of those weapons and neutralize them or, better, set their operation toward new goals or, better still, make them common and thus open to general use. Biopolitical weapons, such as digital algorithms, might in fact be the most important focus of contemporary struggle.

Hephaestus must forge a shield for the multitude like the one he made for Achilles: not just a safeguard against the violence of the ruling powers but also an instrument endowed with magical powers. The face of Achilles's shield is filled with intricately detailed designs that depict in concentric circles the composition of the entire community and its world. Achilles is protected, in effect, by the community as a whole. The concentric circles of the multitude's shield must express a new civilization, new modes of life, a new figure of humanity, and new relations of care among living species and the earth, up to the cosmos.

A three-faced Dionysus to govern the common

The role of a Prince, above all, is to rule, that is, to make decisions over the organization of social life. We have no interest, of course, in merely substituting one ruler for another while maintaining the structures of government. A truly *new* Prince cannot simply take its place on the throne. Our task instead is to transform the structures of rule, uproot them entirely, and in their stead cultivate new forms of social organization. The multitude must constitute a new Prince as a democratic structure.

Three primary paths lead toward a new form of governance, each with its own promises and pitfalls. The strategy of exodus attempts to withdraw from the dominant institutions and establish in miniature new social relations. The strategy of antagonistic reformism engages the existing social and political institutions in order to transform them from within. And, finally, the hegemonic strategy seeks to take power and create the institutions of a new society. It is not a matter of debating which of these three is correct, but rather finding ways to weave them together.

The strategy of exodus is, in certain respects, heir to the strategies of utopian communities. Since the institutions of the dominant society serve to reproduce existing social relations, the logic goes, the means to subvert and transform it must be created outside. On a separate social terrain we can create new ways of doing, new forms of life, producing and reproducing new subjectivities. The rich history of intentional and utopian communities (including monastic orders and urban squats) and theoretical investigations from Charles Fourier to science fiction writers demonstrate the power of creating an alternative outside.

The most inspiring contemporary practices of exodus take the form of prefigurative politics, which create a new outside within the structures of the dominant society. Activists seek to rid themselves of the relations of domination imprinted in them by the ruling social order to create democratic and egalitarian relations among themselves. Prefigurative politics is thus based on a moral and political mandate to match means and ends: it is hypocritical and self-defeating, the argument goes, to strive for a democratic society through undemocratic forms of organization. Activists must be the change they want to see in the world. The creation and reproduction of the community of activists thus becomes a focus of political action. The miniature society created within the social movement is intended not only in anticipation of a better future society but also as a demonstration of its feasibility and desirability.

Prefigurative politics proliferated in various segments of the New Left, particularly feminist and student movements, which posed participatory democracy as a prime criterion for the internal organization of the movement itself.[12] Occupied social centers, which developed throughout Europe and especially in Italy from the 1970s, experimented with autonomous governance structures and the creation of communities within and against the dominant society. Experiences of prefiguration have been multiplied and expanded in recent years. The various encampments of 2011 to 2013, from Tahrir and Puerta del sol to Zuccotti Park and Gezi Park, all serve as inspiring examples, establishing systems of free libraries, food, and medical services as well as (and most important) experiments in democratic decision-making in assemblies on a relatively large scale.[13] Among the greatest accomplishments of prefigurative politics has been its ability to open broader social debates about democracy and equality. The movements not only demonstrate a desire for a different social order but also open avenues for experimentation in the larger society.

The shortcomings of prefigurative approaches, however, are evident in both their internal dynamics and their social effectiveness. It is difficult to live in a prefigurative community while also being part of the larger dominant society (a contradiction like that of trying to maintain socialism in one country surrounded by a capitalist world). Moreover, the mandates of living differently in the community function largely at the moral level, often contradicting the production of subjectivity in the dominant society. As a result moralism and internal policing too often mar the experience of living in such activist communities.

More important than the difficult experiences within such communities, though, is their limited capacities to affect their outside, that is, the inability of prefigurative experiences to transform the broader social order. Generating desires for and posing an example of a new world is already a great accomplishment, but prefigurative experiences in themselves lack the means to engage the dominant institutions, let alone overthrow the ruling order and generate a social alternative.

A second path to a new form of governance leads to engaging with the existing institutions and attempting to transform them from within through a strategy of antagonistic reformism. In contrast to what we might call collaborative reformism, which serves merely to compensate for the ills of the current system, ameliorating its damage, antagonistic reformism sets its sights on fundamental social change. Rudi Dutschke's phrase for antagonistic reformism, a "long march through the institutions" (*Der lange Marsch durch die Institutionen*), is apt in part because it translates the image of Mao's guerrilla war against the Japanese into an internal struggle against the ruling order, a sort of guerrilla warfare from within the existing institutions of power. The phrase also expresses the core of the Gramscian idea of a war of position, conducting political struggle in the realm of culture, the forum of ideas, and the realm of the current structures of power. For Dutschke the goal was to affirm the autonomy of the movements, their strategic power, and, thus, to enlist them in the construction of counterpowers. Palmiro Togliatti also interpreted Gramsci to propose a "long march through the institutions," but he had the opposite path in mind: manage the movements, cage them up, and subordinate them to the command of the party. In order to distinguish between antagonistic reformism and social democratic reformism, between strong and weak reformism, one has to gauge the degree of strategic autonomy: maximal in the case of Dutschke and minimal in that of Togliatti.[14]

The electoral process is one field for antagonistic reformism, with the assumption that once elected a person can substantially and even fundamentally change the structures of power. Innumerable progressive politicians have come to office in recent years with promises of substantial change, from Barack Obama to Ada Colau, and one could draft a balance sheet of their relative success. In some cases the inertia of the office has proven more powerful than the political project for change, and in others substantial changes have been achieved. Another field of antagonistic reformism, which we engaged in chapter 6, involves legal projects working within the confines of existing property law to counter some of the forces of capitalist hierarchies and alleviate some of the damages of poverty and exclusion. Housing projects for the poor, for instance, and rights for workers can be carved out from within the rights of property. There are numerous other legal and institutional fields of antagonistic reformism in play today, including those engaged in environmental issues, protecting against sexual violence, affirming workers' rights, aiding migrants, and many more. A primary criterion for judging these projects as antagonistic reformism, as we said, is whether the reforms they enact support the existing system or set in motion a substantial transformation of the structures of power.

We have no doubt that some projects of antagonistic reformism make important contributions. Even when they appear in the short term as failures, as they most often do, their long-term effects can be significant: the long march requires patience. The limitations of antagonist reformism, however, are also apparent. Too often the long march through the institutions gets lost, and the desired social change never comes about. This, in part, is explained by the production of subjectivity: even if you enter an institution aiming to change it from the inside, often instead it will change you. This is by no means a reason to abandon projects of antagonistic reformism, in our view, but instead highlights how limited they are on their own.

Finally, a third path leads to taking power and achieving hegemony. In contrast to prefigurative strategies, this path does not aim at the small scale and the construction of communities relatively separate from the dominant society (whether outside or inside). The goal instead is to transform directly society as a whole. In contrast to reformist projects, the existing institutions are not the field of action, but rather the object of a "destituent," destructive enterprise. Overthrowing the existing institutions and creating new ones is the primary challenge.

Note that each of the three paths implies a different temporality. Prefigurative strategies, although they live the transformation of the activist community in the present, defer social transformation to a future when the analogy of the small democratic community will be achieved on a large scale. Reformist strategies live the slow temporality of gradual change that constructs the future one brick at a time. Taking power, in contrast, lives in the temporality of the event and thus brings about swift transformation at the social level.

The immediate satisfactions and political clarity of taking power are obvious. Equally obvious, however, should be its many pitfalls. The first concern of anyone intent on taking power is that the new regime not repeat the primary characteristics of the old. Our discussions of sovereignty and constituent power in chapter 3 highlight the practices and structures of domination inherent in sovereignty regardless of who wields it.[15] Taking power, therefore, cannot simply mean taking power as it is; taking power requires *transforming* power. It requires, to use the Marx phrase we explained earlier, "smashing the state," which is to say, in another idiom, that we must create a nonstate public power. Second, taking power (at the national level, for instance) is highly constrained by its environment. The pressures of global capital, the reactions of the dominant nation-states, and the limitations posed by various nonstate external forces, such as the media, all serve to hem in those who take power and reduce to a minimum the room for maneuvering. The drama and the highly constrained choices available to the Syriza government in the summer of 2015 demonstrated some of these limitations, and the agonies of progressive governments in Latin America that came to power in the last two decades provide further scenes of constraint by external and internal forces. Even those who succeed in taking power, in other words, end up having very little of it.

Where does this leave us? Does identifying the pitfalls of all three options mean we have nowhere to go? The first response, which is partial but nonetheless important, is that we must cease viewing these three strategies as divergent and recognize their (potential) complementarity. This involves not just taking a different perspective but also and most important transforming practices. The taking of power, by electoral or other means, must serve to open space for autonomous and prefigurative practices on an ever-larger scale and nourish the slow transformation of institutions, which must continue over the long term. Similarly practices of exodus must find ways to complement and further projects of both antagonistic reform and taking power. This three-faced Dionysus is the coordinated formation of counterpowers and the real creation of a dualism of power, within and against the existing ruling system. This is the realism that Machiavelli teaches us.

A second, more profound response requires that we expand our question from the political to the social terrain. We have insisted throughout this book that viewing politics as an autonomous terrain leads to disasters. The puzzles of democratic governance can be solved only through the transformation of social relations. We traveled this path in part II, recognizing, for example, how property can be opened to the common. The rule of private property is one of the primary mechanisms that maintain social inequality and prevent equal participation in social life. The establishment of the common not only removes the barriers of private property but also creates and institutes new democratic social relations based on freedom and equality. Expansion of our focus from the political to the social terrain allows us to grasp, furthermore, the widespread capacities for organizing social cooperation. The entrepreneurship of the multitude, which we articulated in chapter 9, is one prominent face of the expanded capacities of social and political organization. The ability of people to organize together their productive lives and to plan and innovate future forms of cooperation demonstrates the necessary political capacities. And in the biopolitical context, social organization always spills over into political organization.

Gramsci's concept of hegemony defines something like the path we are describing here. Hegemony, for Gramsci, is not a purely political category (as if it were merely a translation of Lenin's concept of the dictatorship of the proletariat) nor is it purely sociological (as if Gramscian hegemony = Hegelian civil society).[16] Hegemony in Gramsci instead comprises both the party moment (or, rather, the production of subjectivity and the constituent power that gives it flesh) and the dynamic of class and social struggle that transforms society (including modifications of the legal order through trade union counterpowers, for example, and appropriations of machinic knowledges)—and into all of this are interwoven constituent powers. When Gramsci writes in "Americanism and Fordism" that in the United States rationalization has resulted in the need to create a new human type in conformity with the new type of labor and the new productive processes, we can only conclude that this new human type, the Fordist worker, is able to redirect and deploy in struggle what it has learned from the economic crisis and the technological transformations. The ontological deposit of resistance and struggle then becomes the more essential to revolutionary praxis the more it approximates the social figure of the common and interprets, as we will see, the paradigm of "general intellect." This superposition of the political and the social, and of antagonistic reform and taking power, offers us a clear image of how today the construction of a multitudinous democracy of the common can be understood.

At this point, we can now recognize the importance and the possibility of the inversion of strategy and tactics that we advocated in chapter 2. Crucial is the establishment of the multitude's capacity for strategy—to interpret the structures of oppression in all their forms, to form effective counterpowers, to plan with prudence for the future, to organize new social relations. The multitude is gaining the capacities to be a political entrepreneur. The relegation of leadership to tactical deployments follows from the strategic capacities of the multitude. The utility and necessity of the action of leadership, especially in emergency conditions, is clear. What must be established are safeguards that leaders don't outstay their welcome. The strategic power of the multitude is the only guarantee.

A Hermes to forge the coin of the common

Many of those who critique the power and violence of money in contemporary society under the rule of finance, as we do, argue that our primary task is to limit its power: get money out of political elections, restrain the financial power of the wealthy, diminish the power of the banks, and even distribute money more equitably across each society and across the globe. Yes, all that is crucial—but it is only a first step.

The more radical argue that we should abolish money altogether, but they confuse capitalist money with money as such. Money itself is not the problem. As we argued in chapter 11, money institutionalizes a social relation; it is a powerful social technology. The problem, then, as is the case too with other technologies, is not money but rather the social relation it supports.

What we need is to establish a new social relation—based on equality and freedom in the common—and then (and only then) can a new money be created to consolidate and institutionalize that social relation. Local currencies can certainly play a role but we want new social relations that are equally as general and equally as strong as capitalist social relations are today.[17] How can we imagine money that is grounded in the common, instead of being constituted by property relations? This money would not be anonymized title to property (as Heinsohn and Steiger rightly describe capitalist money) but rather plural, singular social bonds in the common. The creation of a new money must proceed hand in hand, then, with the passage from property to the common.

We can begin to imagine a money of the common through concrete shifts in monetary and social policy. A modest proposal, which points in this direction, is a "quantitative easing for the people." Traditionally quantitative easing is a monetary policy by which a central bank, through large-scale purchases of government bonds, commercial debt, mortgage-backed securities, and other assets from financial markets, increases the money supply, effectively printing money in the hope of incentivizing consumption and production. This money, which Milton Friedman sarcastically calls helicopter money, that is, money dropped down as if from a helicopter, is distributed according to the monetary needs of consumption but goes primarily to businesses. Several radical economists today, including Christian Marazzi and Yanis Varoufakis, propose to recast that practice for new ends: a quantitative easing for the people. The idea is to print money (as the current form of quantitative easing does) but distribute the money to the people and, specifically, in the most radical versions, to small and large autonomous initiatives and experiments of social production and reproduction.[18] This proposal creates a useful platform of political training and management of the construction of a real counterpower, but it is only a small step.

Proposals for a guaranteed basic income take us closer to a money of the common. Carlo Vercellone proposes that the establishment of a guaranteed basic income as a primary source of income would be the cornerstone for forging a money of the common by separating income from waged labor and instead linking shared wealth to the cooperative circuits of social production and reproduction. A basic income would recognize the value of unwaged social production and reproduction. Vercellone calls this a money of the common insofar as it grants (a limited) autonomy from capitalist command to existing forms of social production in and of the common: the income gives freedom and time to produce and reproduce social life. Weakening the link between income and labor also undermines the relation between wealth and property, opening spaces for shared wealth in social life.[19] Moreover, a basic income opens possibilities of new forms of social cooperation outside the wage system and fosters imagining a social life beyond capital. Kathi Weeks emphasizes how simply demanding a basic income has antiascetic effects: "Rather than preach the ethics of thrift and savings, the politics of concession, or the economics of sacrifice, the demand for basic income invites the expansion of our needs and desires...[and] points in the direction of a life no longer subordinate to work."[20] In itself a guaranteed basic income, even if it were achieved, would not be sufficient to transform capitalist money, eliminate private property, and institute social relations of the common, but it certainly gestures strongly in that direction.

To grasp the importance and carry further such policy proposals in the direction of a money of the common we should take up the results of our investigations in chapter 11 on the nature of money and try to update them. That means constructing a politics of money that grasps dynamically the new relationships of production and reproduction, interprets the needs that run throughout them (Spinoza would call this an ethics), and combines the analysis of the tendency of capitalist development with a recognition of the forces that traverse and modulate it. We need to identify, first, the monetary form of the relationship among producers and reproducers, as it arises in the regime of finance capital and social production; second, the diverse forms of income that correspond (or should correspond) to the development of this mode of production; and finally, the "regime of virtue" that corresponds to each monetary form. Our problematic is to transform property into the common while grasping the primary social transformations of the passage from industrial command to that of finance capital.

Contemporary capitalist production and its modes of extraction, as we argued in chapter 10, rely on social cooperation. Surplus value is appropriated through financial technologies that organize the extraction of social value. In certain respects, the dissolution of private property and the recognition of the common are, paradoxically, assumed as the basis of the current mode of production by "collective capital" itself. In this context, the immediate object of social and class struggles is to reduce inequality and break with the regimes of austerity. Today, however, this is presented in a particularly dramatic way because in the multitude that resists capitalist power the old and the new live together in a kind of interregnum: an old, unraveling political composition and a new emergent technical composition. Social strike, which combines the traditions of syndicalist and social movements, is the privileged form of struggle on this terrain. Ultimately, the refusal of austerity and inequality must express the demand for a money of cooperation and thus forms of income that correspond to the productivity of social cooperation, income that has both a wage element and an element of welfare. A money of cooperation extends beyond a guaranteed basic income to create a terrain on which new coalitions of social production and reproduction are able to impose a "political income," one that becomes incompatible with capitalist development and the mediations of class relations. The virtue affirmed here, from the standpoint of the struggles of social producers and reproducers, is equality. To all according to their needs, as the old slogan goes, corresponds to the fact that all are engaged and exploited in social production and reproduction.

Since common production is also multitudinous, composed of a set of singularities, the reproduction of the labor force cannot be achieved through forms of massification. Social differences and their powers of innovation have become essential to social production and reproduction. A money of cooperation thus must be accompanied by a money of singularization and what we might call an income of singularization, which underwrites a right to difference and sustains the plural expressions from below of the multitude. From all according to their abilities might thus be translated to from all according to their differences, affirming the virtue of singularity. The income of singularization would have to promote the self-valorization of social producers and reproducers. It is not enough to repropose the neo-Keynesian governance structures and the creation "from above" of effective demand (whatever its measures), but rather it is necessary to subjectivate the social forces of rupture. On this terrain one can create an ample front of what Pascal Nicolas-Le Strat calls "labor of the common," cooperative and democratic platforms of production and services, as well as the creation of experimental currencies for local communities.[21] Moreover, the emerging *economic* capacities of the multitude autonomously to produce and reproduce social relations are immediately *political* capacities: self-valorization implies political autonomy and capacities for self-governance. Finally, whereas the modern bourgeois constitutions were founded on and guaranteed the relations of private property, as Pashukanis argued, the constitution of autonomous social production must be founded on and guarantee the common. This is the leap over the abyss we spoke of in chapter 6, beyond the rule of private property, which can maintain its power even in regimes of equality.

The first two monetary figures interpret the qualities and capacities of the emergent entrepreneurial multitude in the age of social production and general intellect, but that is not enough. We also need a money of social and planetary investment. In the process of growing autonomy we need money, on one hand, to guarantee the expansion of society through education, research, transportation, health, and communication, and, on the other, to preserve life through relations of care, for all species as well as the earth and its ecosystems. The question here is not income but the dedication of social resources for a democratic planning for the future. Capital has proven unable to plan for the flourishing or even survival of social life on the planet, and states have fared little better: the rule of the private and the public have failed.[22] The

CHAPTER 16

PORTOLAN

The calls and responses that have punctuated the rhythm of this book, as we explained at the outset, are not intended as questions and answers, as if the responses could put the calls to rest. Think of them as coordinates on a compass or lines on portolan charts, which as early as the thirteenth century provided sailing instructions for crossing the Mediterranean. We can now look back and gather these coordinates. Our procedure has been to start with the social wealth we already have, consolidate our achievements in lasting institutions, and discover means to organize new subjectivities and social relations. The calls and responses, reshuffled, indicate that design.

Wealth

When W. E. B. Du Bois studied the period of US history after the end of slavery and sought to recognize the potential for an abolition democracy in which blacks and whites could participate equally, he was confronted by the argument that the freed slaves, since they are generally uneducated and poor, should not be allowed to participate politically. He was not satisfied with the obvious reply that ignorant whites have long been participating in US politics. Instead he took the opportunity to pose a more general political challenge. Democracy, he explains, "faces eternal paradox. In all ages, the vast majority of men have been ignorant and poor, and any attempt to arm such classes with political power brings the question: can Ignorance and Poverty rule?" In such arguments, however, Du Bois continues, seldom is taken into account the fact that the ignorant, both black and white, can become intelligent and the poor can attain sufficient wealth. His hopes for an abolition democracy rely on this process, the becoming intelligent and becoming wealthy of all.[1]

Du Bois is certainly right that people are not innately capable of collective self-rule and that democracy is not and cannot be spontaneous. In order to argue for democracy one must verify first that the multitude has the capacities necessary for cooperation and collective political action. He is also right that the requirements for democracy should not be conceived only or even primarily in narrow political terms but rather in the resources (intellectual and material) of social life, which are equally economic and political.

It would be a mistake, however, to view the multitude today as poor and ignorant. We don't merely mean by this, with an inversion typical of various theological traditions, that your worldly wealth is really a form of poverty and the life of the poor, even though now lacking material possessions, will one day be rewarded with riches in heaven. It is true that we need to realign how we understand wealth and poverty: their hoards of money are not really wealth; the fabric of your social relationships, your circuits of cooperation, are. But we should start with how capitalist society presents wealth because even there we can see how wealthy the multitude is, here and now.

We argued above in our **first response** that, when searching for new democratic forms, we must begin by investigating the cooperative networks that animate the production and reproduction of social life. That is where we will recognize the existing forms of wealth (along with intelligence, which is really another form of wealth) that can serve as the foundation for a democratic project.

One way to recognize the wealth and productivity of the multitude is to highlight what is taken from it. You have to be wealthy for so much to be stolen from you. Our living labor, living intelligence, living relationships, and living cooperation are constantly being absorbed into machines, scientific knowledges, social knowledges, the material and cultural structures of the metropolis, and much more. These forms of accumulation in themselves are not a bad thing. On the contrary, accumulated scientific knowledges allow us to think more powerfully just as accumulated social knowledges allow us to act, cooperate, and produce at a higher level. A defining feature of the capitalist mode of production, however, is that such wealth produced and accumulated socially is appropriated in the form of private property.

Sometimes this expropriation is experienced as a kind of theft—why shouldn't the commodities that roll out the factory gates belong to the workers who made them?—but often we are not even conscious of the wealth we are producing and the mechanisms by which it is captured. To return to Google's PageRank algorithm, with each click and each link you make, these expressions of intelligence are absorbed by the algorithm and transformed into fixed capital. The fact that users experience both enjoyment and interest while employing the search engine does not diminish the fact that the algorithm effectively absorbs what they produce to be accumulated by Google. Those astronomical stock valuations of digital and social media corporations are not just fictional. The corporations have sucked up vast reserves of social intelligence and wealth as fixed capital.

Cognizant of the enormous social wealth constantly expropriated, we posed the project in our **fourth call** to reappropriate fixed capital. This is not a matter of struggling against or destroying machines or algorithms or any other forms in which our past production is accumulated, but rather wresting them back from capital, expropriating the expropriators, and opening that wealth to society.

Another way to recognize the existing wealth of the multitude is to highlight that wealth today increasingly appears in the form of the common and not private property. In part this is a movement internal to capitalist development. Culture, knowledge, affective relations, and many other similar productive forms of wealth are difficult to corral and police in the form of private property. Capital relies ever more on the common as a means of production and, in turn, products increasingly take the form of the common. More significant, however, are the ways that people struggle to defend the common against both private and public property. It is not merely that the accumulation of private property is unjust or that politicians are corrupt. The rule of private property and that of public property are increasingly not only fetters on social development but also the authors of enormous disasters. People regard the earth and its ecosystems, for example, as common such that we share not only the effects of its degradation but also the opportunities of its use, and thus they are demanding that global society develop democratic structures for managing our relationship to and care of the earth. Leaving it to the large corporations or state rulers will only compound the existing disasters. Sharing scientific knowledges and cultural products are other examples of fields in which mechanisms of management are already being established to share wealth openly and democratically. All forms of social wealth can be pulled from the rule of private property and from state control to be opened in the form of the common. And, as we argued in our **third response**, the more we share the common, the wealthier we all are.

The existence of shared social wealth, wealth held in common, is not only the necessary basis for organizing a democratic political alternative. It also redefines significantly the concept of the political, with wealth as its central

pillar. Defining the political as wealth, and wealth as the content of the political, may seem paradoxical since the dominant line of modern political
thought taught us to consider wealth and power to be substantially different,
maintaining the "autonomy of the political" from economic pressures and
social needs. And even when wealth and power, the economic and the political, are posed together, it would be a scandal if ethics were drawn down to
that level. But that is no longer paradoxical (and even less, scandalous) when
one considers wealth in terms of the common. The common wealth of social
production implies a direct link between productive powers and political
capacities, as production and reproduction are both oriented toward the production of subjectivity and toward maintaining and expanding social relationships. Ethics, which invests life and is invested by it, becomes a criterion
for the valorization of production and the empowerment of political subjectivities.

Institution

Resistance and protest may force those in power to change policies and may
even in some cases topple regimes, but they are not enough. Resistance and
protest can limit the damage and protect us from the worst, like the force of
Paul the evangelist's *Katechon* that holds evil at bay, but we need also a constructive project.[2] Prefigurative experiments like the various encampments
and occupations in urban squares that have spread since 2011 are extremely
important in this regard. They give a taste of possible democratic social relations and nourish the desire for a different, better world. But they too are not
enough.

We cannot avoid the need to take power, as we proposed in our **third call**.
We are keenly aware of all the disasters that have resulted from the establishment of new sovereign powers, even in revolutionary form. But that recognition should not lead us to shun power and operate only in terms of opposition and resistance. That would concede the place to the current rulers and
merely contain or alleviate in part their damage. It should not lead us either
down the path of exodus and withdrawal whereby we create separate communities in miniature without transforming the society at large. These are
not, however, our only choices. We can take power differently and set in
motion a transformation of society as a whole.

The first key to taking power differently is to understand that sovereignty is not synonymous with freedom, autonomy, and self-determination. On the contrary, sovereignty is always a mechanism for one class to rule over others; it always carries a colonial relation at its heart. To smash the state, as we proposed in our **fourth response**, means finally to be done with sovereignty. When constituent power is posed as sovereign, for example, as it is in modern legal and political traditions, it corrals the plural social forces that compose it and creates of them a political unity. This form of constituent power paves the way for a new constituted power, which terminates the constituent process. Putting an end to sovereignty also requires a reassessment of the relationship between representation and democracy. It is true, of course, that, even in the most virtuous states, the contemporary structures of representation are terribly corrupt: many traditional structures of popular representation, such as trade unions, are in steep decline, and electoral mechanisms of representation are strongly influenced by elites, through money, the media, party structures, and other mechanisms. But even when functioning "properly," representation, defined by a separation between the rulers and the ruled, is a sovereign apparatus. What we need is to complete representation—or destroy representation, depending on your point of view—by reducing to a minimum the separation between rulers and ruled. And if this can never be achieved completely, if we cannot institute an absolute democracy in which we all participate equally and rule ourselves collectively, then we can at least strive to bring closer together the rulers and ruled like an asymptote.

To be done with the sovereignty and unity of rule does not mean disorder. As we proposed in our **second call**, one necessity is to invent nonsovereign institutions that establish and consolidate democratic social relations among a multiplicity of subjectivities. What is an institution? "Every institution imposes a series of models on our bodies," writes Gilles Deleuze, "even in its involuntary structures, and offers our intelligence a sort of knowledge, a possibility of foresight as project."[3] A democratic, nonsovereign institution can be a structure that allows and encourages us to repeat productive and joyful habits and encounters. Repeating our practices and our encounters is what permits us to extend into the future a continuous political project. Remember how free worker institutions—both union and political institutions—sometimes managed to create counterpowers in Fordist society? Today, too, democratic institutions must organize counterpowers and keep open and plural the developments of constituent power.

In more concrete terms, inventing institutions can mean creating nonbu-
reaucratic forms of administration. Modern bureaucracy is in crisis and in its
stead have arisen neoliberal administrative forms that have absorbed some
elements of the struggles for liberation and reproduced them in distorted,
inverted form. One face of neoliberal "freedom," for instance, is that you are
constantly required to administer your own life—within rigid limits, of
course—such that this seeming participation and individual self-management
can be captured and expropriated from above. But this neoliberal administration too is today in crisis. It functions in a permanent state of crisis. Our task
is to create the means for collective self-administration, that is, for the democratic management of our social relations and use of resources. That would be
a real institution of freedom, a promise that neoliberalism offers in only corrupt, distorted form.

Instituting freedom, of course, can require force, especially in a world
where the powers of unfreedom abound. And the defense of freedom is, as
Machiavelli would say, a sacred act: "Pia arma ubi nulla nisi in armis spes
est"—arms are sacred when there is no hope except through arms.[4] Today,
however, almost everywhere, traditional weapons are ineffective and self-
destructive. The multitude must instead forge capacities for social production
and reproduction, its intelligence and its means of cooperation, into weapons
of freedom and equality.

Organization

Activists today are right to resist pressures—in the name of realism and effectiveness—to follow charismatic leaders or accept traditional centralized leadership structures. They know that such promises of political effectiveness are
an illusion and, moreover, that the path to democracy takes a different route.
But those are wrong who make a fetish of horizontalism and, more important, who equate the critique of centralized leadership with the lack of organization. Democracy requires more not less focus on organization, especially
because the adequate and effective forms of organization needed today have
to be invented.

Traditional centralism and absolute horizontalism, thankfully, are not our
only choices. We proposed, in our **first call**, to transform the role of leadership
by inverting strategy and tactics. Strategy, the ability to see far, make decisions,

and enact comprehensive long-term political projects, should no longer be the responsibility of the leaders or the party or even the politicians, but instead should be entrusted to the multitude. This is when the voice skeptical of democracy creeps into your head—and you should listen. People, it whispers, will make a mess of it. They will never agree enough to make a decision; even if they could decide, it would take forever; and even then they don't have the information and intelligence to make good decisions.

We have two responses to these fears. First, leadership should still have a role but it should be relegated to the realm of tactics. It should be deployed temporarily with a limited mandate and when special occasions arise, for example, when specific expertise is required or especially swift action is needed. Such tactical deployments of leadership must always remain strictly subordinate to the strategic decisions of the multitude. Political leaders (even the most authoritarian ones) have long proclaimed themselves "servants of the people." Throughout modernity, though, the multitude was transformed into a people and subordinated to the sovereign. We need, finally, to create democratic structures and institutional frameworks in which leaders are truly servants. In other words, the inversion—strategic direction to the multitude and tactical execution by leadership—must be constitutionalized, maintaining control of government constantly in the hands of the multitude.

Second, to gauge the capacity of the multitude to formulate strategy and execute political decisions brings us back to the need to verify the existing wealth and intelligence of the multitude. In order for the multitude to make decisions effectively, that wealth and intelligence have to be put in motion through circuits of cooperation. For this we have to look at how political capacities are experimented with and developed on the social and economic terrain. In our **fifth call** we articulated the importance of the entrepreneurship of the multitude, which emerges from the forms of cooperation that sustain the production and reproduction of social life. Entrepreneurship names projects to create new combinations, as Schumpeter says, or, better, new and more powerful forms of cooperation. Cooperation, of course, develops within capitalist production but always strains against its limits and points beyond capitalist control. Marx recognized that fact already in the large-scale factory, where the combined working day of workers cooperating created a new power, a social power that went far beyond the power of the individual workers: "When the worker cooperates in a planned way with others, he strips off the fetters of his individuality, and develops the capabilities of his species."[5] Through cooperation we realize the capabilities of the species in the sense that we create a world in which we are no longer forced to choose between our individual good and the good of humanity, between egoism and altruism, but instead can pursue them as one and the same project. Such a project is the highest form of entrepreneurship.

In capitalist industry, however, cooperation, despite pointing beyond, always remains under the thumb of capitalist command: workers are brought together in the factory, given the means to produce together, and forced to obey the discipline that regulates cooperation. In the contemporary circuits of social production, in contrast, cooperation is formed increasingly without the direct imposition of capitalist control. More and more schemes of productive and reproductive cooperation are invented and regulated by the producers themselves in communicative and social networks. These are the conditions in which the multitude can emerge as entrepreneur.

The notion of an entrepreneurial multitude seems to pose a paradox insofar as producers are exhausted by work but at the same time proud of their productive "being together." In the modern factory that tension could be resolved only when the workers came out in struggle—against work and with each other. In contemporary society, the social strike (and often, specifically, the biopolitical struggles for welfare) indicates a potential solution. In the forms of life that the new mode of production generates, the contradiction between working exhaustion and the recognition of the power of being together falls away or is, at least, attenuated. Both Charles Fourier and Paul Lafargue understood this possibility and transformed it into utopian visions. "To all according to their needs" is no longer an ideological and illusory slogan but a political directive for the redistribution of common possibilities, in accordance with common participation in the production and reproduction of social wealth. The refusal of work, the slogan of class struggle repeated by industrial workers, rediscovers here its force in the common organization of emancipation.

When we say the multitude decides we do not mean to imply that the multitude is a homogeneous or unified subject. We find the term *multitude* useful, in fact, precisely because it indicates an irreducible internal multiplicity: the multitude is always many, it is a swarm. In our **second response** we emphasized the plural ontology of social being, and that the political process should not seek to reduce that plurality of subjectivities into a single subject but instead create mechanisms of articulation that allow the multitude, in all its multiplicity, to act politically and make political decisions. The politics of the multitude has its feet planted firmly on the terrain of coalition politics but it never remains merely a collection of identities. Through processes of articulation it sets out on a journey of transformation. Sometimes these articulations stretch across time and space through the formation of a cycle of struggles. A cycle is not formed by a simple repetition of the same struggle among different subjectivities or in different parts of the world. In a new context the struggle is always different. A cycle is formed when the activists are able to operate a political translation by which they both adopt and transform the protest repertoires, modes of action, organizational forms, slogans, and aspirations developed elsewhere. This is how the long cycle of struggles demanding justice and democracy since 2011, whose intelligence has been one of our guides throughout this book, has unfolded—from the Arab Spring to Black Lives Matter, from Gezi Park to Brazil's transport struggles, and from Spain's Indignados to Occupy Wall Street. What begins as coalition must, through processes of articulation and translation, undergo a sea change and assemble as a multitude of powerful new subjectivities.

Exhortatio

The freedom to assemble and associate—consecrated in almost all national constitutions as well as the Universal Declaration of Human Rights—establishes an essential protection against state power. People have a right to gather and form associations without government interference. Today, however, the freedom of assembly is taking on a more substantial meaning.

The general assemblies instituted by social movements in every encampment and occupation of recent years, with their efforts to open participation to all and their rules to encourage those traditionally disadvantaged to speak first, provide a first index of what assembly is becoming. Rather than models, these assemblies should be understood as symptoms of a growing political desire for new democratic modes of participation and decision-making. But the demands and practices of these social movements continually overflow the traditional framework of political rights. Their actions certainly do declare their right to assemble—their right to the streets, the squares, and the city as a whole—but they fill these rights with new social content. The significance of these movements may be best understood, in fact, as an enrichment of the freedom of association central to modern labor movements. From the tradition of strikes at the workplace are emerging forms of social strike that rest on the increasingly social nature of the production.

When conceived only in political terms calls for a fuller, more democratic right to assembly may seem weak in the face of sovereign powers, but the balance of power shifts when assembly is situated on the social terrain. Freedom of assembly here means the right to social cooperation, the right to form new combinations and new productive assemblages. This social right to assembly is not easily denied because circuits of cooperation are increasingly the prime motor of social production and thus the capitalist economy as a whole.

Some concrete demands in wide circulation today already point toward an expanded social right of assembly. For instance, the demand for a basic income, a sum of money granted to all unconditionally, is no longer restricted to the radical Left but is the subject of mainstream debate in nations throughout the world. A basic income would not only institute a more just distribution of the results of social production but also protect against the most extreme forms of poverty and abusive work. A minimum of wealth and time are necessary to participate politically and to create socially. Without them any right to assemble inevitably remains hollow. And as we said earlier, too, basic income already alludes toward a money of the common and its more substantive institutionalization of new, democratic social relations.

Demands for open access to and democratic management of the common are also increasingly widespread. It is clear today that private property will not protect the earth and its ecosystems but instead is hastening their destruction. Neither can it facilitate efficient and productive use of the social forms of wealth we share, such as knowledges, cultural products, and the like. The neoliberal economies of extraction may successfully generate profits for the few but they are fetters to real social development. The freedom to assemble, to cooperate, and to produce social life together requires establishing sustainable relations of care and use regarding the common in all its forms. Access to the common is a prerequisite for social production, and its future can be guaranteed only by democratic schemes of decision-making. Once we understand production in social terms as the creation of forms of life, in fact, then the right to the common overlaps with the right to the reappropriation of the means of social production and reproduction. Increasingly we cannot produce socially without the freedom to assemble.

The freedom of assembly also marks an alternative mode of the production of subjectivity, characterizing both what we do and who we are. Just as neoliberalism involves not only a set of economic and state policies but also the production of a neoliberal subject, *homo economicus*, that sustains and animates these policies, so too a postneoliberal society will not emerge until alternative subjectivities are created. Today, in fact, subjectivities operate increasingly according to a logic of assemblage, defined no longer by their possessions but by their connections. The fact that cooperation has become dominant in social production implies that productive subjectivities must be composed of expansive webs of relations, compositions whose elements even extend beyond the human. The logic of assemblage integrates material and immaterial machines, as well as nature and other nonhuman entities, into cooperative subjectivities. An enriched freedom of assembly generates the subjective assemblages that can animate a new world of cooperative networks and social production.

Freedom of assembly is thus no longer only a defense of individual liberty, or a protection against government abuse, or even a counterweight to state power. It is not a right conceded by the sovereign or the work of representatives but the achievement of the constituents themselves. Assembly is becoming a *constitutive* right, that is, a mechanism for composing a social alternative, for taking power differently, through cooperation in social production. The call to assembly is what Machiavelli would call an exhortation to virtue. More than a normative imperative, this virtue is an active ethics, a constitutive process that on the basis of our social wealth creates lasting institutions and organizes new social relations, accompanied by the force necessary to maintain them. We have not yet seen what is possible when the multitude assembles.

Notes

PREFACE

1. G. W. F. Hegel, *Phenomenology of Spirit*, trans. A. V. Miller, Oxford University Press, 1977, p. 10.
2. Ranajit Guha, preface to *Selected Subaltern Studies*, ed. Ranajit Guha and Gayatri Spivak, Oxford University Press, 1988, p. 35.
3. For an excellent study that gives similar breadth to the concept of assembly, see Judith Butler, *Notes toward a Performative Theory of Assembly*, Harvard University Press, 2015.

CHAPTER I

1. Niccolò Machiavelli, *The Prince*, trans. Peter Bonadella, Oxford University Press, 2005, p. 24.
2. For Karl Marx's judgment of the two errors of the Communards, see *The Civil War in France*, International, 1998, pp. 50–51; and "Letter to Kugelmann," April 12, 1871, in *The Civil War in France*, p. 86. For Lenin's interpretation of the errors of the Communards, see *The Civil War in France*, pp. 91–95. Regarding Chinese interpretations of the Paris Commune and its inspiration during the Cultural Revolution for the 1967 Shanghai Commune, see Hongsheng Jiang, *La commune de Shanghai et la commune de Paris*, La fabrique, 2014.
3. See Marcello Musto, ed., *Workers Unite!*, Bloomsbury, 2014; and Kristin Ross, *Communal Luxury*, Verso, 2015.
4. Jacques Rancière, *Hatred of Democracy*, trans. Steve Corcoran, Verso, 2014, p. 53.
5. The progressive refusal of the figure of the leader in social movements over the last decades stands in inverse relation to the increasingly obsessive affirmation of leadership in mainstream institutions: business and management culture, the universities, the dominant political culture, and so forth. This process appears to form a chiasmus: whereas in the early twentieth century the revolutionary tradition was focused on leadership and the bourgeois ideology was developing bureaucratic institutional forms that displaced centralized leadership, now the poles have reversed. But really, as we will see later, the forms of leadership and its refusal in these different contexts are entirely different.
6. The destructive effects of the mainstream media deserve special attention. When the media selects leaders and transforms them into celebrities, activists who had an integral role in a movement, such as Daniel Cohn-Bendit or Joschka Fischer, are

separated from the movement and integrated into the dominant power structure. If there is no real leader, then even well-meaning journalists feel forced to create one according to their own criteria—generally, someone who looks and sounds the part. The most intelligent activists refuse the mantle of leader conferred by the media, but those who don't quickly become irrelevant. In recent years, activists' use of independent media and, later, social media has served as (partially successful) efforts to avoid or control the destructive media machine. On the destructive effects of the media and the media's transformation of leaders into celebrities, an essential source remains Todd Gitlin, *The Whole World Is Watching*, University of California Press, 1980. On the attempt to create alternative media integrated into the movements, see Todd Wolfson's analysis of the development of Indymedia with particular attention to the experiences in Philadelphia, *Digital Rebellion: The Birth of the Cyber Left*, University of Illinois Press, 2014.

7. For representative accounts of democratic organizing in US feminist groups, see Gainesville Women's Liberation, "What We Do at Meetings," in Rosalyn Baxandall and Linda Gordon, eds., *Dear Sisters: Dispatches from the Women's Liberation Movement*, Basic Books, 2000, pp. 70–72; and Carol Hanisch, "The Liberal Takeover of Women's Liberation," in Redstockings, *Feminist Revolution*, Random House, 1975, pp. 163–167. Jo Freeman recounts how she was criticized and ostracized by other feminists after she allowed a journalist to portray her as a leader of the movement in "Trashing: The Dark Side of Sisterhood," *Ms. Magazine*, April 1976, pp. 49–51, 92–98. For an exemplary history of one Italian experience, see Milan Women's Bookstore Collective, *Sexual Difference*, ed. Teresa De Lauretis, Indiana University Press, 1990 (orig. *Non credere di avere dei diritti*, 1987); and an analysis of the Milan Collective by Linda Zerilli, *The Abyss of Freedom*, University of Chicago Press, 2005, pp. 93–124. For an account of the conflicts of claims to leadership in France, see Christine Delphy, "Les origines du Mouvement de Libération des Femmes en France," *Nouvelles questions féministes*, no. 16–18, 1991, pp. 137–148. Feminist experiences such as these are a key reference, perhaps more important than anarchist traditions, for the organizational practices and prohibition of leaders in the alterglobalization and Occupy movements.

8. There is a vast literature on the critique of representation and the promotion of participation in the US social movements of the 1960s and '70s. For two excellent examples, see Francesca Polletta, *Freedom Is an Endless Meeting*, University of Chicago Press, 2002, especially pp. 12–13; and Tom Hayden, ed., *Inspiring Participatory Democracy*, Paradigm, 2013.

9. Erica Edwards, *Charisma*, University of Minnesota Press, 2012, p. 12. For her explanation of the three types of violence, see pp. 20–21.

10. Marcia Chatelain, "Women and Black Lives Matter: An Interview with Marcia Chatelain," *Dissent*, Summer 2015, pp. 54–61, quote on p. 60.

11. Frederick C. Harris, "The Next Civil Rights Movement?," *Dissent*, Summer 2015, pp. 34–40, quote on p. 36. Glen Ford proclaims similarly, "This Ain't Your

Grandfather's Civil Rights Movement," http://www.blackagendareport.com/ not_your_grandfather's_movement. For the relationship between BLM and the NAACP, see Jamiles Lartey, "NAACP Considers Role alongside Black Lives Matter at Annual Convention," *Guardian*, July 18, 2016, https://www.theguardian .com/world/2016/jul/18/naacp-convention-black-lives-matter-cincinnati.

12. For one account of the role of social media activists in Black Lives Matter, see Jay Caspan Kang, "Our Demand Is Simple: Stop Killing Us," *New York Times Magazine*, May 4, 2015, https://www.nytimes.com/2015/05/10/magazine/our-demand-is-simple-stop-killing-us.html. On the role of social media activists as "choreographers," see Paolo Gerbaudo, *Tweets and Streets: Social Media and Contemporary Activism*, Pluto Press, 2012.

13. Juliet Hooker, "Black Lives Matter and the Paradoxes of U.S. Black Politics: From Democratic Sacrifice to Democratic Repair," *Political Theory*, 44:4, 2016, pp. 448–469, quote on p. 456.

14. See https://policy.m4bl.org.

15. Alicia Garza, "A Herstory of the #BlackLivesMatter Movement," *Feminist Wire*, October 7, 2014, http://www.thefeministwire.com/2014/10/blacklivesmatter-2/. On Black Lives Matter and the queering of black liberation, see also Cathy Cohen's acceptance speech of the Kessler Award, http://fireandink.org/not-the-civil-rights-movement/.

16. Chatelain, "Women and Black Lives Matter," p. 60.

17. For de Certeau's writings on 1968, see *The Capture of Speech and Other Political Writings*, trans. Tom Conley, University of Minnesota Press, 1997, pp. 1–76.

18. For an account from Habermas's perspective on his conflict with the Students for a Democratic Society, Rudi Dutschke, and the student protesters in 1967–69, see Matthew Specter, *Habermas: An Intellectual Biography*, Cambridge University Press, 2010, pp. 101–116.

19. "The function of the intellectual in the party is definitively over" (Mario Tronti, *Operai e capitale*, 4th edition, DeriveApprodi, 2013, p. 111).

20. The experiences of Anonymous are another complex example of the role of the mask in contemporary activism. See Gabriella Coleman, *Hacker, Hoaxer, Whistleblower, Spy: The Many Faces of Anonymous*, Verso, 2014.

21. Subcomandante Marcos, Ejército Zapatista de Liberación Nacional (EZLN) communiqué of May 28, 1994, reprinted in *Zapatistas! Documents of the New Mexican Revolution,* Autonomedia, 1995, pp. 310–311.

22. Beatriz Preciado, "Marcos Forever," *Libération*, June 6, 2014. For an artistic experiment with masks along similar lines, see Zach Blas, "Facial Weaponization Suite," http://www.zachblas.info/projects/facial-weaponization-suite/.

23. Subcomandante Marcos, "Entre la luz y la sombra," May 2014, http://enlacezapatista .ezln.org.mx/2014/05/25/entre-la-luz-y-la-sombra/.

24. Sandro Chignola, "Che cos'è un governo?," http://www.euronomade.info/?p=4417. Chignola borrows the image of the ellipse from Werner Näf.

CHAPTER 2

1. Georg Lukács expresses perhaps the most exaggerated version of the mind-body division described by this version of the centaur: "In this process which it can neither provoke nor escape, the Party is assigned the sublime role of *bearer of the class consciousness of the proletariat and the conscience of its historical vocation*" (*History and Class Consciousness*, trans. Rodney Livingstone, MIT Press, 1971, p. 41).

2. Leon Trotsky, *The History of the Russian Revolution*, trans. Max Eastman, University of Michigan Press, 1957, p. 170. Trotsky adds, "The coordination of the mass insurrection with the conspiracy, the subordination of the conspiracy to the insurrection, the organization of the insurrection through the conspiracy, constitutes that complex and responsible department of revolutionary politics which Marx and Engels called 'the art of insurrection' " (p. 169).

3. Rosa Luxemburg, *Mass Strike*, Harper Books, 1971, pp. 30 and 44.

4. For Lukács's critique of Luxemburg, see *History and Class Consciousness*, p. 279.

5. Luxemburg, *Mass Strike*, p. 68.

6. Although he does not express it with these terms, Karl Marx poses the logic of this relation between technical and political composition at several points in his work—when, for example, he claims that in mid-nineteenth-century France the urban proletariat must represent all the "healthy elements" of French society or lead the peasants. See *The Eighteenth Brumaire of Louis Bonaparte*, International, 1963, p. 128; and *The Civil War in France*, International, 1998, p. 64.

7. Antonio Gramsci, *Quaderni del carcere*, volume 3, ed. Valentino Garratana, Einaudi, 1975, p. 1634.

8. In the early 1960s Mario Tronti proposed an inversion of strategy and tactics as part of his effort to reimagine the relationship between workers' movements and the Italian Communist Party. See *Operai e capitale*, 4th edition, DeriveApprodi, 2013, p. 260. For one application of Tronti's reversal of strategy and tactics to contemporary struggles, see Pablo Ortellado, "Os protestos de junio entre o processo e o resultado," in *Vinte centavos: A luta contra o aumento*, pp. 227–239, especially p. 228; and Bruno Cava, "14 dias," http://www.quadradodosloucos.com.br/3946/14-dias/.

9. See Friedrich Meinecke, *Das Zeitalter, der Deutschen Erhebung (1795–1825)*, Vandenhoeck & Ruprecht, 1963.

10. See Carl Schmitt, *Theory of the Partisan*, trans. G. L. Ulmen, Telos Press, 2007.

11. Aldon Morris, "Black Southern Sit-in Movement: An Analysis of Internal Organization," *American Sociological Review*, 46, December 1981, pp. 744–767.

12. "We didn't expect the revolt," Romano Alquati explains regarding a "spontaneous" worker uprising, "but we organized it" ("Interview with Romano Alquati," in Giuseppe Trotta and Fabio Milana, eds., *L'operaismo degli anni sessanta: Dai "Quaderni Rossi" a "Classe Operaia*," DeriveApprodi, 2008, p. 738). For excellent analyses of autonomous workers' struggles in Turin, see Romano Alquati, *Sulla FIAT ed altri scritti*, Feltrinelli, 1975.

13. Although we share his focus on the need for organization, we part company with Alain Badiou when, in his typology of contemporary revolts, he characterizes "immediate riots," such as those in Greece in 2008 and London in 2011, as spontaneous uprisings. On the ignorance of causes more generally, see Baruch Spinoza, *Ethics*, book 1 appendix.

14. Ernesto Laclau's *On Populist Reason* (Verso, 2007) has been an influential resource for contemporary theories of populism and power.

CHAPTER 3

1. "Sovereign is he who decides on the exception" (Carl Schmitt, *Political Theology: Four Chapters on the Concept of Sovereignty*, trans. George Schwab, University of Chicago Press, 2005, p. 5).

2. See, among the vast literature on this topic, Harold Laski, *The Foundations of Sovereignty*, Harcourt, Brace, 1921; Hans Kelsen, *Das Problem der Souveränität und die Theorie des Völkerrechts*, Mohr, 1920; and Bertrand de Jouvenel, *Sovereignty*, University of Chicago Press, 1957.

3. Alvaro Reyes and Mara Kaufman, "Sovereignty, Indigeneity, Territory: Zapatista Autonomy and the New Practices of Decolonization," *South Atlantic Quarterly*, 110:2, Spring 2011, pp. 505–525, especially pp. 506–512. For Michel Foucault on how the political models of the colonies were transported back to Europe, see *Society Must Be Defended*, trans. David Macey, Picador, 2003, p. 103 (lecture of February 4, 1976).

4. "Sovereignty cannot be represented for the same reason that it cannot be alienated; it consists essentially in the general will, and the will does not admit of being represented: either it is the same or it is different; there is no middle ground" (Jean-Jacques Rousseau, *Of the Social Contract*, in *The Social Contract and Other Later Political Writings*, ed. and trans. Victor Gourevitch, Cambridge University Press, 1997, p. 114). Richard Fralin's *Rousseau and Representation*, Columbia University Press, 1978) is a classic text on this theme. For some more recent and differing views, see Joshua Cohen, *Rousseau: A Free Community of Equals*, Oxford University Press, 2010; Kevin Inston, "Representing the Unrepresentable: Rousseau's Legislator and the Impossible Object of the People," *Contemporary Political Theory*, 9:4, November 2010, pp. 393–413; and Robin Douglass, "Rousseau's Critique of Representative Sovereignty," *American Journal of Political Science*, 57:3, July 2013, pp. 735–747.

5. Rousseau, *Of the Social Contract*, p. 61.

6. "It is important, then, that in order to have the general will expressed well, there be no partial society in the State, and every Citizen state only his own opinion" (Rousseau, *Of the Social Contract*, p. 60).

7. Rousseau, *Discourse on the Origin and Foundations of Inequality among Men*, in *The Discourses and Other Early Political Writings*, ed. and trans. Victor Gourevitch, Cambridge University Press, 1997, p. 161.

8. Robert Michels, *Political Parties*, trans. Eden Paul and Cedar Paul, Free Press, 1915 (German orig. 1911). One might conjecture that he does not challenge the conservative parties of his time because they make no pretense to democracy. Indeed, after the First World War Michels joined the Italian Fascist Party.

9. Marty Cohen, David Karol, Hans Noel, and John Zaller, *The Party Decides*, University of Chicago Press, 2008. The Republican Party establishment's inability to prevent Donald Trump's nomination as presidential candidate in 2016 is a notable exception.

10. Citizens United v. Federal Elections Commission, 558 U.S. 310 (2010). Teachout wonders whether passages like this betray the fact that "some justices have abandoned faith in democratic politics." Zephyr Teachout, *Corruption in America*, Harvard University Press, 2014, p. 267. For an example of a conservative argument that explicitly poses the *Citizens United* decision against the party-media system, see Glenn Hubbard and Tim Kane, "In Defense of Citizens United," *Foreign Affairs*, 92:4, 2013, pp. 126–133. Hubbard and Kane argue that whereas the 1971 campaign finance law put elections effectively in the hands of the two parties and the dominant media, *Citizens United* restores "political competition." The primary focus of their argument is not that the wealthy should have more political power but rather that the political party and media elites should not have a monopoly on it.

11. Perceived dangers of the electoral successes of Donald Trump in Republican primaries inspired many conservative commentators to celebrate the nonrepresentative nature of the party system. "The less-than-democratic side of party nominations," claims Ross Douthat, "is a virtue of our system, not a flaw, and it has often been a necessary check on the passions (Trumpian or otherwise) that mass democracy constantly threatens to unleash" ("The Party Still Decides," *New York Times*, March 13, 2016).

12. Micah White makes a similar point from the perspective of protest movements: "The repertoire of protest tactics…[was] designed to influence elected representatives who had to listen to their constituents. But the breakdown of that paradigm has happened" (*The End of Protest*, Knopf Canada, 2016, p. 36).

13. On constituent power, see Antonio Negri, *Insurgencies*, University of Minnesota Press, 1999. Hannah Arendt emphasizes the political character of constituent power in *On Revolution*, Viking, 1963.

14. Carl Schmitt's conception of constituent power, for instance, rests on the structure of European public law that presumes the sovereignty of the nation-state and its legal order. See Carl Schmitt, *Constitutional Theory*, trans. Jeffrey Seitzer, Duke University Press, 2008.

15. Giorgio Agamben, *The Use of Bodies*, trans. Adam Kotsko, Stanford University Press, 2016, p. 266. See also Agamben, *Homo Sacer*, trans. Daniel Heller-Roazen, Stanford University Press, 1998, pp. 43–44.

16. Jacques Derrida, "Force of Law," in Drucilla Cornell, Michel Rosenfeld, and David Gray Carlson, eds., *Deconstruction and the Possibility of Justice*, Routledge,

1992, pp. 3–67, quote on p. 38. (For the French original text, see *Force de loi*, Galilée, 1994, pp. 93–94.)

17. For an account that poses Black Lives Matter in line with the other struggles in the cycle that began in 2011, see Khaled Beydoun and Pricilla Ocen, "Baltimore and the Emergence of a Black Spring," *Al Jazeera*, May 5, 2015, http://www.aljazeera.com/indepth/opinion/2015/05/baltimore-emergence-black-spring-150504123031263.html.

18. Alexander Weheliye, *Habeas Viscus: Racializing Assemblages, Biopolitics, and Black Feminist Theories of the Human*, Duke University Press, 2014, p. 4.

19. See, for instance, Günther Teubner, "Societal Constitutionalism: Alternatives to State-Centered Constitutional Theory?," in Christian Jeorges, Inger-Johanne Sand, and Teubner, eds., *Transnational Governance and Constitutionalism*, Bloomsbury, 2004, pp. 3–28.

20. Gary Wilder, *Freedom Time*, Duke University Press, 2015, p. 2.

21. Nazan Üstündağ, "Self-Defense as a Revolutionary Practice in Rojava, or How to Unmake the State," *South Atlantic Quarterly*, 115:1, January 2016, pp. 197–210, quote on p. 198. See also Bülent Küçük and Ceren Özselçuk, "Rojava Experience: Possibilities and Challenges of Building a Democratic Life," in the same issue, pp. 184–196; Ali B., "Eroding the State in Rojava," *Theory and Event*, 19:1 supplement, January 2016, https://muse.jhu.edu/article/610227; and Wes Enzinna, "The Rojava Experiment," *New York Times Magazine*, November 29, 2015, pp. 38–49.

22. "Communism is Soviet power plus the electrification of the whole country, since industry cannot be developed without electrification" (Vladimir Lenin, "Our Foreign and Domestic Position and Party Tasks," speech delivered on November 21, 1920, in *Collected Works*, Progress, 1965, volume 31, pp. 408–426).

23. For Marx's periodization, handicrafts–manufacture–large-scale industry, see *Capital*, volume 1, trans. Ben Fowkes, Penguin, 1976, pp. 492–508 and 544–553. For Vercellone's extended periodization, see *Connaissance et division du travail dans la dynamique longue du capitalisme*, thèse d'habilation à diriger des recherches, Université Paris 1 Pantheon Sorbonne, 2014.

24. Wendy Brown, *Edgework*, Princeton University Press, 2005, p. 46.

25. Brown, *Edgework*, p. 44.

26. See, for example, Kenneth Arrow, *Social Choice and Individual Values*, 2nd edition, John Wiley and Sons, 1963.

27. Étienne Balibar, *Equaliberty*, trans. James Ingram, Duke University Press, 2014.

28. On the fact that the conditions of Keynesianism no longer exist, see Giovanni Arrighi, *The Long Twentieth Century*, Verso, 1994.

29. Slavoj Žižek, "The Simple Courage of Decision: A Leftist Tribute to Thatcher," *New Statesman*, April 17, 2013, http://www.newstatesman.com/politics/politics/2013/04/simple-courage-decision-leftist-tribute-thatcher. Žižek cites Badiou's views on "the master" from Alain Badiou and Elisabeth Roudinesco, "Appel aux psychanalystes: Entretien avec Eric Aeschimann," *Le Nouvel Observateur*,

April 19, 2012. On the psychoanalytic dogma regarding the need for the leader in social organization through identification with the ego-ideal in the form of the father figure, see also Sigmund Freud, *Group Psychology and the Analysis of the Ego*, trans. James Strachey, Norton, 1921.

30. Jodi Dean, *The Communist Horizon*, Verso, 2012. For a useful critique of Dean's argument, see Sandro Mezzadra and Brett Neilson, "The Materiality of Communism: Politics beyond Representation and the State," *South Atlantic Quarterly*, 113:4, Fall 2013, pp. 777–790.

CHAPTER 4

1. Corey Robin correctly identifies the reactionary nature of right-wing thought in *The Reactionary Mind*, Oxford University Press, 2011.

2. Carl Schmitt, *State, Movement, People: The Triadic Structure of the Political Unity*, trans. Simona Draghici, Plutarch Press, 2001. Giorgio Agamben reads Schmitt's pamphlet in order to critique progressive and liberation movements, but in our view he misses the essential characteristics that distinguish right-wing movements. See his lecture "Movement," trans. Arianna Bove, http://www.generation-online .org/p/fpagamben3.htm.

3. In Schmitt's analysis, fascist leadership repeats some of the characteristics of leadership developed in liberation and revolutionary movements but now freed of the constant strains between hierarchy and democracy. It should be no surprise that Schmitt admires the political leadership of Lenin and the Bolsheviks, as well as Mao Zedong. See *Theory of the Partisan*, trans. G. L. Ulmen, Telos Press, 2007, pp. 48–60.

4. Schmitt, *State, Movement, People*, p. 37.

5. The movement, he argues, is the pivotal element in any project for political unity between the state (which is political but static in the sense that it cannot engage the people and interpret its needs) and the people (which is dynamic but fundamentally apolitical in the sense that it is incapable of expressing its needs, organizing social structures to meet them, and, above all, making decisions). The movement "penetrates" both the state and the people, shuttling between them and weaving them together. "[N]either the present-day State (in the sense of political unity)," Schmitt writes, "nor the German people of today (the subject of the political entity which is the 'German Reich') would be imaginable without the Movement" (p. 12). Right-wing movements, however, can only perform this mediatory function with a specific configuration of the people, maintained as a unity, bounded by national, religious, or ethnic identity. The people, the object of right-wing movements, must be one.

6. Schmitt, *State, Movement, People*, p. 51.

7. Christopher Parker and Matt Barreto, *Change They Can't Believe In*, Princeton University Press, 2013.

8. Schmitt, *State, Movement, People*, p. 48. Paradoxically, given the racist and fascist core of his thought, Schmitt poses the need for identity between the leader and the people as an anticolonial argument. This identity distinguishes leadership, according to Schmitt, from command and domination, such as British rule in Egypt and India, which are characterized by "alien-transmitted will."

9. Robin, *The Reactionary Mind*, p. 55.

10. Hannah Arendt, *Origins of Totalitarianism*, Harcourt, 1966, p. 72.

11. See David Roediger, *The Wages of Whiteness,* Verso, 1991; and W. E. B. Du Bois, *Black Reconstruction in America*, Oxford University Press, 2014.

12. See Cheryl Harris, "Whiteness as Property," *Harvard Law Review*, 106:8, June 1993, pp. 1707–1791, quote on p. 1758.

13. Property is also gendered in ways parallel to how it is raced, as feminist scholars have long demonstrated. Familial ideologies and legal practices often intersect with religious discourses. Abortion rights, LGBTQ abortion rights, and artificial insemination rights, for example, constitute together a complex framework in which public law is interwoven with defenses of the right to property, inheritance, and identitarian claims.

14. Ernst Troeltsch, *The Social Teaching of the Christian Churches*, 2 volumes, trans. Olive Wyon, Macmillan, 1931.

15. Gershom Sholem, *Sabbatai Sevi: The Mystic Messiah*, trans. R. J. Zwi Werblowsky, Princeton University Press, 1976.

16. Werner Sombart, *Der modern Kapitalismus*, 2 volumes, Duncker & Humblot, 1902; Max Weber, *The Protestant Ethic and the Spirit of Capitalism*, trans. Talcott Parsons, Routledge, 2nd edition, 2001; Ernst Bloch, *Thomas Müntzer als Theologe der Revolution*, Wolff, 1921; Vittorio Lanternari, *The Religions of the Oppressed*, New American Library, 1965; and Ranajit Guha, *Elementary Aspects of Peasant Insurgency in Colonial India*, Duke University Press, 1999.

17. Alain Bertho, *Les enfants du chaos*, La découverte, 2016, p. 13.

18. For a fuller analysis of martyrdom and suicide bombers, see our *Multitude*, Penguin Press, 2004, pp. 45, 54, and 346–347.

19. Voltaire, "The ABC," in *Political Writings*, David Williams, ed., Cambridge University Press, 1994, pp. 85–194, quote on p. 147.

20. Erik Peterson, *Der Monotheismus als politisches Problem*, Hegner, 1935.

21. See Fred Dallmyr, "Gandhi and Islam: A Heart-and-Mind Unity?," in Douglas Allen, ed., *The Philosophy of Mahatma Gandhi for the Twenty-First Century*, Lexington Books, 2008, pp. 143–162.

22. On the passage from Left to Right of progressive populisms, see Zeev Sternhell, *Ni droite ni gauche*, Seuil, 1983; and *Les anti-Lumières: Du XVIIIe siècle à la Guerre Froide*, Gallimard, 2010.

23. See Giovanni Tarello, *Profili giuridici della questione della povertà nel francescanesimo prima di Ockham*, Giuffré, 1964; and Malcolm Lambert, *Franciscan Poverty*, Church Historical Society, 1961.

24. See Herbert Grundmann, *Religious Movements in the Middle Ages*, trans. Steven Rowan, University of Notre Dame Press, 1995.

25. In their arguments against property, Franciscans look all the way back to the Garden of Eden, where there was no "use of right" over property (*usus juris*) but only *usus facti*, that is, use in fact, actual use of goods in a situation of wealth and abundance. And although these uses are lost with the fall from the garden they are won back with the passion of Christ.

26. Giorgio Agamben grasps beautifully the importance of this modern theoretical revolution in *The Highest Poverty*, Stanford University Press, 2013. He recognizes the limits of the ways in which it can subvert the existing order, maintaining that the *usus pauper* does not manage to liberate a "form of bare life" unconstrained by rules. In the Franciscan concept of poverty, he claims, there remains an imposed rule and life is not able to free itself and produce an "authentic form." What we cannot accept in his reading—beyond the claim that in the Franciscan polemic the *usus pauper* expressly demands an *abdicatio iuris*—is that he interprets this as an emptying of subjectivity, of *opera* (praxis), and every common, cooperative, virtuous determination of the concept of *usus*. In fact, once Franciscanism pushed to the limit the relationship between poverty (as a form of life) and *usus facti* as a virtuous relation to things, one can only take the next step and establish a positive connection between poverty and use when the common comes to constitute the mode of production.

27. Karl Marx, *Grundrisse*, trans. Martin Nicolaus, Penguin, 1973, p. 296.

28. See Judith Butler, *Precarious Life*, Verso, 2006; *Frames of War*, Verso, 2010; and *Notes toward a Performative Theory of Assembly*, Harvard University Press, 2015.

29. Spinoza ridicules efforts to ascribe identitarian attributes to the divine: "if a triangle could speak, it would say . . . that God is eminently triangular, while a circle would say that the divine nature is eminently circular. Thus each would ascribe to God its own attributes, would assume itself to be like God, and look on everything else as ill-shaped" (letter 56 to Hugo Boxel, 1674 in *Complete Works*, trans. Samuel Shirley, Hackett, 2002, p. 904, translation modified).

CHAPTER 5

1. We should note some academic trends in critiquing modernity that we regard as allied to our project here. See, for example, Bruno Karsenti's analysis of the history of the modern social sciences in terms of a self-critique of individualism, *D'une philosophie à l'autre*, Gallimard, 2013. From the bourgeois point of view, in fact, the legitimation of individualism would no longer be posed either as Enlightenment individualism or as the so-called organicist theories of the counterrevolution. Karsenti considers the task today, instead, beyond the modern, is to confront the decline of the individualistic human sciences through an archeology of the social sciences. Another important stream of critiques of modernity is represented by the work of Walter Mignolo and the recognition of modernity's intrinsic relation

to coloniality. See, for example, *The Darker Side of Western Modernity*, Duke University Press, 2011.

2. Niccolò Machiavelli, *The Prince*, trans. Peter Bonadella, Oxford University Press, 2005, p. 84.

3. For some important arguments that date the shift in capitalist development to the early 1970s, albeit with different emphases, see Giovanni Arrighi, *The Long Twentieth Century*, Verso, 1994; David Harvey, *A Brief History of Neoliberalism*, Verso, 2007; and Wolfgang Streeck, *Buying Time*, Verso, 2014.

4. Antonio Gramsci, *Further Selections from the Prison Notebooks*, ed. and trans. Derek Boothman, University of Minnesota Press, 1995, p. 347 (cited in Peter Thomas, *The Gramscian Moment*, Brill, 2009 p. 275).

5. Louis Althusser, *Essays in Self-criticism*, trans. Grahame Lock, New Left Books, 1976, p. 155.

6. Wilhelm Dilthey and Paul Yorck von Wartenburg, *Briefwechsel zwischen Wilhelm Dilthey und dem Graf Paul Yorck von Wartenburg*, Niemeyer, 1923.

7. On the cycle of movements that began in 2011, in addition to our *Declaration* (Argo Navis, 2012), see Alain Badiou, *The Rebirth of History: Times of Riots and Uprisings*, trans. Gregory Elliott, Verso, 2012; and Paul Mason, *Why It's Still Kicking Off Everywhere*, Verso, 2013.

8. For an explanation of the concept of multitude as a political project and responses to some critiques of the concept, see Michael Hardt and Antonio Negri, *Multitude*, Penguin Press, 2004, pp. 219–227; and *Commonwealth*, Harvard University Press, 2009, pp. 165–178.

9. See Michael Hardt, "Translator's Foreword: The Anatomy of Power," in Antonio Negri, *The Savage Anomaly: The Power of Spinoza's Metaphysics and Politics*, University of Minnesota Press, 1991, pp. 11–16. Those interested in the philological roots of this distinction can consider the use of potestas and potentia in Boethius's *Consolation of Philosophy*, which is representative in certain respects of the Latin tradition. See Clifford Robinson, "The Longest Transference: Self-Consolation and Politics in Latin Philosophical Literature," PhD dissertation, Duke University, 2014; and Joseph Dane, "Potestas/potentia: Note on Boethius's De Consolatione Philosophiae," *Vivarium*, 17:2, 1979, pp. 81–89. Different German terms for power are used to correspond to the Latin potentia, including die Macht and das Potential. In the philosophical context we prefer the generic translation das Vermögen and also the verb vermögen, such as in this German translation of a well-known Spinoza passage: "Was freilich der Körper alles vermag, hat bis jetzt noch niemand festgestellt" (*Ethik*, trans. Jakob Stern, Holzinger, p. 97).

10. Michel Foucault, "The Subject and Power," *Critical Inquiry*, 8:4, Summer 1982, pp. 777–795, quote on p. 790. For Machiavelli we are thinking primarily of *The Prince*.

11. For two excellent accounts of Western Marxism, see Perry Anderson, *Considerations on Western Marxism*, Verso, 1976; and Fredric Jameson, *Marxism and Form*, Princeton University Press, 1974.

12. Georg Lukács, *History and Class Consciousness*, trans. Rodney Livingstone, MIT Press, 1971, p. 258.

13. Maurice Merleau-Ponty, "'Western' Marxism," in *Adventures of the Dialectic*, trans. Joseph Bien, Northwestern University Press, 1973, pp. 30–58, quotes on pp. 30–31 and 41.

14. Hans-Jürgen Krahl, *Konstitution und Klassenkampf*, Neue Kritik, 1971.

15. Merleau-Ponty, "'Western' Marxism," p. 222.

16. Gilles Deleuze, *Foucault*, trans. Sean Hand, University of Minnesota Press, 1988, p. 27.

17. Deleuze, *Foucault*, p. 144.

PART II

1. Niccolò Machiavelli, *The Prince*, trans. Peter Bonadella, Oxford University Press, 2005, p. 53.

2. See, for instance, E. P. Thompson, "History from Below," *Times Literary Supplement*, April 7, 1966, pp. 279–280.

3. W. E. B. Du Bois, *The Souls of Black Folks*, Dover, 1994, p. 2.

4. James Baldwin, "Encounter on the Seine," *Notes of a Native Son*, Beacon Press, 1955, pp. 119–167, quote on pp. 122–123.

5. On feminist standpoint theory, for example, see Patricia Hill Collins, *Black Feminist Thought*, Routledge, 1991; and Sandra Harding, ed., *The Standpoint Theory Reader*, Routledge, 2004.

6. Max Weber, *Economy and Society*, 2 volumes, ed. Guenther Roth and Claus Wittich, University of California Press, 1978, volume 1, p. 53.

7. Weber, *Economy and Society*, volume 2, p. 946.

8. Hannah Arendt, *On Revolution*, Viking, 1963, p. 193.

9. Raymond Aron claims that Marx, in contrast to Machiavelli, imagines himself to be a "confidant of providence." See "Machiavelli and Marx" in *Politics and History*, trans. Miriam Conant, Transaction, 1984, pp. 87–101, especially, pp. 92–93. On Weber's banishment of the affects, see *Economy and Society*, volume 2, p. 975.

10. Michel Foucault, *The Birth of Biopolitics*, ed. Michel Senellart, trans. Graham Burchell, Picador, 2004, pp. 2–3.

11. Michel Foucault and Noam Chomsky, *The Chomsky-Foucault Debate: On Human Nature*, New Press, 2006, p. 51.

CHAPTER 6

1. Hugo Grotius, *Commentary on the Law of Prize and Booty*, trans. Gwladys Williams and Walter Zeydel, Clarendon, 1950, p. 227 For an original reading of Grotius, particularly sensitive to the colonial and capitalist relations of the modern world system, see Eric Wilson, *The Savage Republic: De Indis of Hugo Grotius, Republicanism*

and Dutch Hegemony within the Early Modern World-System (1600–1619), Martinus Nijhoff, 2008.

2. William Blackstone, *Commentaries on the Laws of England*, 4 volumes, Clarendon, 1765, volume 2, p. 2.

3. Property, writes John Commons, is "not a single absolute right, but a bundle of rights" (*The Distribution of Wealth*, Macmillan, 1893, p. 92). For good histories of the bundle of rights conception, see Daniel Klein and John Robinson, "Property: A Bundle of Rights? Prologue to the Property Symposium," *Econ Journal Watch*, 8:30, September 2011, pp. 193–204; and Fabienne Orsi, "Elinor Ostrom et le faisceaux de droits," *Revue de la régulation*, Autumn 2013, https://regulation.revues.org/10471.

4. Felix Cohen, "Dialogue on Private Property," *Rutgers Law Review*, 9:2, Winter 1954, pp. 357–387, quote on p. 362.

5. Morris Cohen, "Property and Sovereignty," *Cornell Law Review*, 13:1, December 1927, pp. 8–30, quote on p. 29.

6. M. Cohen, "Property and Sovereignty," p. 13.

7. For a recent argument that outlines this connection in the history of European political and legal thought, see Ugo Mattei: "The strong connection between the theories of sovereignty and those of property is easy to see" (*Beni comuni: Un manifesto*, Laterza, 2011, p. 43).

8. Robert Hale, "Coercion and Distribution in a Supposedly Non-coercive State," *Political Science Quarterly*, 38:3, September 1923, pp. 470–494, quote on p. 472.

9. See Duncan Kennedy, "The Stakes of Law, or Hale and Foucault!" *Legal Studies Forum*, 15:4, 1991, pp. 327–366; and Stephen Munzer, "Property as Social Relations," in Munzer, ed., *New Essays in the Legal and Political Theory of Property*, Cambridge University Press, 2001, pp. 36–75.

10. Duncan Kennedy, "The Limited Equity Coop as a Vehicle for Affordable Housing in a Race and Class Divided Society," *Harvard Law Journal*, 46:1, 2002, pp. 85–125; "10 Years of Creative Commons: An Interview with Co-Founder Lawrence Lessig," http://governancexborders.com/2012/12/18/10-years-of-creative-commons-an-interview-with-co-founder-lawrence-lessig/; and Anna di Robilant, "Common Ownership and Equality of Autonomy," *McGill Law Journal*, 58:2, 2012, pp. 263–320, especially pp. 301–319.

11. See Harold Demsetz, "Toward a Theory of Property Rights," *American Economic Review*, 57:2, May 1967, pp. 347–359; and Armen Alchien and Harold Demsetz, "The Property Right Paradigm," *Journal of Economic History*, 33:1, March 1973, pp. 16–27. On the neoliberal use of the bundle of rights conception, see Orsi, "Elinor Ostrom et le faisceaux de droits."

12. Kaiser Aetna v. United States, 444 U.S. 164 (1979).

13. On how progressive property theory counters a neoliberal economics approach, see Timothy Mulvaney, "Progressive Property Moving Forward," *California Law Review*, 5, September 2014, pp. 349–373, especially p. 352.

14. Joseph William Singer, "Property as the Law of Democracy," *Duke Law Journal*, 63, 2014, pp. 1287–1335, quote on pp. 1334–1335.

15. Gregory Alexander, Eduardo Peñalver, Joseph Singer, and Laura Underkuffler, "A Statement of Progressive Property," *Cornell Law Review*, 94, 2009, pp. 743–744, quote on p. 744.

16. "Property implicates plural and incommensurable values"(Alexander, Peñalver, Singer, and Underkuffler, "A Statement of Progressive Property," p. 743). Ezra Rosser argues that the progressive property school is unable to reorient fundamentally the social relations created by property so long as it is unable to address racial hierarchies and injustices. See "The Ambition and Transformative Potential of Progressive Property," *California Law Review*, 101, 2013, pp. 107–171.

17. See, for example, Yochai Benkler, *The Wealth of Networks*, Yale University Press, 2006; and Lawrence Lessig, *Free Culture,* Penguin, 2004. See also Michele Surdi, "Lo spettro di Blanco: Una nota ad Ugo Mattei," *Scienza & Politica*, 24:46, 2012, pp. 69–75. Surdi insists that private property becomes increasingly contradictory as it becomes no longer possession of a material good but the pretense of possession of a service. Such goods can no longer be isolated and individuated. In other words, today, confronting forms of production that are socialized, individual private property appears as merely the residue of a previous era.

18. John Locke, *Second Treatise*, chapter 5, section 27.

19. See, for example, Title 35 of the US Code, paragraph 101.

20. Karl Marx, *Capital*, volume 1, trans. Ben Fowkes, Penguin, 1976, p. 928.

21. Karl Marx, "Draft of an Article on Friedrich List's Book, *Das Nationale System der Politischen Oekonomie*," in Karl Marx and Frederick Engels, *Collected Works,* International, 1975, volume 4, 265. See also Roman Szporluk, *Communism and Nationalism: Karl Marx versus Friedrich List*, Oxford University Press, 1988.

22. Jean-Marie Harribey, "André Orléan, *L'empire de la valeur*," book review, *Revue de la régulation*, Fall 2011, http://regulation.revues.org/9483.

23. See Antonio Negri, "Labor in the Constitution," in Michael Hardt and Antonio Negri, *Labor of Dionysus*, University of Minnesota Press, 1994, pp. 53–138. On how the New Deal and the Keynesian state were responses to the militancy of radical labor organizing, see Antonio Negri, "Keynes and the Capitalist Theory of the State," in Hardt and Negri, *Labor of Dionysus*, pp. 23–51; and Richard Hurd, "New Deal Labor Policy and the Containment of Radical Union Activity," *Review of Radical Political Economists*, 8:3, 1976, pp. 32–43.

24. See, among others, Alain Supiot, *The Spirit of Philadelphia: Social Justice versus the Total Market*, Verso, 2012.

25. See Stefano Rodotà, *Il diritto di avere diritti*, Laterza, 2012; and Ugo Mattei, *Beni comuni: Un manifesto*, Laterza, 2011; as well as Ugo Mattei, "Protecting the Commons," *South Atlantic Quarterly*, 112:2, Spring 2013, pp. 366–376.

26. See Stefano Rodotà, "La grande trasformazione sociale," *Alfabeta2*, 29, May 2013, p. 20; and Giso Amendola, "Per un costituzionalismo dei bisogni," *Alfabeta2*, 29, May 2013, p. 23.

27. See Karl Marx, *The Eighteenth Brumaire of Louis Bonaparte*, International, 1963, pp. 65–66 and 118.

28. One should construct for each country and region a specific history of the destruction of common forms of land tenure and the transformation of the land into private property. Some examples of what should be a very long list include, regarding Europe, Marx's analysis of primitive accumulation, *Capital*, volume 1, pp. 871–940; and Peter Linebaugh, *The Magna Carta Manifesto*, University of California Press, 2008; regarding indigenous land tenure in Latin America, José Maria Maríategui, *Seven Interpretive Essays on Peruvian Reality*, trans. Marjory Urquidi, University of Texas Press, 1971; and regarding South Asia, Ranajit Guha, *A Rule of Property for Bengal*, Duke University Press, 1996.

29. Maria Rosaria Marella provides a useful categorization of objects of legal thought of the common in "I beni comuni," *Libro del anno del diritto*, 2013, pp. 13–16. See also, on the common as *tertium genus*, Maria Rosaria Marella, "Beni comuni: Oltre l'opposizione natura/cultura," *Lettera internazionale*, 113:3, 2012, pp. 9–14. For a general treatment of the common, see Antonio Hardt and Michael Negri, *Commonwealth*, Harvard University Press, 2009, and for a specific focus on the metropolis as common, pp. 249–260. For a contrast between the limited nature of the earth as common and the reproducible character of immaterial common wealth, see Michael Hardt, "Two Faces of Apocalypse," *Polygraph*, 22, 2010, pp. 264–274.

30. Elinor Ostrom, *Governing the Commons: The Evolution of Institutions for Collective Action*, Cambridge University Press, 1990, p. 20.

31. Quoted in Albert O. Hirschman, *The Passions and the Interests*, Princeton University Press, 1977, p. 101.

32. "The *value*, or WORTH of a man," Thomas Hobbes claims, "is as of all other things, his price; that is to say, so much as would be given for the use of his Power" (*Leviathan*, Oxford University Press, 1998, p. 51).

33. Baruch Spinoza, *Ethics*, part III, proposition 18, scolium 2, in *Complete Works*, ed. Samuel Shirley, Hackett, 2002, pp. 188–189.

34. Rebecca Solnit, *A Paradise Built in Hell: The Extraordinary Communities That Arise in Disaster*, Penguin, 2009, p. 6. For some among the numerous examples of relative security created in the common in times of social and economic crisis, see Anne Alison, *Precarious Japan*, Duke University Press, 2013, pp. 180–206 (on life after the Fukushima disaster); and Naomi Klein, *The Shock Doctrine*, Metropolitan Books, 2007, pp. 533–561; and *This Changes Everything*, Simon & Schuster, 2014, pp. 291–448.

35. Joseph Schumpeter, *Capitalism, Socialism, and Democracy*, Harper, 1942, p. 142.

36. Karl Marx, *Economic and Philosophical Manuscripts*, in *Early Writings*, trans. Rodney Livingstone, Penguin Classics, 1974, pp. 297–400, quote on p. 361.

37. "The ability for enjoyment [*Die Fähigkeit des Genusses*] is a condition of enjoyment, hence its primary means, and this ability is the development of an individual potential, a force of production" (Karl Marx, *Grundrisse*, trans. Martin

Nicolaus, Penguin, 1973, p. 711, translation modified. Original text: "Die Fähigkeit des Genusses ist Bedingung für denselben, als erstes Mittel desselben, und diese Fähigkeit ist Entwicklung einer individuellen Anlage, Produktivkraft.").

38. The literature on precarious labor in Europe (and somewhat less in North America and Japan) is enormous. For an excellent analysis of precarious work in South Africa, see Franco Barchiesi, *Precarious Liberation*, SUNY Press, 2011.

39. Judith Butler, *Notes toward a Performative Theory of Assembly*, Harvard University Press, 2015, p. 150.

40. Among the many excellent analyses of the construction of institutions of the common, see Pascal Nicolas-Le Strat, "Agir en commun / agir le commun," May 1, 2014, http://blog.le-commun.fr/?p=738.

41. Duncan Kennedy, "The Stakes of Law, or Hale and Foucault," in *Sexy Dressing Etc.*, Harvard University Press, 1993, pp. 83–125, quote on p. 85.

42. C. B. Macpherson, *The Political Theory of Possessive Individualism*, Oxford University Press, 1969.

43. Alexandra Kollontai, "Sexual Relations and the Class Struggle," in Alix Holt, ed., *Selected Writings of Alexandra Kollontai*, Allison & Busby, 1977, pp. 237–249.

44. Mattei, *Beni comuni*, p. 99.

CHAPTER 7

1. Max Horkheimer and Theodor Adorno, *The Dialectic of Enlightenment*, trans. John Cumming, Continuum, 1972, p. xvi.

2. Martin Heidegger, "The Question concerning Technology," in *The Question Concerning Technology and Other Essays*, trans. William Lovitt, Garland, 1977, pp. 3–35, quote on p. 14.

3. Heidegger, "The Question concerning Technology," p. 28.

4. In some respects the pessimistic anthropology of Arnold Gehlen, another Nazi, is a variant on Heidegger's view of the relation of humans to technology. Gehlen maintains that technology, which has accompanied humanity from its origins, addresses a radical lack or insufficiency in humans, who are unable to exist on their own. See, for example, Arnold Gehlen, *Man in the Age of Technology*, trans. Patrice Lipscomb, Columbia University Press, 1980. And even when other German anthropologists contest Gehlen's anthropological pessimism, they seldom go beyond a functionalism that refers human technology, just beyond lack and insufficiency, to some organic disposition. See, for instance, Heinrich Popitz in *Der Aufbruch Zur Artifiziellen Gesellschaft: Zur Anthropologie Der Technik*, Mohr Siebeck, 1995, who constructs an "optimistic" [*sic*!] perspective insisting on the fact that the relationship of humanity to the world is already in some sense naturally determined by material or physiological predispositions. For excellent interpretations of Gehlen and these developments in anthropology, see Ubaldo Fadini, *Configurazioni antropologiche*, Liguori, 1991; and *Sviluppo tecnologico e identità personali*, Dedalo, 2000.

5. Günther Anders, *Die Antiquiertheit des Menschen*, 3rd edition, C. H. Beck, 2009.

6. "But just as men, in the beginning, were able to make the easiest things with the tools they were born with (however laboriously and imperfectly), and once these had been made, made other, more difficult things with less labor and more perfectly, and so, proceeding gradually from the simplest works to tools, and from tools to other works and tools, reached the point where they accomplished so many and so difficult things with little labor, in the same way the intellect, by its inborn power, makes intellectual tools for itself, by which it acquires other powers for other intellectual works, and from these works still other tools, or the power of searching further, and so proceeds by stages, until it reaches the pinnacle of wisdom" (Baruch Spinoza, *The Emendation of the Intellect*, in *The Collected Works of Spinoza*, ed. Edwin Curley, volume 1, Princeton University Press, 1985, p. 17).

7. N. Katherine Hayles, *How We Became Postmodern*, University of Chicago Press, 1999, p. 7.

8. Hayles, *How We Became Postmodern*, pp. 283–291.

9. Gilbert Simondon, *Du mode d'existence des objets techniques*, Aubier, 1958, p. 12. For a development along these lines, see also Bernard Stiegler, *Technics and Time 1: The Fault of Epimetheus*, trans. Richard Beardsworth and George Collins, Stanford University Press, 1998.

10. Gilles Deleuze and Félix Guattari, "Balance-Sheet for 'Desiring Machines,'" in Guattari, *Chaosophy: Texts and Interviews, 1972–1977*, ed. Sylvère Lotringer, trans. David L. Sweet, Jarred Becker, and Taylor Adkins, Semiotext(e), 2009, p. 91. Original French, *L'anti-oedipe*, 2nd edition, Minuit, 1972, p. 464.

11. Walter Benjamin, "One Way Street," in *One Way Street and Other Writings*, trans. Edmund Jeffcott and Kingsley Shorter, New Left Books, 1979, pp. 45–104, quote on p. 104.

12. Popitz, *Der Aufbruch*.

13. Karl Marx, *Capital*, trans. Ben Fowkes, Penguin, 1976, volume 1, p. 773.

14. Marx, *Capital*, volume 2, p. 187.

15. Marx, *Capital*, volume 3, p. 373.

16. See, for example, Marx, *Capital*, volume 3, p. 322.

17. For a general discussion of the countervailing factors, see Marx, *Capital*, volume 3, chapter 14.

18. Karl Marx, *Grundrisse*, trans. Matin Nicolaus, Penguin, 1973, p. 749.

19. Carlo Vercellone, "Composizione organica di capitale e composizione di classe," in *La crisi messa a valore*, CW Press and Sfumature, 2015, pp. 103–118, quote on p. 114.

20. "From the standpoint of the direct production process it can be regarded as the production of *fixed capital*, this fixed capital being man himself." Marx, *Grundrisse*, p. 712 ("being man himself" in English in original).

21. See Emmanuel Renault, *L'expérience de l'injustice: Reconnaissance et clinique de l'injustice*, La découverte, 2004.

22. On the added alienation of emotional work, see Arlie Hochschild, *The Managed Heart*, University of California Press, 1983.

23. Christophe Dejours, *Souffrance en France: La banalisation de l'injustice sociale*, Seuil, 1998, p. 115.

24. Paolo Virno, "Virtuosity and Revolution," in Virno and Michael Hardt, eds., *Radical Thought in Italy*, University of Minnesota Press, 1994, pp. 13–37.

25. Luc Boltanski and Eve Chiapello, *The New Spirit of Capitalism*, Verso, 2006.

26. Matteo Pasquinelli, "Google's PageRank Algorithm," in Konrad Becker and Felix Stalder, eds., *Deep Search: The Politics of Search beyond Google*, Studien Verlag, 2009, pp. 152–162, quote on p. 155. See also Sergey Brin and Lawrence Page, "The Anatomy of a Large-Scale Hypertextual Web Search Engine," http://infolab .stanford.edu/~backrub/google.html; and Christian Fuchs, "A Contribution to the Critique of the Political Economy of Google," *Fast Capitalism*, 8:1, 2011, http:// www.fastcapitalism.com/.

27. Marx, *Capital*, volume 3, p. 927.

28. See, for example, Christian Fuchs, "Labor in Informational Capitalism and on the Internet," *Information Society*, 26:3, 2010, pp. 179–196.

29. Félix Guattari, "On Machines," trans. Vivian Constantinopoulos, "Complexity," ed., Andrew Benjamin, special issue, *Journal of Philosophy and Visual Arts*, no. 6, 1995 pp. 8–12. (Originally published as "A propos des machines" in *Chimères*, no 19, Spring 1993, pp. 85–96.) For an excellent analysis of the concept of machine in Guattari, see Gerald Raunig, "A Few Fragments on Machines," http://eipcp.net/ transversal/1106/raunig/en/#_ftnref39; and *Tausend Maschinen*, Klappen, 2008.

30. Louis Althusser, "Ideology and State Ideological Apparatuses," in *On Ideology*, Verso, 1971, pp. 1–60, quote on p. 56.

31. This dilemma is not solved when followers such as Étienne Balibar amend Althusser's affirmation: "it is [only] *in the process without a subject* as a historical process that the 'constitution of the subject' can have meaning" ("L'objet d'Althusser," in Sylvain Lazarus, ed., *Politique et philosophie dans l'œuvre d'Althusser*, Presses Universitaire de France, 1993, pp. 81–116, quote on p. 98).

32. See Donna Haraway, "A Cyborg Manifesto," in *Simians, Cyborgs, and Women*, Routledge, 1991, pp. 149–182; and, more recently, "Anthropocene, Capitalocene, Plantationoscene, Chthulucene: Making Kin," *Environmental Humanities*, 6, 2015, pp. 159–165.

33. On the anthropogenetic model, see Robert Boyer, *La croissance, début de siècle*, Albin Michel, 2002; and Christian Marazzi, "Capitalismo digitale e modello antropogenetico del lavoro," in Jean-Louis Laville, Christian Marazzi, Michele La Rosa, and Federico Chicchi, eds., *Reinventare il lavoro*, Sapere, 2000, pp. 107–126.

CHAPTER 8

1. James Scott, *Seeing Like a State*, Yale University Press, 1998.

2. See Antonio Negri, *The Political Descartes*, trans. Matteo Mandarini and Alberto Toscano, Verso, 2006.

3. On the need for an organization to have a leader, see Max Weber, *Economy and Society*, 2 volumes, ed. Guenther Roth and Claus Wittich, University of California Press, 1978, p. 48. On the translation of *Herrschaft*, see p. 61, note 31.

4. Weber, *Economy and Society*, p. 225.

5. On the separation of administrative staff from the means of production and administration, see pp. 218–219. On administration as a career, see p. 220. On the segregation of "official activity from the sphere of private life" of the bureaucrat, see p. 957. On the replacement of the "cultivated" administrator with the expert, see p. 1001.

6. Franz Kafka, "Before the Law," in *The Complete Stories*, ed. Nahum Glatzer, Schocken Books, 1946, pp. 3–4; and *The Castle*, trans. Anthea Bell, Oxford University Press, 2009. One of the innovative aspects of Deleuze and Guattari's reading of Kafka is that against the gray, impersonal domination of modern power they recognize creative minoritarian forces in Kafka's thought. See Gilles Deleuze and Félix Guattari, *Kafka: Toward a Minor Literature*, trans. Dana Polan, University of Minnesota Press, 1986.

7. Weber, *Economy and Society*, p. 225.

8. On rational, traditional, and charismatic forms of authority, see Weber, *Economy and Society*, pp. 212–302 and pp. 1111–1157.

9. Weber, *Economy and Society*, p. 972.

10. Weber certainly does understand the power of affects and even the necessity of engaging them in administration and politics. His study of charisma is one field for exploring this. More interesting might be his assessments of the importance of the 1905 and 1917 Russian Revolutions. See Max Weber, *The Russian Revolutions*, trans. Gordon Wells and Peter Baehr, Cornell University Press, 1995.

11. For one excellent investigation of the importance of political affects, which are completely inextricable from political reason, and an exploration of political action that is thoroughly interwoven with our powers to be affected, see Lauren Berlant, *Cruel Optimism*, Duke University Press, 2001. For the need to understand emotions and reasons together in social movements, see Deborah Gould, *Moving Politics: Emotion and ACT UP's Fight against AIDS*, University of Chicago Press, 2009.

12. Weber, *Economy and Society*, p. 973.

13. Karl Marx, *Capital*, trans. Ben Fowkes, Penguin, 1976, volume 1, pp. 546–548.

14. See Ursula Huws, *The Making of a Cybertariat*, Monthly Review Press, 2003. On digital Taylorism, see Hugh Lauder, Phillip Brown, and Gerbrand Tholen, "The Global Auction Model, Skill Bias Theory and Graduate Incomes," in *Educating for the Knowledge Economy?*, Routledge, 2012, pp. 43–65; and "Digital Taylorism," *Economist*, September 12, 2015, http://www.economist.com/news/business/2166 4190-modern-version-scientific-management-threatens-dehumanise-workplace -digital. For an analysis of Amazon's Mechanical Turk, a mechanism for outsourcing routine digital work, see Lilly Irani, "Difference and Dependence

among Digital Workers: The Case of Amazon Mechanical Turk," *South Atlantic Quarterly*, 114:1, January 2014, pp. 225–234.

15. Our insistence on "Weber in reverse" is also meant to challenge the way many political theorists identify Weber and Schmitt, citing their coincidence in *Jus publicum europeum*, as if state violence and the absolute nature of sovereign decision-making were the only basis on which power and administration can rely. Today, in fact, Schmitt's conception of sovereignty is dissolving, not only because it sustained totalitarian regimes in the past but especially because society is increasingly able to throw off its structures of command. In this context, a counterproject of nonsovereign administration, "Weber in reverse," emerges clearly. For arguments that put together Weber and Schmitt, see Massimo Cacciari, *Walther Rathenau e il suo ambiente*, De Donato, 1979; and Carlo Galli, *Genealogia della politica*, Il mulino, 1996.

16. Karl Marx, *The Civil War in France*, International, 1998, pp. 54–55; and "Letter to Kugelmann," April 12, 1871, in the same volume, p. 86.

17. Europe, of course, also pursued internal colonial relations in the eighteenth and nineteenth centuries, in Ireland, for example, and southern Italy. The colonial projects of Mitteleuropa were focused on eastern Europe, territories of uncertain nationalities and ancient cultural mixtures: economic projects of latifundium agriculture and enormous mines, along with the drafting of mercenary troops by the Austro-Hungarian bourgeoisie and the Prussian nobility. Rosa Luxemburg and the young Max Weber denounced these brutal forms of exploitation and accumulation.

18. Thomas Mann, "Goethe as a Representative of the Bourgeois Age," cited in Franco Moretti, *The Bourgeois*, Verso, 2013, p. 20.

19. Moretti, *The Bourgeois*, p. 20.

CHAPTER 9

1. Imre Szeman, "Entrepreneurship as the New Common Sense," *South Atlantic Quarterly*, 114:3, July 2015, pp. 471–490, quote on pp. 472–473.

2. Joseph Schumpeter, "The Creative Response in Economic History," in *Essays*, ed. Richard Clemence, Addison-Wesley Press, 1951, pp. 216–226, quote on p. 219.

3. Schumpeter, "The Creative Response in Economic History," p. 217.

4. Karl Marx, *Capital*, trans. Ben Fowkes, Penguin, 1976, volume 1, p. 447.

5. Joseph Schumpeter, "Theorie der wirtschaftlichen Entwicklung," trans. Markus Becker and Thorbjørn Knudsen (of selection from 1911 edition of *Theory of Economic Development*), *American Journal of Economics and Sociology*, 61:2, April 2002, pp. 405–437, quote on p. 415.

6. Marx, *Capital*, volume 1, p. 450.

7. Schumpeter, "Theorie der wirtschaftlichen Entwicklung," p. 413.

8. On Schumpeter's notion of the "Man of Action" in the 1911 edition, see Richard Swedberg, "Rebuilding Schumpeter's Theory of Entrepreneurship," in Yuichi

Shionoya and Tamotsu Nishizawa, eds., *Marshall and Schumpeter on Evolution*, Edward Elgar, 2008, pp. 188–203, especially pp. 190–191. On the "weight of personality" of the entrepreneur, see "Theorie der wirtschaftlichen Entwicklung," p. 414.

9. Joseph Schumpeter, *Theory of Economic Development*, Harvard University Press, 1934, p. 89.

10. Joseph Schumpeter, *Capitalism, Socialism, and Democracy*, Harper, 1942, p. 142.

11. Karl Marx himself critiques making historical relations of production into eternal categories (*Grundrisse*, trans. Martin Nicolaus, Penguin, 1973, p. 85) even though he flirts with such a stage conception both in the *German Ideology* and the *Grundrisse*.

12. For an argument that the effects of social entrepreneurship are ultimately indistinguishable from neoliberalism, specifically with respect to unemployment in Australia, see Beth Cook, Chris Dodds, and William Mitchell, "Social Entrepreneurship: False Premises and Dangerous Forebodings," *Australian Journal of Social Issues*, 38:1, February 2003, pp. 57–72.

13. Charles Leadbeater, *The Rise of the Social Entrepreneur*, Demos, 1997, p. 23.

14. For a feminist critique of microcredit, see Christine Keating, Claire Rasmussen, and Pooja Rishi, "The Rationality of Empowerment: Microcredit, Accumulation by Dispossession, and the Gendered Economy," *Signs*, 36:1, Autumn 2010, pp. 153–176. On "neoliberalism from below," see our discussion of Verónica Gago's work in chapter 12.

15. On the Millenium Villages, see Lia Haro, "The End(s) of the End of Poverty," PhD dissertation, Duke University, 2014. For an analysis of the neoliberal logic of development in an irrigation project in Ecuador, see Roberto Adolina, "The Values of Water: Development Cultures and Indigenous Cultures in Highland Ecuador," *Latin American Research Review*, 47:2, 2012, pp. 3–36.

16. For our analysis of the Bolivian social movements for water and gas in the name of the common, see *Commonwealth*, Harvard University Press, 2009, pp. 107–112. In *Declaration*, Argo Navis, 2012, we interpret the encampments created by the cycle of struggles that began in 2011, from the Arab Spring to Occupy, as struggles for the common.

17. Alberto De Nicola and Biagio Quattrocchi, "La torsione neoliberale del sindicato tradizionale e l'imagginazione del 'sindicalismo sociale': Appunti per una discussione," http://www.euronomade.info/?p=2482. See also Alberto De Nicola and Biagio Quattrocchi, eds, *Sindacalismo sociale*, DeriveApprodi, 2016, especially their introduction.

18. Kim Moody summarizes with wonderful clarity the argument for a shift from political unionism to social-movement unionism. See Kim Moody, "Towards an International Social-Movement Unionism," *New Left Review*, September 1997, pp. 52–72. See also Peter Waterman, "Social-Movement Unionism: A New Union Model for a New World Order?" *Review (Fernand Braudel Center)*, 16:3,

Summer 1993, pp. 245–278; Stephanie Ross, "Varieties of Social Unionism: Towards a Framework for Comparison," *Just Labour*, 11, Autumn 2007, pp. 16–34; and Anthony Ince, "Beyond 'Social Movement Unionism'? Understanding and Assessing New Wave Labour Movement Organising," June 5, 2010, https://reinventinglabour.wordpress.com/2010/06/05/beyond-social-movement-unionism-ince/.

19. The tripartite alliance continued after the ANC assumed power in 1994, but its character changed significantly as the trade unions were oriented no longer toward social movements but instead the ruling government. Recently new alliances of social unionism have emerged against the ANC and the congress of unions, a development that results in part from anger over the 2012 Marikana massacre of striking miners. Early in 2014 the National Union of Metalworkers broke with the ANC and the Communist Party, critiquing what it considers the Soviet model of demanding allegiance from trade unions. The breakaway union declared that instead of being faithful to the ruling party it would, at least temporarily, orient its activities toward social movements, some of which continue the antineoliberalism and antiprivatization struggles that challenged ANC policies in the early 2000s. On the developments of labor and social movement challenges to the ANC, see the group of essays edited by Ahmed Veriava, "Reconfigurations on the Left in South Africa," *South Atlantic Quarterly*, 114:2, April 2015, pp. 426–466.

20. On the experiences of the Service Employees International Union, see, for example, Valery Alzaga, "Justice for Janitors Campaign: Open-Sourcing Labour Conflicts against Global Neo-liberalism," *Open Democracy*, February 7, 2011, https://www.opendemocracy.net/valery-alzaga/justice-for-janitors-campaign-open-sourcing-labour-conflicts-against-global-neo-libera.

21. Frances Fox Piven and Richard Cloward, *Poor People's Movements*, Vintage, 1977, p. 25.

22. Paolo Donadio, "La nuova lingua del New Labour," PhD dissertation, Università Federico II, Naples, 2001.

23. See Naoki Sakai, *Translation and Subjectivity*, University of Minnesota Press, 1997; Sandro Mezzadra, "Living in Transition: Toward a Heterolingual Theory of the Multitude," http://eipcp.net/transversal/1107/mezzadra/en; and Sandro Mezzadra and Brett Neilson, *Border as Method*, Duke University Press, 2013.

24. James C. Scott, *The Art of Not Being Governed*, Yale University Press, 2009.

25. Adolfo Muñoz's video installation "Midas" presents such an animated visual representation that transforms the frontispiece of Hobbes, *Leviathan*, http://amunyoz.webs.upv.es/blog/midas/.

PART III

1. Michel Foucault claims that the revulsion toward Keynes and the Keynesian state unites the German and US variants of neoliberalism (*The Birth of Biopolitics*,

Picador, 2004, p. 79). The creation of the Keynesian state was itself the fruit of an earlier reaction on the part of capital. In the first half of the twentieth century it sought to block and interiorize the workers' struggles and the economic-political projects that emerged from the orbit of communist movements across the world in the period of the Soviet Revolution. The Keynesian project, in other words, acknowledged the challenge of revolutionary movements, but sought to neutralize them politically by appropriating in distorted form some of their demands—for democracy, workers' control, the egalitarian redistribution of wealth, and so forth. See Antonio Negri, "Keynes and the Capitalist Theory of the State," in Michael Hardt and Antonio Negri, *Labor of Dionysus*, University of Minnesota Press, 1994, pp. 23–52.

2. Samuel Huntington, "The Democratic Distemper," *Public Interest*, no. 41, Fall 1975, pp. 9–38, quote on p. 10; see the full version of Huntington's text in the Trilateral Commission report: Michel Crozier, Samuel Huntington, and Joji Watanuki, *The Crisis of Democracy*, New York University Press, 1975.

3. Fareed Zakaria claims that the crisis of democracy that Huntington diagnosed never went away: the problems have mounted and the crisis has merely been deferred. See "Can America Be Fixed? The New Crisis of Democracy," *Foreign Affairs*, 92:1, 2013, pp. 22–33.

4. See Joseph Schumpeter, *Capitalism, Socialism, and Democracy*, Harper & Row, 3rd edition, 1950; and Karl Polanyi, *The Great Transformation*, Farrar & Rinehart, 1944.

5. Nancy Fraser, "Feminism's Two Legacies: A Tale of Ambivalence," *South Atlantic Quarterly*, 114:4, October 2015, pp. 699–712, quote on p. 707. See also Nancy Fraser, "Feminism, Capitalism, and the Cunning of History," *New Left Review*, no. 56, March–April 2009, pp. 97–117.

6. On the warlike violence intrinsic to neoliberalism, see, among others, Naomi Klein, *The Shock Doctrine*, Metropolitan Books, 2007; Retort, *Afflicted Powers*, Verso, 2005; and our *Multitude*, Penguin, 2004.

CHAPTER 10

1. Christian Marazzi, *Il comunismo del capitale*, Ombre corte, 2010, p. 64.

2. We presented a similar argument in *Empire*, Harvard University Press, 2000, chapters 3.3 and 3.4. See also, Luc Boltanski and Eve Chiapello, *The New Spirit of Capitalism*, Verso, 2006.

3. David Harvey, *A Brief History of Neoliberalism*, Oxford University Press, 2007, p. 48. See also Roger E. Alcaly and David Mermelstein, eds., *The Fiscal Crisis of American Cities: Essays on the Political Economy of Urban America with Special Reference to New York*, Vintage Books, 1977.

4. On the continuing fiscal crisis of Detroit as a political response to social struggles, see Scott Kurashige, *The Fifty-Year Rebellion: How the U.S. Political Crisis Began in Detroit*, forthcoming from University of California Press.

5. Rudolf Hilferding, *Finance Capital*, ed. Tom Bottomore, trans. Morris Watnick and Sam Gordon, Routledge & Kegan Paul, 1981, pp. 107 and 225.

6. Vladimir Lenin, *Imperialism: The Highest Stage of Capitalism*, International, 1939, p. 59.

7. On concentration and centralization in the banks, see Hilferding, *Finance Capital*, p. 180. Lenin criticizes Hilferding for not recognizing monopoly as the result of this process. See *Imperialism*, p. 47.

8. Karl Marx, *Capital*, trans. David Fernbach, Penguin, 1981, volume 3, p. 275.

9. Marx, *Capital*, volume 3, p. 275. "But it is only foreign trade, the development of the market to a world market, which causes money to develop into world money and *abstract labour* into social labour. Abstract wealth, value, money, hence *abstract labour*, develop in the measure that concrete labour becomes a totality of different modes of labour that comprise the world market." Marx, *Theories of Surplus Value*, volume 3, chapter 21: "Opposition to the Economists (Based on the Ricardian Theory)," originally published in 1968 by Progress; currently available from Marxists.org, https://www.marxists.org/archive/marx/works/1863/theories-surplus-value/ (translation modified).

10. On the origins of futures markets in Chicago, see Marco d'Eramo, *The Pig and the Skyscraper*, trans. Graeme Thomson, Verso, 2002, pp. 41–51. D'Eramo explains that futures trading requires uniform measures of goods: "Without standardization, the futures market cannot exist" (p. 45).

11. On the crisis of the law of measure, see Antonio Negri, "Twenty Theses on Marx," in Saree Makdisi, Cesare Casarino, and Rebecca Karl, eds., *Marxism beyond Marxism*, Routledge, 1996, pp. 149–180; and Negri, *Marx beyond Marx*, Autonomedia, 1992. For a range of discussions regarding measure and value from sociological perspectives, see Lisa Adkins and Celia Lury, eds., *Measure and Value*, Blackwell, 2012.

12. Dick Bryan and Michael Rafferty, *Capitalism with Derivatives*, Palgrave Macmillan, 2006, p. 37.

13. Dick Bryan and Michael Rafferty, "Financial Derivatives and the Theory of Money," *Economy and Society*, 36:1, pp. 134–158, quote on p. 141.

14. Randy Martin, "After Economy? Social Logics of the Derivative," *Social Text*, 31:1, Spring 2013, pp. 83–106, quote on p. 88. See also Lawrence Grossberg, "Modernity and Commensuration," *Cultural Studies*, 24:3, 2010, pp. 295–332.

15. For an analysis of the different qualities of these two forms of the common, see Michael Hardt, "Two Faces of Apocalypse: A Letter from Copenhagen," *Polygraph*, no. 22, 2010, pp. 265–274.

16. On the "reprimarization" of the economy in Latin America, see Maristella Svampa, "Commodities Consensus," *South Atlantic Quarterly*, 114:1, January 2015, pp. 65–82, quote on p. 66.

17. Bill McKibben, "Global Warming's Terrifying Math," *Rolling Stone*, July 19, 2012, http://www.rollingstone.com/politics/news/global-warmings-terrifying-new-math-20120719.

18. Sandro Mezzadra and Brett Neilson, "On the Multiple Frontiers of Extraction," forthcoming in *Cultural Studies*. Mezzadra and Neilson have developed a rich conception of extraction through several recent essays. In addition to "On the Multiple Frontiers," see "Operations of Capital," *South Atlantic Quarterly*, 114:1, January 2015, pp. 1–9; and "Extraction, Logistics, Finance," *Radical Philosophy*, no. 178, March–April 2013, pp. 8–18.

19. Vandana Shiva, *Biopiracy*, South End, 1999.

20. Mezzadra and Neilson analyze the metaphors of data mining and data extraction in "On the Multiple Frontiers of Extraction," pp. 13–14.

21. On the metropolis as a field of the common, see Hardt and Negri, *Commonwealth*, Harvard University Press, 2009, pp. 249–260.

22. Anna Tsing, *The Mushroom at the End of the World*, Princeton University Press, 2015, p. 63.

23. Finance sets in motion an "ongoing and violent tendency," Mezzadra and Neilson write, "to penetrate and subsume economic activity and social life as a whole" ("Operations of Capital," p. 2).

24. Matthew Desmond, *Evicted: Poverty and Profit in the American City*, Crown, 2016, p. 306.

25. Verónica Gago, "Financialization of Popular Life and the Extractive Operations of Capital," *South Atlantic Quarterly*, 114:1, January 2015, pp. 11–28, quote on p. 16. See also Verónica Gago and Sandro Mezzadra, "Para una crítica de las operaciones estractivas del capital," *Nueva sociedad*, no. 255, January–February 2015, pp. 38–52.

26. On the passage from Fordism to post-Fordism and the increasingly central role of knowledge, cooperation, and subjectivity in production, see Antonio Negri and Carlo Vercellone, "Le rapport capital/travail dans le capitalisme cognitif," *Multitudes*, Spring 2008, pp. 39–50, especially pp. 40–41.

27. The results of "general scientific labour, technological application of natural sciences, on one side, and…the general productive force arising from social combination [*Gliederung*] in total production on the other side," Marx writes, appear "as a natural fruit of social labour (although it is a historic product)" (*Grundrisse*, trans. Martin Nicolaus, Penguin, 1973, p. 700).

28. For an excellent account of the concept of cognitive capitalism, see Carlo Vercellone, "The Hypothesis of Cognitive Capitalism," paper presented at SOAS conference, Birkbeck College, November 4, 2005. Standard theories about digital revolutions, which conceive capitalist innovation as the primary creative force animating the development of information and communication technologies, are blind to the real motor of these processes, that is, living knowledge, intelligence, and subjectivity. Information and communication would remain sterile without them, just as, in general, capital would without labor.

29. Carla Freeman, *High Tech and High Heels in the Global Economy*, Duke University Press, 2000. See also Andrew Ross, *No Collar*, Basic Books, 2003.

30. Marx, *Grundrisse*, p. 297.

31. Some Marxists view abstraction entirely in negative terms and make it the cornerstone of their critique of capital. See, for example, John Holloway, *Crack Capitalism*, Pluto Press, 2010.

32. Marx, *Grundrisse*, p. 296.

33. Marx, *Grundrisse*, p. 172.

34. Marx, *Grundrisse*, p. 296.

35. Marx, *Grundrisse*, p. 706.

36. Deborah Cowen, *The Deadly Life of Logistics*, University of Minnesota Press, 2014.

37. Marx, *Capital*, volume 2, p. 135.

38. See Marx, *Capital*, volume 2, p. 229.

39. "[T]he production of the means of communication, of the physical conditions of circulation, is put into a category of the production of fixed capital, and hence does not constitute a special case. Meanwhile, and incidentally, there opened up for us the prospect... *of a specific relation of capital to the communal, general conditions of social production*, as distinct from the conditions of *particular capital* and its *particular production* process" (Marx, *Grundrisse*, p. 533). See also *Capital*, volume 2, p. 429.

40. Brett Neilson and Ned Rossiter, "Logistical Worlds: Territorial Governance in Piraeus and the New Silk Road," *Logistical Worlds*, no. 1, November 2014, pp. 4–10, quote on p. 5.

41. Keller Easterling, *Extrastatecraft: The Power of Infrastructure*, Verso, 2014, p. 27.

42. Cowen, *The Deadly Life of Logistics*, p. 41.

43. Stefano Harney and Fred Moten, *The Undercommons*, Autonomedia, 2013, p. 92.

44. See, for example, Niccolò Cuppini, Mattia Frapporti, and Maurilio Pirone, "Logistics Struggles in the Po Valley Region: Territorial Transformations and Processes of Antagonistic Subjectivation," *South Atlantic Quarterly*, 114:1, January 2015, pp. 119–134.

45. Harry Harootunian, *Marx after Marx: History and Time in the Expansion of Capitalism*, Columbia University Press, 2015, p. 2.

46. For Marx's analysis of primitive accumulation, see *Capital*, volume 1, pp. 873–931.

47. On accumulation as dispossession, see Harvey, *A Brief History of Neoliberalism*. For an excellent appraisal of Marx's concept of primitive accumulation in light of contemporary capitalist production, see Sandro Mezzadra, "The *Topicality* of Prehistory: A New Reading of Marx's Analysis of 'So-called Primitive Accumulation,'" *Rethinking Marxism* 23: 3, 2011, pp. 302–321.

48. See Christopher Arthus, *The New Dialectic and Marx's Capital*, Brill, 2002. Note also that several excellent Marxist histories of seventeenth-century England demonstrate that the radical socioeconomic transformation that Marx calls primitive accumulation unfolds in an uneven way, with a variety of forms of property and modes of the organization of labor. See Maurice Dobb, *Studies in the Development of Capitalism*, Routledge, 1947; E. P. Thompson, *The Making of the English Working Class*, revised edition, Penguin, 1991; and, in contrast to these, Ellen Meiksins Wood, *The Origins of Capitalism: A Longer View*, Verso, 2002.

49. For Marx's explanations of formal and real subsumption, see "Results of the Immediate Process of Production," included as the appendix to the English version of *Capital*, volume 1, trans. Ben Fowkes, Penguin, 1976, pp. 943–1084, especially pp. 1019–1038. For our previous analyses of formal and real subsumption, see Negri, *Marx beyond Marx*, pp. xvi, 113–123, and 142; and Hardt and Negri, *Empire*, pp. 254–256.

50. Praful Bidwai, *The Phoenix Moment: Challenges Confronting the Indian Left*, HarperCollins India, 2015, p. 365. For an excellent summary of the "mode of production debate" in India, see pp. 353–365.

51. Jairus Banaji, *Theory and History*, Brill, 2010, p. 282. The essay from which this chapter is derived was published originally in 1977. See also Harootunian's excellent interpretation of Banaji in *Marx after Marx*, pp. 210–225.

52. For a history of debates over semifeudalism and semicolonialism among Chinese intellectuals, see Rebecca Karl, "On Comparability and Continuity: China, circa 1930s and 1990s," *boundary 2*, 32:2, 2005, pp. 169–200. Karl argues that the anti-imperialist content of the 1930s debates has been expunged such that these concepts came in the 1990s to signal "the inevitability of capitalism through the mutation of semicolonialism into a theory of perpetual transition" (p. 187).

53. Álvaro García Linera, *Nueve tesis sobre el capitalismo y la comunidad universal*, Ministerio de trabajo, empleo, y previsión social, 2015, especially p. 8. For García Linera's extended analysis of formal and real subsumption in the context of indigenous community, see *Forma valor y forma comunidad*, 2nd edition, Muela del Diablo, 2009.

54. Harootunian, *Marx after Marx*. On formal subsumption as the general rule of capitalist development, see specifically pp. 9 and 38.

CHAPTER 11

1. "Money is the supreme form of social being," claim Michael Neary and Graham Taylor, "yet bourgeois science makes no investigation into its social life" (*Money and the Human Condition*, Macmillan, 1998, p. 1). On money as a social relation, see also Geoffrey Ingham, *The Nature of Money*, Polity, 2004, p. 12.

2. John Maynard Keynes, *A Treatise on Money*, Harcourt, Brace, 1930, p. 3.

3. "The history of money," writes J. K. Galbraith, "teaches much or it can be made to teach much. It is, indeed, exceedingly doubtful if much that is durable can be learned about money in any other way" (*Money*, rev. ed., Houghton Mifflin, 1995 [orig. 1975], p. 1). See also Carlo Boffito, *Teoria della moneta: Ricardo, Wicksell, Marx*, Einaudi, 1973; and Antonio Negri, *Libri del rogo*, Derive Approdi, 2006, pp. 42, 52, and 53.

4. Karl Marx, *Grundrisse*, trans. Martin Nicolaus, Penguin, 1973, p. 225.

5. E. P. Thompson, "Time, Work-Discipline, and Industrial Capitalism," *Past and Present*, no. 38, December 1967, pp. 56–97.

6. See Steffen Böhm and Chris Land, "The New 'Hidden Abode': Reflections on Value and Labour in the New Economy," *Sociological Review*, 60:2, May 2012, pp. 217–240.

7. Jonathan Crary, *24/7*, Verso, 2013, p. 88.

8. Gilles Deleuze, "Postscript on the Societies of Control," *October*, Winter 1992, pp. 3–7, quote on p. 5.

9. Melinda Cooper, "Shadow Money and the Shadow Workforce," *South Atlantic Quarterly*, 114:2, April 2015, pp. 395–423. Dick Bryan, Michael Rafferty, and Chris Jefferis make a similar point: "So just as that post-war monetary stability gave way to more fluid forms of finance following the floating of exchange rates and the invention of the Black-Scholes options pricing model (to name two different dimensions of the rise to prominence of financial risk), at the same time, and for broadly the same reasons, permanent, full time employment went into decline to be replaced increasingly by precarious, casual and immaterial forms of labor" ("Risk and Value: Risk, Labor, and Production," *South Atlantic Quarterly*, 114:2, April 2015, pp. 307–329, quote on pp. 308–309).

10. Christian Marazzi, *E il denaro va*, Bollati Borighieri, 1998, p. 64.

11. Gunnar Heinsohn and Otto Steiger, "The Property Theory of Interest and Money," in John Smithin, ed., *What Is Money?*, Routledge, 2000, pp. 67–100, quote on p. 67.

12. Carlo Vercellone, "Composizione organica del capitale e composizione di classe," in Commonware, Effimera, Unipop, eds., *La crisi messa a valore*, CW Press & Edizioni Sfumature, 2015, pp. 104–119, quote on p. 112.

13. Karl Marx, *Capital*, trans. Ben Fowkes, Penguin, 1976, volume 1, p. 226.

14. See *Proletari e stato*, thesis 2 and thesis 8 in Negri, *Libri del rogo*, pp. 146–150 and 169.

15. Bernard Schmitt, *Monnaie, salaires et profits*, Presses universitaires de France, 1966, p. 11. See also Negri, *Libri del rogo*, p. 210.

16. Simmel "expressly conceptualizes money as an institution" (Gianfranco Poggi, *Money and the Modern Mind: Georg Simmel's Philosophy of Money*, University of California Press, 1983, p. 132).

17. Georg Simmel, *The Philosophy of Money*, trans. Charles Lemert, Routledge Classics, reprint edition, 2011, p. 461.

18. Simmel, The Philosophy of Money, pp. 150, 62–70, and 127.

19. Simmel, The Philosophy of Money, pp. 285 and 348.

20. Georg Lukács, *Notes on Georg Simmel's Lessons*, Documenta, 2011.

21. See Jerome Roos, "In Each Other We Trust: Coining Alternatives to Capitalism," March 31, 2014, https://roarmag.org/essays/moneylab-conference-alternative-currencies/.

22. David Harvey argues that value "is a social relation established between the laboring activities of millions of people around the world. As a social relation, it is immaterial and invisible." And being "immaterial and invisible, value requires some material representation. This material representation is money. Money is a tangible form of appearance as well as a symbol and representation of the

immateriality of social value" (*Seventeen Contradictions*, Oxford University Press, 2014, pp. 26–27).

23. Harvey, *Seventeen Contradictions*, p. 27.

24. Heinsohn and Steiger, "The Property Theory of Interest and Money," p. 86. See also Gunnar Heinsohn and Otto Steiger, *Ownership Economics*, trans. Frank Decker, Routledge, 2012. When reading Heinsohn and Steiner one should keep in mind the work of the institutionalist sociologists, such as Marcel Mauss, Karl Polanyi, and Marshall Sahlins.

25. See Serge Audier, *Neoliberalisme(s): Une archéologie intellectuelle*, Grasset, 2012. The notion of property as a sphere of rights resonates strongly with the work of Hayek.

26. Wilhelm Röpke, *A Humane Economy*, Intercollegiate Studies Institute, 1998.

27. On Walter Euken, see Stephan Kuhnert, "The Man Who Heated Up Economic Discussion with a Stove: Walter Euken's Challenge to the Social Sciences," in Mark Sproule-Jones, Barbara Allen, and Filippo Sabetti, eds., *The Struggle to Constitute and Sustain Productive Orders*, Lexington Books, 2008, pp. 111–123; and Viktor Vanberg, "The Freiburg School: Walter Euken and Ordoliberalism," *Freiburg Discussion Papers in Constitutional Economics*, 4:11, 2004.

28. Christian Marazzi, *The Violence of Financial Capitalism*, trans. Kristina Lebedeva and Jason McGimsey, Semiotext(e), 2010, pp. 48, 64, and 106.

29. On disaster capitalism, see Naomi Klein, *The Shock Doctrine*, Metropolitan Books, 2007.

30. See, among others, Nico Poulantzas, *Political Power and Social Classes*, Verso, 1975; Claus Offe, *Strukturprobleme des kapitalistischen Staates*, Suhrkamp, 1972; Joachim Hirsch, *Wissenschaftlich-technischer Fortschritt und politisches System*, Suhrkamp, 1970; and James O'Connor, *The Fiscal Crisis of the State*, St. Martin's Press, 1973.

31. Lapo Berti, *Moneta, crisi e stato capitalistico*, Feltrinelli, 1978, p. 33.

32. Wolfgang Streeck, *Buying Time*, Verso, 2014.

33. Streeck, *Buying Time*, p. 72.

34. Streeck foresees the end of capitalism without any social subject (revolutionary or otherwise) able to construct a viable alternative. See "How Will Capitalism End?," *New Left Review*, 87, May–June 2014, pp. 35–64.

35. For a more detailed analysis of Marx's theories of crisis, see Antonio Negri, "Marx on Cycle and Crisis," in *Revolution Retrieved*, Red Notes, 1988 pp. 43–90.

36. Marx, *Theories of Surplus Value*, volume 3, p. 447, originally published by Progress, currently available from Marxists.org, https://www.marxists.org/archive/marx/works/1863/theories-surplus-value/.

CHAPTER 12

1. Sheldon Wolin, *Democracy Inc.*, Princeton University Press, 2008. On different aspects of constitutional corruption in the United States, see also Bruce Ackermann, *The Decline and Fall of the American Republic*, Harvard University

Press, 2010; and Zephyr Teachout, *Corruption in America*, Harvard University Press, 2014.

2. Robert Hale, "Coercion and Distribution in a Supposedly Non-Coercive State," *Political Science Quarterly*, 38:3, September 1923, pp. 470–494. See our argument on property law in chapter 6.

3. Michel Foucault, *The Birth of Biopolitics*, Picador, 2004, p. 145.

4. Foucault, *The Birth of Biopolitics*, pp. 226 and 241.

5. Foucault, *The Birth of Biopolitics*, p. 270.

6. Peter Drucker, *Innovation and Entrepreneurship*, Harper & Row, 1985, p. 264. On trade unions, see pp. 257–259; on public institutions, see pp. 259–260.

7. See David Slater, "The Making of Japan's New Working Class: 'Freeters' and the Progression from Middle School to the Labor Market," *Asia-Pacific Journal*, 8:1, January 2010, pp. 1–37; and Anne Allison, *Precarious Japan*, Duke University Press, 2013, especially pp. 64–71.

8. Jonathan Crary, *24/7*, Verso, 2013, p. 46.

9. Verónica Gago, "Financialization of Popular Life and the Extractive Operations of Capital," *South Atlantic Quarterly* 114:1, January 2015, pp. 11–28, quote on p. 15.

10. Michel Foucault, "The Subject and Power," *Critical Inquiry*, 8:4, Summer 1982, pp. 777–795, quote on p. 790.

11. Andreas Fischer-Lescano and Günther Teubner, "Regime-Collisions: The Vain Search for Legal Unity in the Fragmentation of Global Law," *Michigan Journal of International Law*, 25:4, 2004, pp. 999–1046, quote on p. 1004. On neoliberal governance see also our analysis in *Commonwealth*, Harvard University Press, 2009, pp. 223–228 and 371–375; Sandro Mezzadra, "Seizing Europe—Crisis Management, Constitutional Transformation, Constituent Movements," in Óscar García Agustín and Christian Ydesen, eds., *Post-Crisis Perspectives*, Peter Lang, 2013, pp. 99–118; and Marco Fioravanti, "Costituzionalismo dei beni comuni," *Storica*, no. 55, 2013, pp. 103–137.

12. Christian Marazzi, *Il comunismo del capitale*, Ombre corte, 2010, p. 66.

13. For country-by-country accounts of abuses against freedom of information and journalistic freedom, see the Reporters without Borders website, en.rsf.org.

14. Paul Mason, *Why It's Kicking Off Everywhere*, Verso, 2012, p. 75. On social media and social movements, see also Paolo Gerbaudo, *Tweets and Streets*, Pluto, 2012; and Todd Wolfson, *Digital Rebellion: The Birth of the Cyber Left*, University of Illinois Press, 2014.

15. United Nations High Commissioner for Refugees, *World at War: Global Trends 2014*, http://www.unhcr.org/556725e69.html.

16. United Nations High Commissioner for Refugees, "Worldwide Displacement Hits All-time High as War and Persecution Increase," June 18 2015, http://www.unhcr.org/558193896.html.

17. As of 2013, a total of 232 million people live outside their country of origin according to the United Nations Population Fund, http://www.unfpa.org/migration.

18. This figure is reported by the International Labour Organization on the basis of Chinese national statistics in 2009. See "Labor Migration in China and Mongolia," http://www.ilo.org/beijing/areas-of-work/labour-migration/lang--en/index.htm.

19. See Marco Bascetta and Sandro Mezzadra, "L'Europa: Ce la facciamo?," *Il manifesto*, November 7, 2015; and Martina Tazzioli, "Da Calais a Marsiglia," *Tutmondo*, November 7, 2015.

20. Sandro Mezzadra and Brett Neilson, "Né qui, né altrove—Migration, Detention, Desertion: A Dialogue," *Borderlands*, 2:1, 2003, www.borderlands.net.au/vol2no1_2003/mezzadra_neilson.html. See also Sandro Mezzadra, *Diritto di fuga*, Ombre corte, 2001.

21. "The only part of the so-called national wealth," Marx writes, "that actually enters into the collective possession of a modern nation is—the national debt.... The public debt becomes one of the most powerful levers of primitive accumulation" (Karl Marx, *Capital*, trans. Ben Fowkes, Penguin, 1976, volume 1, p. 919).

22. Wendy Brown, *Undoing the Demos*, Zone Books, 2015, p. 108.

23. Brown, *Undoing the Demos*, p. 151. On neoliberalism and law, see also Corinne Blalock, "Neoliberalism and the Crisis of Legal Theory," *Law and Contemporary Problems*, 77:4, 2014, pp. 71–103; and David Grewal and Jedediah Purdy, "Law and Neoliberalism," *Law and Contemporary Problems*, 77:4, 2014, pp. 1–24.

24. "[P]ower is tolerable only on condition that it masks a substantial part of itself," Michel Foucault claims. "Its success is proportional to its ability to hide its own mechanisms" (*History of Sexuality*, trans. Robert Hurley, Vintage, 1980, volume 1, p. 86).

25. See Antonio Negri, "Reflections on the 'Manifesto for an Accelerationist Politics,'" trans. Matteo Pasquinelli, http://www.e-flux.com/journal/53/59877/reflections-on-the-manifesto-for-an-accelerationist-politics/.

26. Foucault, "The Subject and Power," p. 789.

27. Pedro Biscay, "Ipotesi d'inchiesta," 2015, http://www.euronomade.info/?p=4712.

PART IV

1. Heinrich von Kleist, "The Puppet Theatre," in *Selected Writings*, ed. and trans. David Constantine, Hackett, 2004, p. 414.

2. Margaret Atwood, "Song of the Worms," in *You Are Happy*, Harper & Row, 1974. Thanks to Sumeet Patwardhan for suggesting this poem as a characterization of the multitude.

CHAPTER 13

1. Like us, both Ernesto Laclau and Alain Badiou grasp the crisis of modern politics and the urgency posed by the movements to discover an alternative political framework. They arrive, however, at conclusions that are different than ours and, to an extent, opposed to one another.

Ernesto Laclau's conception of populism starts, as does our concept of multitude, from the recognition of the heterogeneity of the social field, that is, the fact that there is no single subject that can or should unify all of those in struggle. He departs from us, though, when he rejects the terrain of immanence, that is, the prospect that the multiplicity of social subjectivities in struggle can organize themselves effectively, create lasting institutions, and eventually constitute new social relations. Instead Laclau maintains that a transcendent motor, a hegemonic force, is necessary to organize from above the plural social subjectivities into "the people," which he emphasizes, rightly, is an empty signifier. This creation of the people, he claims, is the political act par excellence. Our primary objection is that the multitude of social subjectivities should not (and ultimately today cannot) be organized as a united subject from above, by a hegemonic power; we maintain, instead, that social subjectivities have the potential to organize themselves as a multitude (not a people) and create lasting institutions. In effect, we fault Laclau for hanging on to the categories of modern politics and modern sovereignty, without being able to transform them sufficiently. See, primarily, Laclau, *On Populist Reason*, Verso, 2005.

Alain Badiou, like Laclau, focuses on the contemporary lack of a unifying political instance, but for him the force to recompose the parts depends on the flash of the event. The revolutionary event in Badiou can only be conceived in its purity—another "empty signifier," empty of the accumulation of resistances and struggles. In essence, the event for Badiou comes from the outside, like a god descended on earth, not a Christ constructed by the refusal of slavery and suffering under imperial command, not a Robespierre that transforms hatred of the ancien régime into justice, not a Lenin who is the product of a century of class struggles for bread and popular hatred for war. In our view, the event is not an extraordinary thing but a daily production of those who struggle. Revolutionary power is critically constructed through subversive practices and a patient excavation that penetrates into the viscera of social production and social struggles, which produce subjectivities and wealth. From that continuous movement of resistance derives the crisis of the modern state, which we have described at various points above. For Badiou, like Laclau, the scheme of modern conceptions of the state, politics, and sovereignty remain intact. See primarily, Badiou, *Being and Event*, trans. Oliver Feltham, Continuum, 2005; and *Logic of Worlds*, trans. Alberto Toscano, Continuum, 2009.

2. Cornelius Castoriadis, *L'institution imaginaire de la société*, Seuil, 1975, pp. 7–8. For an analogous argument, founded on a "historico-descriptive" rather than an "analytical" basis, see Claude Lefort, *L'invention démocratique*, Fayard, 1981.

3. Furthermore, whereas the recognition of the overlap and admixture of private and public affords the legal realists a means to recognize the rights of others and legitimate state action, the link leads Pashukanis to maintain that the abolition of private property requires too the abolition of the state, a position that certainly

drew him no favor with Stalin and his inner circle. Perhaps the subterranean connection between Cohen and Pashukanis is not so paradoxical when we remember that the orthodoxy of the Soviet state, against which the legal realists position themselves, was hostile to Pashukanis, who was executed on Stalin's order in 1937.

4. See Evgeny Pashukanis, *The General Theory of Law and Marxism*, Transaction, 2007, especially chapter 4, "Commodity and Subject." For a systematic reading of Pashukanis and on the importance of private property to the general framework of bourgeois law, see Antonio Negri, "Rileggendo Pasukanis," in *La forma stato*, Feltrinelli, 1977, pp. 161–193. Regarding Hans Kelsen's view of Pashukanis, see *The Communist Theory of Law*, Stevens & Sons, 1955, pp. 93–94.

5. Walter Benjamin, "Critique of Violence," in *Reflections*, trans. Edmund Jephcott, Schocken Books, 1986, p. 281.

6. Carl Schmitt, "Nehmen, Teilen, Weiden," in Ernst Forsthoff, ed., *Rechtsstaatlichkeit und Sozialstaatlichkeit*, Wissenschaftliche Buchgesellschaft, 1953, pp. 95–113.

7. Félix Guattari, *The Three Ecologies*, trans. Ian Pindar and Paul Sutton, Athlone, 2000.

8. See Georg Lukács, *The Young Hegel*, trans. Rodney Livingston, MIT Press, 1976; and Antonio Negri, *Stato e diritto nel giovane Hegel*, CEDAM, 1958.

9. Georges Sorel, *Reflections on Violence*, ed. Jeremy Jennings, Cambridge University Press, 1999.

10. W. E. B. Du Bois, *Black Reconstruction in America*, Oxford University Press, 2014, p. 51.

11. Karl Marx, *Capital*, trans. Ben Fowkes, Penguin, 1976, volume 1, p. 415.

12. Rosa Luxemburg, "Introduction to Political Economy," in *The Complete Works of Rosa Luxemburg*, volume 1, ed. Peter Hudis, trans. David Fernbach, Joseph Fracchia, and George Shriver, Verso, 2013, pp. 89–300, quote on p. 286.

13. For similar arguments regarding the extremism of the center, see Tariq Ali, *The Extreme Centre: A Warning*, Verso, 2015; and Étienne Balibar, who uses the term in several works, including in the preface to Carl Schmitt, *Le léviathan dans la doctrine de l'état de Thomas Hobbes*, Seuil, 2002, p. 11; and *Politics and the Other Scene*, Verso, 2002, pp. 44–45. The term is also used in earlier eras by Seymour Lipset and Theodor Geiger to analyze the roots of fascism. See Lipset, *Political Man*, Doubleday, 1960; and Geiger, "Panik im Mittelstand," *Die Arbeit*, 7, 1930, pp. 637-639.

14. See Paolo Prodi, *Il tramonto della rivoluzione*, Il Mulino, 2015.

15. Giorgos Katsambekis and Yannis Stavrakakis, "Populism, Anti-populism and European Democracy: A View from the South," July 23, 2013, https://www.opendemocracy.net/can-europe-make-it/giorgos-katsambekis-yannis-stavrakakis/populism-anti-populism-and-european-democr.

16. Martin Luther, "To John Rühel at Mansfeld," May 23, 1525, in Preserved Smith, *The Life and Letters of Martin Luther*, Houghton Mifflin, 1914, pp. 163–164.

17. See our reading of Machiavelli on the revolt of the Ciompi in *Commonwealth*, Harvard University Press, 2009, pp. 51–53. On this general theme see also the insert above in the opening text to Part II on what "from below" means.

18. On "the part of those who have no part," see Jacques Rancière, *Disagreement*, trans. Julie Rose, University of Minnesota Press, 1999.

CHAPTER 14

1. On the Tiananmen repression as a response to struggles against neoliberalism in China, see, for example, Wang Hui, *China's New Order*, trans. Theodore Huters and Rebecca Karl, Harvard University Press, 2006.

2. On Lenin's conception of the dualism of power, see Antonio Negri, *The Factory of Strategy: Thirty-Three Lessons on Lenin*, trans. Arianna Bove, Columbia University Press, 2015. The 1967 Shanghai Commune is an example of a counterpower in the Chinese context. See Hongsheng Jiang, *La commune de Shanghai et la commune de Paris*, trans. Eric Hazan, La fabrique, 2014.

3. We give a more complete discussion of altermodernity in *Commonwealth*, pp. 101–118.

4. See Antonio Negri, *Insurgencies*, trans. Maurizia Boscagli, University of Minnesota Press, 1999.

5. Several important authors, such as Giorgio Agamben and Massimo Cacciari, analyze the theological foundations of modern political thought, but the most important advocate of political theology, especially with regard to sovereignty, is, of course, Carl Schmitt. In addition to *Political Theology* (trans. George Schwab, University of Chicago Press, 2006), see his affirmation of the Christian concept of Katechon: "The belief that a restrainer [*Aufhalter*] holds back the end of the world provides the only bridge between the notion of an eschatological paralysis of all human events and a tremendous historical monolith, like that of the Christian empire of the Germanic kings" (*Nomos of the Earth*, trans. G. L. Ulmen, Telos Press, 2006, p. 60). The Katechon, which restrains evil, is necessarily a sovereign power. For our critique of contemporary uses of Katechon, see *Commonwealth*, Harvard University Press, 2009, pp. 197–198.

6. Pierre Bourdieu, *Pascalian Meditations*, trans. Richard Nice, Stanford University Press, 2000.

7. Carl von Clausewitz, *On War*, Princeton University Press, 1976, p. 101.

8. Slavoj Žižek, *Violence*, Picador, 2008.

9. In *Commonwealth* we make a similar argument against excessive focus among some contemporary authors on states of exception (and the acts of sovereign power), arguing instead for greater attention to the daily, unexceptional activities of power through the critique of law and the critique of capital. See pp. 3–8.

10. "Le motif de la résistance," as Stephane Hessel says, "c'est l'indignation" (Stephane Hessel, *Indignez-vous*, Ce qui marche contre le vent, 2010, p. 11).

11. For its impressive ability to catalogue and analyze the myriad contemporary forms of violence, see the Histories of Violence project, organized by Brad Evans, www.historiesofviolence.com.

12. Angela Davis has been an intelligent and consistent advocate for creating coalitions in an international and intersectional frame. See *Freedom Is a Constant Struggle*, ed. Frank Barat, Haymarket, 2016; and Angela Davis and Elizabeth Martinez, "Coalition Building among People of Color," in *The Angela Davis Reader*, ed. Joy James, Blackwell, 1998, pp. 297–306.

13. Ignacio Cano quoted in Justin Salhani, "Police Brutality in Brazil Is Out of Control," August 4, 2015, https://thinkprogress.org/police-brutality-in-brazil-is-out-of-control-dc8a98278c0d#.uu3kqrlyi.

14. See, for example, Dylan Rodriguez, "Beyond 'Police Brutality': Racist State Violence and the University of California," *American Quarterly*, 64:2, June 2012, pp. 303–313.

15. In this regard protest movements against police violence dovetail with the work of various struggles against institutionalized racial violence, such as the prison abolition movement. See, for example, Angela Davis, *Are Prisons Obsolete?*, Seven Stories Press, 2003. For an international view of the violence of prison systems, see "Prison Realities," ed. Leonidas Cheliotis, special issue, *South Atlantic Quarterly*, 113:3, Summer 2014.

16. Roberto Bolaño, *2666*, trans. Natasha Wimmer, Farrar, Straus, and Giroux, 2004, p. 348. We are grateful to Jaime Gonzalez for pointing us to this passage in Bolaño's novel. Alice Driver calls these killings "feminicide" rather than "femicide" to indicate they are more than individual murders but hate crimes against the female gender. See Alice Driver, *More or Less Dead: Feminicide, Hauntings, and the Ethics of Representation in Mexico*, University of Arizona Press, 2nd edition, 2015.

17. Kristin Bumiller, *In an Abusive State*, Duke University Press, 2008, p. 19.

18. On the Polish demonstration for reproductive rights, see Mark Bergfeld, Aleksandra Wolke, and Mikolaj Ratajczak, "The #czarnyprotest and Monday's Women Strike Might Be a Turning Point in Polish Politics," https://rs21.org.uk/2016/09/30/interview-the-czarnyprotest-and-mondays-women-strike-might-be-a-turning-point-in-polish-politics/. On the movement against sexual violence in Argentina, see http://niunamenos.com.ar/.

19. Rachel Carson, *Silent Spring*, Houghton Mifflin, 1992, p. 32, quoted in Rob Nixon, *Slow Violence and the Environmentalism of the Poor*, Harvard University Press, 2011, p. 10.

20. Nixon, *Slow Violence and the Environmentalism of the Poor*.

21. See http://standwithstandingrock.net/. Indigenous movements against environmental threats proliferate around the world. Idle No More, born in Canada in 2012, for instance, protests the dangers and devastations of tar sands oil extraction, pipeline construction, water contamination, and other forms of degradation of the land. See the dossier "Idle No More," ed. Dina Gilio-Whitaker, *South Atlantic*

Quarterly, 114:4, October 2015, pp. 862–906. For examples of indigenous environmental activism in the Pacific, see the dossier "Environmental Activism across the Pacific," ed. Teresa Shewry, *South Atlantic Quarterly*, 116:1, January 2017, pp. 170–217. For an excellent synthetic account of resistance movements against environmental degradation, see Naomi Klein, *This Changes Everything*, Simon and Schuster, 2014, pp. 293–336.

22. On Foxconn suicides, see Jenny Chan, "A Suicide Survivor: The Life of a Chinese Worker," *New Technology, Work and Employment*, 28:2, July 2013, pp. 84–99; and Ralph Litzinger, "The Labor Question in China: Apple and Beyond," *South Atlantic Quarterly*, 112:1, Winter 2013, pp. 172–178. On the *hikikomori*, see Anne Allison, *Precarious Japan*, Duke University Press, 2013, pp. 71–76.

23. On the power of debt to produce passive, stunted subjectivities, see our *Declaration*, Argo Navis, 2012, pp. 10–14; and Maurizio Lazzarato, *The Making of Indebted Man*, trans. Joshua David Jordan, Semiotext(e), 2012. Regarding US movements to combat student debt, housing debt, and health care debt, see "Dossier from Strike Debt," ed. Andrew Ross, *South Atlantic Quarterly*, 112:4, Fall 2013, pp. 782–838. Unions of precarious workers in Japan and France, such as the Intermittents du spectacle, like the tradition of Movements of Unemployed Workers in Argentina (Movimientos de trabajadores disocupados) have been important not only for gaining rights for precarious or unemployed workers in a specific sector but also for their pedagogical value, revealing the increasing precarity of the working classes as a whole. See Antonella Corsani and Maurizio Lazzarato, *Intermittents et précaires*, Editions Amsterdam, 2008.

24. See Jeremy Scahill, *Dirty Wars*, Nation Books, 2013; and Grégoire Chamayou, *Théorie du drone*, La fabrique, 2013.

25. Military strategists and politicians shouldn't need Machiavelli to remind them that the successful use of weapons must do much more than kill: they must transform the subjectivity of the Prince's enemies, making them accept and even desire a new form of life, and they must engage too the subjectivity of the Prince's own population. Weapons may kill, in other words, but that is only a vehicle to their real purpose, to transform the living. The US invasions and the subsequent, escalated strategies of drone warfare certainly succeed in killing enemies but have proven counterproductive with regard to the living. This is not a surprise. Many recognized at the time that the visions of a peaceful, remade Middle East painted by George W. Bush, Tony Blair, Dick Cheney, Donald Rumsfeld, Paul Wolfowitz, and the other proponents of war would be quickly revealed as a nightmare. For our analysis of the "revolution in military affairs" and related strategies at the outset of the US war on terror, see *Multitude*, Penguin, 2004, pp. 41–51.

26. "We are witnessing today the dissolution of the Empire described in 2000 by Michael Hardt and Toni Negri, as a form beyond classical imperialism, tied to a modality of accumulation of capital that (in the course of the preceding thirty years) had gone beyond the dialectic between center and periphery. It had

extended the peripheries to the center and the center to the peripheries, under the articulated and hierarchical command that pivoted on the financial markets and the interests of the great multinational corporations on a planetary scale" (Christian Marazzi, "Dentro e contro la normalità della guerra," interview with Antonio Alia and Anna Curcio, December 9, 2015, http://effimera.org/dentro-e-contro-la-normalita-della-guerra-intervista-a-christian-marazzi-di-antonio-alia-e-anna-curcio/).

27. Giovanni Arrighi, *Adam Smith in Beijing*, Verso, 2007, p. 185.

28. Saskia Sassen, *Territory, Authority, Rights*, Princeton University Press, 2006.

29. Sandro Mezzadra and Brett Neilson, *Border as Method*, Duke University Press, 2013.

30. Keller Easterling, *Extrastatecraft*, Verso, 2014.

31. For our analysis of the failed US attempt to return to imperialist rule, see *Commonwealth*, Harvard University Press, 2009, pp. 203–218. For an excellent review of some mainstream arguments about the decline of US global hegemony, see Robert Keohane, "Hegemony and After," *Foreign Affairs*, 91:4, July–August 2012, pp. 114–118.

32. See, for example, Alberto Acosta, "El retorno del estado," *La Tendencia*, April–May 2012, pp. 62–72.

33. Henry Kissinger, "The End of NATO as We Know It?," *Washington Post*, August 15, 1999, https://www.washingtonpost.com/archive/opinions/1999/08/15/the-end-of-nato-as-we-know-it/354a60e6-bdb7-43a8-b5fb-d66a4cc73a62/.

CHAPTER 15

1. Karl Marx, *The Civil War in France*, International, 1998, p. 36.

2. Mao Zedong, *Problems of War and Strategy*, 2nd edition, Foreign Languages Press, 1960, p. 13. Mao quickly adds that the party controls the gun and the gun will not be allowed to control the party.

3. Kristin Ross, *Communal Luxury*, Verso, 2015, pp. 11–29.

4. On the Black Panther health clinics, see Alondra Nelson, *Body and Soul: The Black Panther Party and the Fights against Medical Discrimination*, University of Minnesota Press, 2013.

5. On the experiment in democratic autonomy in Rojava in the midst of war, see the dossier of essays edited by Bülent Küçük and Ceren Özselçuk, "Struggling for Democratic Autonomy in Kurdistan," *South Atlantic Quarterly*, 115:1, January 2016, pp. 184–196.

6. René Char, *Dans l'atelier du poète*, ed. Marie-Claude Char, Quarto Gallimard, 2007, pp. 373–374.

7. For a historical analysis of the Val d'Ossola and the other "partisan republics," see Carlo Vallauri, ed., *Le repubbliche partigiane: Esperienze di autogoverno democratico*, Laterza, 2013.

8. Franco Fortini, *Un dialogo ininterotto*, Bollati Borighieri, 2009, pp. 63–64.

9. Jean-Paul Sartre, at various points in his work, poses the problem of the relationship between figures of subjectivity and their existential, situated, historically determinate production—a relationship generally between the subjectivity and historicity of the organizational processes of revolutionary movements. The theme of "totalization," which is so dear to Sartre, is posed as the key to the synthesis of the possible differences of this dialectic. The analysis of the transformation of individual praxis and its totalization, as many have noted, constitutes the heart of Sartre's problem. But the more interesting part, at least for us, is Sartre's reasoning when he discovers the residues or products of alienation that can disturb and destroy this process. Inertia undermines it and terror can destroy it. Here we are faced with a process that remains bogged down in difficulties and has no happy ending. But isn't this the real situation we always face—when, in the process of totalization, we grasp the inevitable aporias and recognize that there is no subject that can realize that process? Which means that only struggle can lead to a solution. When Sartre analyzes the failure of that repressive or counterrepressive process "from series to fusion" in the Algerian Revolution, he confirms this conclusion: the relationship between the production of subjectivity and its social constitution remains open. See Jean-Paul Sartre, *Critique of Dialectical Reason*, volume 1, trans. Alan Sheridan-Smith, ed. Jonathan Rée, New Left Books, 1976, on individual praxis and totalization, pp. 79–94, on alienation and inertia, pp. 228–252, and on the Algerian Revolution, pp. 721–734.

10. Karl Marx, *Capital*, trans. Ben Fowkes, Penguin, volume 1, p. 563.

11. On the introduction of the standard shipping container, see Deborah Cowen, *The Deadly Life of Logistics*, University of Minnesota Press, 2014, pp. 31 and 40–42.

12. On prefigurative politics in the New Left, see Wini Breines, *Community and Organization in the New Left, 1962–1968*, 2nd edition, Rutgers University Press, 1989, especially pp. 46–66.

13. On prefigurative politics in Occupy Wall Street, see David Graeber, *The Democracy Project*, Penguin, 2013.

14. One might object that the historical situations of these two cases were so different that they cannot be compared in this way. That is indeed what the "Togliattians" claimed every time they were confronted by struggles based on autonomous strategic projects. They justified, for example, their submission to the formal rules of constitutional democracy on the basis of insuperable international conditions, such as the Yalta Treaty, which left the Italian Communist Party (as well as the French) at the mercy of NATO. How could one deny it? That was not the problem, however, but rather the refusal of the Togliattians to confront this necessity with honesty and truth: the honesty to continue to produce communist subjectivity not subordinated to bourgeois rule and its economic pact, and the truth that reveals critically the reasons for that obstacle to praxis. They instead subordinated the truth to a perpetual regime of mystifications and falsifications. If they were to have acted honestly, the Togliattians would have probably been able to bring together (even in a fragile way) the relationship between the social formations of the movements and the production of subjectivity, and they would

have in the successive years been able to hand down their terrific antifascist and democratic legacy to the next generation of activists, creating a continuous line in the history of European revolutionary movements.

15. We recognize the validity of some of John Holloway's critiques of the practices of taking power, although we do not endorse his conclusions, in *Change the World without Taking Power*, Pluto Press, 2002.

16. Peter Thomas provides excellent critiques of the dominant interpretations of hegemony in Gramsci, particularly those of Laclau and Mouffe, and Perry Anderson. See *The Gramscian Moment*, Brill, 2009.

17. For one important local currency proposal, see Eduardo Garzón Espinosa, "Ventajas y riesgos de la moneda local qua propone crear Barcelona en Comú," *El diario*, June 13, 2016.

18. See, for example, Christian Marazzi, *Che cos'è il plusvalore*, Casagrande, 2016, pp. 81–83; and Marie Charrel, "Da la monnaie pour le peuple," *Le monde*, February 20, 2016.

19. See, for example, Laurent Baronian and Carlo Vercellone, "Monnaie du commun et revenu social garanti," *Terrains/Théories*, 1, 2015, http://teth.revues.org/377, doi: 10.4000/teth.377. For our earlier proposal of a guaranteed basic income, see *Empire*, Harvard University Press, 2000, pp. 401–403.

20. Kathi Weeks, *The Problem with Work*, Duke University Press, 2011, p. 146.

21. See Pascal Nicolas-Le Strat, *Le travail du comun*, Éditions du commun, 2016. For a range of excellent discussions of a money of the common, see Emanuele Braga and Andrea Fumagalli, eds., *La moneta del comune*, DeriveApprodi, 2015.

22. Marx argued that capital's inability to plan for social needs leads continually to disaster: "The matter would be simply reduced to the fact that the society must reckon in advance how much labour, means of production and means of subsistence it can spend, without dislocation, on branches of industry which, like the building of railways, for instance, supply neither means of production nor means of subsistence, nor any kind of useful effect, for a long period, a year or more, though they certainly do withdraw labour, means of production and means of subsistence from the total annual product. In capitalist society, on the other hand, where any kind of social rationality asserts itself only *post festum*, major disturbances can and must occur constantly" (*Capital*, volume 2, p. 390).

CHAPTER 16

1. W. E. B. Du Bois, *Black Reconstruction*, Oxford University Press, 2014, p. 169.

2. Paul, 2 Thessalonians 2:6–7.

3. Gilles Deleuze, "Instincts and Institutions," in *Desert Islands and Other Texts, 1953–1974*, Semiotext(e), 2004, pp. 19–21, quote on p. 21.

4. Niccolò Machiavelli, *Prince*, trans. Peter Bonadella, Oxford University Press, 2005, p. 88.

5. Karl Marx, *Capital*, trans. Ben Fowkes, Penguin, volume 1, p. 447.

Acknowledgments

We are grateful to the many friends who read portions of the manuscript and helped us with the arguments, including Corinne Blalock, Angela Chnapko, Grant Farred, Michael Gaffney, Lisl Hampton, Mark Hansen, Melanie Jackson, Fred Jameson, Naomi Klein, Christian Marazzi, Sandro Mezzadra, Ruth O'Brien, Jed Purdy, Judith Revel, Carlo Vercellone, Kathi Weeks, and the editorial collective of Euronomade.

Index

machinic assemblage, 140, 146
  defined, 120–121
  See also administration, machinic;
    subjectivity, machinic
Macpherson, C. B., 105
Madison, James, 40
Mahler, Gustav, 135
Malcolm X, 10
Mandela, Nelson, 9
Mann, Thomas, 136
Manning, Chelsea, 215
Marazzi, Christian, 122, 160, 187, 199, 214, 281
Marcos. See Subcomandante Marcos
mareas (Spanish social movements),
    22, 149–150
Martin, Randy, 165
martyrs, 8, 56, 60
Marx, Karl, 24, 40–41, 59, 120, 163, 165, 171,
    173–174, 176, 243–244
  on cooperation, 140–141, 291–292
  on crisis, 203–205
  on fixed capital, 110, 115–116
  on money, 184, 189
  on property, 92–94, 103
  on technology, 112–115, 273
  on the Paris Commune, 4–5, 134,
    269, 278
  See also, primitive accumulation;
    subsumption, formal and real
Marxism, 30, 66, 70, 82
  Western, 72–76
Mason, Paul, 214
Mattei, Ugo, 95–96, 100, 105
Maturana, Humberto, 110
Mazzini, Giuseppe, 5
Mckesson, DeRay, 11
McKibben, Bill, 168
media and social movements, 7, 9–10, 11, 69,
    214
Merkel, Angela, 130
Merleau-Ponty, Maurice, 74–75
metropolis, 101, 196, 242
  as site of production, 28, 98, 149, 169, 286
Mezzadra, Sandro, 168, 216, 264
Michaloliakos, Nikolaos, 49
Michels, Robert, 30–31
migrants, 130, 170, 178, 262–263, 272

precarity and power of, 60, 152–153, 215–217
  See also, antimigrant movements
money, 183–184, 193–196
  in relation to property, 196–200
  of the common, 224–225, 237,
    280–284, 294
  social relations of, 184–193
  See also, banks; capital, finance
Mont Pellerin Society, 198
Montesquieu, Charles-Louis de Secondat,
    100, 245
Mill, John Stuart, 43
Moretti, Franco, 136
Morris, Aldon, 21
Morris, William, 241
Mosca, Gaetano, 30
Moten, Fred, 178
Movement for Socialism (Bolivia), 22
multitude, 39, 78, 228, 234, 269–274
  and strategy, 20–22
  defined, 69
  wealth of, 285–287
  See also, entrepreneurship, of the
    multitude
Musil, Robert, 135
Muslims, 54, 56–57 (see also, anti-Muslim
    movements)

native peoples, 166, 191
Nazis, 48, 136, 271
necropolitics, 36
Neilson, Brett, 168, 176, 216, 264
neoliberalism, 42–45, 179–180, 200–201,
    247–248
  and entrepreneurship, 144–146
  and freedom, 208–212, 290
  and legal theory, 89–90, 95–97, 100
  and private property, 197–199
  and reformism, 151, 251, 253–254, 257
  as a reaction, 78, 114, 134, 155–158
  origins of, 64
  resistance to, 22, 36, 59–60, 222–225,
    244–245, 265
  social, 145
  See also, administration, neoliberal
Newton, Huey, 10
Nicolas-Le Strat, Pascal, 283